RACE
Are We So Different?

Alan H. Goodman

Yolanda T. Moses

Joseph L. Jones

WILEY-BLACKWELL

A John Wiley & Sons, Ltd., Publication

FOUNDED · 1902

A·M·E·R·I·C·A·N
ANTHROPOLOGICAL
ASSOCIATION

This edition first published 2012
© 2012 American Anthropological Association

Blackwell Publishing was acquired by John Wiley & Sons, in February 2007. Blackwell's publishing program has been merged with Wiley's global Scientific, Technical, and Medical business to form Wiley-Blackwell.

Registered Office
John Wiley & Sons, Ltd, The Atrium, Southern Gate, Chichester, West Sussex, PO19 8SQ, UK

Editorial Offices
350 Main Street, Malden, MA 02148-5020, USA
9600 Garsington Road, Oxford, OX4 2DQ, UK
The Atrium, Southern Gate, Chichester, West Sussex, PO19 8SQ, UK

For details of our global editorial offices, for customer services, and for information about how to apply for permission to reuse the copyright material in this book please see our website at www.wiley.com/wiley-blackwell.

The right of Alan H. Goodman, Yolanda T. Moses, and Joseph L. Jones, to be identified as the authors of this has been asserted in accordance with the UK Copyright, Designs and Patents Act 1988.

Wiley also publishes its books in a variety of electronic formats. Some content that appears in print may not be available in electronic books.

Designations used by companies to distinguish their products are often claimed as trademarks. All brand names and product names used in this book are trade names, service marks, trademarks or registered trademarks of their respective owners. The publisher is not associated with any product or vendor mentioned in this book. This publication is designed to provide accurate and authoritative information in regard to the subject matter covered. It is sold on the understanding that the publisher is not engaged in rendering professional services. If professional advice or other expert assistance is required, the services of a competent professional should be sought.

Library of Congress Cataloging-in-Publication Data

Goodman, Alan H.
  Race : are we so different? / Alan H. Goodman, Yolanda T. Moses, Joseph L. Jones.
      p.   cm.
  Includes bibliographical references and index.
  ISBN 978-0-470-65713-3 (hardback : alk. paper) – ISBN 978-0-470-65714-0 (pbk. : alk. paper)
1. Race–Social aspects–United States.   2. Race–Social aspects.   3. Racism–United States.   4. Racism.
I. Moses, Yolanda T.   II. Jones, Joseph L.   III. Title.
  E185.86.G637 2012
  305.800973–dc23

                                      2011044946

A catalogue record for this book is available from the British Library

Cover image: Courtesy American Anthropological Association
Cover design by Cyan
Timeline design by Design Deluxe

Set in 10/12pt Bembo by SPi Publisher Services, Pondicherry, India
Printed and bound in Singapore by Markono Print Media Pte Ltd

1   2012

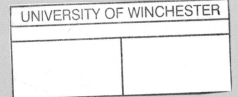

Contents

Illustrations

Preface

Figure 0.1 Are we so different?.

Not unlike the networks of meaning and actions that coalesce and continually refashion the powerful idea of race, writing a multiauthored book on race comes about through the synergies of multiple personal, institutional, and professional connections. Invaluable to us, we have also had a large, complex, active, and supportive beehive of supporters. This is especially true of this project and this book.

Race also looks different depending on one's experience, place, and history. We expect, then, that this book will strike each reader in slightly different ways. As is the tendency with the exhibit and website, readers may gravitate to areas of the book that have particular, individual interest and meaning. However, we have designed this book with a clear beginning, middle sections, and conclusions to best develop knowledge and analysis. As a companion to the larger project called RACE: Are We So Different? the book is meant to be read from front to back, and as a sort of primer on race (as well as human biological variations and racism). We hope that our main messages are expressed in ways that resonate with all readers.

The project that led to this book first took recognizable shape in 1997. One of us, Yolanda Moses, then president of the American Anthropological Association (AAA), the world's largest and foremost organization of professional anthropologists, called together a group of scholars from the subfields of anthropology to talk to each other about what race means in their subfields.

The participants came out of that session at the annual meeting of the AAA with a clear consensus that, rather than occupying conceptually different universes, we had many points of agreement: much more agreement than difference. We came to our points of agreement from different intellectual histories and with different observations and data. We found that subfields of anthropology, such as linguistic anthropology, archaeology, biological anthropology, and political anthropology, highlighted diverse aspects of the complexly protean idea of race and the dynamics of racism.

Remember the parable of blindfolded individuals touching different parts of an elephant? One touches the tail and thinks she has a snake. Another touches the trunk and thinks he is feeling a wall. It was much like that. It was clear that working together, and ultimately with colleagues from other fields from physics to the humanities, we could best describe and understand the whole of the elephant in our midst that is race and racism.

Finally, it was clear just how harmful the idea of race had been in the hands of individuals with the power to maintain and benefit from a racial status quo. Systems of inequalities was built and maintained around the unchallenged idea that racial differences and inequalities were biological and natural. These notions reverberate today. However, it is clear that they are refutable and simply based on bad science. This is why we felt compelled to educate that *race is powerful, but not based in genes or biology, rather than a cultural and changeable concept.*

We concluded then that a necessary step toward change had taken place: we had talked to each other and realized that we could communicate and, in combination, we could articulate a complex idea. However, the necessary step is not sufficient to make changes. We needed as well to do more than talk to our colleagues and college students. This book would not be possible without them, and we hope that with it, we will reach more college classrooms. We also

need to elevate the public discussions about race, bringing it back to fundamental issues, such as how race came about in history and was invented and how race and human variation are different. And we needed to try and include everyone in the discussion.

The RACE public education program, of which this book is a part, was launched by a steering committee under the guidance of the AAA and the staff leadership of Dr. Peggy Overbey. The tangible results include a website (www.understandingrace. org) that was created by S2N Media, Inc. (led by Kathy Prusinksi) and a museum exhibit that was designed and built with our museum partners, the exceptional staff of the Science Museum of Minnesota (SMM), led by President Eric Jolly and the project headed by Robert Garfinkle and Joanne Jones-Rizzi. To them we owe our first and deepest gratitude. This book would simply never, never happen if not for Robert, Joanne, their creative and resourceful team, and their courageous and collaborative spirit.

The museum exhibit, originally a huge undertaking of over nearly fifty components and 5,000 square feet is currently touring the country until 2015. It has been such a huge success that a similarly sized and nearly identical exhibit was recently constructed as well as a smaller version of 1,500 square feet for smaller, community venues.

Acknowledgments

This book is an outgrowth of the ten years of work that went into the conceptualization, research, and construction of the website and especially into the creation of the components of the museum exhibit. Many people and organizations assisted AAA in developing, producing, and implementing the RACE: Are We So Different? public education program. They include the Project Advisory Board members: Michael L. Blakey (College of William and Mary), Louis Casagrande (Children's Museum of Boston), Robert Hahn (Centers for Disease Control and Prevention), Faye Harrison (University of Florida), Thomas Holt (University of Chicago), Janis Hutchinson (University of Houston), Marvin Krislov (Oberlin College), Richard Lewontin (Harvard University), Jeffrey Long (University of New Mexico), Shirley Malcom (American Association for the Advancement of Science), Carol Mukhopadhyay (San Jose State University), Michael Omi (University of California–Berkeley), Kyeyoung Park (University of California–Los Angeles), Kenneth Prewitt (Columbia University), Enid Schildkrout (Museum for African Art), Theodore Shaw (NAACP Legal Defense and Education Fund), Marcelo Suarez-Orozco (New York University), David Hurst Thomas (American Museum of Natural History), Russell Thornton (University of California–Los Angeles), and Arlene Torres (City University of New York).

Additionally, AAA staff contributed extensively to the project. They include William Davis, executive director; Elaine Lynch, deputy executive director; Suzanne Mattingly, controller; Susannah Bodman and Lauren Schwartz, former media relations associates; Lucille Horn, former meetings director; Khara Minter, former meetings coordinator; Stacy Lathrop and Dinah Winnick, former managing editors, Anthropology News; Oona Schmid, director of publishing; Damon Dozier, director of public affairs; Amy Goldenberg, managing editor, Anthropology News; Mark Booker, production editor, Anthropology News; and Carla Fernandez, meetings planner and exhibits manager.

Felica Gomez worked as an intern on the project and coauthored the family guide published on the RACE Project website. Amy Beckrich served as project assistant, helping to coordinate the massive project and keep everyone in line. Because of her excitement about the project, Mary Margaret Overbey left a permanent position at AAA and was for many years the force behind the project as its director through to the completion of the website and exhibit.

The exhibit and the book have benefited immensely from collaborations with California Newsreel. Under the directorship of Larry Adelman, California Newsreel produced the exceptional video "Race: The Power of an Illusion" (see www.pbs.org/race). This award-winning documentary film has been an inspiration to our project, and in fact we have portions of two interviews in this book.

A number of eminent scholars from a cross-section of disciplines graciously agreed, under tight deadlines and time constraints, to write and include their voices in the form of guest essays; our profound thanks go to Kamari Clarke, Faye Harrison, Nina Jablonski, Kenneth Kidd, Ian Haney López, Carol Mukhopadhyay, Michael Omi, Nell Irvin Painter, Mica Pollock, Susan Reverby, Audrey Smedley, Deborah Thomas, Arlene

Torres, Bonnie Urciuoli, and Joseph Watkins. Other individuals have been directly quoted or featured in the book via excerpts from "Race: The Power of an Illusion" or via their inclusion in the museum exhibit. These include scientists Joseph Graves and Richard Lewontin. The story of sickle cell is movingly told by Frank and Vickie Giacomazza.

At Wiley-Blackwell, we have been guided and encouraged by Rosalie Robertson and Julia Kirk. Rosalie saw at the very start the importance of our project. In an incredibly efficient manner, she and Julia were able to elicit seven insightful and very constructive manuscript reviews that we used, hopefully to enhance our final product. We also wish to thank these anonymous reviewers. Julia Kirk has been a fabulous work partner as she stewarded us through the complexities of soliciting over a hundred permissions for the plethora of photos and images for the book and for the many other logistics of producing a book as multifaceted as this one. Charlotte Frost took a very complex book and turned it into one with a pleasing layout and colour scheme. Felicity Marsh was a great work partner in editing and design work.

Neither would this project have come about without the financial support of many individuals who have allowed us to use images and text (see individual credits). Major financial support for the project was provided by the AAA and the National Science Foundation (NSF). The Ford Foundation specifically provided funding to start this project and to produce the book that you are now holding. We express our deep gratitude to the funding Program Officers: Al Desena at NSF and Margaret Wilkerson, Gertrude Fraser, Irma McClaurin, and Irene Korenfield at the Ford Foundation.

In the course of this project, we have all benefited from help in many forms and from many people. Alan Goodman wishes to thank numerous students, staff, and faculty at Hampshire College and other venues, not least the 8th graders at Amherst Regional Middle School, Massachusetts, who helped in thinking through the best way to communicate ideas around race and human variation: In the early 1990s my colleagues and I helped organized "teach-ins" on race, not because of any crisis but just to educate about the myriad ways that race permeates our (mostly white) lives. My father taught me to be critical and always question my position.

I have learned immensely about the power of stories from filmmakers Larry Adelman, Christine Sommers, and Lew Smith and exhibit developers including Joanne Jones-Rizzi and Robert Garfinkle. In addition to advisory board members, many colleagues have helped me personally, including, but not limited to, Larry Adelman, George Armelagos, Lee Baker, Michael Blakey, Joseph Graves, Faye Harrison, Evelynn Hammonds, Thomas Leatherman, Richard Lewontin, Jonathan Marks, Michael Montoya, Lynn Morgan, Leith Mullings, Dean Robinson and Banu Subramanian. Chaia Heller, my spouse and cultural anthropologists, added tremendous insight into how to communicate the power of the idea of race, not to mention giving daily moral support. Some comfort that ideas permeate comes about when my daughter Ruby Goodman, age 8, explains to Stella Gordon, age 5, that her dad is going to Texas to talk about racism. Stella asks what racism is and Ruby replies that "it is when white people are mean to black people." Stella responds "what if a black person is mean to a white person" and Ruby says "that's also racism but it is less common and less hurtful than white people being mean to black people." We hope this book will help to unveil some of the systems behind race and racism and why racism hurts.

Yolanda Moses wishes to thank the many people who have helped to make this project a reality for her and who have given her personal support over the years. At UC Riverside, the intellectual contributions of Tom Patterson, Wendy Ashmore, Christine Gailey, Sang Hee Lee, and T. S. Harvey have been invaluable to me as I have worked on ideas for this book. I thank them for that support. A special thanks goes to the students in my classes who challenged me to explain the intricacies of the social construction of race and human variation in ways that tracked with their everyday experiences of race and racism. I want to thank the following graduate students who helped me with various tasks connected to this book from basic research to helping to track down numerous permissions. They are Scott Smith, John Gust, Jenny Banh, Priscilla LoForte, Isabel Placentia, Richard Alvarez, and Doris Logan. Special thanks to staff members Felecia Garrett and Sonia

Zamora who helped me to type early drafts. And finally to my family, my husband Jamrs F. Bawek, of almost forty years, and my two grown daughters, Shana and Toni, who have been my sounding board for my ideas, research, and activities for this project since its inception. To my 90-year-old mother, Willie Lee Moses, I give thanks for her encouragement to complete this project so that others may know what it means "to not live a day of your life without thinking about race."

Joseph Jones would first like to thank Alan Goodman and Yolanda Moses for their invaluable support and guidance towards realizing a vision of public anthropology and social justice. Numerous others who share this vision gave generously of their time and knowledge and helped me to understand better the uses and limits of race in human culture and biology. They include Michael Blakey and Mark Mack (who together introduced me to the worlds of anthropology at Howard University), Faye Harrison, Audrey Smedley, R. Brooke Thomas, Alan Swedlund, Bob Paynter, John Bracey, Maddie Marquez, Dula Amarasiriwardena, Warren Perry, John Higginson, and many more at University of Massachusetts–Amherst and outside of the academy. I hope their varied insights and influences come through as you read this text.

My family has been a well of support and inspiration. Danielle, my wife, graciously provided necessary time, encouragement, and feedback as the manuscript took form. In typically honest, 5-year-old fashion, my curious little Nia has begun to ask straightforward questions about human diversity. Her questions reaffirm the need to educate young children proactively about difference and race. To my mother and late father, Mary and Robert Jones, I am grateful for so many enduring lessons and of course for your decades of steady love, support, and confidence. My efforts here are an extension of your inability to settle for racism. May this book help others to see through social inequality to the truth of human equality.

1

Regarding Race

Figure 1.1 "Seward Montessori Graduation" (part of Lake Street USA series, 1997–2000). Photograph by Wing Young Huie.

Race: Are We So Different?, First Edition. Alan H. Goodman, Yolanda T. Moses, and Joseph L. Jones.
© 2012 American Anthropological Association. Published 2012 by Blackwell Publishing Ltd.

Is race real? Sometimes, it depends – obviously?

Talking about race or afraid to talk about race; talking too much or too little. It does not matter. We never seem to get very far.

How do we get out of this gridlock?

Our answer: start asking and resolving different questions about race. Most people think race is real, and they are obviously right. *Race is real*. But race is not real in the way we think of it: as deep, primordial, and biological. Rather, race is a foundational idea with devastating consequences because we, through our history and culture, made it so.

The purpose of this book is to lead readers to understand how race is and is not real. Simply focusing on diversity and acceptance, as is common today, misses the deeper roots of race, racial thinking, and overt racism. On the other hand, a purely scientific and objective approach fails to tell the full story of how race has shaped historical events and continues to be a powerful influence on individual lives. It certainly does not tell all about the variation in how race is experienced among individuals and over time and place.

In this book we aim to bring together a combination of science, history, and personal experiences. The result we are hoping for is surprisingly liberating. Race has come to be a knotted ball of history, culture, identity, and biology. We aim to untangle that ball. Once unraveled, one understands much more about the physical differences among us, and how race became such a powerful force.

We know that race seems obviously real to anyone immersed in North America's dominant culture. Race seems visually real. Every day, one can observe difference in outward form between individuals. Interestingly, rather than biology, race is real because of the everyday ways in which we interpret differences and invest *meaning* into those biological differences. It might seem counterintuitive, but race is also biological in that the idea of race, and specifically living in a racial society with differential access to resources, has effects on the body that are manifest in infant and adult mortality. If race is an illusion, then it is an unusually powerful one.

Yet, what we have internalized as evidence that we have seen with our own eyes of the "facts" of race such as differences in skin color and other so-called

markers of race, simply have no inherent or deeper sociopolitical significance other than what our culture attaches to them. There is human linguistic, cultural, biological, and genetic variation. But these variations are not racial in that they do not "naturally" partition individuals into races.

A key insight from anthropology is that what we see as real is often due to what our worldviews predispose our minds to see. In much the same way that we used to think the sun revolved around the earth, we see variation as race only because the idea is all around us and is unquestioned. As Spellman president Beverly Tatum says, race is like smog. If we are in it, it is all we see. Moreover, it obstructs clear vision of the true nature of difference. It is time to lift the smog.

In this book, the companion to an award-winning website and museum exhibit, we hope to show how the idea of race continues to have consequences, every day, for all of our lives. Race is not only a *social construct*, it is a powerful *social contract*. The Constitution of the United States listed enslaved Africans as three-fifths of a person. While the Thirteenth Amendment changed this formulation,[1] the racial contract is much deeper than laws and "official" statements. It is particularly enduring because the idea of race is deeply etched into our minds and institutions. We want to expose the social contract and thereby expose the deep roots of racial thinking. Just as weeds will return if they are not pulled out by the roots, we will not get beyond racism unless we pay attention to the roots – to its foundational ideas.

As fundamentally woven into our minds and institutions as the idea of race became and is still, we can change the way that we understand race, and even how race is embedded in institutions. We will not do so by avoiding race or pretending that it is not salient. Rather, we do so by engaging with the science of human variation, the history, culture, and politics of race and the everyday lived experiences of race and racism.

Our students and those who visit the exhibit often have "ah ha" moments in which they come to forever see race differently. Suddenly, race is seen to not be natural but an idea and product of culture. Amazing!

---

[1] Additional laws were also passed by most states against miscegenation (interracial marriage).

Fortunately, too, those insightful moments do not require advanced training in genomics, anthropology, philosophy, or any other discipline. Rather, the only requirement is openness to questioning assumptions that we thought were obviously true.

Imagine that you have lived your life in a landscape that has never led you or those around you to question that the earth is anything but flat. You go to a mountaintop and you look into the clear distance and notice that the horizon appears to bend down. That bend is a sign that the earth is round. It is time to pay attention to signs like that. However, be forewarned. The results are mind bending. Changes from seeing the earth as flat to round are what scientists call paradigm shifts. A paradigm shift, or a change in worldview, can be disorienting, and it takes a while to readjust.

In addition to making a novel argument, this book has another unique feature: it is a companion to the hugely successful national public education project, RACE: Are We So Different? Developed by the AAA, this project consists of a set of traveling exhibits,[2] a website, and additional educational materials. The project is organized around three powerful themes: (1) race is a recent human invention, (2) race is about culture and not about biology,[3] and (3) race and racism are imbedded in institutions and in everyday life. The book is similarly organized with a section on history, followed by one on science and another on lived experience.

We hope that this book will be engaging to those who have visited the website or exhibit as well as to those new readers. For those who have visited the website and exhibit, here you will find more detailed explanations and the back stories that could not be explained in a walkthrough of an exhibit. With over one hundred images and photographs, we aim to capture the sense that images explain and illustrate and also enhance what can best be explained by succinct writing.

The book in your hands aims to be a fundamental primer on the idea and reality of race and how the idea connects to institutional and everyday racism.

[2] Currently, there are two 5000 square foot exhibit traveling around the country and a smaller exhibit of nearly 1500 square feet.

[3] Paradoxically, race is not a biological or genetic construct, but it does have biological consequences. Some of these consequences of race, especially for health and wealth, will be highlighted in this book.

Human races, we argue, are not "out there in nature." Rather, humans invented race.

Combining insights and examples from the realms of science, history, and individual stories, our aim was to write and assemble a book that is serious yet engaging and lively. Our main goal is to move readers beyond the false dichotomy of human races as being real or not. We want readers to appreciate *how* contemporary social and biological analyses show that race is real and ways that they show that race is surprisingly outmoded (chiefly as a way to think about genetic differences among us). We want this to be a book that deeply transforms its readers. We want everyone to have an "ah ha" moment.

Five central arguments of this book are as follows:

1 *The idea of race was invented.* Race was invented as a way to categorize and rank groups and by extension, individuals. The invention did not happen in an isolated laboratory or at one place in time. Rather, this scientific and social idea slowly took hold and became more and more real through European exploration and colonization and slavery in the Americas. In the 18th century race might have made sense because the physical (or phenotypic) differences between Europeans and others seemed to be great.

While just a human invention that is explored in the first section of this book, the idea was politically powerful because the belief in separate and unequal races was the only potentially moral and ethical justification for the inhumanities of colonization and slavery. In the first section of this book we will tell the gripping story of the interlinked social, religious, political, and scientific histories of race. Closely following the exhibit, the story is outlined in four parts.

2 *Human biological variation is real, obvious, wonderful, and necessary.* We do vary. The second section of this book provides a primer of human genetic variation; that is, how variation is patterned within individuals and among individuals and groups. Evolutionarily speaking, even if it is not the spice of life, variety is certainly a required ingredient for the survival of our species.

3 *The idea of race does not explain human variation.* The biggest myth of race is that we humans have biological races and that on a biological or, more precisely,

on a genetic level our race determines a good deal about how we differ from each other and our potentialities. The science of human variation, however, tells us otherwise. Race-as-genetic-variation is a myth. Race neither explains variation nor is a useful genetic construct. In this book, we will use a number of interrelated examples to show why this is so.

4   *Race is both stable and protean.* The idea of race is something we all share – to a degree. We argue that race today is much the same, on a fundamental level, as it was a hundred or even three hundred years ago. But the realities of race – how the ideas get into lived experiences – morph from place to place and time to time. Here, we have the opportunity to share how some of those diverse lives were lived racially. What was it like to be a Native American and to see Europeans for the first time? What was it like to be a Japanese American during World War II? It is our expectation that understanding how race differs among diverse groups provides a deeper understanding of each group and about race itself.

5   *We own the future of race.* How we continue to understand and use race is up to us. We hold the core belief that our book will contribute to a fundamental overhaul of how various publics think and talk about race. By explaining how the power of race was used in the past to divide us, in this book we will show how this new knowledge is power to understand and reunite. Once we understand what race is and is not, race ceases to become a ready excuse for the intolerable differences in our wealth, health, and other core indicators of equality and experiences of life.

Race is a recent human invention.

It's only a few hundred years old, in comparison to the lengthy span of human history. Although not scientific, the idea of race proposed that there were significant differences among people that allowed them to be grouped into a limited number of categories or races. Yet, are we so different? All humans share a common ancestry and, because each of us represents a unique combination of ancestral traits, all humans exhibit biological variation.

From the beginning, the idea of race was tied to power and hierarchy among people, with one group being viewed as superior and others as inferior. Despite disproving notions of hierarchy and removing social, economic and political barriers, the legacy of race continues to shape the lives and relationships of people in the U.S. and around the world.

This book may challenge popular understandings about race, raise questions, and spark critical thinking. We hope the exhibition, public website and educational materials produced by the *RACE* Project will foster dialogue in families and communities around the U.S. and help better relations among us all.
American Anthropological Association

RACE Exhibit Introductory Video Transcript

Race.

What is race?

What do we really know about race?

Here's what we do know: Race is a short word with a long history in the United States of America. Think of the history of America and our ideas of race together, mixed-up, and ever-changing. Just like this painting, race was created. It is a powerful idea that was invented by society.

Race is an enduring concept that has molded our nation's economy, laws, and social institutions. It is a complex notion that has shaped each of our destinies. Many of the ideas we now associate with race originated during the European era of exploration.

Europeans like Christopher Columbus traveled overseas and encountered, and then colonized or conquered peoples in Africa, Asia, and the Americas who looked, talked, and acted much differently from them. Naturalists and scientists then classified these differences into systems that became the foundation for the notion of race as we know it today.

In the American colonies, the first laborers were European indentured servants.

When African laborers were forcibly brought to Virginia beginning in 1619, status was defined by wealth and religion, not by physical characteristics such as skin color.

But this would change.

Over time, physical difference mattered, and with the development of the transatlantic slave trade, landowners began replacing their temporary European laborers with enslaved Africans who were held in permanent bondage. Soon a new social structure emerged based primarily on skin color, with those of English ancestry at the top and African slaves and American Indians at the bottom.

By 1776, when "all men are created equal" was written into the Declaration of Independence by a slaveholder named Thomas Jefferson, a democratic nation was born with a major contradiction about race at its core. As our new nation asserted its independence from European tyranny, blacks and American Indians were viewed as less than human and not deserving of the same liberties as whites.

In the 19th and 20th centuries, the notion of race continued to shape life in the United States. The rise of "race science" supported the common belief that people who were not white were biologically inferior. The removal of Native Americans from their lands, legalized segregation, and the internment of Japanese Americans during World War II are legacies of where this thinking led.

Today, science tells us that all humans share a common ancestry. And while there are differences among us, we're also very much alike.

Changing demographics in the United States and across the globe are resulting in new patterns of marriage, housing, education, employment, and new thinking about race.

Despite these advances, the legacy of race continues to affect us in a variety of ways.

Deeply held assumptions about race and enduring stereotypes make us think that gaps in wealth, health, housing, education, employment, or physical ability in sports are natural. And we fail to see the privileges that some have been granted and others denied because of skin color.

This creation, called race, has fostered inequality and discrimination for centuries.

It has influenced how we relate to each other as human beings. The American Anthropological Association has developed this exhibit to share the complicated story of race, to unravel fiction from fact, and to encourage meaningful discussions about race in schools, in the workplace, within families and communities.

Consider how your view of a painting can change as you examine it more closely.

We invite you to do the same with race. Examine and re-examine your thoughts and beliefs about race.

PART 1

HISTORIES OF RACE, DIFFERENCE, AND RACISM

The imaginary of whiteness, captured here, is too often not considered part of the invention of races. Whiteness is taken for granted as a standard of beauty and normalcy, thus providing access to power, yet is a relatively recent invention. Courtesy of the Science Museum of Minnesota/C. Thiesen.

2

Introducing Race

The world got along without race for the overwhelming majority
of its history. The U.S. has never been without it.
David Roediger, *How Race Survived U.S. History:*
From Settlement and Slavery to the Obama Phenomenon

Realizing Race

A social contract … cognitive smog … a dangerous myth … a powerful illusion … Race metaphors abound, and these examples express as well as any the reality of race in contemporary society in the United States. Race, today, is everywhere. Whatever confusion and disagreements exist around its definitions or delineations, few would argue this point. And understandably so! We live in a society saturated with race. Racial thinking has infiltrated and now influences in some way or another everyone's experiences of health, education, romance, friendship, work, religion, politics – virtually every arena and aspect of our lives. These influences can be painfully obvious or virtually imperceptible, but they are ever present. As a result, over time most of us develop strongly held racial beliefs based on these accumulated experiences and a steady stream of images and other forms of information that reinforce confidence in our ability to see race. Eventually, we become race experts, or at least experts on how we see and experience "the races" – their physical characteristics, their behaviors, and especially their inherent or *essential* differences.

We debate the nature and extent of contemporary racism among family and friends, in online forums, and even through intermittent "national conversations," usually prompted by current events and plagued by predictable sound bites. Occasionally, the shared experiences and beliefs of others may cause us to revisit and rethink our own. Yet, rarely do these exchanges reveal or probe the powerful cultural underpinnings of our collective commitments to race and racism. Think about it. How often do the second glances required to guess someone's "proper" race lead us to second-guess the premise of race-as-biology or the notion of racial *phenotypes* – or to question our desire to "race" them in the first place? We are much more likely to puzzle over such individuals' nonconformity to racial criteria disproven long ago. Sure, those of us still counting may quibble over whether humanity divides into three, four, five, or more races. However, few take the logical leap of allowing this apparently minor detail to challenge our belief in race as a way of defining, categorizing, and inevitably ranking human difference. Taking this step can prove challenging even for those of us who struggle to void the "racial contract" (Mills 1997) and reject notions of

Race: Are We So Different?, First Edition. Alan H. Goodman, Yolanda T. Moses, and Joseph L. Jones.
© 2012 American Anthropological Association. Published 2012 by Blackwell Publishing Ltd.

racial supremacy. In failing to engage such basic questions and issues, or in doing so only superficially, we undermine our ability to understand race and unlearn racism.

Coming to terms with our varied and shared histories of race and racism is a good starting point for those who would reverse this trend. There is more at stake in our collective ability or failure to face our racial pasts squarely than the repetition of past mistakes or misdeeds because these are living histories. They live with and within us, and keep us from moving forward together as equals. At times, historic episodes of race and racism resurface, quite literally, to reshape both past and present. This was the case in the early 1990s when construction workers "rediscovered" Lower Manhattan's 17th- and 18th-century New York African Burial Ground. The subsequent unearthing of artifacts and skeletal remains of over four hundred individuals from this early African American cemetery helped to spur broad interest in the underexplored and underappreciated history of northern slavery (Blakey 2010).

More often, our racial legacies persist in classrooms, workplaces, banks, courtrooms, and a host of other institutional spaces where life chances and material realities are significantly enhanced or diminished. In such settings, the seemingly impersonal nature of procedures and interactions may easily conceal underlying race-infused assumptions, biases, and power relations. Especially through the enactment of "race neutral" and "colorblind" policies, these routine interactions can invoke and reinforce racial stereotypes and power relations in subtle but potent ways (Haney López, chapter 6 this volume). We embody our racial pasts most profoundly through contemporary identity formations and classifications and associated health, wealth, and educational opportunity disparities discussed in part 3 of this book. Thus, while some today are eager to declare the United States a "postracial" society, this refrain rings untrue and problematic for many, especially those targeted by and dedicated to eradicating racism (Harrison 2005; chapter 17 this volume). Indeed, perhaps for better and worse, most find it difficult to imagine a time before race or to envision life without it. Instead, we tend to extrapolate from its current pervasiveness and power – in institutions, popular culture, language, etc. – that race always

has been and always will be with us. Race, it appears, is an inevitable part of our own past and destiny.

Is this truly the case? Just how deep into human history do the roots of race run?

A Recent Human Invention

As the epigraph suggests, and as impossible as it now seems, there was a time before race colored perceptions of human diversity. In fact, most anthropologists, historians, and others who study and compare cultural and societal systems agree that time was not so long ago (Smedley 2007). They do not recognize race among humans as the product of biological evolution or divine design. Instead, scholars have produced a vast and growing literature that documents race as a social/historical/*cultural construct*: a system of ideas, identities, and material relations that emerged slowly in the context of Western European imperialism and colonial expansion beginning in the 15th century. In contrast to the popular belief in race as an empirically validated, innate, and defining human quality, they point out that the first laws designed to establish and patrol racial boundaries and hierarchy did not appear until the middle of the 17th century, when the "racial worldview" was a new thing under the sun (Smedley 2007). From this perspective, human races are not biological units. Although referenced through presumably shared physical (and, increasingly, cultural) attributes, races are in fact political entities resulting from our social actions (Blakey 1999; Mukhopadhyay et al. 2007; Harrison 1995).

We concur. The information in the chapters and sections that follow clearly supports this view of race as a recent human invention. Current scholarship suggests that *human races exist solely because we created them and only in the forms that we perpetuate them.* Furthermore, echoing historian Barbara Fields (1990; 2003), we emphasize that recognizing race and racism as sociocultural rather than biological facts is only the tip of the analytical iceberg. What academics call the "constructivist" approach affords a perspective from which to investigate critically the ideological and material manifestations, connections, and consequences of race, racism, and related phenomena (Smedley 2007; Harrison 2005). Simply put, this approach represents the means, not an end, to understanding race. Thus, it is not our intention simply to convince the reader *that* human races are sociocultural constructs; rather, our goal in this section of the book is to show precisely *how* and *why* race – like class, gender, and other "axes of oppression" (Farmer 2003) – came to be and continues to be such a durable and dynamic stratifying element in US society and culture. As the title of this section implies, the difficult history of race in this country is in actuality a set of stories or interwoven narratives illustrating how forces of tradition, religion, law, and science conspired, and at times competed, to define and influence human diversity (e.g. through miscegenation laws). Realizing its "unnatural" political origins and ongoing development as the product of human activity is the vital *first* step towards a comprehensive understanding of race: what it has been, what it is today, and what we might make of it in years to come.

In this book, we chart our journey through the historical origins and evolution of the very idea of human races. First, however, a brief excursion into that "time before race" is in order. Surely, the claim that race enters the scene so late in human history, perhaps just several hundred years ago, leaves wide open the question of how earlier peoples processed human difference. How *did* our ancestors understand cultural and biological diversity until then? If race is recent in human experience, what preceded racial thinking?

To be sure, past peoples were *ethnocentric*. They frequently believed themselves culturally superior to others and sometimes exhibited the nasty habit of painting others as uncultured and brutish or savage, even to the point of justifying enslavement and killing on this basis. Yet, as any introductory cultural anthropology text will illustrate, ethnocentric and later racial logics differed significantly. These differences are most obvious with respect to characterization of human potential and the perceived connection, or lack thereof, of cultural and physical traits. Prior to the inception of race, people were much less likely to link cultural practices instinctively and irrevocably to physical differences, which were often attributed to distinct environmental conditions (Brace 2005). Nor were people necessarily inclined to believe that phenotypic diversity across groups represented inherent or essential – i.e., unbridgeable – differences in ability or character. Indeed, before race, people more readily saw through phenotypes to find deeper, behavioral similarities if not common ground. Moreover, where they deemed others to be culturally backwards in language, religion, food, adornment, or other behaviors, they tended to view these deficits as correctable. With time, learned behavioral deficiencies could be overwritten through "proper" *enculturation*, while inherent racial inferiority, by definition, could not.

Again, cultural biases are far from benign and it is not our intent to rank stratification systems according to their perniciousness. In fact, it is sometimes difficult to distinguish between ethnocentrism and racism because of the increasing conflation of culture and race (Harrison, chapter 17 this volume). The point here is to show the critical shift that race represents in the nature of human relations; an unfortunate shift in primary focus from learned practices and traditions toward static or fixed notions of physical and essential characteristics. In general, pre-racial conceptions of diversity did not inhibit one from recognizing and acknowledging the shared human capacity to learn and participate fully in *any* culture or society – irrespective of phenotypic characteristics later used to distinguish races.

Classicist Frank Snowden (1983) clearly illustrates this fact in *Before Color Prejudice*, his seminal study of "the black image" in Egyptian, Greek, Roman, and early Christian art and literature. Warning against the temptation to read contemporary social issues into the historical record, Snowden observes that interactions in the ancient Mediterranean between peoples today classified as black or white – even among political and military rivals – were devoid of "acute" color consciousness and any type of racial discrimination. He points out that these societies never observed blackness as the basis of slave status.

Nor is ancient history white race history (Painter 2010). Not surprisingly, the argument against race and racism as fixed or ancient elements of human relations permeates the writings of W. E. B. Du Bois (1939), Anna Julia Cooper (1988), Saint Clair Drake (1987; 1990), and others who sought to defend and "vindicate" African Americans and others against claims of their inherent and immutable inferiority.

Their careful historical and anthropological treatments of the race concept and related phenomena of skin color prejudice and sexism help form the intellectual basis for current constructivist interpretations. As noted above, however, one need not visit antiquity to appreciate a time when correctable culture trumped intractable race as the accident of birth in the view of those with the power to decide such things. From the 18th through the early 20th centuries, for example, white Americans were fascinated with the idea of "civilizing" and "elevating" Native Americans by wiping out indigenous cultural practices.

Our historical examination of race unfolds over four chapters, each of which mirrors in focus and content one of the core history components of the RACE: Are We So Different? traveling museum exhibit. The topics we cover include origins of the human race concept; race and racism in science; history and meaning of the "white" racial category and whiteness; and the role of legal racialization/racism in creating and maintaining social inequality and privilege. Each chapter includes a time line of key concepts, events, and individuals as well as essays and other supporting features that yield deeper insights into these topics. These histories help to reveal race as both social reality and one of science's greatest fictions, subjects we explore in detail in later sections of the book. To convey them, we enlist numerous voices representing multiple perspectives. We hear from historical figures, some of today's leading scholars, and others whose personal experiences and insights illustrate the contradictions and flexibility that have made both race and racism so very compelling over time. Some individuals, like Pocahontas, Thomas Jefferson, and Frederick Douglass, are no doubt familiar to readers. Others such as Takao Ozawa, John Punch, and Franz Boas may prove less so outside academic circles.

In chapter 3, "Creating Race," we reconstruct the unique social and economic circumstances that gave rise to the beginnings of race "as we know it" in colonial North America. In an essay on the origins of racial ideology, Smedley observes that the advent of race was not an automatic process upon the arrival of Europeans and Africans to American shores. Rather, what we typically find in the early colonies are distinctive medleys of "Old" and "New" World

ethnicities fighting, loving, and living together without resort to race or racism (Berlin 2003). Differences of religion (Christians versus heathens) and nationality initially weighed more heavily on the minds of the first colonists than did those of skin color. Smedley describes how all of this changed when wealthy landowners created race for the purposes of justifying chattel slavery, claiming indigenous peoples' land, and promoting division among an increasingly rebellious class of Native American, European, and African laborers. The development of a heritable and permanent slave status for blacks contrasted starkly with slavery as practiced in other societies and the nation's founding principles, including the burgeoning notion of freedom and liberty as inalienable human rights.

Chapter 4, "Human Mismeasure," is an historical primer for our discussion of the science of human variation (part 2), in which we rule out the possibility that human races *ever* existed from an evolutionary perspective. The chapter takes its name from evolutionary biologist Stephen Jay Gould's *The Mismeasure of Man*, a classic refutation of race-based intelligence studies. Here, we examine how scientists and others nonetheless reverse-engineered the myth of biological race from human variation. We recount the rise, fall, and return of race science and scientific racism as scientists predisposed to look for racial differences either found or manufactured them. Meanwhile, other scientists contested racial studies by redirecting their foci from deterministic ends (sometimes leaving unchallenged the biological race concept) or developing nonracial means of studying human variation (e.g. Livingstone 1962; Brace 2005). Consequently, there exists within most sciences a triple legacy of racialism/racism/antiracism evident as one follows the time line for this chapter (Mukhopadhyay and Moses 1997; Armelagos and Goodman 1998; Mullings 2005; Marks 2010). In this chapter, archaeologist Joe Watkins tackles an important dimension of anthropology's conflicted racial legacy in an essay on the traditionally contentious relationship between Native Americans and the practice of archaeology in the United States of America.

Chapter 5 is an exploration of the origins and expansion of racial whiteness throughout the history of the United States. Over the past several decades, some historians, sociologists, and cultural analysts have developed whiteness studies as a rich field of inquiry into the historical and cultural construction and maintenance of the racial category "white." These scholars detail the early political and economic difficulties faced by European immigrants along their various paths to "becoming white," as well as the social and material privileges ultimately afforded them, and denied racial others, through these processes (Brodkin 1998; Jacobson 1998; Dominguez 1986; Roediger 1999; 2008; Haney López 1996). We approach the topic of personal whiteness from several perspectives. Historian Nell Painter compares the views of Thomas Jefferson and contemporary Michel-Guillame-Jean de Crèvecoeur, a French soldier-diplomat and writer, regarding racial (Anglo-Saxon) purity as the basis of early American whiteness. Linking past and present, anthropologist Carol Mukhopadhyay contributes to this chapter an enlightening essay on the persistence of the term "Caucasian" in U.S. culture. Mukhopadhyay argues compellingly that retirement of this relic of racial *typology* is long overdue. Indeed, shifting boundaries of whiteness remind us that racial identities and categories, as products of historical and social tensions, are at once salient and perhaps less stable than they seem.

In chapter 6, "Separate and Unequal," the final chapter of part 1, we consider how those with the power to do so legislated race, racism, and racial privilege. This is a topic explored in our discussion of whiteness and expanded here to include the experiences of various nonwhites. We recount key aspects of our shared histories of Native American land dispossession, race-based slavery, anti-immigration efforts, anti-Semitism, segregation, Japanese American internment, redlining, and other legal forms of discrimination and oppression. Of course, such measures never went unanswered, and we illustrate how proponents of racial justice resisted, modified and/or appropriated them. Therefore, we also present milestones in the painstaking and ongoing expansion of human and civil rights that inform racial identities that many today justifiably celebrate. Author Jonathan Odell provides an honest and moving account of his indoctrination as a young boy into 1950s' Jim Crow culture and white privilege. Along with the discussion of contemporary experiences of race and racism found in part 3, this chapter reminds us how far we as a nation have come, and how far we must go in order to establish full racial equality.

In a short book, the histories presented in this section are necessarily scanty. Fortunately, excellent historical treatments of many aspects of the race concept are readily available — some written by contributors to this volume. However, connecting dots across time and space in order to understand human experiences and problems as fully as possible is what anthropologists do best. We believe the many and deep connections between culture, science, and society that we begin to explore in this section provide a novel conceptual framework for appreciating human diversity or variation within the greater context of our shared humanity. Furthermore, the information presented here is indispensable for anyone willing to rethink race and unlearn racism. It is our hope that as you read you will gain a greater appreciation for race and history as living forces that drive contemporary inequalities and identities. Let's begin …

References

Armelagos, George J., and Alan H. Goodman
1998   Race, Racism and Anthropology. *In* Building a New Biocultural Synthesis: Political-Economic Perspectives on Human Biology. Alan H. Goodman and Thomas L. Leatherman, eds. pp. 359–377. Ann Arbor: The University of Michigan Press.

Berlin, Ira
2003   Generations of Captivity: A History of African-American Slaves. Cambridge, MA: The Belknap Press of Harvard University Press.

Blakey, Michael L.
1999   Scientific Racism and the Biological Concept of Race. Literature and Psychology 45: 29–43.

Blakey, Michael L.
2010   African Burial Ground Project: Paradigm for Cooperation. Museum International 62: 61–68.

Brace, C. Loring
2005   "Race" Is a Four-Letter Word: The Genesis of the Concept. New York: Oxford University Press.

Brodkin, Karen
1998   How Jews Became White Folks And What That Says about Race in America. New Brunswick: Rutgers University Press.

Cooper, Anna Julia
1988 A Voice from the South. New York: Oxford University Press.

Dominguez, Virginia R.
1986 White By Definition: Social Classification in Creole Louisiana. New Brunswick: Rutgers University Press.

Drake, St. Clair
1987 Black Folk Here and There: An Essay in History and Anthropology, vol. 1. Los Angeles: Center for Afro-American Studies, University of California.

Drake, St. Clair
1990 Black Folk Here and There: An Essay in History and Anthropology, vol. 2. Los Angeles: Center for Afro-American Studies, University of California.

Du Bois, W. E. B.
1939 Black Folk Then and Now: An Essay in the History and Sociology of the Negro Race. New York: Henry Holt and Company.

Farmer, Paul
2003 Pathologies of Power: Health, Human Rights and the New War on the Poor. Berkeley: University of California Press.

Fields, Barbara J.
1990 Slavery, Race and Ideology in the United States of America. New Left Review 181: 95–118.

Fields, Barbara J.
2003 Of Rogues and Geldings. The American Historical Review 108: 1397–1405.

Haney López, Ian F.
1996 White by Law: The Legal Construction of Race. New York: New York University Press.

Harrison, Faye V.
1995 The Persistent Power of "Race" in the Cultural and Political Economy of Racism. Annual Review of Anthropology 24: 47–74.

Harrison, Faye V., ed.
2005 Resisting Racism and Xenophobia: Global Perspectives on Race, Gender, and Human Rights. Walnut Creek, CA: Altamira Press.

Jacobson, Matthew Frye
1998 Whiteness of a Different Color: European Immigrants and the Alchemy of Race. Cambridge, MA: Harvard University Press.

Livingstone, Frank
1962 On the Nonexistence of Races. Current Anthropology 3: 279–281.

Marks, Jonathan
2010 The Two 20th-Century Crises of Racial Anthropology. In Histories of American Physical Anthropology in the Twentieth Century. Michael A. Little and Kenneth A. R. Kennedy, eds. pp. 187–206.

Mills, Charles W.
1997 The Racial Contract. Ithaca and London: Cornell University Press.

Mukhopadhyay, Carol C., and Yolanda T. Moses
1997 Reestablishing "Race" in Anthropological Discourse. American Anthropologist 99: 517–533.

Mukhopadhyay, Carol C., Henze, Rosemary, and Yolanda T. Moses
2007 How Real Is Race: A Sourcebook on Race, Culture, and Biology. Lanham, MD: Rowman and Littlefield Education Press.

Mullings, Leith
2005 Interrogating Racism: Toward an Antiracist Anthropology. Annual Review of Anthropology 34: 667–693.

Painter, Nell Irvin
2010 The History of White People. New York: W. W. Norton and Company.

Roediger, David R.
1999 The Wages of Whiteness: Race in the Making of the American Working Class. Rev. edition. London: Verso.

Roediger, David R.
2008 How Race Survived U.S. History: From Settlement and Slavery to the Obama Phenomenon. London: Verso.

Smedley, Audrey
2007 Race in North America: Origin and Evolution of a Worldview. 3rd edition. Boulder: Westview Press.

Snowden, Frank M., Jr.
1983 Before Color Prejudice: The Ancient View of Blacks. Cambridge, MA: Harvard University Press.

3

Creating Race

Race was not found in nature but made by people in power.
RACE exhibit, SMM

Today, most scholars recognize race as an idea or set of ideas about human difference. Often, these ideas are inaccurate and woefully inadequate for understanding or explaining the nature and various mechanisms of human diversity. Nonetheless, they play a major role in shaping our interpretations of individual and group differences as well as our social networks and material relations. In other words, we do not identify human races – at least not through any objective means. We create them. Human races did not evolve in nature but from folk beliefs through cultural and social practices.

How did the idea of race begin? The answer resides in the complex interplay of science, government, and culture within the history of Spanish colonial expansion into the Americas. When European colonists first arrived on North American shores beginning in the 1500s, Native Americans already inhabited the land. The Spanish, French, and English frequently clashed with indigenous peoples as they established settlements in Florida, the northeast area bordering Canada, the Virginia colony, and the southwest. Initially, Europeans viewed various indigenous tribes as separate "nations," not as "races." Nor did the earliest English colonists describe blacks in racial terms when they established a labor system of indentured servitude that included both Europeans and Africans. However, by the mid-1600s, the status of Africans began to

change dramatically. They were no longer servants with the prospect of freedom following a period of servitude, like their European counterparts. Instead, colonial leaders relegated Africans to a status of permanent slavery. For a time, enslaved Africans *and* Native Americans labored side by side (with indentured European servants) to produce rice, cotton, indigo, and other cash crops, but eventually slavery was limited to blacks. It was only with their increased reliance upon slavery and ambitions for Native American lands that English colonists began to develop a racial hierarchy. Slavery and Native American land dispossession did not begin, but *became*, racial or race-based projects.

By now, you may be wondering why slavery and military campaigns against indigenous peoples required rationalization in the first place. Sure, we *now* see slavery as a moral stain, our nation's "original sin," yet societies change and today's moral bearings differ markedly from those of yesterday. Didn't colonization and slavery align with the majority values of that time? Wasn't slavery practiced the world over – including in Africa and the Americas – prior to and during the colonial era? Why, then, were English colonists compelled to justify these millennia-old practices, whether through race or any other means?

While one may be inclined to view slavery as the same institution whether practiced in ancient Rome, the 17th-century Gold Coast (Ghana), or 19th-century Virginia, this, in fact, was not the case. Race-based slavery in the Americas was without historical precedent, the

Race: Are We So Different?, First Edition. Alan H. Goodman, Yolanda T. Moses, and Joseph L. Jones.
© 2012 American Anthropological Association. Published 2012 by Blackwell Publishing Ltd.

foundation of the burgeoning "Atlantic World" economy. For example, one major difference between American "slave societies" and those other "societies with slaves" was the extent of social alienation between the enslaved and those who "owned" them (Berlin 2003; Meillasoux 1991). In the former, enslaved individuals generally found themselves integrated into the social fabric as occupants of the bottom rung of a biological and fictive kinship ladder. However farfetched the notion of human equality may have seemed to elites in these societies, they usually did not deem it necessary to call into question the fundamental humanity of those they enslaved, whether through conquest, debt, or other means. Nor was slave status necessarily inherited, an intergenerational curse designed to ensure an enslaved labor force, as was eventually the case in the colonial Americas. Thus, the prospect of freedom was more likely in "societies with slaves" – if not for the individual, then for their children.

Race emerged specifically to justify this new form of dehumanizing slavery and the characterization of Native Americans as (sometimes "noble") savages undeserving of their lands. During the 1770s, when English colonists in the United States fought a war for independence from the British Crown, they were acutely aware of their moral contradictions. Indeed, as time passed, their constant fear was that enslaved communities might draw inspiration for large-scale rebellion from successful freedom struggles on both sides of the Atlantic, particularly the Haitian Revolution (James 1989). Yet, they continued to deny Africans their freedom and withhold rights from Native Americans. Ironically, one of the first casualties of the Revolutionary War was Crispus Attucks, a runaway enslaved individual of African and Indian ancestry.

Perhaps no historical figure exemplifies the inherent political and personal contradictions of race and racism like Thomas Jefferson, the nation's third president. A Virginia slave owner who helped draft the Declaration of Independence, Jefferson actually penned a lengthy indictment of slavery removed from the document's final version. Today it is common knowledge that Jefferson in all likelihood fathered children with enslaved Sarah "Sally" Hemings, a claim that actually dates to his first presidential term (Gordon-Reed 2008). In addition to his political career, Jefferson was a prominent natural historian, a role in which he encouraged the scientific exploration of racial origins and black inferiority specifically. In *Notes on the State of Virginia* (1776), Jefferson observes that blacks possess "inferior … endowments both of body and mind" in comparison to whites and, to a lesser degree, Native Americans. He wonders whether this state, proposed "as a suspicion only," reflects separate natural origins for the races or is instead the result of racial divergence from a common origin (either as separate species or subspecies) due to "time and circumstances." As we discuss in the following chapter, scientists eagerly took up this challenge. Some, like Swedish naturalist Carolus Linnaeus – whose tenth edition of *Systema Naturae* (1758) introduced the familiar binomial (genus, species) nomenclature system of taxonomy (e.g. *Homo sapiens*) – had already endeavored to investigate and classify the "races of man."

CREATING RACE, 1400–1800, A TIME LINE

> ❝ Race was never just a matter of categories. It was a matter of creating hierarchies. ❞
>
> ROBIN D. G. KELLEY, historian,
> University of Southern California: RACE exhibit, SMM

A time before race Prior to the advent of racial slavery in the colonial Americas, the concept of race – defined as a way to divide and rank peoples of the world – does not exist in Europe. The primary measure of difference is religion. There are Christian peoples and there are heathens, which include Jews, Muslims and pagans. Slavery exists but slave status is based on religious affiliation as a non-Christian, not skin color or "race."

> ❝ Expansion, conquest, exploitation, and enslavement have characterized much of human history over the past 5,000 years or so, but none of these events before the modern era resulted in the development of ideologies or social systems based on race. ❞ SMEDLEY 1999

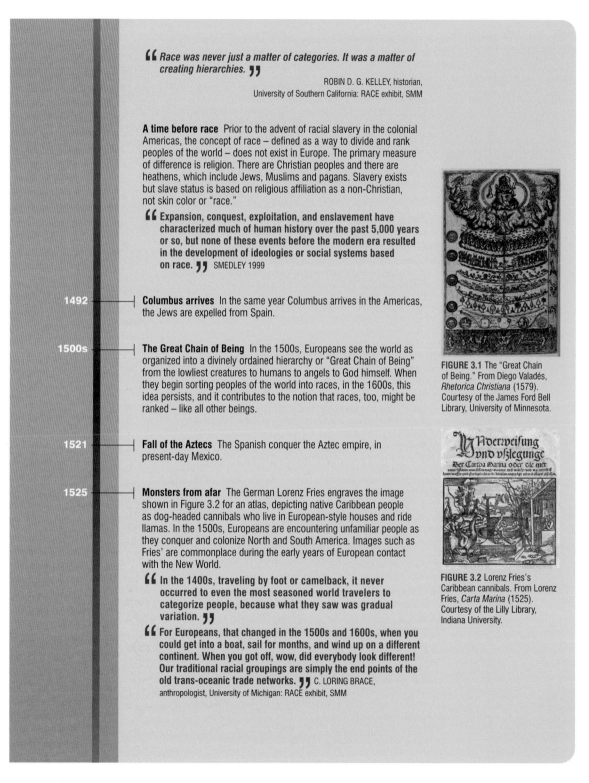

1492 **Columbus arrives** In the same year Columbus arrives in the Americas, the Jews are expelled from Spain.

1500s **The Great Chain of Being** In the 1500s, Europeans see the world as organized into a divinely ordained hierarchy or "Great Chain of Being" from the lowliest creatures to humans to angels to God himself. When they begin sorting peoples of the world into races, in the 1600s, this idea persists, and it contributes to the notion that races, too, might be ranked – like all other beings.

FIGURE 3.1 The "Great Chain of Being." From Diego Valadés, *Rhetorica Christiana* (1579). Courtesy of the James Ford Bell Library, University of Minnesota.

1521 **Fall of the Aztecs** The Spanish conquer the Aztec empire, in present-day Mexico.

1525 **Monsters from afar** The German Lorenz Fries engraves the image shown in Figure 3.2 for an atlas, depicting native Caribbean people as dog-headed cannibals who live in European-style houses and ride llamas. In the 1500s, Europeans are encountering unfamiliar people as they conquer and colonize North and South America. Images such as Fries' are commonplace during the early years of European contact with the New World.

> ❝ In the 1400s, traveling by foot or camelback, it never occurred to even the most seasoned world travelers to categorize people, because what they saw was gradual variation. ❞

> ❝ For Europeans, that changed in the 1500s and 1600s, when you could get into a boat, sail for months, and wind up on a different continent. When you got off, wow, did everybody look different! Our traditional racial groupings are simply the end points of the old trans-oceanic trade networks. ❞ C. LORING BRACE, anthropologist, University of Michigan: RACE exhibit, SMM

FIGURE 3.2 Lorenz Fries's Caribbean cannibals. From Lorenz Fries, *Carta Marina* (1525). Courtesy of the Lilly Library, Indiana University.

1513–1604

Early Spanish and French colonies The Spanish and French explore and establish colonies in North America. St Augustine is founded in 1565, and, under the Spanish Crown, the settlement provides refuge and freedom for enslaved individuals who accept Catholicism. In 1604 the French establish the colonial territory of Acadia, which includes parts of eastern Quebec, the Maritime provinces and present-day New England. Both Spanish and French colonizers work to convert American Indians to Catholicism.

FIGURE 3.3 *The Landing of the Pilgrims at Plymouth*. Courtesy of the Library of Congress.

1607

English colonization begins England's first successful colony in America is established in Jamestown.

1617

Pocahontas visits the British king Pocahontas, the daughter of Chief Powhatan and wife of early Jamestown settler John Rolfe, visits England and is presented at the court of King James I.

❝ In the early 1600s the English did not yet think in racial terms. Status and religion were more important. Pocahontas was received so well in London because she was royalty. ❞ KAREN KUPPERMAN, historian, New York University: RACE exhibit, SMM

FIGURE 3.4 Pocahontas. Courtesy of the Library of Congress.

1619

First Africans in Virginia The first Africans in the English colonies arrive in Jamestown. Africans are already held as slaves in the Portuguese and Spanish colonies of South America and the Caribbean, but their status in early Virginia is less clear.

❝ The first Africans who arrived in Jamestown in 1619 were not initially perceived as slaves; slavery had to be created and established as a new institution in these colonies. ❞ AUDREY SMEDLEY, anthropologist, Virginia Commonwealth University: RACE exhibit, SMM

1600s

Indentured servitude Many who come to the colonies, both Africans and Europeans, arrive as indentured servants, bound to work for a set period – usually four to seven years – in exchange for meals and housing. The English force the poor and destitute, convicts, and Irish prisoners of war into service. It is a life of hard labor, little food, and few rights. Many die before completing their time. In colonial Virginia, until the late 1600s, indentured servitude – not slavery – is the dominant form of labor. In the colonies, white and black servants work side by side.

❝ [Black and white servants] ran away together, played together and revolted together. ❞

❝ They mated and married, siring a sizable mixed population. In the process, black and white servants – the majority of the colonial population – created a racial wonderland. ... The basic division ... was between servants and free people, and there were whites and blacks on both sides of the line. ❞ BENNETT 1987

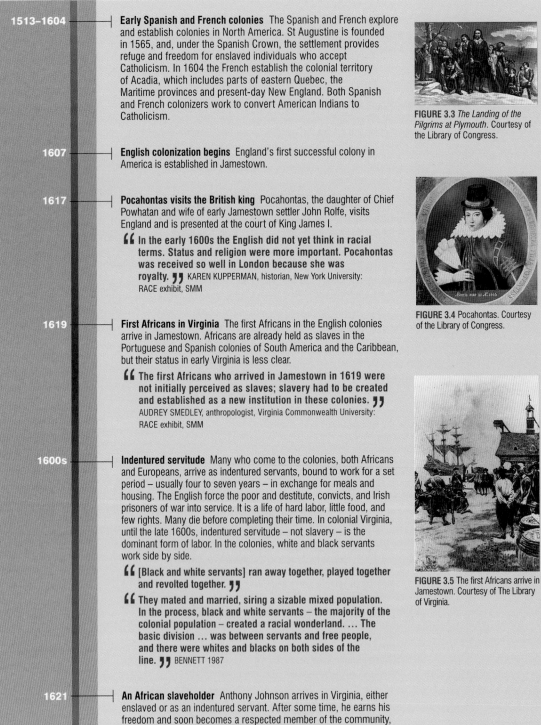

FIGURE 3.5 The first Africans arrive in Jamestown. Courtesy of The Library of Virginia.

1621

An African slaveholder Anthony Johnson arrives in Virginia, either enslaved or as an indentured servant. After some time, he earns his freedom and soon becomes a respected member of the community, with a large farm, livestock, and slaves of his own. In 1655, he successfully challenges a white farmer who has illegally taken one of his enslaved laborers, winning his case in the colonial courts.

1640

Unequal punishment As punishment for escaping, a black indentured servant, John Punch, is sentenced to servitude for life. However, his two indentured white companions are ordered to serve only one additional year.

> ❝ [This is] the first definite indication of outright enslavement. ... No white servant in any English colony, so far as is known, ever received a like sentence. ❞ JORDAN 1968

1675–76

King Philip's War Metacom, the chief of the Wampanoag Indians (called King Philip by the English colonists), frustrated by growing competition over land and humiliating treatment by the colonists, declares war. King Philip is defeated, tribes throughout the region are decimated, and colonists jail many neutral Indians who are Christian converts.

> ❝ When permanent settlement became the primary English concern ... and land the object of desire, the image of the Indian as a hostile savage became ascendant in the English mind. ... To typecast the Indian as a brutish savage was to solve a moral dilemma. If the Indian was truly cordial, generous, and eager to trade, what justification could there be for taking his land? But if he was a savage, without religion or culture, perhaps the colonists' actions were defensible. ❞ NASH 1970

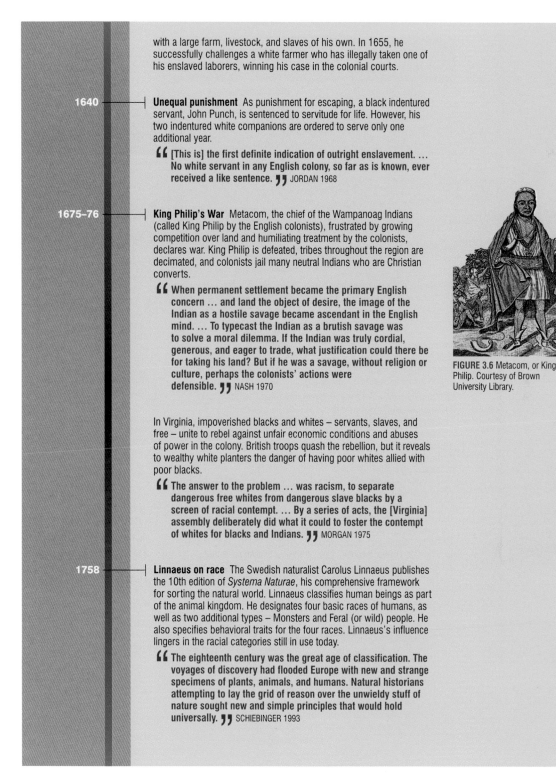

FIGURE 3.6 Metacom, or King Philip. Courtesy of Brown University Library.

In Virginia, impoverished blacks and whites – servants, slaves, and free – unite to rebel against unfair economic conditions and abuses of power in the colony. British troops quash the rebellion, but it reveals to wealthy white planters the danger of having poor whites allied with poor blacks.

> ❝ The answer to the problem ... was racism, to separate dangerous free whites from dangerous slave blacks by a screen of racial contempt. ... By a series of acts, the [Virginia] assembly deliberately did what it could to foster the contempt of whites for blacks and Indians. ❞ MORGAN 1975

1758

Linnaeus on race The Swedish naturalist Carolus Linnaeus publishes the 10th edition of *Systema Naturae*, his comprehensive framework for sorting the natural world. Linnaeus classifies human beings as part of the animal kingdom. He designates four basic races of humans, as well as two additional types – Monsters and Feral (or wild) people. He also specifies behavioral traits for the four races. Linnaeus's influence lingers in the racial categories still in use today.

> ❝ The eighteenth century was the great age of classification. The voyages of discovery had flooded Europe with new and strange specimens of plants, animals, and humans. Natural historians attempting to lay the grid of reason over the unwieldy stuff of nature sought new and simple principles that would hold universally. ❞ SCHIEBINGER 1993

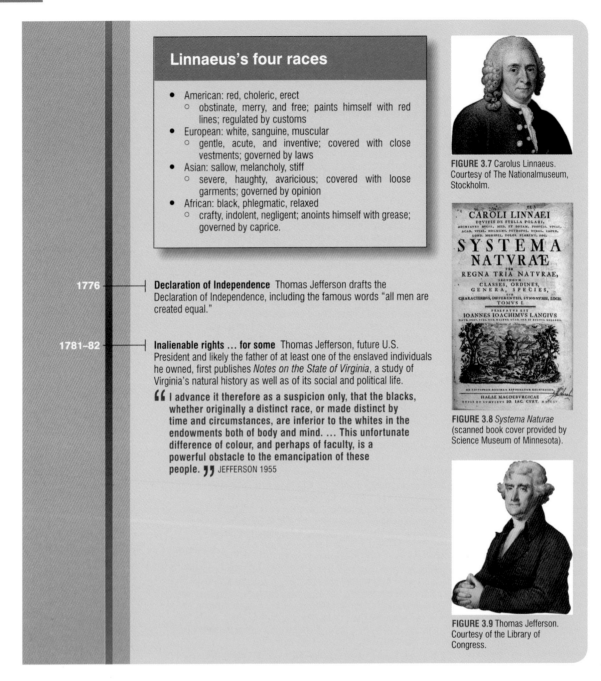

Linnaeus's four races

- American: red, choleric, erect
    - obstinate, merry, and free; paints himself with red lines; regulated by customs
- European: white, sanguine, muscular
    - gentle, acute, and inventive; covered with close vestments; governed by laws
- Asian: sallow, melancholy, stiff
    - severe, haughty, avaricious; covered with loose garments; governed by opinion
- African: black, phlegmatic, relaxed
    - crafty, indolent, negligent; anoints himself with grease; governed by caprice.

FIGURE 3.7 Carolus Linnaeus. Courtesy of The Nationalmuseum, Stockholm.

FIGURE 3.8 *Systema Naturae* (scanned book cover provided by Science Museum of Minnesota).

1776 — **Declaration of Independence** Thomas Jefferson drafts the Declaration of Independence, including the famous words "all men are created equal."

1781–82 — **Inalienable rights ... for some** Thomas Jefferson, future U.S. President and likely the father of at least one of the enslaved individuals he owned, first publishes *Notes on the State of Virginia*, a study of Virginia's natural history as well as of its social and political life.

> ❝ I advance it therefore as a suspicion only, that the blacks, whether originally a distinct race, or made distinct by time and circumstances, are inferior to the whites in the endowments both of body and mind. ... This unfortunate difference of colour, and perhaps of faculty, is a powerful obstacle to the emancipation of these people. ❞ JEFFERSON 1955

FIGURE 3.9 Thomas Jefferson. Courtesy of the Library of Congress.

AUDREY SMEDLEY
The Origin of the Ideology of Race

Audrey Smedley *is Professor of Anthropology Emerita, Virginia Commonwealth University and Binghamtom University. She is the author of* Race in North America: Origin and Evolution of a Worldview. *Application of the term "race" to humans certainly predates the colonial American experiment. However, it is not until the latter part of the 17th century that we witness the beginnings of a full-blown ideological system predicated on, and dedicated to reproducing, the idea of irreconcilable racial differences. In this essay, Smedley describes the critical social and economic forces and events – the decisions – that gave rise to race in colonial America.* Photograph courtesy of Joseph Jones.

Contemporary historical studies have revealed that "race" was a relatively recent invention in human history (Allen 1994; 1997; Fredrickson 2002; Hannaford 1996; Smedley 2007. Historians point out that our popular beliefs about human races did not exist before the late 17th century. These authors agree that race was essentially a cultural invention about human differences that had its basis in social, political, and economic conditions. Although most Americans still believe that physical differences reflected in skin color are the basis for racial categories, such differences tell us nothing about the real nature of human physical diversity and obscure bio-genetic realities. Modern science now holds that there is no basis in science for the categories of people we call races (Part 2).

"Race" originated as a folk ideology about human differences and was constituted of beliefs and attitudes about these differences. These attitudes and beliefs emerged over a period roughly beginning in the 1690s and continued over the 18th century, a period which also coincides with numerous laws establishing American slavery. From the late 18th century on, these popular beliefs were buttressed by the appearance of scientific arguments that were designed to confirm them.

The significance of history

In 1607, the English began settling colonies in North America, following the pattern of the Spanish and Portuguese, with the objective of acquiring wealth. The early colonists, who took over most of the land, unsuccessfully tried to force conquered Indians to work. However, the Indians did not take well to forced labor; many died of European diseases and others escaped to unknown territories. The English then turned to importing indentured servants from the British Isles, many of them Irishmen captured in wars. These were poor men and some women who were allowed to work off their transportation debts and subsequently obtain their freedom. The need for labor was acute: early colonists barely survived on what they could produce themselves, and we know the death rate was high. They soon learned that the one product that would bring them considerable wealth was tobacco, a highly labor-intensive crop.

The first Africans who arrived in Virginia colony in 1619 were not initially considered slaves. They had Spanish or Portuguese names and were familiar with European culture. Like other poor laborers, they were treated as indentured servants who could also achieve their freedom after paying their debts. Some of these Africans worked hard and acquired land, houses, live-stock, and tools on their own. Historians now agree that true slavery did not exist in the early decades of the English North American colonies (see Allen 1997; Fredrickson 2002; E. Morgan 1975; P. Morgan 1998; Parent, Jr. 2003). Moreover, there is little or no evidence that Africans were treated differently from other people of the same class. They were assimilated into colonial society as were others. When they acquired land, they participated in the assembly, the governing body of the colony, voted, served on juries, and socialized with white planters.

Historian Edmund Morgan writes,

> There is more than a little evidence that Virginians during these years were ready to think of Negroes as members or potential members of the community on the same terms as other men and to demand of them the same standards of behavior. Black men and white serving the same master worked, ate, and slept together, and together shared in escapades, escapes, and punishments. (1975:327)

He adds, "It was common for servants and slaves to run away together, steal hogs together, get drunk together. It was not uncommon for them to make love together" (327). Indeed, there was no stigma associated with what we today call "interracial" marriages.

Until the early 18th century, the image of Africans among most Europeans was generally positive. They were farmers and cattle-breeders; they had industries, arts and crafts, governments, and commerce. Moreover, they had immunities to Old World diseases, they were better laborers under the tropical conditions of the southern settlements; and they had nowhere to run and hide once transplanted to the New World (E. Morgan 1975; Smedley 2007).

There were critical reasons for the preference for Africans. As early as the 1630s, planters expressed a desire for African laborers ("If only we had some Africans!" they wrote). Records of plantation owners in the Caribbean and in the colonies of Virginia and Maryland reveal that Africans were initially considered a civilized and docile people who had knowledge of, and experience with, tropical cultivation. They were accustomed to discipline, one of the hallmarks of civilized behavior, as well as working cooperatively in groups. They knew how to grow corn, tobacco, sugar cane, and cotton in their native lands; these crops were unknown in Europe. And many Africans had knowledge of metalwork, carpentry, cattle-keeping, brick-making, weaving, rope making, leather tanning, and many other skills. Colonists soon realized that without Africans, their enterprises would fail. "We cannot survive without Africans!" they claimed.

By mid-century, the colonies were in crisis. A few men from among the earliest settlers had taken over most of the fertile land; they had established large plantations and made huge fortunes growing tobacco when they had enough workers. Poor servants who achieved their freedom found it difficult to acquire land. The freed poor and servants, among whom were now included Europeans, Africans, mulattoes, and a few Indians, became unhappy with their lot and especially the corruption and abuse of power on the part of wealthy men who ruled the colony. They threatened rebellions, plundered their neighbors, showed contempt for colony leaders, and generated unrest throughout the settlement.

In 1676, the most famous rebellion took place. Led by Nathaniel Bacon, this uprising of thousands of poor workers in Virginia was the first major threat to social stability. The rebellion dissipated after Bacon's death, but British royal commissioners sent out to suppress the uprising realized the population at large had supported the rebellion and were "sullen and obstinate." On one occasion they faced a dissatisfied "rabble" of "400 African and 600 or 700 European bond laborers, chiefly Irish" (Allen 1994:218). The colony leaders soon recognized the need for a strategy to prevent such occurrences in the future and to ensure that a sufficient number of easily controlled laborers were made available to plantation owners.

Establishing slavery

The decisions that the rulers of the colony made during the last decades of the 17th century and the first quarter of the 18th century resulted in the establishment of racial slavery. These leaders began to pass a series of laws separating out Africans and their descendants, restricting their rights and mobility, and imposing a condition of permanent slavery on them. Africans were now being brought directly from Africa rather than from African communities established in Europe or other European colonies. They were different from earlier Africans in that they were heathens, that is, not Christians, and were unfamiliar with European languages, customs, and traditions. They were vulnerable to any restrictions placed on them. Some colony leaders began to argue that Africans had no rights under British laws and therefore could be subject to forced and permanent labor with impunity.

Sources of English servants began to decline in the latter part of the 17th century, as jobs became available at home. The slave trade with Africa increased as internal warfare in Africa made more and more people available for the slave trade. Leaders of the colonies, all large planters, had two objectives: to impose effective social controls over the population and prevent rebellions; and to provide themselves with cheap and easily controlled workers. They readily perceived that, given the varied physical characteristics of the working population, they could separate them and demarcate some for permanent slavery. Anthony Parent (2003) argues that a powerful planter class, acting to further its own economic interests, deliberately brought a new form of servitude, racial slavery, to Virginia over the period 1690–1725. In this period, dozens of laws were passed restricting the rights of Africans and their descendents, imposing permanent slavery on them, and forbidding masters to set them free. By 1725, even free Negroes were prohibited from voting.

Colonial leaders were simultaneously doing something else: they were laying the basis for the invention of the idea of race and racial identities. They began to homogenize all Europeans, regardless of ethnicity, status, or social class, into a new category. The first time the term "white," rather than "Christian" or an ethnic name (English, Irish, Scots, Portuguese, German, Spanish, Swede), appeared in the public record was seen in a law passed in 1691 that prohibited the marriages of Europeans ("whites") with Negroes, Indians, and mulattoes (Smedley 2007:118). A clearly separated category of Negroes as slaves allowed newly freed European servants opportunities to realize their ambitions and to identify common interests with the wealthy and powerful. New laws offered material advantages and social privileges to poor whites. In this way, colony leaders consciously contrived a social control mechanism to prevent the unification of the working poor (Allen 1997). Physical features became markers of racial (social) status. As Virginia's governor William Gooch asserted, the assembly sought to "fix a perpetual Brand upon Free Negroes and Mulattos" (Allen 1997:242).

Rationalizing slavery

The earliest rationale for racial slavery did not invoke differences in physical features, but rather identified Africans as uncivilized heathens. The first "savages" that the English had created in their minds were the "wild Irish." In the late 16th century, after centuries of conflict and brutal warfare with the Irish, Queen Elizabeth declared that the Irish were natural "savages" incapable of civilization. In fact, the Elizabethans came very near to racializing the Irish. Indeed, in the 18th century the term "race" and facets of the ideology of race were imposed on them by many historical writers.

Native Americans had been deemed "savages" when they resisted English appropriation of their lands, but this image began to change in the late 18th century to a more benign "noble savage." By then most Native Americans were dying out or had been forcibly driven onto reservations, a process begun in the previous century in the northeast colonies. Now,

by reducing Africans to permanent slavery, prohibiting owners from freeing slaves, and preventing their education and training, the English invented a new savage. From the 18th century on, negative characterizations of Africans formed part of a new rationalization for enslavement. These became the stereotypes of races and race differences that we inherited in the 19th and 20th centuries. *What colony leaders were doing was establishing unequal groups, called races, and imposing different social meanings on them.* As they created the institutional and behavioral aspects of slavery, the colonists were simultaneously structuring the ideological components of race. The defenders of slavery exaggerated human group differences and developed an ideology about these differences that dehumanized "the Negro" and demoted him in popular eyes to a status closer to the apes, placing the onus of slavery on its victims.

In 1865, following the Civil War, slavery officially ended in the South, but "race" as social status and the basis of our human identities remained. Race ideology was based in a belief in the existence of separate, distinct, and exclusive groups that were made unequal by God or nature. African Americans, the most inferior, were at the bottom of the hierarchy, European whites (some of them) were at the top. Each race was thought to have distinct physical and behavioral traits. Thus, we have the continuing stereotype of African Americans as lacking in intelligence, lazy, overly sexed, loud, irrational, musical, emotional, and superstitious. Finally, it was believed that these race differences were inherited and immutable; thus, they could not be transformed or transcended (see Smedley 2007).

After the Civil War, white Americans had been so deeply conditioned to the beliefs in the inferiority of the low-status races (blacks and Indians) that they could not accept them as equal citizens. They made enormous efforts to keep them separate and inferior and were largely successful as the statistics regarding the well-being and social and economic status of blacks and Indians demonstrate even today (Jones 2009; Macartney 2011). With the election of Barack Obama as president of the United States, on the other hand, and numerous social changes taking place, many people believe that the power of the ideology of race is declining in the United States, and some forecast its demise everywhere.

Creating Race

A Conversation

We conclude each chapter in this section with the words of leading thinkers on race. These "conversations" are edited transcripts of videos from the RACE: Are We So Different? traveling museum exhibit provided by California Newsreel (www.newsreel.org). To close our discussion on the origins of race, we turn to a group of distinguished historians who discuss the multiethnic composition of early colonial America and the transition from ethnic to racial identities. **Mia Bay** *is Professor of History and Associate Director of the Center for Race and Ethnicity at Rutgers University.* **Ira Berlin** *is Distinguished University Professor at University of Maryland, College Park.* **James Horton** *is Benjamin Banneker Professor of American Studies and History at George Washington University and Historian Emeritus of the Smithsonian Institution's National Museum of American History.* **Robin Kelley** *is Professor of American Studies and Ethnicity at the University of Southern California.* **Theda Perdue** *is Atlanta Distinguished Professor of Southern Culture at University of North Carolina at Chapel Hill.*

MIA BAY: The word "race" doesn't really appear until the 15th century and doesn't mean what we think it means, or even what it meant in the 19th century, then. It sort of begins as a notion of lineage. Who you are related to is your race. Your family is your race; your extended family is your race.

THEDA PERDUE: One of the things that happens with the Age of Discovery is that Europeans had to confront the presence of people in the world about whom they'd never known anything before. And so, the result is that they have to account for their presence. Genesis is not very clear on this. That is, you have to stretch it a good bit to account for people who look quite different from Europeans. And so, Europeans began to search for reasons to explain why people not only look different, but why they live in different ways, why they have different beliefs.

People in the 17th century did not think about differences between human beings in the way that we

think about those differences today. They were more likely to distinguish between Christians and heathens than they were between people of color and people who were white. That is, they regarded a person's [religious] status in life as somehow more fundamental than what color they were or what their particular background was. And so, in the 17th century, certainly Europeans had a concept of difference, but it was not a concept that is analogous to modern notions of race.

JAMES HORTON: Think about it for a second. If you had interviewed the first slave to get off the first slave ship in Jamestown, there was no way that that person would have said to you, "I am from Africa." He would have identified a nation, an ethnic group, a familial group, a political group. He would have had something far more specific to say about his identify.

IRA BERLIN: In the 17th century we can say that the Chesapeake area is indeed a multiracial society, that it is a society in which Native America has come together with Africa with people of a European descent. They are jumbled up in a variety of ways, and they do the kinds of things that people do when they get jumbled up together. That is, they work together. They play together. They fight. They sleep together.

ROBIN KELLEY: Over time those alliances were broken up, and as the alliances were broken up, it became clear that many of the European-descended poor whites began to identify themselves, if not directly with the rich whites, certainly with being white … as a way to distinguish themselves from those dark-skinned people who they associate with perpetual slavery.

MIA BAY: There is a racial divide emerging that people begin to see as natural, and that's part of where the idea of race comes from. It's just in the tendency for people to see existing power relationships as having some sort of natural quality to them.

ROBIN KELLEY: The problem that they had to figure out is how can we promote liberty, freedom, democracy on the one hand and a system of slavery and exploitation of people who are nonwhite on the other.

JAMES HORTON: And the way you do that is to say, "Yeah, but you know, there is something different about these people. This whole business of inalienable rights … that's fine but it only applies to certain people."

IRA BERLIN: It seems to me that what's most painful about this process is that these are two sides to the same coin; that the very process of defining who's in also is a process of defining who's out.

JAMES HORTON: Thomas Jefferson is in many ways a personification of America. He is a person with lofty ideals. He writes them down in the sacred document of American society, the Declaration of Independence. Those are the magic words of American society … wonderfully lofty aims and goals … but, like America, Jefferson does not live up to his principles. He knows it. And he is bothered by it. He is … he lives in a kind of anxiety, actually, between what he says and what he does. This is a person committed to human freedom who holds over two hundred human beings in the state of slavery. And he knows that that is a massive contradiction.

America is exactly the same way. I mean, we are a society based on principles literally to die for, principles that are so wonderful it brings tears to your eyes. But we are a society that so often allows itself to not live by those principles.

References

Berlin, Ira
2003   Generations of Captivity: A History of African-American Slaves. Cambridge, MA: The Belknap Press of Harvard University Press.
Gordon-Reed, Annette
2008   The Hemingses of Monticello: An American Family. New York: W. W. Norton and Company.
James, C. L. R.
1989   The Black Jacobins: Toussaint L'Ouvrture and the San Domingo Revolution. Rev. 2nd edition. New York: Vintage Books.
Meillasoux, Claude
1991 [1986]   The Anthropology of Slavery: The Womb of Iron and Gold. A. Dasnois, trans. Chicago: The University of Chicago Press.

Commerce. http://www.census.gov/prod/2011pubs/acsbr10-05.pdf, accessed January 4, 2012.
Morgan, Edmund
1975   American Slavery, American Freedom: The Ordeal of Colonial Virginia. New York: W. W. Norton.
Morgan, Philip D.
1998   Slave Counterpoint: Black Culture in the Eighteenth-Century Chesapeake and Lowcountry. Chapel Hill: University of North Carolina Press.
Parent, Anthony S., Jr.
2003   Foul Means: The Formation of Slave Society in Virginia, 1660–1740. Chapel Hill: University of North Carolina Press.
Smedley, Audrey
2007 [1993]   Race in North America: Origin and Evolution of a Worldview. 3rd edition. Boulder: Westview Press.

Audrey Smedley: The Origin of the Ideology of Race

Allen, Theodore W.
1994   The Invention of the White Race, vol. 1: Racial Oppression and Social Control. London: Verso.
Allen, Theodore W.
1997   The Invention of the White Race, vol. 2: The Origin of Racial Oppression in Anglo America. New York: Verso.
Fredrickson, George M.
2002   Racism: A Short History. Princeton: Princeton University Press.
Hannaford, Ivan
1996   Race: The History of an Idea in the West. Washington, D.C.: Woodrow Wilson Center Press; Baltimore: The Johns Hopkins University Press.
Jones, Stephanie J., ed.
2009   The State of Black America: Message to the President. New York: National Urban League.
Macartney, Suzanne
2011   Child Poverty in the United States 2009 and 2010: Selected Race Groups and Hispanic Origin. American Community Survey Briefs. United States Department of

Creating Race, 1400–1800

Bennett, Jr., Lerone
1987   Before the Mayflower: A History of Black America. 6th edition. Chicago: Johnson Publishing Company.
Jefferson, Thomas
1955 [1787]   Notes on the State of Virginia. 2nd edition. William Peden, ed. Chapel Hill: University of North Carolina Press.
Jordan, Winthrop D.
1968   White over Black: American Attitudes toward the Negro, 1550–1812. Baltimore: Penguin Books Incorporated.
Nash, Gary
1970   Red, White, and Black: Origins of Racism in Colonial America. In The Great Fear: Race in the Mind of America. Gary Nash and Richard Weiss, eds. New York: Holt, Rinehart and Winston.
Schiebinger, Londa
1993   Nature's Body: Gender in the Making of Modern Science. Boston: Beacon Press.
Smedley, Audrey
1999 [1993]   Race in North America: Origin and Evolution of a Worldview. 2nd edition.

4

Human Mismeasure

The history of science includes many attempts to justify race and racial hierarchies.

RACE exhibit, SMM

Historically, sciences of race were less concerned with understanding biological diversity as a product of environment or, later, evolution than with parsing that diversity for political purposes. This may seem a fantastic claim, as it challenges the common assumption of a longstanding empirical basis for our racial categories in the natural sciences. However, as geneticist Richard Lewontin reminds us, race was imported into science from social practice and not vice versa. It was not until the late 18th century that naturalists influenced by European Enlightenment models of rationality and empiricism enlisted science to justify the folk taxonomy of race. Science, they hoped, could rationalize these contradictions of freedom, slavery, and genocide by establishing a basis in nature for the existing social order.

At its outset, the specific charge for race science was twofold. Scientists were to establish objectively (1) whether all races were fully human, and (2) whether all human races were equal. By the 19th century, debate centered around two theories of racial origins: polygeny and monogeny. Polygenists such as Josiah Nott, George Gliddon, and Louis Agassiz saw human races as separate species. Meanwhile, monogenists like Charles Darwin proposed that races represented variation within a single human species. Underlying these forays into natural

history was the question of the nature of racial differences. Were apparent differences innate and immutable or were they reducible, possibly erased, through the elimination of discriminatory social practices? Explicit challenges to the idea of human races would come later.

Although polygenists initially supported their arguments with scriptural references to non-Adamic people in the land of Nod or the Hamitic myth, many American scientists were Christians who found the monogenist argument for one human species more compatible with biblical creationism (Fredrickson 1987). Thus, religion was a major early barrier to widespread acceptance of polygenism in particular, but also to scientific arguments for human origins from both camps.

In 1859, this paradigm began to shift. That year, Darwin published *On the Origin of the Species*, in which he articulated the theory of *natural selection*. Darwin's explanation of the actual mechanism through which environmental factors select for biological diversity within a species was a critical step in rendering evolution as a credible alternative to creationism within the scientific community and the broader public.

Scientific debates over humanity and equality focused primarily on intelligence, with polygenists in particular contending that cognitive ability was unevenly distributed among the races. The primary method for determining these differences was craniometry, the measurement of skulls. Predictably, polygenists reported larger skull size and greater cranial/cognitive capacity for Europeans and white

Race: Are We So Different?, First Edition. Alan H. Goodman, Yolanda T. Moses, and Joseph L. Jones.
© 2012 American Anthropological Association. Published 2012 by Blackwell Publishing Ltd.

Americans in comparison with Native Americans and African Americans. Around the middle of the 19th century, polygenist arguments gained credence in the scientific community and beyond, prompting the formerly enslaved abolitionist Frederick Douglass to offer perhaps the earliest systematic refutation of scientific racism. In an 1854 commencement address delivered at Western Reserve College, Douglass dismissed craniometric claims as "anti-Negro propaganda," arguing that social environment better explained the unfortunate conditions of blacks and impoverished peoples throughout the world.

While crania drew most of their attention, "objective" race scientists investigated virtually every human anatomical and physiological feature, as well as real and imagined diseases (Hammonds and Herzig 2008). Prominent physician Samuel Cartwright, for example, coined the term *drapetomania* to explain enslaved Africans' tendency to attempt escape and prescribed whipping as a method of treatment. Even more unsettling were the actions of J. Marion Sims, the "father of gynecology," who exploited poor white and enslaved black women to develop gynecologic techniques and surgical procedures. Describing them as more resistant to pain than white women, Sims purchased enslaved women for the purpose of surgical experimentation and operated on them without anesthesia (Byrd and Clayton 2000). Nor was racial mismeasure of human bodies and minds limited to enslaved blacks and Native Americans. During the latter half of the century, as their population grew rapidly in California and other western states, medical authorities labeled immigrant Chinese workers as vectors of contagious diseases such as diphtheria, typhoid, and the more ambiguous condition "mental alienation" (Hammonds and Herzig 2008).

In the early 20th century, the field of physical anthropology emerged, largely as the study of racial types and differences (Blakey 1987; Armelagos and Goodman 1998; Marks 2010). Yet, some leaders in the discipline countered mainstream ideas about race. Among the latter was Franz Boas, considered by many to be the founder of modern American anthropology. In 1912, Boas reported significant changes in cranial shape and size between Jewish and Sicilian immigrants and their United States-born children. Boas's results revealed that cranial development was responsive to environmental conditions, discrediting the notion of stable racial "types" defined by heritable racial traits. With craniometric studies under attack, psychologists and other scientists began to base their arguments for race-based intelligence on the results of intelligence quotient (IQ) tests. In the United States, IQ tests were heavily culturally biased and used to justify discrimination against southern and eastern Europeans in immigration policy as well as racial segregation in public education.

During the Great Depression, race scientists further sought to justify economic and social inequality by establishing a genetic basis for the transmission of intelligence and other characteristics such as criminal behavior and work ethic. These negative traits were "in the genes" and thus inevitable, inherited as a legacy and predictor of low social status. Hereditarian theory was the foundation of the United States *eugenics* movement that inspired ideals of racial hygiene in Nazi Germany. It would in fact take the tragedy of the Holocaust, which involved the state-sanctioned murder of approximately six million Jews as well as other "undesirables" by the Nazi regime and its allies, to force the retreat of scientific racism (Barkan 1992).

Following World War II, hereditarianism fell out of favor as a basis for public policy in the United States in large part thanks to the concerted efforts of anthropologists such as Boas, William Montague Cobb (1936), Ruth Benedict (1945), and Ashley Montagu (1964). In growing numbers, evolutionary scientists rejected biological race, agreeing that racial categories lacked taxonomic validity. They argued that these categories were arbitrary (to nature, not socially) and imprecise (lacking cross-cultural stability), and they developed alternative concepts more appropriate for studying human biological variation. Some population geneticists and anthropologists, for example, replaced race with concepts of populations and clines, which mapped the continuous (as opposed to discrete or race-specific) distribution of physical traits and trait frequencies (Livingstone 1962; Brace 2005; see chapter 7, this volume). From the 1950s through the early 1960s, these events coincided with the Civil Rights Movement, which eventually helped to foster a political environment that was less hostile to scientific racism.

Although the idea of biological race never truly expired, by the 1980s the concept was relatively dormant, more or less abandoned by scientists as a proxy for human differences (Armelagos and Goodman 1998). In 1994, however, the public debate over race and intelligence reignited with the publication of *The Bell Curve*, a controversial book in which psychologist Richard J. Herrnstein and political scientist Charles Murray chronicled the rise of a "cognitive elite" in the United States composed mostly of individuals of European and Asian ancestry. The title was a reference to the bell-shaped graph of IQ scores and, once again, scientists were embroiled in debate over the extent to which purported racial intelligence differentials explain or reflect social inequality. Within the scientific community and the mainstream media, people rallied in both support and criticism of Herrnstein and Murray. Some, like evolutionary biologist Stephen Jay Gould, took issue with the premise of intelligence as "a measurable, genetically fixed, and unitary" entity – an unalterable *thing* reducible to a single number useful for ranking individuals, races, genders, and classes. In his revised edition of *The Mismeasure of Man* (1996), Gould identified efforts to rank human intelligence as part of the long, broader tradition of *biological determinism*, an ideology that attributes differences in human behavior and ability – and by extension, social organization and stratification – primarily to innate biogenetic characteristics.

The cultural pervasiveness of biological determinism unfortunately ensures the staying power and popular appeal of race science and other forms of social Darwinism. Indeed, the renewed debate over race and intelligence in the 1990s signaled a broader revival of the biogenetic race concept that has intensified in the genomic age (Koenig et al. 2008; Social Science Research Council 2005; Keita et al. 2004). Ironically, President Bill Clinton's famous announcement in 2000 that decoding of the human genome revealed human genetic sequences as 99.9 percent identical – surely the death knell of biological race – seems only to have inspired proponents of racial genetics.

Today, efforts to "geneticize" race are most evident in biomedicine and other health-related fields. Race-based studies of disease susceptibility and pharmacological response seldom take into account social scientific findings concerning the health consequences of racism or racialization, or critical histories of race science (Harding 1993; Duster 2005; Montoya 2007; Krieger 2003). Instead, such studies often recycle and conflate outmoded typological and geographic conceptions of race (Feldman and Lewontin 2008; Kahn 2004), as do attempts to locate propensity for criminal or violent behavior "in the genes" (Ossorio and Duster 2005). We appear unable to escape the limits of the racial imagination. Biological anthropologist Alan Swedlund has described this inability to decouple the possibilities of genomic science from uncritical conceptions of race as "21st-century technology applied to 19th-century biology" (cited in Armelagos and Van Gerven 2003). Nonetheless, some anthropologists and other scientists are forging new understandings of how race does, or does not, relate to complex patterns of real human cultural, genetic, and environmental variation (Templeton 2003; Jackson 2004; Gravlee et al. 2009; Kuzawa and Sweet 2009; Long et al. 2009).

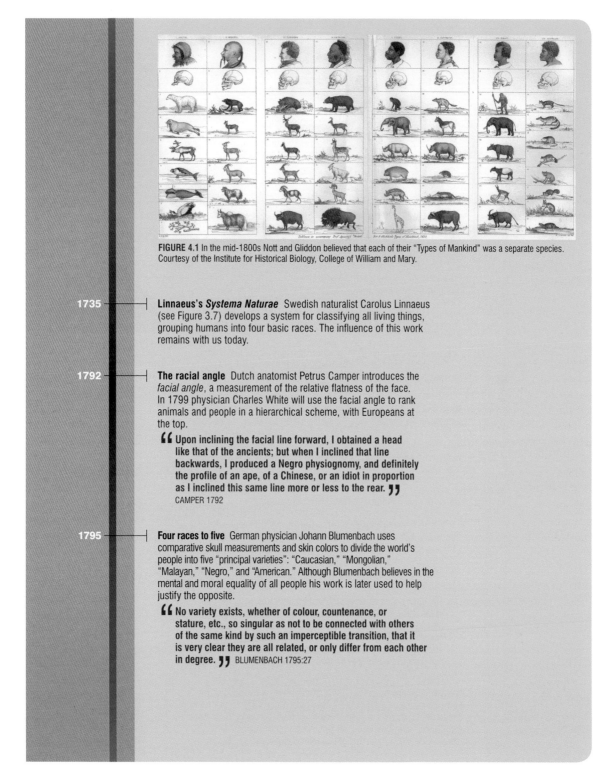

FIGURE 4.1 In the mid-1800s Nott and Gliddon believed that each of their "Types of Mankind" was a separate species. Courtesy of the Institute for Historical Biology, College of William and Mary.

1735

Linnaeus's *Systema Naturae* Swedish naturalist Carolus Linnaeus (see Figure 3.7) develops a system for classifying all living things, grouping humans into four basic races. The influence of this work remains with us today.

1792

The racial angle Dutch anatomist Petrus Camper introduces the *facial angle*, a measurement of the relative flatness of the face. In 1799 physician Charles White will use the facial angle to rank animals and people in a hierarchical scheme, with Europeans at the top.

> **" Upon inclining the facial line forward, I obtained a head like that of the ancients; but when I inclined that line backwards, I produced a Negro physiognomy, and definitely the profile of an ape, of a Chinese, or an idiot in proportion as I inclined this same line more or less to the rear. "**
> CAMPER 1792

1795

Four races to five German physician Johann Blumenbach uses comparative skull measurements and skin colors to divide the world's people into five "principal varieties": "Caucasian," "Mongolian," "Malayan," "Negro," and "American." Although Blumenbach believes in the mental and moral equality of all people his work is later used to help justify the opposite.

> **" No variety exists, whether of colour, countenance, or stature, etc., so singular as not to be connected with others of the same kind by such an imperceptible transition, that it is very clear they are all related, or only differ from each other in degree. "** BLUMENBACH 1795:27

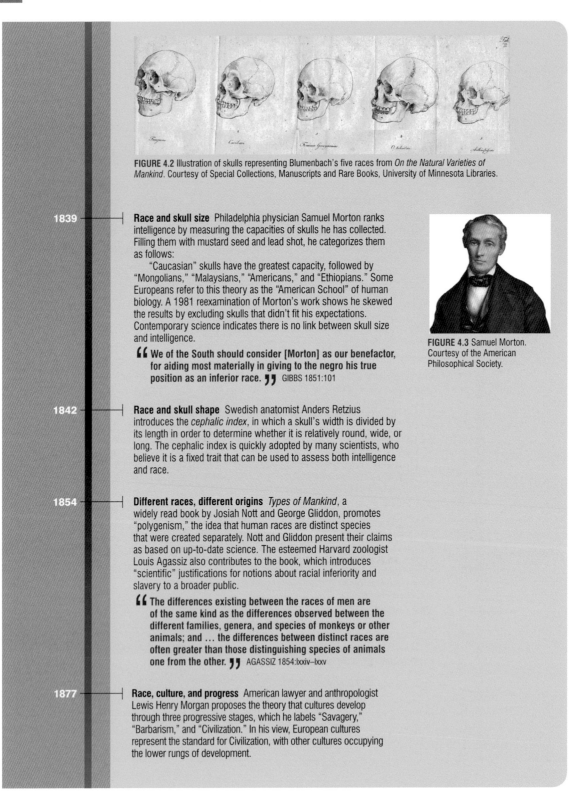

FIGURE 4.2 Illustration of skulls representing Blumenbach's five races from *On the Natural Varieties of Mankind*. Courtesy of Special Collections, Manuscripts and Rare Books, University of Minnesota Libraries.

1839

Race and skull size Philadelphia physician Samuel Morton ranks intelligence by measuring the capacities of skulls he has collected. Filling them with mustard seed and lead shot, he categorizes them as follows:

"Caucasian" skulls have the greatest capacity, followed by "Mongolians," "Malaysians," "Americans," and "Ethiopians." Some Europeans refer to this theory as the "American School" of human biology. A 1981 reexamination of Morton's work shows he skewed the results by excluding skulls that didn't fit his expectations. Contemporary science indicates there is no link between skull size and intelligence.

❝ We of the South should consider [Morton] as our benefactor, for aiding most materially in giving to the negro his true position as an inferior race. ❞ GIBBS 1851:101

FIGURE 4.3 Samuel Morton. Courtesy of the American Philosophical Society.

1842

Race and skull shape Swedish anatomist Anders Retzius introduces the *cephalic index*, in which a skull's width is divided by its length in order to determine whether it is relatively round, wide, or long. The cephalic index is quickly adopted by many scientists, who believe it is a fixed trait that can be used to assess both intelligence and race.

1854

Different races, different origins *Types of Mankind*, a widely read book by Josiah Nott and George Gliddon, promotes "polygenism," the idea that human races are distinct species that were created separately. Nott and Gliddon present their claims as based on up-to-date science. The esteemed Harvard zoologist Louis Agassiz also contributes to the book, which introduces "scientific" justifications for notions about racial inferiority and slavery to a broader public.

❝ The differences existing between the races of men are of the same kind as the differences observed between the different families, genera, and species of monkeys or other animals; and … the differences between distinct races are often greater than those distinguishing species of animals one from the other. ❞ AGASSIZ 1854:lxxiv–lxxv

1877

Race, culture, and progress American lawyer and anthropologist Lewis Henry Morgan proposes the theory that cultures develop through three progressive stages, which he labels "Savagery," "Barbarism," and "Civilization." In his view, European cultures represent the standard for Civilization, with other cultures occupying the lower rungs of development.

❝ Thus, while Africa was and is an ethnical chaos of savagery and barbarism, Australia and Polynesia were in savagery, pure and simple, with the arts and institutions belonging to that condition. In like manner, the Indian family of America … illustrated, when discovered, each of these conditions, and especially those of the Lower and of the Middle Status of barbarism, more elaborately and completely than any other portion of mankind. ❞ MORGAN 1877:16

Frederick Douglass, an early critic of "race science"

In 1854, Frederick Douglass, who escaped slavery to become an abolitionist and renowned intellectual, published *The Claims of the Negro, Ethnologically Considered*, a critical review of race science conducted by Nott, Gliddon, Morton, Agassiz, and others. In this work, Douglass articulates the case for "nurture" at the origin of an American "nature versus nurture" debate.

❝ I think it will ever be found, that the well or ill condition of any part of mankind, will leave its mark on the physical as well as on the intellectual part of man. A hundred instances might be cited, of whole families who have degenerated, and others who have improved in personal appearance, by a change of circumstances. A man is worked upon by what he works on. He may carve out his circumstances, but his circumstances will carve him out as well ❞ DOUGLASS 1854:294

FIGURE 4.4 Frederick Douglass. Courtesy of the Library of Congress.

George Horse Capture

There is no other group that is as patriotic as we are. When we have a veteran's dance almost every adult [male] gets up and dances, because we have all served our country as volunteers – it's part of the way we are. Because of the way we are treated in this country people often confuse our reason for this intense devotion … We are dedicated to our country – the physical land. … It makes no difference whose name is on the deed. We are the landlords. GEORGE HORSE CAPTURE in POHRT 1975

1879 **Anthropology takes on the "Indian problem"** As it expands its system of Indian reservations, the U.S. government seeks to gain a better understanding of the tribes under its control. In 1879 it establishes the Bureau of Ethnology to document and study American Indian history, customs and language.

1885 **The equality of human races** In his book *The Equality of Human Races*, the Haitian politician and intellectual Anténor Firmin criticizes European and American scientists for allowing ideas about the inequality of races to shape their work. Firmin carefully refutes their theories and proposes alternate ones about the development of human variation.

FIGURE 4.5 Native American lifeways on display at the American Museum of Natural History, c. 1902. © American Museum of Natural History.

FIGURE 4.6 Anténor Firmin. Courtesy of the CIDIHCA Collection.

“ The notion of a hierarchy of the human races, one of the doctrinal inventions of modern times … will be seen some day as one of the greatest proofs of the imperfection of the human mind and of the imperfection … of the arrogant race that made it into a scientific doctrine. ” FIRMIN 2002

1897

Living collections Famed polar explorer Robert Peary brings 7-year-old Minik, his father, Qisuk, and four other Greenland Inuit to the American Museum of Natural History in New York to be studied. Peary has promised to return them to Greenland, but once they are in New York, four of them, including Qisuk, become ill and die. Minik is adopted by a museum superintendent, and his father's bones are "de-fleshed" and added to the museum's collections. Almost a century later, Kenn Harper, author of a biography of Minik, successfully fights for the return of the father's skeleton to Greenland.

Salvage Ethnology

Around the turn of the last century, many anthropologists believed that Native American cultures would soon be extinct. Desperate to salvage knowledge about these groups, anthropologists and private collectors gathered everyday utensils, religious objects, clothing and even skeletal remains for museums and personal collections.

But American Indians did not die out, and in recent years many of the objects and human remains collected during this period have been returned to the tribes to which they belonged. "Now or never is the time in which to collect from the natives what is still available for study. What is lost now will never be recovered again. SAPIR 1911

FIGURE 4.7 In 1897, Minik, along with several relatives, was brought to New York City from Greenland for anthropologists to study. Courtesy of the Peabody Museum of Archaeology and Ethnology, Harvard University.

1899 **The races of Europe** This popular book by the economist William Z. Ripley classifies Europeans as comprising three distinct races: "Teutonic," "Alpine," and "Mediterranean." Ripley relies on Anders Retzius's long-accepted cephalic index head-measurement standard as a basis for his work. He wins a prestigious award from the Royal Anthropological Institute of Great Britain for his work, and his ideas pave the way for later efforts by scientists and writers such as Charles Davenport, Madison Grant, and Carleton Coon.

1911 **Undermining the cephalic index** Studying the skull shape of immigrants and their American-born children, Columbia University anthropologist Franz Boas finds that this feature can vary from one generation to the next. His work undermines the wide use of the cephalic index as a stable marker of race. Boas shows that the human form is more susceptible to environmental factors than most people at the time believe.

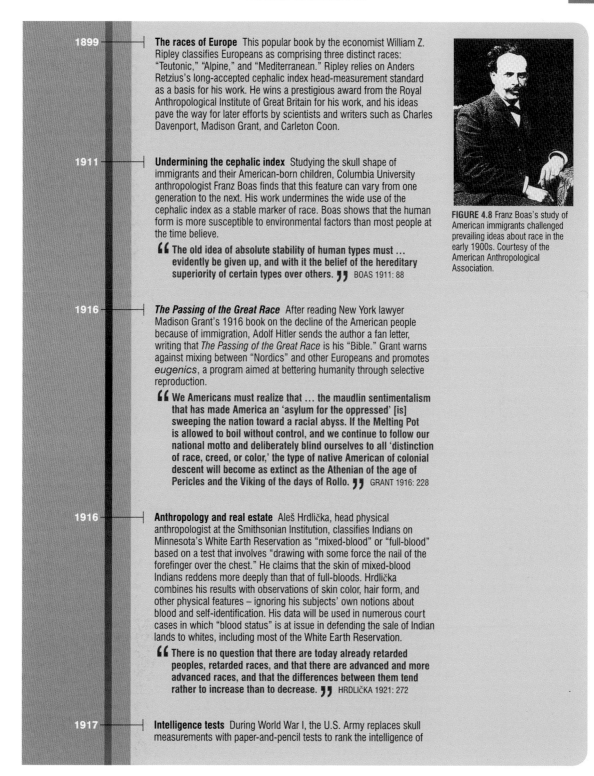

FIGURE 4.8 Franz Boas's study of American immigrants challenged prevailing ideas about race in the early 1900s. Courtesy of the American Anthropological Association.

> **The old idea of absolute stability of human types must … evidently be given up, and with it the belief of the hereditary superiority of certain types over others.** BOAS 1911: 88

1916 ***The Passing of the Great Race*** After reading New York lawyer Madison Grant's 1916 book on the decline of the American people because of immigration, Adolf Hitler sends the author a fan letter, writing that *The Passing of the Great Race* is his "Bible." Grant warns against mixing between "Nordics" and other Europeans and promotes *eugenics*, a program aimed at bettering humanity through selective reproduction.

> **We Americans must realize that … the maudlin sentimentalism that has made America an 'asylum for the oppressed' [is] sweeping the nation toward a racial abyss. If the Melting Pot is allowed to boil without control, and we continue to follow our national motto and deliberately blind ourselves to all 'distinction of race, creed, or color,' the type of native American of colonial descent will become as extinct as the Athenian of the age of Pericles and the Viking of the days of Rollo.** GRANT 1916: 228

1916 **Anthropology and real estate** Aleš Hrdlička, head physical anthropologist at the Smithsonian Institution, classifies Indians on Minnesota's White Earth Reservation as "mixed-blood" or "full-blood" based on a test that involves "drawing with some force the nail of the forefinger over the chest." He claims that the skin of mixed-blood Indians reddens more deeply than that of full-bloods. Hrdlička combines his results with observations of skin color, hair form, and other physical features – ignoring his subjects' own notions about blood and self-identification. His data will be used in numerous court cases in which "blood status" is at issue in defending the sale of Indian lands to whites, including most of the White Earth Reservation.

> **There is no question that there are today already retarded peoples, retarded races, and that there are advanced and more advanced races, and that the differences between them tend rather to increase than to decrease.** HRDLIČKA 1921: 272

1917 **Intelligence tests** During World War I, the U.S. Army replaces skull measurements with paper-and-pencil tests to rank the intelligence of

American recruits. The Army Alpha test is used for those who can read, while the Beta test is used for those who are illiterate or do not know English. In the early 1920s, Congress uses results from these tests to justify new legislation that greatly restricts immigration from Southern and Eastern Europe.

❝ Our own data from the army tests indicate clearly the intellectual superiority of the Nordic race group. ... The Alpine race, according to our figures ... seems to be considerably below the Nordic type intellectually. ❞ BRIGHAM 1923:207

1924 **IQ tests and propaganda** Nineteen-year-old college student Horace Mann Bond critiques the reasoning behind the idea that race explains differences in intelligence test scores. Later in life he becomes a prominent educator, eventually serving as president of Lincoln University, his alma mater.

❝ A perusal of those nationalities whom [Brigham] classifies as inferior will be found to have a close correlation existing between the sums of money expended for education and their relatively low standing. ❞ BOND 1924

❝ When ... we read ... that the greatest and most masterful personalities have had blond hair and blue eyes, we can make a shrewd guess at its author's complexion. ❞ HUXLEY and HADDON 1935:133

FIGURE 4.9 Test-takers were asked to draw the missing element of each picture in this 1917 Army Beta test for "innate intelligence." From Robert Yerkes, ed. (1921) "Psychological Examining in the United States Army," *Memoirs of the National Academy of Sciences* 15.

1936 **Race and the Olympics** The African American runner and long-jumper Jesse Owens wins four gold medals at the 1936 Berlin Olympics, dashing Nazi expectations that white Northern Europeans would triumph. Many believe this dominance proves that athletic ability is linked to race and, perhaps, inversely related to intelligence.

To challenge these beliefs, Howard University physical anthropologist W. Montague Cobb compares Owens's physical measurements to those of others. He concludes that Owens has few of the characteristics believed to be associated with African Americans, such as a relatively short calf muscle. He also shows that measurements of African Americans' and whites' physical features are too similar to permit any meaningful comparisons of athletic performance. Cobb finds that differences in training and experience, not race, probably account for differences in athletic performance.

FIGURE 4.10 Jesse Owens at start of record-breaking 200 meter race in the 1936 Olympics. From Altona-Bahrenfeld and Cigaretten-Bilderdienst (1936) *Die Olympischen Spiele 1936 in Berlin und Garmisch-Partenkirchen*, p. 27. Courtesy of the Library of Congress.

1939 **A Jewish race?** Adolf Hitler threatens "the annihilation of the Jewish race in Europe." On September 1, he invades Poland, sparking World War II. The racializing of Jews isn't unique to Germany. That same year, two Harvard anthropology professors note traits that supposedly set Jews apart from others.

❝ The Jewish look seems to be one of the most noticeable and most easily distinguished of characteristic facial expressions found within the racial family of white people. ❞ COON 1939:442

❝ Anti-Semitic outbreaks will recur whenever societies get into economic messes and politicians are looking for scapegoats, as long as there dwell in our midst physically distinctive Jewish minorities who, by their intelligence, out-strip their non-Jewish competitors and thrive under adversities which crush the majority of lesser natural endowment. ❞ HOOTON 1939

1910–45

The rise of eugenics In the early 1900s, many scientists worldwide support eugenics as a tool to help speed human progress. Eugenicists believe in controlling reproduction to improve the *germ plasm* of the population, what today we would call the human gene pool. In the U.S. some eugenicists worry that miscegenation, or "race-mixing," could degrade the American population.

In Nazi Germany, racism and eugenic ideals fuel the Holocaust. Between 1933 and 1945, Nazis murder more than six million Jews and an untold number of Roma (Gypsies) in programs to eliminate those seen as racially inferior. Nazi extermination policies also target Poles, Russians, Ukrainians, those with mental and physical disabilities, homosexuals, and political and religious dissidents.

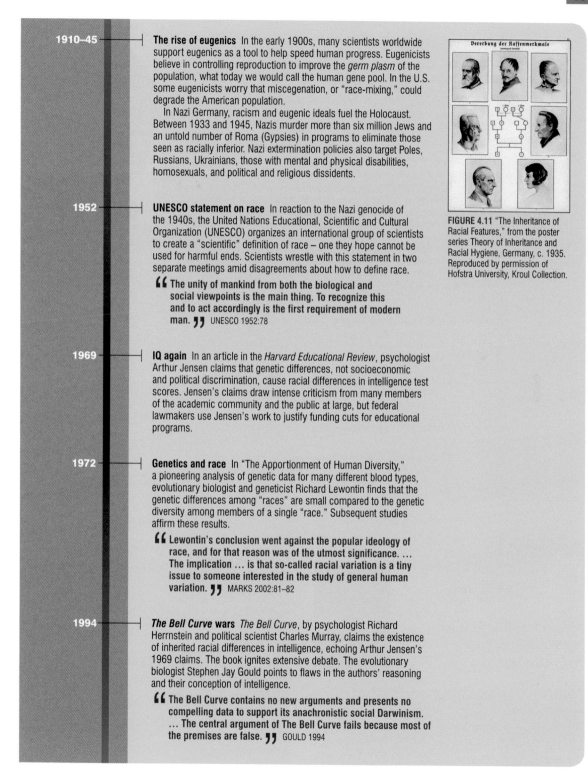

FIGURE 4.11 "The Inheritance of Racial Features," from the poster series Theory of Inheritance and Racial Hygiene, Germany, c. 1935. Reproduced by permission of Hofstra University, Kroul Collection.

1952

UNESCO statement on race In reaction to the Nazi genocide of the 1940s, the United Nations Educational, Scientific and Cultural Organization (UNESCO) organizes an international group of scientists to create a "scientific" definition of race – one they hope cannot be used for harmful ends. Scientists wrestle with this statement in two separate meetings amid disagreements about how to define race.

❝ The unity of mankind from both the biological and social viewpoints is the main thing. To recognize this and to act accordingly is the first requirement of modern man. ❞ UNESCO 1952:78

1969

IQ again In an article in the *Harvard Educational Review*, psychologist Arthur Jensen claims that genetic differences, not socioeconomic and political discrimination, cause racial differences in intelligence test scores. Jensen's claims draw intense criticism from many members of the academic community and the public at large, but federal lawmakers use Jensen's work to justify funding cuts for educational programs.

1972

Genetics and race In "The Apportionment of Human Diversity," a pioneering analysis of genetic data for many different blood types, evolutionary biologist and geneticist Richard Lewontin finds that the genetic differences among "races" are small compared to the genetic diversity among members of a single "race." Subsequent studies affirm these results.

❝ Lewontin's conclusion went against the popular ideology of race, and for that reason was of the utmost significance. ... The implication ... is that so-called racial variation is a tiny issue to someone interested in the study of general human variation. ❞ MARKS 2002:81–82

1994

***The Bell Curve* wars** *The Bell Curve*, by psychologist Richard Herrnstein and political scientist Charles Murray, claims the existence of inherited racial differences in intelligence, echoing Arthur Jensen's 1969 claims. The book ignites extensive debate. The evolutionary biologist Stephen Jay Gould points to flaws in the authors' reasoning and their conception of intelligence.

❝ The Bell Curve contains no new arguments and presents no compelling data to support its anachronistic social Darwinism. ... The central argument of The Bell Curve fails because most of the premises are false. ❞ GOULD 1994

1996 — **Kennewick Man** The skeleton of a 9,200-year-old man is found near Kennewick, Washington. Examining the skull, archaeologist James Chatters uses the outdated term *Caucasoid* to characterize it. This angers some Native Americans, who contend that the bones are those of an American Indian.

Scientists, wishing to continue their study of the remains, wage a long-running legal struggle with Native American tribes who want to rebury the skeleton as their ancestor. Further study showed Kennewick Man to have anatomical features similar to some ancient Asians. These racial distinctions were employed by anthropologists to oppose Native American rights of reburial. In 2004 a federal appeals court decides to allow scientists to carry on with their study.

❝ Scientists have dug up and studied Native Americans for decades. We view this practice as desecration of the body and a violation of our most deeply held religious beliefs. Today thousands of native human remains sit on the shelves of museums and institutions, waiting for the day when they can return to the earth, and waiting for the day that scientists and others pay them the respect they are due. ❞ ARMAND MINTHORN, a leader of the Confederated Tribes of the Umatilla Indian Reservation, MINTHORN 1996

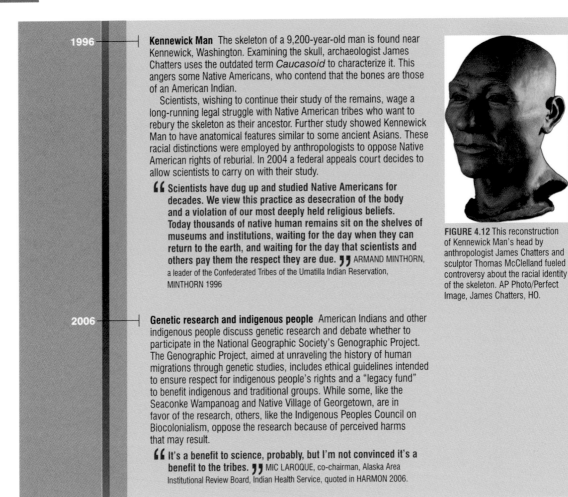

FIGURE 4.12 This reconstruction of Kennewick Man's head by anthropologist James Chatters and sculptor Thomas McClelland fueled controversy about the racial identity of the skeleton. AP Photo/Perfect Image, James Chatters, HO.

2006 — **Genetic research and indigenous people** American Indians and other indigenous people discuss genetic research and debate whether to participate in the National Geographic Society's Genographic Project. The Genographic Project, aimed at unraveling the history of human migrations through genetic studies, includes ethical guidelines intended to ensure respect for indigenous people's rights and a "legacy fund" to benefit indigenous and traditional groups. While some, like the Seaconke Wampanoag and Native Village of Georgetown, are in favor of the research, others, like the Indigenous Peoples Council on Biocolonialism, oppose the research because of perceived harms that may result.

❝ It's a benefit to science, probably, but I'm not convinced it's a benefit to the tribes. ❞ MIC LAROQUE, co-chairman, Alaska Area Institutional Review Board, Indian Health Service, quoted in HARMON 2006.

JOE WATKINS

Deracializing the Past

Archaeologists and Native American Relationships in the Age of Racialization

Joe Watkins *is Director of the Native American Studies Program at the University of Oklahoma. He is Choctaw Indian, and has been involved in archaeology* *for more than forty years. Watkins has published numerous articles on the ethical practice of anthropology and the discipline's relationships with descendant communities and aboriginal populations. Here, he discusses the relationship between Native Americans and the practice of archaeology in the United States, drawing upon contemporary issues such as the Native American Graves Protection and Repatriation Act (NAGPRA), the controversy over Kennewick Man, and the rise of Indigenous Archaeology. Photograph courtesy of Joseph Watkins, photograph by Jacquelyn D. Slater.*

Race versus ethnicity

"Race," as anthropologists will assert, is a social construct rather than a physiological one, but the public misunderstanding of this difference continues to create issues between the various ethnic groups and descendant communities. Today, "American Indian" is a politically created ethnicity rather than a racial one. American Indians are defined by their relationship with a political organization – a "tribe" – and not by any genetic relationship. Even tribal groups whose membership is based on "blood quantum" (generalized percentages of "tribal" versus "non-tribal" blood) do not use genetic measures to identify their members.

Anthropology and American Indians

Much of the negative history between anthropologists and American Indians hinges around the excavation and retention of ancient, historic, and recent American Indian human remains. I have presented brief histories of the relationships between American anthropologists and American Indians elsewhere (Watkins 2000; 2003; 2004; 2005a; 2005b). American Indian authors such as Deloria (1969), Echo-Hawk (1997; 2000), Mihesuah (1996); Riding In (1992), and Trope and Echo-Hawk (1992), among others, have written on these relationships as well, but the impact of the excavation and removal of human remains by anthropologists is brought into strong focus by Devon Mihesuah's comparison of grave looters and archaeologists. She writes, "the only difference between an illegal ransacking of a burial ground and a scientific one is the time element, sun screen, little whisk brooms, and the neatness of the area when finished" (1996:233). Working from this perspective, one can see how easy it becomes for American Indian concerns with archaeology to take on a more personal tone than the perspective of other descendant communities.

As a means to try to ameliorate some of the issues related to the retention of American Indian human remains within government sponsored museum collections, Congress passed legislation in 1989 and 1990 that aimed to give American Indians tribes the opportunity to regain the skeletal remains of their ancestors. Some anthropologists saw this legislation – NAGPRA – as an opportunity to further their field of study, noting that "NAGPRA will allow bioarcheology to emerge as a vigorous and possibly more publicly relevant and responsible profession" (Rose et al. 1996: 82), while others, such as Rob Bonnichsen, saw it as a threat to archaeology, noting "Repatriation has taken on a life of its own and is about to put us out of business as a profession" (as quoted in Johnson 1996). For many anthropologists, repatriation of human remains that could be easily identified to historic or near-historic American Indian groups was understandable and justifiable; however, once the age of the materials reaches into the "deep past" the justification for repatriating those remains became more difficult. The Kennewick case was a perfect example.

The Kennewick case involved a set of human remains radiocarbon dated to about 8,000 to 8,500 years before present, one of the oldest dated sets of human remains from the Western Hemisphere. The age of the remains suggested to some archaeologists that repatriation was allowable under NAGPRA; to others, the scientific information likely to be held within the remains made repatriation scientifically untenable. The human remains recovered from the Columbia River in Washington had physical characteristics that led Dr. James Chatters, an archaeologist in the area tasked with recovering the remains, to categorize the remains as "Caucasoid," one of the three outmoded "racial types." However, when Dr. Chatters was mistakenly quoted in local newspapers as saying the remains appeared to be "Caucasian," a term commonly used in the United States to describe "white Americans," the case and remains became racialized.

Physical anthropologists have classified human remains based on a suite of measurements made on human skeletal components. Taken together, the measurements produced statistical "modes" that were used to define characteristics of human populations. These "modes" are used by physical anthropologists and forensic scientists to place individuals within likely "ethnic backgrounds" primarily as a means of discussion rather than being based in any racial realities.

Once the Kennewick skeleton became "white," the racialism followed. Right-wing political writer Lowell Ponte wrote that Kennewick Man might prove that "some of the first 'Native Americans' had white skin and European ancestry" (Ponte 1999). Additionally, he proposed that perhaps "white-skinned Americans were exterminated by invading ancestors of today's Indians" and that, had the genocide not taken place, "Columbus might have been greeted by natives with faces whiter than his own."

The political implications of this racialization of the past are enormous in terms of the political aspects of Native American sovereignty and social structure. If the "true" inhabitants of America were white, and their land was stolen by invading "Native Americans" then the "rediscovery" of America by Europeans was merely a re-conquest of lands that were already theirs – and thus the treaties made with the Indians could be deemed unnecessary and void.

When a request for repatriation of the human remains by local American Indian tribes was filed, eight scientists sued for access to the human remains for study. The remains, because of their antiquity, are important for the information they might hold regarding the earliest inhabitants of this hemisphere. In support of this suit, a non-profit group – The Friends of America's Past – initiated a campaign to influence the public perception that the "past" belongs to everyone and should not be "controlled" by any one particular group. This idea of shared heritage is prevalent within Western culture, and archaeologists benefit from this concept. However, to be succinct, the rights of indigenous groups to the ownership and control of their archaeological and cultural heritage is rarely equivalent to those of the nations within which they exist.

Larry Zimmerman (2001:169) makes an important point about the issue within the United States: "it is difficult to see the historical relationship between archaeologists and Native Americans as anything but scientific colonialism": whereby knowledge about a people is acquired and then "exported" out of the "country of origin" to be used for "processing" into intellectual material.

Indigenous archaeology

Recently, a movement within archaeology termed "indigenous archaeology" has drawn into question not only the basics of archaeology but also the utility of it to indigenous groups. The most recent and succinct discussion of this idea has been presented by Nicholas as growing "out of efforts by marginalized peoples worldwide to challenge the imposition of archaeology on their lives and heritage" (2008:1668). Opponents of indigenous archaeology, (cf. McGhee 2008) however, argue it bases its argument of utility on an "essentialism" that privileges "indigenous" people over non-indigenous researchers based somehow on the "indigeneity" of the native.

A recent edition of the Society for American Archaeology's *Archaeological Record* contained a group of papers on the issue of "Working Together on Race and Racialism in American Archaeology" (Dongoske and Zimmerman 2010:3–25) which examined the idea of indigenous archaeology as a racialized concept. The impetus for the discussion was led by Roger Echo-Hawk, a member of the Pawnee Nation but a self-professed "former Indian," who notes, "in recent years ever-increasing numbers of stake-holding Indians – self-identified adherents to racial Indianhood – have appeared in archaeology, wielding Ph.D.s and trowels as they circle the archaeological meta-narrative" (2010:21). This "racial Indianness," Echo-Hawk believes, makes "Indians" as racialist as the Western academy they seem to be fighting against. His own essentialism of practitioners of indigenous archaeology as racialist archaeologists is at times troubling, but it will hopefully lead to a fuller questioning of underlying ideas about such sub-disciplinary precepts.

Repatriation and the control of the past

This brief essay is not intended to explore every relationship between American Indians and archaeologists, but merely to draw attention to some of the underlying reasons for conflicts. The issues of repatriation of American Indian human remains and the control of the past by academic groups rather than the descendants of those who created them are emotionally laden and controversial. Some groups see American Indian human remains as scientific resources containing information about this country's earliest inhabitants while other groups see the disproportional number of American Indian human remains within scientific and museum collections as a shameful legacy of 18th-century racialist attitudes.

Regardless of where repatriation leads archaeology or where the collaboration between archaeologists and American Indians leads, there will always be an uneasy truce between the scientists who study "the past" and those whose ancestors created it. NAGPRA is here and will likely create more issues as its interpretation through the courts continues and as further legislation actions expand its purview. While it is not race per se that underlies these different perspectives, the ease with which the entrenched *idea* of race so often arises remains problematic and must be altered.

Mismeasuring Humans

A Conversation

To conclude this chapter, we hear from several historians, a geneticist, and a legal scholar on the colonial imperative to naturalize the social order through race science. **Mia Bay** *is Professor of History and Associate Director of the Center for Race and Ethnicity at Rutgers University.* **Evelyn Hammonds** *is Dean of Harvard College and Barbara Gutman Rosenkrantz Professor of History of Science and of African and African American Studies at Harvard University.* **James Horton** *is Benjamin Banneker Professor of American Studies and History at George Washington University and Historian Emeritus of the Smithsonian Institution's National Museum of American History.* **Richard Lewontin** *is Professor of Biology Emeritus and Alexander Agassiz Professor of Zoology in the Museum of Comparative Zoology Emeritus at Harvard University.* **Pilar Ossorio** *is Associate Professor of Law and Bioethics at the University of Wisconsin at Madison.*

MIA BAY: During the 19th century there were lots of public lectures on the races of Man. [Race science] was, because it was new, something people were avidly interested in. Science in the 19th century was expected to reveal all the mysteries of the universe.

RICHARD LEWONTIN: Everyone was concerned with explaining tremendous social inequalities, despite the fact that they were living in these societies in which revolutions had occurred to make equality.

JAMES HORTON: There were scientists who argued that there were special physical and medical characteristics of blacks that made them particularly suited to slavery.

Reproduced courtesy of California Newsreel.

In fact, there is one scientist, I will put this in quotes, there is one "scientist" that postulated that it was a disease that could account for runaway slaves. He called it "The Runaway Sickness." You got this sickness, and it made you want to run away from slavery, so you wouldn't run away from slavery unless you had the sickness.

EVELYNN HAMMONDS: And by the end of the 19th century, if we just take African Americans as an example, there's not a single body part that hasn't been subjected to this kind of analysis. So you'll find articles in the medical literature about the Negro ear, and the Negro nose, and the Negro leg, and the Negro heart, and the Negro eye, and the Negro foot. And it's every single body part. It is this endless catalogue of differences.

JAMES HORTON: Sometimes it would have been better if America had just looked the world in the eye and said, "Look, we hold these people in slavery because we need their labor, and we have got the power to do it." Now that would have been much better, because then when the power was gone, when slavery was over, it's over. But what we said was, there is [something] different about these people. Well, and by doing [that] it means that when slavery is over, that rationalization for slavery remains.

EVELYNN HAMMONDS: Those that looked wanted to confirm what they saw, which is to say that the proper place of, say, the Negro, is at the bottom of our society. And they naturalized that position through their search for these fundamental physical and biological differences. The thing about looking for differences is once you look, you find them. So they find differences in sizes of chests, breadth of chests, length of limbs, capacity of lungs, these kinds of things. And of course, they read those differences through the lens of race.

PILAR OSSORIO: Anthropologists, during the 18th and early 19th century, one of the things they did was to go around and try and categorize people by race. And they did this by trying to take all sorts of physical measurements. And they eventually came to the understanding, in the early 1900s, that it wasn't possible to define a set of measurements and criteria that could clearly categorize all the people that we think of as being in one race and separate them from all the people we think of as being in another race. So even in the early 1900s, anthropologists were already coming to the conclusion that there were not distinct races, and our genetic [studies are] backing that up.

References

Armelagos, George J., and Alan H. Goodman
1998   Race, Racism and Anthropology. *In* Building a New Biocultural Synthesis: Political-Economic Perspectives on Human Biology. Alan H. Goodman and Thomas L. Leatherman, eds. pp. 359–377. Ann Arbor: The University of Michigan Press.

Armelagos, George J., and Dennis P. Van Gerven
2003   A Century of Skeletal Biology and Paleopathology: Contrasts, Contradictions, and Conflicts. American Anthropologist 105:53-64.

Barkan, E.
1992   The Retreat of Scientific Racism: Changing Concepts of Race in Britain and the United States between the World Wars. New York: Cambridge University Press.

Benedict, Ruth
1945   Race: Science and Politics. Rev. edition. New York: Viking Press.

Blakey Michael L.
1987   Skull Doctors: Intrinsic Social and Political Bias in the History of American Physical Anthropology. With special reference to the work of Aleš Hrdlička. Critique of Anthropology 7:7–35.

Brace, C. Loring
2005   "Race" Is a Four-Letter Word: The Genesis of the Concept. New York: Oxford University Press.

Byrd, W. Michael, and Linda A. Clayton
2000   An American Health Dilemma, vol. 1: A Medical History of African Americans and the Problem of Race: Beginnings to 1900. New York: Routledge.

Cigaretten-Bilderdienst, and Altona-Bahrenfeld
1936   Die Olympischen Spiele 1936 in Berlin und Garmisch-Partenkirchen. p. 27: Cigaretten-Bilderdienst and Altona-Bahrenfeld.

Cobb, William Montague
1936   Race and Runners. The Journal of Health and Physical Education 7:3–7, 52–56.

Duster, Troy
2005   Race and Reification in Science. Science 307:1050-1051.

Ossorio, Pilar, and Troy Duster
2005   Race and Genetics: Controversies in Biomedical, Behavioral and Forensic Sciences. American Psychologist 60:115–128.

Feldman, Marcus W., and Richard C. Lewontin
2008   Race, Ancestry, and Medicine. *In* Revisiting Race in a Genomic Age. Barbara A. Koenig, Sandra Soo-Jin Lee, and Sarah S. Richardson, eds. pp. 89–101. New Brunswick: Rutgers University Press.

Fredrickson, George M.
1987   The Black Image in the White Mind: The Debate on Afro-American Character and Destiny, 1817–1914. Wesleyan edition. Hanover, NH: Wesleyan University Press.

Gould, Stephen Jay
1996   The Mismeasure of Man. Rev. and expanded edition. New York: W. W. Norton and Company.

Gravlee, Clarence C., Amy Non, and Connie Mulligan
2009 Genetic Ancestry, Social Classification, and Racial Inequalities in Blood Pressure in Southeastern Puerto Rico. PLoS ONE 4: e6821.

Hammonds, Evelyn M., and Rebecca M. Herzig, eds.
2008   The Nature of Difference: Sciences of Race in the United States from Jefferson to Genomics. Cambridge, MA: The MIT Press.

Harding, Sandra, ed.
1993   The Political Economy of Science: Toward a Democratic Future. Bloomington: Indiana University Press.

Jackson, Fatimah L. C.
2004   Human Genetic Variation and Health: New Assessment Approaches Based on Ethnogenetic Layering. British Medical Journal 69:215–235.

Kahn, Jonathan
2004   How a Drug Becomes "Ethnic": Law, Commerce, and the Production of Racial Categories in Medicine. Yale Journal of Health Policy, Law, and Ethics 4:1–46.

Keita, Shomarka, R. A. Kittles, C. D. M. Royal, G. E. Bonney, P. Furbert-Harris, G. M. Dunston, and C. M. Rotimi
2004   Conceptualizing Human Variation. Nature Genetics 36:S17–S20.

Koenig, Barbara A., Sandra Soo-Jin Lee, and Sarah S. Richardson, eds.
2008 Revisiting Race in a Genomic Age. New Brunswick: Rutgers University Press.

Krieger, Nancy
2003 Does Racism Harm Health? Did Child Abuse Exist Before 1962? On Explicit Questions, Critical Science, and Current Controversies: An Ecosocial Perspective. American Journal of Public Health 93(2):194–199.

Kuzawa, Christopher, and E. Sweet
2009 Epigenetics and the Embodiment of Race: Developmental Origins of U.S. Racial Disparities in Cardiovascular Health. American Journal of Human Biology 21:2–15.

Livingstone, Frank
1962 On the Nonexistence of Races. Current Anthropology 3:279–281.

Long, Jeff C., J. Li, and M. E. Healy
2009 Human DNA Sequences: More Variation and Less Race. American Journal of Physical Anthropology 139:23–34.

Marks, Jonathan
2010 The Two 20th-Century Crises of Racial Anthropology. In Histories of American Physical Anthropology in the Twentieth Century. Michael A. Little and Kenneth A. R. Kennedy, eds. pp. 187–206.

Montagu, Ashley, ed.
1964 The Concept of Race. New York: Collier Books.

Montoya, Michael
2007 Bioethnic Conscription: Genes, Race, and Mexicana/o Ethnicity in Diabetes Research. Cultural Anthropology 22:94–128.

Social Science Research Council
2005 Is Race Real?: A Web Forum Organized by the Social Science Research Council. http://raceandgenomics. ssrc.org/, accessed November 17, 2011.

Templeton, Alan R.
2003 Human Races in Context of Recent Human Evolution: A Molecular Genetic Perspective. In Genetic Nature/Culture: Anthropology and Science beyond the Two-Culture Divide. Alan H. Goodman, Deborah Heath, and M. Susan Lindee, eds. pp. 258–277. Berkeley: University of California Press.

Joe Watkins, Deracializing the Past

Deloria, Vine, Jr.
1969 Custer died for your sins: An Indian Manifesto. London: The Macmillan Company.

Dongoske, Kurt, and Larry Zimmerman
2010 Working Together on Race and Racialism in American Archaeology. The SAA Archaeological Record 10(3):3–4.

Echo-Hawk Roger
1997 Forging a New Ancient History for Native America. In Native Americans and Archaeologists: Stepping Stones to Common Ground. N. Swidler, K. Dongoske, R. Anyon, and A. Downer, eds. pp. 88–102. Walnut Creek, CA: AltaMira Press.

Echo-Hawk Roger
2000 Exploring Ancient Worlds. In Working Together: Native Americans and Archaeologists. Kurt E. Dongoske, Mark Aldenderfer & Karen Doehner, eds. pp. 3–7. Washington, D.C.: Society for American Archaeology.

Echo-Hawk, Roger
2010 Merciless Greetings, Wicked Servants of the Age of Archaeoracialism. The SAA Archaeological Record 10(3):21–25.

Johnson, George
1996 Indian Tribes' Creationists Thwart Archeologists. New York Times October 22.

McGhee, Robert
2008 Aboriginalism and the Problems of Indigenous Archaeology. American Antiquity 73(4):579–597.

Mihesuah, Devon A.
1996 American Indians, Anthropologists, Pothunters, and Repatriation: Ethical, Religious, and Political Differences. Special issue, "Repatriation: An Interdisciplinary Dialogue," American Indian Quarterly 20(2):229–250.

Nicholas George P.
2008 Encyclopedia of Archaeology, vol. 3: Native Peoples and Archaeology. Deborah M. Pearsall, ed. pp. 1660–1669. New York: Academic Press.

Ponte, Lowell
1999 Politically Incorrect Genocide, Part 2. FrontPageMagazine.com, October 5. On line edition at http://archive.frontpagemag.com/readArticle.aspx? ARTID=22976, accessed November 17, 2011.

Riding In, James
1992 Without Ethics and Morality: A Historical Overview of Imperial Archaeology and American Indians. Arizona State Law Journal 24(1):11–34.

Rose, Jerome C., Thomas J. Green, and Victoria D. Green
1996 NAGPRA is Forever: The Future of Osteology and the Repatriation of Skeletons. Annual Review of Anthropology 25:81–103.

Trope, Jack F., and Walter Echo-Hawk
1992 The Native American Graves Protection and Repatriation Act: Background and Legislative History. Arizona State Law Journal 24(1):35–77.

Watkins, Joe
2000 Indigenous Archaeology: American Indian Values and Scientific Practice. Walnut Creek, CA; AltaMira Press.

Watkins, Joe
2003   Beyond the Margin: American Indians, First Nations, and Archaeology in North America. American Antiquity 68(2):273–285.

Watkins, Joe
2004   Representing and Repatriating the Past. *In* North American Archaeology. Timothy Pauketat and Diana Loren, eds. Malden, MA: Blackwell Press.

Watkins, Joe
2005a   Sacred Sites and Repatriation. Contemporary Native American Issue. Philadelphia: Chelsea House Publishers.

Watkins, Joe
2005b   The Politics of American Archaeology: Cultural Resources, Cultural Affiliation and Kennewick. *In* Indigenous Peoples and Archaeology: Decolonizing Theory and Practice. Claire Smith and Martin Wobst, eds. pp. 189–203, Routledge Press, London.

Yerkes, Robert ed.
1921   Psychological Examining in the United States Army. Memoirs of the National Academy of Sciences 15. Washington, DC: Government Printing Office.

Zimmerman, Larry J.
2001   Usurping Native American Voice. *In* The Future of the Past: Archaeologists, Native Americans, and Repatriation, Tamara Bray, ed. pp. 169–184. New York: Garland Publishing, Inc.

Human Mismeasure, 1700–2000

Agassiz, Louis
1854   Sketch – of the natural provinces of the animal world and their relation to the different types of man *In* Types of Mankind: or, Ethnological researches based upon the ancient monuments, paintings, sculptures, and crania of races, and upon their natural, geographical, philological and Biblical history : illustrated by selections from the inedited papers of Samuel George Morton and by additional contributions from L. Agassiz, W. Usher, and H.S. Patterson. 2nd Edition. Josiah Nott and George Gliddon. Philadelphia: J.B. Lippincott, Grambo and Company.

Blumenbach, Johann
1795   [2000] On the natural varieties of mankind. *Cited in* The Idea of Race Robert Bernasconi and Tommy Lee Lott, eds. Indianapolis: Hackett Publishing Company, Inc.

Franz Boas
1911   [2000] The Instability of Human Types. *In* The Idea of Race. Robert Bernasconi and Tommy Lee Lott, eds. Indianapolis: Hackett Publishing Company, Inc.

Bond, Horace Mann
1924   Intelligence Tests and Propaganda. The Crisis 25(2):61–64.

Brigham, Carl C.
1923   A Study of American Intelligence. Princeton: Princeton University Press.

Camper, Petrus
1792   [1974]   Dissertation sur les variétés naturelles qui caracterisent la physionomie des divers climates et es differens ages. Henri J. Jansen, trans. (Paris). *Cited in* Coleridge's speculations on race. Studies in Romanticism. J. H. Haeger. 13(4):339.

Coon, Carleton
1939   The Races of Europe. New York: The Macmillan Company.

Douglass, Frederick
1854   [1999]   The claims of the negro, ethnologically considered. *In* Frederick Douglass: Selected Speeches and Writings. Philip S. Foner, ed. Adapted by Yuval Taylor. Chicago: Lawrence Hill Books.

Firmin, Anténor
2002[1885]   The Equality of Human Races. Asselin Charles, trans. Champaign, IL: University of Illinois Press.

Gibbs, R. W.
1851   [1996]   Death of Samuel George Morton, M.D. Charleston Medical Journal. *Cited in* The Mismeasure of Man. Rev. and exp. edition. Stephen Jay Gould. New York: W.W. Norton and Company.

Gould, Stephen Jay
1994   Curveball. New Yorker, November 28.

Grant, Madison
1916   [1994]   The Passing of the Great Race or The Racial Basis of European History. New York: Charles Scribner's Sons.

Harmon Amy
2006   DNA Gatherers Hit a Snag: The Tribes Don't Trust Them. New York Times. December 10: A1, A38.

Hooton, Earnest A.
1939   Why the Jew Grows Stronger. Collier's Weekly, May 4.

Hrdlička, Aleš
1921   [1994]   American university lecture 27. Cited in Race. Steven Gregory and Roger Sanjek, eds. New Brunswick, NJ: Rutgers University Press.

Huxley, Julian and A. C. Haddon
1935   [1985]   We Europeans. *Cited in* In the Name of Eugenics: Genetics and the Uses of Human Heredity. Daniel J. Kevles. Berkeley and Los Angeles: University of California Press.

Marks, Jonathan
2002   What it means to be 98% chimpanzee. Berkeley and Los Angeles: University of California Press.

Minthorn, Armand

1996   Human remains should be reburied. http://www.
umatilla.nsn.us/kman1.html, accessed January 25, 2012.

Morgan, Lewis Henry

1877   Ancient Society, or Researches in the Lines of
Human Progress from Savagery through Barbarism to
Civilization. New York: Henry Holt and Company.

Pohrt, Richard A.

1975   The American Indian, the American Flag. Flint,
MI: Flint Institute of Art.

Sapir, Edward

1911   An Anthropological Survey of Canada. Science,
December 8.

UNESCO

1952   What Is Race? Paris: UNESCO Department of
Mass Communication. http://unesdoc.unesco.org/images/
0006/000678/067867eb.pdf, accessed January 25, 2012.

5

Inventing Whiteness

Like other racial categories, "white" was created by those in power and contested by those who were not.

RACE exhibit, SMM

Why devote an entire chapter to the invention of racial whiteness? For once, the answer is simple. In the United States, "white" is what linguistic anthropologists refer to as an "unmarked" racial category. Although seldom explicitly or officially acknowledged as such by their members, unmarked categories represent the "normal" standard against which others are measured. They serve as a "north star," orienting us all to other categories as exceptions (see Mukhopadhyay, this chapter; Urciuoli, this volume, chapter 12). Hence, some today still equate white racial identity with true or authentic "American-ness." Yet, the history (or histories, as we shall see) of those we now consider white Americans is little understood outside of the grand narratives of American history taught in primary schools. This is unfortunate but not surprising because racial whiteness often operates above the mainstream public and academic scrutiny often afforded other racial identities. The history of race in America is grossly incomplete without the stories of how white folks came to be.

The first legal use of the term "white" appears in a 1691 colonial Virginian statute that, among other things, expanded the range and severity of punishments for interracial marriage and sexual relations. This statute is an early example of how colonial leaders attempted to preserve the boundaries of whiteness *as they understood*

them. Many individuals considered white today would not have been so in 1691. As explained in previous chapters, religious and national affiliations strongly influenced early white identity, which essentially was limited to Protestant Anglo-Americans at this time. Others, such as German and Irish immigrants and their children, were not yet white, and only the landowning class enjoyed the full benefits of citizenship. Like all racial formations, however, the development of whiteness is an ongoing process or "project" (Winant 2001). Hence, definitions and boundaries of whiteness have changed throughout American history, expanding strategically from time to time usually as scientists, policymakers, and others attempted to balance nativist and anti-immigrant prejudices with the labor needs of a growing nation.

To understand contemporary racial whiteness, we begin like numerous others with W. E. B. Du Bois, the source of many crucial insights into both realities and unrealities of race in America. In *Black Reconstruction* (1970), Du Bois explains that racial whiteness was neither natural (based on phenotype) nor a foregone cultural conclusion in the United States, even in the context of racial slavery. Instead, whiteness defined through European ancestry was a calculated racial solution developed by colonial leaders to the economic and physical threat of laboring-class solidarity. As lawmakers fashioned and imposed the legal apparatus of racial slavery during the 17th and 18th centuries, it was not unusual for European workers to consort, conspire, and revolt with blacks (enslaved and free) and Native Americans against their common exploitation at the hands of white landowners. Bacon's Rebellion of 1676 in Virginia (see chapter 3) and the 1741 "conspiracy" to destroy New York illustrate the seriousness of this threat to the propertied class. In response, white elites resolved to undermine interracial working-class solidarity. They succeeded by granting virtually all European men full access to political or legal whiteness. During the first half of the 19th century, colonial legislators removed tax, property ownership, employment, and other requirements that had previously limited suffrage to male landowners. As labor historian David Roediger (1999; 2008) notes, this legal expansion of whiteness was not an expression of extant white unity based on European ancestry but a successful attempt on the part of colonial elites to create it.

For Du Bois, racial alliance with elites on these terms was disastrous because newfound working-class whiteness was based on the betrayal and suppression of shared class interests for the purposes of white supremacy and privilege. European laborers' acceptance of "personal whiteness" as "something that could be owned as an asset and as an identity" (Roediger 2008) ensured continued political and economic dominance by the propertied class. In return, they received material benefits associated with full citizenship as well as the "public and psychological wage" (Du Bois 1970) of codified social distance and deference from their former allies. The white worker's political independence existed in contrast to the black worker's lack of such. By agreeing and helping to ensure that the lowest social stratum consists exclusively of nonwhites (and primarily of blacks), they also established a powerful and enduring economic incentive for *systematic* working-class racism. The Du Boisian assessment of political, personal whiteness as the polar opposite of racial blackness continues to inform critical analyses of the legal and economic consequences of white racial formations on their nonwhite complements (e.g. Harris 1993; Lipsitz 2006).

In a fascinating survey, *The History of White People*, historian Nell Painter (2010, excerpted in this chapter) identifies extension of suffrage on the part of 19th-century elites to (most) European males – this trumping of class by race – as only the first

"enlargement of American whiteness." These are periods in the history of the United States when definitions of racial whiteness expanded primarily in response to large-scale demographic shifts and cultural pressures. A second expansion occurred during the late 19th and early 20th centuries when the Irish, Germans, and other "Nordics" gained greater acceptance as "true" Americans (although still decidedly less true than Anglo-Americans). Already possessing legal and political privileges afforded white males, their enhanced racial standing was meant to reaffirm and reinforce – quite literally, with their bodies – the boundaries of whiteness against a wave of immigration from southern and eastern Europe.

These "new immigrants," for example, Jews, Poles, Russians, and Italians, brought with them customs and traditions that were different from the "old immigrants" of northwestern Europe. Often cast as racial inferiors in Europe (e.g. Ripley 1899), in the United States they were victims of discriminatory restrictive immigration policies designed to limit their numbers through quotas. Once in the country, they resumed their roles as racial inferiors, now alongside indigenous peoples, Hispanics, Asians, and African Americans. Consider, for example, these depictions of various European immigrant "races" by William Cook (1929), from his book *American Institutions and Their Preservation*:

Italian

> a fiery temper quick to take offence and to revenge an insult real or fancied; an utter absence of scruple in the weapons chosen to attack an enemy … Some one in America must do the hard, repelling physical toil of the mines, the railroads, the ditch, the streets, and elsewhere. They do that, but can hardly be called desirable citizens … they remain a hopeless mass in their relations to American institutions. (pp. 202, 203–204)

Jewish

> A strange race … they have lowered the standards of the theater and moving pictures … not a fighter and he has never shown any enthusiastic partiality for American institutions. As a dweller in the cities, as adverse to agriculture and hard labor, as of little physical courage, as opposed to conflict and controversy, he will never really enter American life. (pp. 160, 173, 184)

Russian

> But there can be no substantial mingling of the two races. The differences are too great. ... They do not and never will cut any figure in America, except as hewers of wood and drawers of water. (pp. 205–206)

Polish

> He does not rise to intellectual heights and leadership and is a very doubtful asset, except industrially. ... If anything displeases them, it is the fault of the country; never their fault. ... Their ethics are apt to be no ethics. They require a strong hand. (pp. 208–209)

Cook's cynical assessments of new immigrants' abilities and prospects as future Americans were hardly fringe or inconsequential. He first published *American Institutions* privately in 1927 when he was the nation's leading scholar of corporation law. A decade earlier, Madison Grant had outlined the popular nativist case against southeastern Europeans' recognition as white Americans in his influential book *The Passing of the Great Race* (1916). The basic argument was a familiar one. Grant held that older immigrants were skilled, thrifty, and hardworking like native-born (i.e. Anglo-) Americans (although the Irish in particular still received constant reminders of their second-tier status in the hierarchy of whiteness). Meanwhile the new immigrants were unskilled and ignorant, poor cultural candidates for assimilation into American society. Grant and other eugenicists served as expert advisors during congressional debates over the Immigration Restriction Act (or Johnson–Reed Act) of 1924, designed to limit the national threat of "inferior stock" Europeans via highly restrictive quotas.

Despite these barriers, new immigrants groups' racial profiles, rooted in their European experiences, eventually gave way to new ethnic distinctions within a shared white racial identity. Of course, legal and political recognition as white and even economic success did not translate immediately into social or cultural acceptance. As in the past, when acceptance came it did so unevenly, more slowly for some groups than for others. At the turn of the century, for example, many Anglo-Americans had found it easier to receive Germans, Scandinavians, and other old immigrants into the white racial fold than they did the Irish. Their prejudices reflected a history of Irish political subjugation by the British in Europe as well as concerns over Catholicism and its doctrine of papal supremacy, which contradicted professed U.S. ideals of political and religious freedom (Franklin 1988). Now, Jewish and Italian Americans remained somewhat in flux between non-white and white racial identities. Until World War II, these groups, the primary targets of the 1924 immigration quotas, were deemed somewhat less white than other European descended groups.

By the middle of the 20th century, however, all southern and eastern European immigrants and their children saw themselves and were largely recognized politically and culturally as white people – a third "enlargement" of whiteness. During the 1940s and 1950s, these groups benefited from discriminatory federal housing policies that helped create and nurture suburban middle-class whiteness in contrast to increasingly "colored" inner cities. They also enjoyed increasingly favorable popular portrayals as "normal" whites, even if popular culture also served to remind them that they did not match up to the idealized aesthetics of Anglo-Americans (Brodkin 1998). This was a crucial period in U.S. history, when white became synonymous with pan-European ancestry and new immigrants became "ethnics." From this point, only Hispanics, Asians, African Americans, and Native peoples have been marked and measured as racially different.

In this chapter, we have illustrated that a white/nonwhite racial divide based upon European ancestry is more recent and less rational than one might think. Whiteness, it turns out, is fundamentally cultural and political and cannot be understood through resort to biological or other fictional purities. We also have explained why white racial identity over time has proven desirable and attainable for some and not others. Whiteness pays ... literally, and in ways that other racial formations do not. These observations are central to the academic field of whiteness studies as developed over the past few decades by historians, anthropologists, legal theorists, and others. By exploring historical and evolving white racial formations critically and in conjunction with nonwhite formations, these scholars continue a tradition that extends to the earliest critiques of racial inequality in the U.S. (e.g. see Roediger 1998).

Cultural analysis allows anthropologists and others to build upon knowledge of historical whiteness by revealing racial logics embedded, sometimes encrypted, within routine activities (Thomas and Jackson 2009; Hargrove 2009). In addition to knowing who became "officially" white and when, these scholars are interested in understanding the many specific channels and mechanisms through which racial formations are maintained, challenged, and reworked. Anthropologists, for example, explore ideological and material manifestations of whiteness across a broad range of sites and activities. These range from plantation and other contested historical landscapes (Epperson 1997; Paynter 2001) to contemporary discourse and policies related to diverse issues including education (Lee 2004), "appropriate" residential behavior (Low 2009), urban development (Hargrove 2009), and reproductive rights (Davis 2009). These cultural approaches to white racial formation enable and push us to link analyses of race, class, and gender critically and organically, and to seek out and interpret new meanings of whiteness within and, ideally, beyond our shared histories and experiences of racial inequality.

INVENTING WHITENESS, 1650–2000, A TIME LINE

1691 — **First legal use of the term "white"** The Virginia colony enacts a law prohibiting marriage between whites and blacks.

> ❝ And for prevention of that abominable mixture and spurious issue which hereafter may encrease … whatsoever English or other white man or woman being free shall intermarry with a negroe, mulatto, or Indian … shall … be banished and removed from this dominion forever. ❞ *The Laws of Virginia*, April 1691 (3:86–88)

1790 — **Naturalization Act** This law allows only "free white persons" to become U.S. citizens. It is enacted at a time when one-fifth of the population is either African or descended from Africans – the highest proportion in the nation's history.

1792 — **Militia Act** Congress provides for an armed militia, consisting of "free and able-bodied white male" citizens ages 18 to 45, to be called into service when national need arises.

> ❝ The idea of citizenship had become thoroughly entwined with the idea of 'whiteness' … because what a citizen really was, at bottom, was someone who could help put down a slave rebellion or participate in Indian wars. ❞ JACOBSON 1998:25

1795 — **The Caucasian Race** German scientist Johann Blumenbach uses a skull from his collection to exemplify the "white" race. It comes from a woman who lived in the Caucasus Mountains, between the Black and the Caspian seas, the home territory, Blumenbach writes, of the world's most beautiful people. With this, the nonscientific term "Caucasian" begins to be used as an alternate word for white.

> ❝ Of all the odd myths that have arisen in the scientific world, the 'Caucasian mystery' invented quite innocently by Blumenbach is the oddest. … It became his model exemplar of human skulls, from which all others might be regarded as deviations. ❞ HUXLEY 1865:244–245

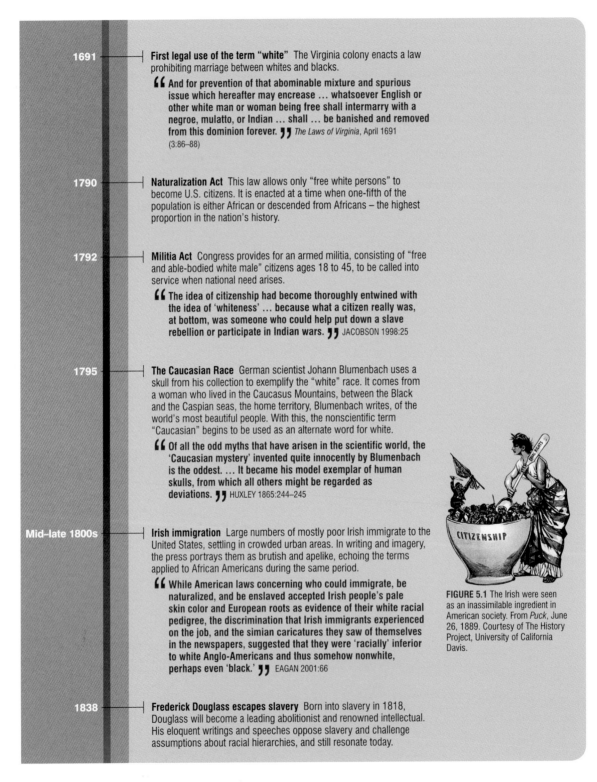

Mid–late 1800s — **Irish immigration** Large numbers of mostly poor Irish immigrate to the United States, settling in crowded urban areas. In writing and imagery, the press portrays them as brutish and apelike, echoing the terms applied to African Americans during the same period.

> ❝ While American laws concerning who could immigrate, be naturalized, and be enslaved accepted Irish people's pale skin color and European roots as evidence of their white racial pedigree, the discrimination that Irish immigrants experienced on the job, and the simian caricatures they saw of themselves in the newspapers, suggested that they were 'racially' inferior to white Anglo-Americans and thus somehow nonwhite, perhaps even 'black.' ❞ EAGAN 2001:66

FIGURE 5.1 The Irish were seen as an inassimilable ingredient in American society. From *Puck*, June 26, 1889. Courtesy of The History Project, University of California Davis.

1838 — **Frederick Douglass escapes slavery** Born into slavery in 1818, Douglass will become a leading abolitionist and renowned intellectual. His eloquent writings and speeches oppose slavery and challenge assumptions about racial hierarchies, and still resonate today.

❝ One drop of Teutonic blood is enough to account for all good and great qualities occasionally coupled with a colored skin; and on the other hand, one drop of negro blood, though in the veins of a man of Teutonic whiteness, is enough on which to predicate all offensive and ignoble qualities. ❞ DOUGLASS 1881:650.

1866 **Ku Klux Klan founded** The Klan uses elaborate rituals and disguises to terrorize blacks and their supporters during the post–Civil War Reconstruction in the South. It recruits poor whites by playing on the idea that their economic troubles are caused by recently freed blacks.

FIGURE 5.2 *Visit of the Ku-Klux*. Courtesy of the Library of Congress.

❝ The most important thing about races was the boundaries between them. ... If one were a member of the race at the top, then it was essential to maintain the boundaries that defined one's superiority, to keep people from the lower categories from slipping surreptitiously upward. ❞ SPICKARD 1992:15

1879 **First Native American boarding school** The Carlisle Industrial Training School opens in Pennsylvania. Seeking to "Americanize" Native American children, the school removes them from their homes, cuts their hair, and dresses them like white people. They are forbidden to speak their language or practice their cultural traditions.

❝ My friend ... Judéwin knew a few words of English, and she had overheard the paleface woman talk about cutting our long, heavy hair. ... We discussed our fate some moments and when Judéwin said, 'We have to submit, because they are strong,' I rebelled. 'No, I will not submit! I will struggle first!' I answered. ❞ ZITKALA-SA (Dakota) 1900:314

❝ Transfer the savage-born infant to the surroundings of civilization, and he will grow to possess a civilized language and habit. ❞ RICHARD HENRY PRATT, Carlisle School founder, 1892: RACE exhibit, SMM

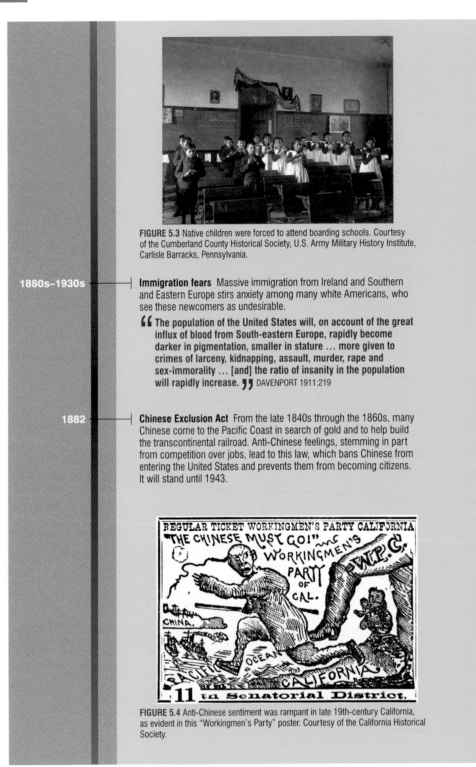

FIGURE 5.3 Native children were forced to attend boarding schools. Courtesy of the Cumberland County Historical Society, U.S. Army Military History Institute, Carlisle Barracks, Pennsylvania.

1880s–1930s

Immigration fears Massive immigration from Ireland and Southern and Eastern Europe stirs anxiety among many white Americans, who see these newcomers as undesirable.

❝ The population of the United States will, on account of the great influx of blood from South-eastern Europe, rapidly become darker in pigmentation, smaller in stature … more given to crimes of larceny, kidnapping, assault, murder, rape and sex-immorality … [and] the ratio of insanity in the population will rapidly increase. ❞ DAVENPORT 1911:219

1882

Chinese Exclusion Act From the late 1840s through the 1860s, many Chinese come to the Pacific Coast in search of gold and to help build the transcontinental railroad. Anti-Chinese feelings, stemming in part from competition over jobs, lead to this law, which bans Chinese from entering the United States and prevents them from becoming citizens. It will stand until 1943.

FIGURE 5.4 Anti-Chinese sentiment was rampant in late 19th-century California, as evident in this "Workingmen's Party" poster. Courtesy of the California Historical Society.

" I ... a Chinaman, a republican, and a lover of free institutions; am much attached to the principles of the government of the United States. ... You argue that this is a republic of a particular race – that the Constitution of the United States admits of no asylum to any other than the pale face. This proposition is false to the extreme, and you know it. The declaration of your independence, and all the acts of your government, your people, and your history are all against you. **"** ASING 1852

1890s–1910s

World's Fairs Vast fairs such as the Chicago World's Columbian Exposition (1893) and the St Louis Louisiana Purchase Exposition (1904) are billed as important educational experiences, and they draw millions of people from across the United States.

At the St Louis fair, race and human progress are prominent themes and exhibits include entire "living villages." According to W. J. McGee, an anthropologist who organizes what he calls a "Congress of Races," these exhibits are intended to reaffirm the hierarchy of races.

" The aim of the Department of Anthropology at the World's Fair will be to represent human progress from the dark prime to the highest enlightenment, from savagery to civic organization, from egoism to altruism. **"** MCGEE 1903

" When a white man comes to our country, we give him presents, sometimes of sheep, goats, or birds, and divide our elephant meat with them. The Americans treat us as they do our pet monkey. They laugh at us and poke their umbrellas into our faces. **"** LATUNA, Pygmy village resident, quoted in the *St. Louis Republic*, August 6, 1904: RACE exhibit, SMM

FIGURE 5.5 The Cliff Dwellers' Village at the 1904 World's Fair. Courtesy of the Saint Louis Public Library.

1896

Plessy v. Ferguson In 1892 Homer A. Plessy, a black, is jailed after boarding a railroad car reserved for white people only. Four years later, his case reaches the U.S. Supreme Court, which decides against him, ruling that states may provide blacks with "separate but equal" facilities for transportation, education, and public accommodations such as hotels and theaters.

1904

White orphans removed The New York Foundling Hospital, a Catholic-run orphanage, sends 40 young Irish orphans to two Arizona copper-mining towns for adoption by Mexican-immigrant Catholic families. Whites in the towns are outraged, taking the children from their new families by force. The Catholic Church sues to get the children back, but in 1906 the U.S. Supreme Court rules that the abduction was legal. Interestingly, these children "became" white only after being adopted by Mexican families in Arizona. Like Jews, Italians and other "white ethnics" and "new immigrants," Irish people usually were not considered truly or fully white in early twentieth-century New York.

> ❝ The child in question is a white Caucasian child ... abandoned ... to the keeping of a Mexican Indian, [who is] by reason of his race, mode of living, habits and education, unfit to have the custody, care and education of the child. ❞ JUSTICE WILLIAM R. DAY, majority opinion, 1906

> ❝ Religion has influenced and shaped concepts of race. This event illustrates how race and religion intersect ❞ MARY MARGARET OVERBEY, anthropologist, American Anthropological Association: RACE exhibit, SMM

Early 1900s

"One drop rule" According to this belief a person thought to have any amount of African blood – even "one drop" – is classified as black. The notion, which has no scientific basis, dates back to American colonial times, when any child born of a slave was automatically considered a slave, even if one parent was white. During the segregation era, the "one drop rule" becomes codified in law and custom, appearing on legal documents ranging from birth records to marriage licenses to census forms.

> ❝ If it is proven that a man has even 1 per cent of African blood, he becomes a Negro every time; the 99 per cent of Anglo-Saxon blood counts for nothing – the man always falls to our pile in the count of the races. It takes 100 per cent to make a white man, and 1 per cent will make a Negro every time. So, you see, we are a stronger race than the white race. ❞ WASHINGTON 1900:115

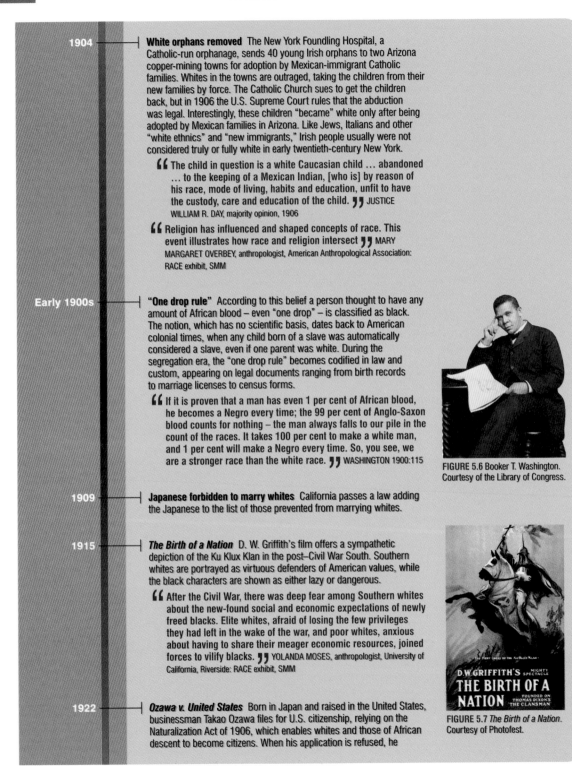

FIGURE 5.6 Booker T. Washington. Courtesy of the Library of Congress.

1909

Japanese forbidden to marry whites California passes a law adding the Japanese to the list of those prevented from marrying whites.

1915

The Birth of a Nation D. W. Griffith's film offers a sympathetic depiction of the Ku Klux Klan in the post–Civil War South. Southern whites are portrayed as virtuous defenders of American values, while the black characters are shown as either lazy or dangerous.

> ❝ After the Civil War, there was deep fear among Southern whites about the new-found social and economic expectations of newly freed blacks. Elite whites, afraid of losing the few privileges they had left in the wake of the war, and poor whites, anxious about having to share their meager economic resources, joined forces to vilify blacks. ❞ YOLANDA MOSES, anthropologist, University of California, Riverside: RACE exhibit, SMM

D.W. GRIFFITH'S MIGHTY SPECTACLE

THE BIRTH OF A NATION FOUNDED ON THOMAS DIXON'S THE CLANSMAN

FIGURE 5.7 The Birth of a Nation. Courtesy of Photofest.

1922

Ozawa v. United States Born in Japan and raised in the United States, businessman Takao Ozawa files for U.S. citizenship, relying on the Naturalization Act of 1906, which enables whites and those of African descent to become citizens. When his application is refused, he goes to court. The case reaches the U.S. Supreme Court, which unanimously rules that, as a person of Japanese descent, he is not white and therefore ineligible for citizenship.

1923 ┤ *United States v. Thind* The U.S. Supreme Court rules that Bhagat Singh Thind, a religious scholar from India who served in the U.S. Army during World War I, cannot become a citizen because U.S. law allows only "free white persons" to become naturalized. While the court concedes that Thind is "Caucasian" because anthropologists consider Indians to belong to the same race as white Americans, it argues that Thind does not fit the common understanding of the term "white."

> **It may be true that the blond Scandinavian and the brown Hindu have a common ancestor in the dim reaches of antiquity, but the average man knows perfectly well that there are unmistakable and profound differences between them today.** JUSTICE GEORGE SUTHERLAND, majority opinion, 1923

1924 ┤ **Virginia's Racial Integrity Act** This law prohibits marriage between whites and nonwhites. It will stand until 1967, when the U.S. Supreme Court overturns it. The law is part of a growing eugenics movement, which stresses the improvement of humanity through controlled reproduction.

> **For the purpose of this act, the term 'white person' shall apply only to the person who has no trace whatsoever of any blood other than Caucasian; but persons who have one-sixteenth or less of the blood of the American Indian and have no other non-Caucasian blood shall be deemed to be white persons.** Racial Integrity Act of 1924

FIGURE 5.8 Lucky Brown Pressing Oil. Courtesy of the Jim Crow Museum of Racist Memorabilia, Ferris State University, Big Rapids, Michigan.

1930s ┤ **Products to look more "white"** "Whiteness" defines the standard of beauty. African Americans used Lucky Brown, and other products like it, to aid in straightening their hair with a hot comb.

1948 ┤ **Armed forces integrated** President Harry Truman signs an executive order integrating the U.S. Armed Forces. "There shall be equality of treatment and opportunity for all persons in the armed services," the order states, "without regard to race, color, religion or national origin."

1950s–1970s ┤ **White TV** Popular television series such as *Leave It to Beaver*, *Father Knows Best*, and, later, *The Brady Bunch* offer idealized images of middle-class American families – all of whom are white.

> **White people can think of themselves as just 'American,' but other people must be labeled as 'African American' or 'Mexican American,' etc.** ELIZABETH BRUMFIEL, anthropologist, Northwestern University: RACE exhibit, SMM

FIGURE 5.9 The cast of *Leave It to Beaver*. Courtesy of James Berman.

1967 ┤ *Loving v. Virginia* Virginia residents Richard Loving (white) and Mildred Jeter (African American) leave the state to marry in

Washington, D.C. Returning home, they are charged with violating Virginia's Racial Integrity Act of 1924 and plead guilty. They are sentenced to a year in prison, but the sentence is suspended on condition that they move out of state. The Lovings settle in Washington and begin petitioning to have the Virginia law overturned. In 1967 the U.S. Supreme Court unanimously rules to strike down the Virginia law, a decision that also extends to similar laws in 15 other states.

1970s–2000s

Immigration in the United States   Immigration from around the world to the United States changes patterns of marriage, housing, education, and employment and redefines ideas about race and whiteness.

❝ As a white person, I realized I had been taught about racism as something which puts others at a disadvantage, but had been taught not to see one of its corollary aspects, white privilege, which puts me at an advantage. ❞ MCINTOSH 1988:10

The 12 White steps

Step 1: Admit you have a race. Whiteness comes with advantages. You know it. So why not admit it? If you have a jar full of cookies, you can spend your whole life denying you have them … or you can share them. The thing is, everyone already knows you have the cookies. We can smell the sugar and see the crumbs on your chin. Yep, the secret is out. So maybe it's time to offer some of the sweet dessert to others. (damali ayo, "The 12 White Steps" (2005))

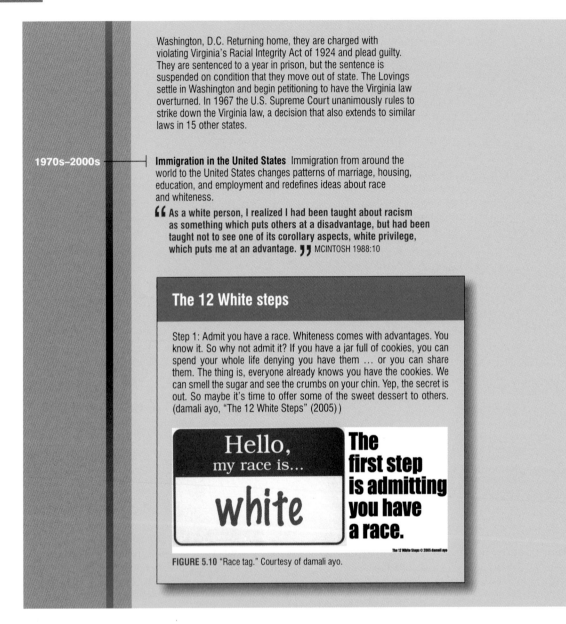

FIGURE 5.10 "Race tag." Courtesy of damali ayo.

Nell Irvin Painter
Early American White People Observed

Nell Irvin Painter *is Edwards Professor of American History Emerita at Princeton University, past president of the Organization of American Historians and the Southern Historical Association, and a Fellow of the American Academy of Arts and Sciences. In this excerpt from her recent book* The History of White People *(2010), Painter explains intersecting race and gender dimensions of the early U.S. censuses and contrasts the opinions of Thomas Jefferson and French soldier-diplomat Michel-Guillame-Jean de Crèvecoeur regarding the constitution of (white) American identity. While Jefferson defines the true American narrowly in terms of the myth of Anglo-Saxon purity, de Crèvecoeur observes stark class division and notes the presence of other white Americans from varied European backgrounds.* Photograph by Robin Holland, courtesy of Nell Irvin Painter.

North America's unique jumble of peoples appealed to Western intellectuals as a test case for humanity. Who are the Americans? What are they like? Might the United States, so far across the western sea, reveal mankind's future? Or at least Europeans' future? Some observers saw Americans as white and egalitarian; others perceived a more varied and multiracial assortment of oppressors and oppressed. Meanwhile, the government of this new republic went about its own everyday business, answering its own questions by counting its people according to its own devices.

In article 1, sections 2 and 9, of the Constitution, the United States created a novel way of apportioning representation and direct taxation: a national census every ten years. The first U.S. census, taken in 1790, recognized six categories within the population: (1) the head of each household, (2) free white males over sixteen, (3) free white males under sixteen, (4) free

white females, (5) all other free persons by sex and color, and (6) slaves.[i] U.S. marshals conducted this first census, recording results on whatever scraps of paper lay at hand. The effort required eighteen months and counted 3.9 million people, incidentally a number George Washington called too low. The first undercount.

Three terms parsed the only race mentioned – white – and two categories demarcated slave and free legal statuses. Unfree white persons, of whom there were many in the new union, seem to have fallen through the cracks in 1790, though the fourfold mention of the qualifier "free" by inference recognizes the existence of nonfree whites in servitude. Had all whites been free and whiteness meant freedom, as is often assumed today, no need would have existed to add "free" to "white." The 1800 census fixed this problem through an enumeration of "all other persons, except Indians not taxed."[ii] For these early censuses, "free" formed a meaningful classification not identical with "white."

Counting free white males by age sprang from a need to identify men eligible for militia service, the only armed service of the time. To calculate each state's congressional representation, Congress counted all the free persons (women, too, although they did not have the vote) and three-fifths of "others," that is, indentured laborers and slaves. Later on, realities behind the census's careful separation of bondage and race changed, calling for new categories. As politics freed all white people and ideology whitened the face of freedom, "free white males" seemed a useless redundancy.[iii]

---

[i] Margo J. Anderson, *The American Census: A Social History*. New Haven: Yale University Press, 1988:9, 12–14; and Bureau of the Census, U.S. Department of Commerce [Frederick G. Boheme], *200 Years of U.S. Census Taking: Population and Housing Questions, 1790–1990*. Washington, D.C., 1989:1.

[ii] Indians appeared in the census of 1800, and colored people gained their own category in 1820; thereafter, the races broke down into white, black, and mulatto in 1850. Chinese people appeared in 1870.

[iii] The census of 1840 asked for the number of "free white males and females" and "free colored males and females." By 1850 the question addressed simply "each free person in a household." The three-fifths clause remains in article 1, section 2, paragraph 3 of the U.S. Constitution, however, in which people bound to a term of servitude – presumably white – are counted as whole persons.

Census categories kept changing every ten years, as governmental needs changed and taxonomical categories shifted, including taxonomies of race. Throughout American census history, non-Europeans and part-Europeans have been counted as part of the American population, usually lumped as "nonwhite," but occasionally disaggregated into black and mulatto, as in the censuses of 1850 and 1860.

During the early nineteenth century, when "free white males" was losing its usefulness because fewer and fewer whites were not free, another phrase was coming into use, one with a much longer life: "universal suffrage." The United States was the first nation to drastically lower economic barriers to voting. Between 1790 and the mid-1850s the ideology of democracy gained wide acceptance, so that active citizenship was opened to virtually all adult white men, including most immigrant settlers. Mere adult white maleness thus replaced eighteenth-century requirements of a stake in society (property ownership, tax paying) and political independence (one's own steady income) before a man could vote. With the vote came inclusion in public life, so that the antebellum period associated with the rise of the Jacksonian common man witnessed the first major extension of the meaning of what it meant to be American.[iv]

All women, people ineligible to become citizens (Native American Indians and Asians), the enslaved, and free people of African descent outside New England continued to be excluded, as well as paupers, felons, and transients such as canal workers and sailors. (Even today, children, non-citizens, and most convicted felons cannot vote. People who cannot meet residency requirements and do not register prior to voting are also disenfranchised.) In this situation, "universal suffrage" meant adult white male suffrage, though from time to time the definition of "white" came into question. Were men with one black and one white parent or three white and

one black grandparent "white"? Did "white" mean only Anglo-Saxons, or all men considered Caucasian, including those classed as Celts?[v]

The abolition of economic barriers to voting by white men made the United States, in the then common parlance, "a white man's country," a polity defined by race and limited to white men. Once prerequisites for active citizenship came down to maleness and whiteness, poor men could be welcomed into the definition of American, as long as they could be defined as white – the first enlargement of American whiteness.

We can date the pairing of "American" with descendants of Europeans to the quickly translated, widely read, and endlessly quoted *Letters from an American Farmer* of 1782, by the French soldier-diplomat-author Michel-Guillaume-Jean de Crèvecoeur (1735–1813). Crèvecoeur inaugurated a hardy tradition, that of contrasting class-riven Europe, the land of opulent aristocrats and destitute peasants, with the egalitarian United States, home of mobility and democracy.

Crèvecoeur's road to fame meandered far and wide. After immigrating to Canada and fighting on the French side during the Seven Years'/French and Indian War of 1754–63, he moved to New York and changed his name to J. Hector St. John. The gratifying picture of Americans in *Letters from an American Farmer* and Crèvecoeur's subsequent success as a French diplomat in the United States raised him high, earning election to the exclusive American Philosophical Society, plus many a local honor. The Vermont legislature so revered Crèvecoeur that it named a town St. Johnsbury after him; it became the largest city in Vermont's impoverished and deeply conservative northeast region.

Crèvecoeur's letter 3 asks, "What then is the American, this new man?" – and answers,

> He is either an European or the descendant of an European, hence that strange mixture of blood, which you will find in no other country. I could point out to you a family whose grandfather was an Englishman, whose wife was Dutch, whose son married a French woman, and whose present four sons have now four wives of different nations. He is an American who, leaving behind him all

iv Alexander Keyssar, *The Right to Vote: The Contested History of Democracy in the United States* (New York: Basic, 2000), xxii–xxiii, 20–34, 52–76, 102, and Sean Wilentz, *The Rise of American Democracy: Jefferson to Lincoln* (New York: W. W. Norton, 2005), 27–28, 82–83, 17, 485. Keyssar and Wilentz both note historians' long neglect of the basic history of the right to vote, especially with regard to class. See also Wilentz, "On Class and Politics and Jacksonian America," *Reviews in American History* 10, no. 4 (Dec. 1982), 45–48, 59.

v Rhode Island delayed ratification of the Fifteenth Amendment to the Constitution until 1870 because legislators feared it might enfranchise members of the Celtic race. Black men had been able to vote there since 1840.

his ancient prejudices and manners, receives new ones from the new mode of life he has embraced, the new government he obeys, and the new rank he holds. ... Here individuals of all nations are melted into a new race whose labors and posterity will one day cause great changes in the world. ... From involuntary idleness, service dependence, penury, and useless labor [in Europe], he has passed to toils of a very different nature, rewarded by ample subsistence. – This is an American.[vi]

In addition to a willingness to innovate and to think new thoughts, heterogeneous – but purely European – ancestry characterizes the American.

This "new man" escapes old Europe's oppression, embraces new opportunity, and glories in freedom of thought and economic mobility. Now a classic description of *the* American, Crèvecoeur's paragraph constantly reappears as an objective eyewitness account of American identity. But letter 3 is only one part of the story. When other classes, races, sexes, and the South entered Crèvecoeur's picture, all sorts of revisions became necessary. For instance, poor and untamed white people, particularly southerners, occupy a separate category well below *the* American. While *the* American and the poor white might both be judged white according to American law, poor white poverty and apparent wildness kept him at a remove from the charmed circle. Such complexity ensured that the *who* question could not be answered clearly. But European and American observers never stopped pursuing it.

Crèvecoeur conceded the existence of other Americans – other white Americans – who do "not afford a very pleasing spectacle." He offers a hope that the march of American progress would soon displace or civilize these drunken idlers; meanwhile, white families living beyond the reach of law and order "exhibit the most hideous parts of our society." Crèvecoeur cannot decide whether untamed frontier families represent a temporary stage or a degeneration beyond redemption: "once hunters, farewell to the plow." Indians appear positively respectable beside mongrelized, half-savage, slothful, and drunken white hunting families.

Concerning slavery, ugly scenes in Charleston, South Carolina, break Crèvecoeur's heart, but his pessimism arises most from the shock of his hosts' callousness. The rich slaveholders entertaining Crèvecoeur are the "gayest" people in America – but gay at the cost of their humanity: "They neither see, hear, nor feel the woes" of their slaves or the blood-curdling violence of their social arrangements. Crèvecoeur can only marvel at such insouciance. In their situation, he says,

never could I rest in peace; my sleep would be perpetually disturbed by a retrospect of the frauds committed in Africa in order to entrap them, frauds surpassing in enormity everything which a common mind can possibly conceive. ... Can it be possible that the force of custom should ever make me deaf to all these reflections, and as insensible to the injustice of that [slave] trade, and to [slaves'] miseries, as the rich inhabitants of this town seem to be?[vii]

Face-to-face with the realities of southern slavery, Crèvecoeur becomes the first to predict slave insurrection as an inevitable consequence of "inveterate resentment" and a "wish of perpetual revenge." This is a European thinking in terms of rampant poverty and obscene wealth and seeing the enslaved as the poor, not simply as a race of people. Thus Crèvecoeur's America is split as much by class as by race, a society in contrast with the sunny, democratic image of his more popular pronouncement.

Writing a few years after Crèvecoeur, Thomas Jefferson (1743–1826) missed the class dimension that so alarmed Crèvecoeur. Born and raised in Virginia, Jefferson never questioned that American society was structured according to race, not class; to him, the poor people who served, including most prominently his slaves, belonged to a naturally servile race. By taking note of black people, he did not concede them status as Americans, who are "our people."

Like many other intellectuals, Jefferson held that slavery harms whites more than blacks. "Query XVIII: Manners," in *Notes on the State of Virginia* (1787), reflects upon the "unhappy" influence of slavery on

vi   J. Hector St. John de Crèvecoeur, Letters from an American Farmer and Sketches of Eighteenth-Century America (originally published 1782) AS@UVA Hypertexts, Letter 3, 54, http://xroads. virginia.edu/~HYPER/CREV/letter03.html. Post-industrial St. Johnsbury now figures as Vermont's capital of heroin addiction.

vii   J. Hector St. John de Crèvecoeur, Letters from an American Farmer and Sketches of Eighteenth-Century America (originally published 1782) AS@UVA Hypertexts, 170. Letter 9, 223–25, 229, http://xroads.virginia.edu/ ~HYPER/CREV/letter09.html.

the slave-owning class, scarcely mentioning the suffering of the enslaved. Rather it dwells on the price paid by the South's white slave owners. Slave-owning children mimic their parents' abuse of the people they own, coarsening their character and, thereby, their society. The white child, "thus nursed and educated, and daily exercised in tyranny," Jefferson warns, "cannot but be stamped by it with odious peculiarities. The man must be a prodigy who can retain his manner and morals undepraved by such circumstances."[viii]

In apportioning the injuries of slavery, Jefferson and Crèvecoeur mostly agreed. But their theories of American ancestry conflict, for the eloquent Jefferson rejected any idea of a mongrel American, even though he fathered seven of them with Sally Hemings, a woman he owned. He also rejected Crèvecoeur's "Dutch" man – probably meaning a *deutsch* man, or German – as essential to the American family tree. Jefferson's family tree was pure and sturdy oak, the Saxons of England.

Throughout his life Thomas Jefferson believed in the Saxon myth, a story of American descent from Saxons by way of England. He had conceived a fascination with it as a student at William and Mary College in 1762 and never wavered in it. Over fifty years of book collecting – his personal library formed the basis of the Library of Congress – Jefferson came to own the country's largest collection of Anglo-Saxon and Old English documents.[ix]

As a founding father, Jefferson theorized Americans' right to independence on the basis of Saxon ancestry. Laying out that claim in July of 1774, he makes English people "our ancestors," and the creators of the Magna Carta "our Saxon ancestors." Though the Magna Carta dates from 1215 and the Norman Conquest from 1066, Jefferson maintains that system of rights of "our ancestors" was already in place when "Norman lawyers" connived to saddle the Saxons with unfair burdens.[x] He continued to associate

Saxons with the liberal Whigs and Normans with the conservative Tories, as though liberal and reactionary parties had existed from time immemorial, almost as a matter of blood.[xi] For Jefferson, English-style Saxon liberty was not a trait to be found in Germans.

Jefferson's Saxon genealogy ignored a number of inconvenient facts. The oppressive English king George III was actually a Saxon and also the duke of Brunswick-Lüneburg as well as elector of Hanover in Lower Saxony. Furthermore, George the III's father and grandfather, Hanoverian kings of England before him, had been born in Germany and spoke German as a first language. It hardly mattered. To Jefferson, whatever genius for liberty Dark Age Saxons had bequeathed the English somehow thrived on English soil but died in Germany.[xii]

In the Philadelphia Continental Congress of 1776, Jefferson went so far as to propose his heroic Saxon ancestors for the great seal of the United States. Images of "Hengist and Horsa, the Saxon chiefs from whom we claim the honor of being descended,"[xiii] would aptly commemorate the new nation's political principles, government, and physical descent.[xiv] This proposition did not win approval, but Jefferson soldiered on. In 1798 he wrote *Essay on the Anglo-Saxon Language*, which equates language with biological descent, a confusion then common among philologists. In this essay Jefferson runs together Old English and Middle

---

[viii] Thomas Jefferson, Notes on the State of Virginia (originally published 1787), AS@UVA Hypertexts, Query 18, http://xroads.virginia.edu/~HYPER/JEFFERSON/ch18.html.

[ix] Stanley R. Hauer, "Thomas Jefferson and the Anglo-Saxon Language," *PMLA* 98, No. 5 (October 1983):879, 881.

[x] Thomas Jefferson, "A Summary View of the Rights of British America," July 1774 *The Papers of Thomas Jefferson*. Edited by Julian P. Boyd et al. Princeton: Princeton University Press, 1950–.1:121–35. http://press-pubs.uchicago.edu/founders/documents/v1ch14s10.html.

[xi] Dumas Malone, *The Sage of Monticello. Jefferson and His Time, Vol. 6*. Boston: Little, Brown: 1981:202–203.

[xii] [The tangled history of the two Saxon regions in Germany would have put Jefferson off, had he sought to trace a the relationship between Hengist and Horsa – who, according to Bede (ca.730) were Jutes – and the English and Americans of his own time. Until German unification under the Prussians, provincial borders changed with the marriages, wars, and alliances of practically every new generation of rulers.]

[xiii] Hengist ("Stallion") and Horsa ("Horse"), legendary founders of Saxon England, were said to have come from Jutland (now part of Denmark). According to Bede in his *Ecclesiastical History* (731), King Vortigern invited them from Jutland to England in 449 to help repulse attacks by the Picts and Scots. Vortigern gave them the Isle of Thanet in gratitude. The *Anglo-Saxon Chronicle* makes Hengist and Horsa joint kings of Kent.

[xiv] John Adams to Abigail Adams, Philadelphia 14 August 1776, in Charles Francis Adams, *Familiar Letters of John Adams and His Wife Abigail Adams, During the Revolution, with a Memoir of Mrs. Adams*. Boston: Houghton Mifflin, 1875:210–211. See also Malone, *Sage of Monticello*, vol. 6:202. For the other side of the seal, Jefferson suggested the children of Israel in the wilderness.

English, creating a long era of Anglo-Saxon greatness stretching from the sixth century to the thirteenth.

With its emphasis on blood purity, this smacks of race talk. Not only had Jefferson's Saxons remained racially pure during the Roman occupation (there was "little familiar mixture with the native Britons"), but, amazingly, their language had stayed pristine two centuries after the Norman Conquest: Anglo Saxon "was the language of all England, properly so called, from the Saxon possession of that country in the sixth century to the time of Henry III in the thirteenth, and was spoken pure and unmixed with any other."[xv] Therefore Anglo-Saxon/Old English deserved study as the basis of American thought.

One of Jefferson's last great achievements, his founding of the University of Virginia in 1818, institutionalized his interest in Anglo-Saxon as the language of American culture, law, and politics. On opening in 1825, it was the only college in the United States to offer instruction in Anglo-Saxon, and Anglo-Saxon was the only course it offered on the English language. *Beowulf*, naturally, became a staple of instruction. Ironically, the teacher hailed from Leipzig, in eastern German Saxony. An intensely unpopular disciplinarian, Georg Blaettermann also taught French, German, Spanish, Italian, Danish, Swedish, Dutch, and Portuguese. After surviving years of student riots and protests, Blaettermann was fired in 1840 for horsewhipping his wife in public.[xvi]

CAROL C. MUKHOPADHYAY

"Caucasian"

Carol C. Mukhopadhyay *is Professor of Anthropology at San Jose State University and a member of the RACE Project Scholarly Advisory Board. A cultural anthropologist, her research interests include gendered activities in households, politics, and particularly in science and engineering. She has 40 years of experience in teaching, research, consulting, and publishing in the area of race–gender– education–culture. Here, Mukhopadhyay recounts the 18th-century origins of the word "Caucasian" as a reference to white or European Americans. She explains how the term's continued use, often under the mistaken belief that it conveys scientific precision, perpetuates the belief that only whites are authentic Americans. Photograph courtesy of Carol Mukhopadhyay.*

Language reflects and shapes how we perceive and experience the world around us. The "race" concept is a particularly powerful example, referencing an elaborate U.S. "worldview" rooted in colonialism and slavery and a "race"-based system of inequality. As we go about dismantling this ideology, especially scientific racism and the false notion that races are naturally occurring, biologically-rooted, ranked subdivisions of the human species, we must also critically examine the language historically associated with these outmoded systems of racial classification, the labels we use for "races."

One of the most pernicious, and surprisingly persistent, remnants of the old ideology is the term "Caucasian."[1] Over the past decades many labels associated with racial science have been challenged. Terms such as "Mongoloid" and Negroid, along with

[xvi]   Hauer, "Thomas Jefferson and the Anglo-Saxon Language": 883–886, 891.

This is a significantly revised version of an earlier article, see Mukhopadhyay 2008.

[1]   [There are many others, including the persistence of "color" linked terminology, such as *white* and *black*; the collapse of multiple, complex world of U.S. ethnicity/race/communities into the familiar dualistic, oppositional frame (white–others) even if it takes new forms (People of Color-White); the continuation of a race/ethnicity distinction, despite the tortuous and confusing definitions that result ; and the persistence of language inconsistent with what we know to be continuous, gradations of biological traits like skin color ("darker" v. "dark," "lighter" v. "light" (aka "fair"!) skin.]

[xv]   Thomas Jefferson, *Essay on the Anglo-Saxon Language*, in Andrew A. Lipscomb, ed. Thomas Jefferson, *The Writings of Thomas Jefferson*. Washington, DC: Thomas Jefferson Memorial Association of the United States, 1903–1904. Vol. XVIII, 1904:365–366.

"The Red Man" and "The Yellow Race" have essentially disappeared from our vocabulary. Today, employing such linguistic fossils would immediately mark the user as seriously out of touch with modern understandings of race. Yet the word "Caucasian" is surprisingly alive and well in both scientific and popular usage.

Isn't it time we got rid of the word Caucasian? Some would argue that it's "only a label" and we shouldn't quibble over mere semantics!

Language is one of the most systematic, subtle, and significant vehicles for transmitting cultural knowledge, including racial ideology. The word "Caucasian" encapsulates the old racial science, carries a misplaced scientific "cache" and precision, and evokes a different and problematic set of images than other racial labels. Caucasian also conveys broader messages about who has "culture" and "ethnicity" and what constitutes real "Americaness." Every time we use "Caucasian," I would argue, we are reinforcing – rather than unraveling – the old U.S. racial worldview.

Caucasians and 18th–20th century racial science

The term Caucasian originated in the 18th century as part of the developing European science of racial classification (Mukhopadhyay et al. 2007, with especial reference to part 2). After visiting the Caucasus Mountains region, between the Caspian and Black Seas, German anatomist Johann Blumenbach declared its inhabitants the most beautiful in the world, created in "God's Image," and deemed this area the likely site of human origins (wrong – it was Africa). He decided all light-skinned peoples from this region, plus Europeans, belonged to the same race, which he labeled Caucasian.

Blumenbach proposed four other races, all considered physically and morally "degenerate" forms of "God's original creation." He classified Africans (excepting lighter-skinned North Africans) as "Ethiopians" (black). He split non-Caucasus Asians into two separate races: the "Mongoloid" or "yellow" race of China and Japan and the "Malayan" or "brown" race which included Aboriginal Australians and Pacific Islanders. Native Americans were the fifth or "red" race.

Blumenbach's system of racial classification was adopted in the United States. The RACE exhibit's Scientific Racism section shows how American scientists measured skull size to try to prove that Caucasians had larger brains and were smarter than other races (see chapter 4). Racial science dovetailed with 19th-century evolutionary theories, which ranked races from more "primitive" ("savages") to more "advanced" ("civilized"), with Caucasians on top. Racial hierarchies were used to justify slavery and other forms of racial discrimination.

The U.S. legal system drew upon Blumenbach's definitions to decide who was eligible to be a naturalized citizen, a privilege the 1790 Naturalization Act restricted to "whites." This created dilemmas. The courts and other powerful U.S. elites had hoped that racial science could provide a "scientific" basis for racism, including a racially restrictive citizenship policy. Yet Blumenbach's Caucasians included groups like Armenians, Persians, North Indians, and some North Africans. Clearly these were not the "whites" envisioned by lawmakers in 1790 – that is, Europeans, especially northern and western European Christians. White and Caucasian had to be reinterpreted! In 1923, the Court rejected the naturalization petition of an immigrant from North India, saying he was Caucasian but *not* white, citing, among other things, his skin color and his non-Christian religion.[2]

This constant reinvention of what was meant by "white" and "Caucasian" for political goals continued in the 20th century, as millions of new immigrants threatened to change the face (and religion) of the United States. How were newcomers to fit into a racialized, unequal social system? Once again, racial science came to the rescue. By the 1920s, U.S. eugenicists had divided Caucasians into four ranked sub-races: Nordic, Alpine, Mediterranean, and Jew (Semitic), with Nordics ranked highest intellectually and morally.[3] These allegedly scientific subdivisions (which still left "Caucasians" superior to the other four races) were used to justify discriminatory immigration laws that preserved the U.S. ethnic dominance of Nordics (and Protestant Christians).

---

[2] See also Race Exhibit section, "The Invention of Whiteness."

[3] Eugenics sought to "improve" the human species, including through race-related breeding practices such as sterilizing women from "inferior" races and preventing "superior" race women from gaining access to contraception and other methods of birth reduction.

It was not until after World War II, and the horrors of Nazi racism, that racial science and eugenics were discredited. Distinctions among European Americans gradually dissolved, at least legally, in housing, education, occupations; and even Jews became "White Folks." Caucasian, rather than disappearing, replaced the thoroughly tainted, Nazi-linked "Aryan" race label, becoming equivalent to "white," that is to say, European-Americans.

The U.S. racial classification system continues to shift in response to historical, economic, and political events. Surprisingly, Blumenbach's conceptual framework of five major macro-racial categories remains today (cf. U.S. Census). Yet the labels, definitions, and overall discourse surrounding most contemporary racial categories have altered to reflect new understandings of race (and its fuzzy boundary with "ethnicity"). Most "color" labels, such as the Yellow Race, or pseudo-scientific remnants of racial science, like "Mongoloid," have been replaced by labels that more appropriately reference geographic region, political entities, language, and cultural features, rather than biological traits (e.g. African American, Asian American, Pacific Islanders, etc.).

Yet the word Caucasian persists despite being embedded in discredited racial science. Indeed, it seems to carry a scientific, authoritative weight not associated with other racial labels, nor with the increasingly popular "white." A sampling of major government websites (Department of Education, Census Bureau, NIH) produced an astonishing number of formal reports that employed the term Caucasian, sometimes along with "white." I found Education-related performance and accountability reports, NCLB applications, school-district and state-wide documents, and research studies which used Caucasian, especially in "formal" contexts and data summaries. The Census Bureau website contained a major focus group study which used Caucasian [and only Caucasian] throughout. Most striking were the results from the U.S. National Library of Medicine. Over 56,000 scientific articles included Caucasian in the title or abstract, referring to European-ancestry populations, mainly European Americans. The vast majority were published between 2000 and 2010, in major scientific, medical, and health-related journals, and were reporting research results by ethnicity/race,

sometimes also using the term "white."[4] Even my own culturally diverse and "aware" university uses "Caucasian" regularly, in the campus newspaper, student theses, and major administrative/department reports (e.g. 2004 WASC report, a 2008 Department Planning Document, Counseling Center presentations), especially in race/ethnic statistics (e.g. Caucasian/White, 74%).

An empty category

Beyond its association with racial science, Caucasian, as a word and concept, conveys a false scientific precision and scientific authority. It is esoteric, a complex three-syllable word whose meaning is not obvious or easily inferred. Other contemporary racial labels, like Asian American, describe a geographic region from which people originated. But Caucasian, as used in the United States, bears virtually no resemblance to the ancestry or national origins of those designated Caucasian. There are, of course, "real" Caucasians … people from the Caucasus, although that includes a myriad of languages, cultures, diverse histories. But few U.S. Americans could locate the Caucasus on a map nor specify its countries, regions, or linguistic groups (e.g. Georgia, Armenia, Azerbaijan, parts of North Iran, and central southern Russia, including Chechnya).

So … what associations does Caucasian invoke? Virtually none … not national origins, ancestral home, language. Indeed, it does not suggest anything cultural, anything learned, shared, invented by humans. U.S. Caucasians do not speak Caucasian, there is no (in the U.S.) Caucasian music or Caucasian dancing. Caucasian is a rather empty category, at least culturally. As a consequence, it is easy to infer that it's biologically "real" rather than a cultural invention. The old fallacy of racial categories as biologically rooted and "natural" is reinforced.

---

[4] Compare Methotrexate (MTX) Pathway Gene Polymorphisms and Their Effects on MTX Toxicity in Caucasian and African American Patients with Rheumatoid Arthritis. (J Rheumatol. 2008); Changes in Caucasian Eyes after Laser Peripheral Iridotomy: An Anterior Segment Optical Coherence Tomography. Clin Experiment Ophthalmol. 2010 Jun 21. (Epub ahead of print).

Of course, there is no single language, food, religion, or unitary culture for "Asians," "Africans," "Pacific Islanders," or "Native Americans." All U.S. macro-racial categories, even if linked to geographically or historically politically contiguous regions, are artificial, human-made classifications that lack clear boundaries and contain enormous diversity. No clearly demarcated, unambiguous land masses constitute "Asia," "Europe," or even "Africa". Where is the western boundary of Asia, the eastern or southern boundary of Africa?

Similarly, macro-racial categories mask enormous cultural and historical complexity. Consider the racial category "Asian" or "Asian American," or "Pacific Islander," with hundreds of languages, ethnic groups, nations, cultures. Fortunately, this diversity is becoming acknowledged. The 2010 census question on race offered many options for "Asians": "Asian Indian, Chinese, Filipino, Japanese, Korean, Vietnamese along with Other Asian," a write-in section for Thai, Pakistani, etc. Pacific Islanders could be Hawaiians, Samoans, Guamanian or Chamorro, or "Other" with a write-in space. And American Indians or Alaska Natives were asked to specify their tribe. Only two macro-racial categories lacked sub-groups: "Black, African American or Negro" and "White." Implicitly, these are homogenous racial groups/identities (except "Latino," an "ethnicity") although Irish, Norwegian, Nigerian, and Haitian Americans might feel otherwise.

Significantly, white, alone, has a single color-based label with no geographic reference (versus "*African American*"). All other U.S. macro-racial group labels evoke a geographic–cultural–political reference point and a set of diverse culture-bearing entities within Asia or Africa or the Pacific Islands.

Like "white," the term "Caucasian" (versus European American) does not evoke geography–culture–history. It masks the arbitrary and culturally invented history of this racial category. It renders invisible the diverse ethnic, linguistic, religious, and political groups that make up Europe. Such subdivisions probably constituted the significant identities of most European Americans until the past half century. Caucasian implies that the European-descended population is a coherent, stable, fixed, homogenous, biologically distinct entity, reinforcing obsolete biological notions of "race."

"Real" versus hyphenated Americans

"Caucasian" (versus European American) also suggests a different and unique relationship to "America" and "Americaness." European Americans, like most other Americans, originally came from some other place. Today, they are no more authentically "American" than any other race/ethnic group. Compared to Native Americans, all European Americans are recent immigrants. Most African Americans' ancestors were brought to these shores before the ancestors of most European Americans arrived. Indeed, the majority of "Caucasians" in the United States today probably had no ancestors in the country before the 20th century! Yet the term Caucasian subtly masks this group's foreign ancestry while other labels, like Asian American or African American, highlight these groups' foreign roots.

The word Caucasian in other ways exacerbates the U.S. tendency to equate "American" with those of European descent (e.g. "American" food). As a one-word designation, it reinforces the "hyphenated" or marginal status of other American groups. Linguistically, adding a modifier to a generic term (e.g. adding *Asian or African* to American) signifies that the modified form is less "normal", more marginal. The more fundamental, typical, "normal" form is left unmarked. (For example, we add the gender modifier "male" to mark the unusual, abnormal category of "male" nurses. "Nurse" refers to the typical, taken-for-granted, "normal" nurse who is female nurse.)

Most standard U.S. racial category labels today *other* than Caucasian (or "white") add a modifier, such as Asian- or African- or Native, to "American." Why the asymmetry? Why are immigrant origins of Caucasians (or whites) hidden while other groups are highlighted? Such modifiers, unless used for all racial–ethnic groups, subtly marginalize the "marked" groups, implying they are not fully Americans. Some groups remain framed, through language, as eternal immigrants, regardless of how many generations they have been in the United States.

Who has "ethnicity," "culture," and an "ethnic identity"?

Finally, for those designated Caucasian, the term subtly erases their ethnicity, ancestry, and cultural traditions. Ironically, we are starting to talk as if "ethnicity" and "culture" are attributes of only some racial–ethnic groups, usually traditionally marginalized groups. Many campuses have "cultural" organizations on campus – or events to celebrate "cultural" diversity. But such events usually do not include European American ethno-cultural groups. But then, what is "Caucasian" culture? The category is empty.

In a world where ethnic identities are a significant and often positive dimension of personal identity, where does this leave Caucasians? Of course, the dominant institutionalized culture in the United States remains overwhelmingly of European (northwestern, Christian) origin. But … we don't call these cultural traditions "Caucasian." And it makes no sense to do so. They should be explicitly labeled European, or preferably, linked to specific cultural or linguistic regions, such as English, German, Italian, and so forth. This situates them as *one among many* cultural traditions brought to the United States by immigrants. At the same time, being more specific about origins allows European Americans to explore their ethnic identities and ancestries.

How can we eradicate Caucasian, this pernicious remnant of the past? Fortunately, the term is becoming less prevalent, although the usual substitute, white, has its own problems. Labels like "white," "black," and "people of color" linguistically (and thus perceptually) reinforce race as biology and false notions of homogeneous, distinctly bounded groups. They also preserve the long-standing white/not-white (colored) racial frame.

European American is a more precise substitute for Caucasian than white. It parallels the language for other macro-racial U.S. groups, highlighting national origins rather than biology, allowing for diverse experiences while not ignoring privileges historically accorded those of European ancestry. The label European American may sound too bulky or formal at first (versus, for example, "white" or "black"), but we have managed to cope with African American, Asian American, Mexican American, Pacific Islanders, and other multi-syllabic labels. And we can easily come up with shorter versions, such as Euro. We humans are able to accommodate new terminology rather quickly, especially if we make a conscious effort or are around others using it.

Whiteness
A Conversation

Here, our panel of experts discusses the implications, structural and personal, of being "raced" as white or nonwhite. **Eduardo Bonilla-Silva** *is Professor of Sociology at Duke University.* **Dalton Conley** *is Senior Vice Provost and Dean for the Social Sciences and University Professor at New York University.* **Alan Goodman** *is Vice President for Academic Affairs and Dean of Faculty and Professor of Biological Anthropology at Hampshire College.* **Evelyn Hammonds** *is Dean of Harvard College and Barbara Gutman Rosenkrantz Professor of History of Science and of African and African American Studies at Harvard University.* **Pilar Ossorio** *is Associate Professor of Law and Bioethics at the University of Wisconsin at Madison.* **john a. powell** *is Executive Director of the Kirwan Institute for the Study of Race and Ethnicity at The Ohio State University.*

john a. powell: America is a country made up of immigrants. And part of creating a national identity was to decide, first of all, who comes, but [also] how those immigrants are going to be stitched together. And it really was stitched together along the concept of whiteness that really emanated from Anglo-Saxons.

ROBIN KELLEY: And that's why what happens in the 18th and early 19th century, with the invention of whiteness, is that suddenly all these people who were considered hybrid – the Portuguese and the Spanish, the Germans, the Italians, people from Eastern Europe – suddenly gets, get crushed together in this grouping we call white.

EDUARDO BONILLA-SILVA: The idea of the melting pot … really was a notion that was extended exclusively to white immigrants, whether they're white Italian, Irish, Polish, etc. Because they didn't have the language skills, etc., they were, they didn't … Well, the idea was you will assimilate or melt into the American pot, but that pot never included people of color. Blacks, Chinese, Puerto Ricans, etc., could not melt into the pot. They could be used as wood to produce the fire for the pot, but they could not be used as material to be melted into the pot.

john a. powell: So I think that that question of how whites think about race … First of all, they don't think about it in terms of themselves. They think about race as something that belongs to somebody else. The blacks have race. Maybe Latinos have race. Maybe Asians have race. They're just white. They're just people.

DALTON CONLEY: And that's part of what whiteness is. It's not having to think about being in the normative or dominant group. It is also, beyond that, a sense of privilege, a sense that this society is stacked in your favor, and that you can do anything because the American society, the American economy, is sort of like a banquet, and you can keep going up for more helpings. That's your system. It belongs to you. So that there is a sense of entitlement that comes with whiteness as well.

ALAN GOODMAN: And personally I'd have to say that I'm not very aware of my skin color, and I think that's probably typical of a lot of white people who have grown up amongst white people. That it becomes less salient to them.

EVELYNN HAMMONDS: When I was a child, certainly growing up in Atlanta in the black community, there certainly was to some extent a value placed on people who were lighter-skinned versus people who were darker-skinned in the African American community. And I saw, as a child, the ways in which some people felt very hurt by those kinds of assessments, that lighter-skinned black people were somehow better than darker-skinned black peoples. I grew up reading *Ebony* magazine, seeing the ads for skin lighteners. I grew up watching people, women in my family, go through all kinds of contortions to make sure that their hair was always straight and appropriate. Of course, you can see I rebelled very much against that notion. But I think the idea that African Americans were being subjected to a kind of pressure on this social and cultural level to be more white, and that white was somehow valued, it makes perfect sense in a society structured around race as the way ours is.

Reproduced courtesy of California Newsreel.

ALAN GOODMAN: This is not an individual thing as much as it simply is we live in racial smog. This is a world of racial smog. We can't help it, we can't help but breath that smog. Everybody breathes it. But what's nice to know is that you are breathing that smog, to recognize it, and that's the first step.

EVELYNN HAMMONDS: And I think everybody probably has a kind of Crayola crayon story. But when I was a kid, it was really troubling that you had white crayon, you had a flesh-tone, and you had various shades of brown. And flesh was not what the color that people were in my life. And it was very troubling to draw a picture, and I'd say, "But you know, mom, this is you." And, you know, color her in with the flesh-tone, of course, or then change it and color it in with the brown. And none of the browns ever quite fit. And so I was very disturbed that the color of flesh was not a color I recognized among the people I loved.

PILAR OSSARIO: If people can't tell what race you are, they feel very uncomfortable. And I know, because I get that all the time. People ask me all the time, because I'm a little bit indeterminate. And I ask people sometimes, "Why do you need to know?" And I think they need to know because they feel uncomfortable, and they don't realize that the way they treat people is partially based on race.

EVELYNN HAMMONDS: I can remember when I was watching, say, something like *Father Knows Best* or *Leave It To Beaver* when I was a child, thinking that they were people just like me, that I lived in a neighborhood like that. My parents went off to work, except that my mother went to work every day. But those are the kinds of things I thought about as different.

But I didn't realize that the fact that I was brown and not pink – and my sister and I used to have very long conversations about that white people really weren't white, they were pink – is that, we were confused about it, but it was, but we really still, I think I really saw myself as the same. I really thought color was simply the surface.

References

Asing, Norman
1852   letter to the editor. Daily Alta California, May 15.
Brodkin, Karen
1998   How Jews Became White Folks And What That Says about Race in America. New Brunswick: Rutgers University Press.

Cook, William W.
1929   American Institutions and Their Preservation. 2nd edition. Norwood, MA: Norwood Press.
Davis, Dana-Ain
2009   The Politics of Reproduction: The Troubling Case of Nadya Suleman and Assisted Reproductive Technology. Theme issue, "Whiteness: The Series," Transforming Anthropology 17:105–116.

Du Bois, W. E. B.

1970 [1935] Black Reconstruction: An Essay Toward a History of the Part which Black Folk Played in the Attempt to Reconstruct Democracy in America, 1860–1880. New York: Atheneum.

Epperson, Terrence

1997 Whiteness in Early Virginia. Race Traitor 7:9–20.

Franklin, John Hope

1988 Ethnicity in American Life: The Historical Perspective. *In* Race and History: Selected Essays, 1938–1988, pp. 321–331. Baton Rouge: Louisiana State University Press.

Hargrove, Melissa D.

2009 Mapping the "Social Field of Whiteness": White Racism as Habitus in the City Where History Lives. Theme Issue, "Whiteness: The Series," Transforming Anthropology 17:93–104.

Harris, Cheryl I.

1993 Whiteness as Property. Harvard Law Review 106:1707–1791.

Lee, Stacey J.

2004 Up against Whiteness: Students of Color in Our Schools. Anthropology & Education Quarterly 35:121–125.

Lipsitz, George

2006 The Possessive Investment in Whiteness: How White People Profit from Identity Politics. Rev. and expanded edition. Philadelphia: Temple University Press.

Low, Setha

2009 Maintaining Whiteness: The Fear of Others and Niceness. Theme Issue, "Whiteness: The Series," Transforming Anthropology 17:79–92.

Painter, Nell Irvin

2010 The History of White People. New York: W. W. Norton and Company.

Paynter, Robert

2001 The Cult of Whiteness in Western New England. *In* Race and the Archaeology of Identity. Charles E. Orser, Jr., ed. pp. 125–142. Salt Lake City: University of Utah Press.

Ripley, William Z.

1899 The Races of Europe: A Sociological Study. New York: D. Appleton and Company.

Roediger, David R., ed.

1998 Black on White: Black Writers on What It Means to Be White. New York: Shocken Books.

Roediger, David R.

1999 The Wages of Whiteness: Race in the Making of the American Working Class. Rev. edition. London and New York: Verso.

Roediger, David R.

2008 How Race Survived U.S. History: From Settlement and Slavery to the Obama Phenomenon. London: Verso.

Thomas, Deborah A., and John L. Jackson

2009 Racialized Publics. Theme Issue, "Whiteness: The Series," Transforming Anthropology 17:77–78.

Winant, Howard

2001 White Racial Projects. *In* The Making and Unmaking of Whiteness. Birgit Rasmussen, Eric Klineberg, Irene Nexica, and Matt Wray, eds. pp. 97–112. Durham, NC: Duke University Press.

Carol C. Mukhopadhyay, "Caucasian"

Mukhopadhyay, Carol C.

2008 Getting Rid of the Word "Caucasian." *In* Everyday Antiracism: Getting Real about Race in School. Mica Pollock, ed. pp. 12–16. New York: The New Press.

Mukhopadhyay, Carol C., Rosemary Henze, and Yolanda T. Moses

2007 *How Real Is Race? A Sourcebook on Race, Culture, and Biology*. Lanham, MD: Rowman and Littlefield Education Press.

Inventing Whiteness, 1650–2000

Asing, Norman

1852 Letter to the editor. Daily Alta California, May 15.

Davenport, Charles

1911 Heredity in Relation to Eugenics. New York: Henry Holt and Company.

Douglass, Frederick

1881 [1999] The Color Line. *Cited in* Frederick Douglass: Selected Speeches and Writings. Philip S. Foner, ed. Adapted by Yuval Taylor. Chicago: Lawrence Hill Books.

Eagan, Catherine M.

2001 "White," if "Not Quite": Irish Whiteness in the Nineteenth-Century Irish-American Novel. Eire-Ireland: Journal of Irish Studies, 36 (Spring/Summer):66–81.

Huxley, Thomas Henry

1865 On the Methods and Results of Ethnology. *In* Collected Essays, vol. 7. London: Macmillan and Company.

Jacobson, Matthew Frye

1998 Whiteness of a Different Color: European Immigrants and the Alchemy of Race. Cambridge, MA: Harvard University Press.

McGee, W. J.

1903 *Cited in* Prof. WJ. M'Gee. Appointed Chief of the Department of Anthropology. Anonymous. World's Fair Bulletin 4(10):29.

McIntosh, Peggy

1989 White Privilege: Unpacking the Invisible Knapsack. Peace and Freedom Magazine (July/August):10–12. Women's International League for Peace and Freedom, Philadelphia.

Spickard, Paul R.
1992 The Illogic of American Racial Categories. *In* Racially Mixed People in America. Maria P. P. Root, ed. pp. 12–23. Newbury Park, CA: Sage Publications.

Washington, Booker T.
1900 The Problem of the South. Journal of Proceedings and Addresses of the Thirty-ninth Annual Meeting of the National Educational Association. Chicago: The University of Chicago Press for the National Educational Association.

Zitkala-Sa (Dakota)
1900 [2000] The School Days of an Indian Girl *In* Native American Women's Writing: An Anthology c. 1800–1924. Karen L. Kilcup, ed. Oxford: Blackwell.

6

Separate and Unequal

Laws favoring whites over others helped create the social and economic inequalities we see in the United States today.
                    RACE exhibit, SMM

In the previous chapter we saw that lawmakers wield tremendous power to define racial difference – power historically used to foster racial unity amongst whites by granting them privileged access to political and economic resources. In this, the final chapter of the history section, we consider other sides of this story, namely the inverse processes through which colonial, state, and federal laws forbade or restricted access to equal resources for people of non-European descent. We explore legal constructions of race and especially racism around issues of citizenship and civil rights, land ownership and access, and the regulation of human biological and cultural diversity.

In this chapter, we do not emphasize antiracist social or political movements. We do not discuss racial identities that make race more than a failed attempt at classifying human difference. This intentional omission is a temporary state, in recognition that "the targets of racism do not 'make' racism, nor are they free to 'negotiate' it, though they may challenge it or its perpetrators and try to navigate the obstacles it places in their way. … There is no voluntary and affirmative side to racism as far as its victims are concerned, and it has no respect for symmetry at all" (Fields 2001:48). In the sections that follow, as throughout the book, we encounter important voices and forces of antiracist

dissent that create a more complete picture of racist and other racial formations. For the moment, however, we wish to convey the power and historical consequences of state-sanctioned racism. Our primary focus is on the foundational experiences that successfully and variously defined people of color as racially vulnerable under the law. These experiences – of slavery, warfare, immigration, and so forth – in many ways continue to define these communities' common obstacles and distinct paths to social, political, and economic equality.

During the 17th and 18th centuries, Virginia was the most influential of the English colonies in defining British North America socially and culturally. Beginning in the 1660s, the colony's leadership role included being the first to establish a legal system for controlling enslaved laborers. Until this point, the legal status of colonial Africans had been ambiguous. A. Leon Higginbotham's (1978) *In the Matter of Color* provides a detailed account of this process, which began with individual laws that often addressed specific issues such as whether enslaved individuals became free upon conversion to Christianity. (They did not according to a 1667 act.) Between 1680 and 1682, legislators in Virginia established the first major slave codes. These more comprehensive laws

> not only synthesized all the piecemeal legislative deprivations of the previous twenty years but introduced others incorporating some of the harshest customs and traditions

Race: Are We So Different?, First Edition. Alan H. Goodman, Yolanda T. Moses, and Joseph L. Jones.
© 2012 American Anthropological Association. Published 2012 by Blackwell Publishing Ltd.

that had evolved to control the colony's indentured servants. At the same time the codes were emphatic in denying slaves any of the privileges or rights that had accrued to white indentured servants in the same period. (Higginbotham 1978:38)

A 1705 statute established firmly that blacks were due no protection under the law, and subsequent acts passed through 1792 further defined and clarified slave status in contrast to that of white servants.

Additionally, the slave codes limited employment opportunities, mobility and other rights of free blacks and called for more severe punishments for interracial couples, especially those seeking to legalize their unions. Other colonies and slave states adopted and modified the Virginia slave codes, which provided an underlying legal uniformity to regionally distinct systems of slavery. Following the passage of the Thirteenth Amendment to the U.S. Constitution in 1865, legal slavery would morph into sharecropping, debt bondage, convict leasing, and other strategies for maintaining control of black labor (Jaynes 1986). Some of these practices continued well into the 20th century, overlapping with the period of Jim Crow segregation discussed throughout this chapter (Blackmon 2008).

Laws concerning slavery sometimes revealed similarities and differences in the status of American Indians and African Americans. For example, the aforementioned 1667 act declaring baptism an inadequate pathway to freedom for blacks also pertained to Indians in bondage, and two acts passed in 1682 collapsed both groups as "negroes and other slaves." Quite naturally, colonial whites' perceptions of Indians reflected the "problem" of tribal sovereignty and resistance to white conquest and settlement of their lands. Hence, the lone exception to a 1639 law prohibiting enslaved Africans from carrying firearms except in the event of their defending the colony against Indian raids. Indeed, Bacon's Rebellion of 1676, which brought together workers across the nascent black–white racial divide, was stridently anti-Indian in its demands for the implementation of more aggressive policies to settle and provide those workers greater access to indigenous lands (Higginbotham 1978; Roediger 2008).

From the 17th through the 19th centuries, relations between the colonies/United States and various Indian peoples deteriorated steadily as the U.S. military fulfilled the "manifest destiny" of its white citizenry through a series of wars and broken treaties (Borden 1970; Thornton 1987). During this period, portrayals of Indians as savages and narratives of Indian captivity flourished as justification for their dispossession and forced resettlement on reservations from the northeast to Florida and throughout the West. Such characterizations called into question whether the two races would ever coexist peacefully. White Americans' tended to vacillate in their assessments, a reflection of their often-conflated ideas about racial and/versus cultural Indian inferiority. As Roediger notes,

"Heathen," "barbarian," and "savage" – words applied in various ways and degrees to victims of modern colonialism in its Irish testing grounds and in North America – did not directly refer to biology, the hallmark of nineteenth-century white supremacy, nor even to skin color. Instead, these totalizing views emerged from colonizers' discussions about indigenous peoples' lack of Christianity, or the absence of what colonizers could recognize as the practice of settled agricultural production. (2008:18)

In other words, culture – not race – was the main culprit rendering American Indians fundamentally undeserving of their land or the right to self-determination. For some romantic intellectuals dating to the 16th century, the "traditional" or "primitive" cultural practices of these "noble savages" recalled an earlier, more open and honest period of human relations, and even compared favorably in many regards to those of their own "civilized" societies (Patterson 1997). Since the 18th century, however, many white Americans had reversed this logic. They believed that Indians could be "elevated" through proper (Anglo-American) enculturation, a possibility entertained by Thomas Jefferson in contrast to his ideas about innate and irredeemable black inferiority. Indeed, for some, saving Indians from Indian culture was a matter of Christian obligation. Thus, the situation, while bleak, was salvageable. The solution lay in the Indian's ability to follow the cultural examples set by whites regarding matters of religion, subsistence, language, etc. Whether or not they were willing to do so was a non-factor.

Not surprisingly, the idea of Indian uplift gained greater purchase over the course of the 19th century as the U.S. attained military and political dominance over Native American lands. The practice of recognizing Indian tribes as sovereign nations ended in 1871 when Congress approved the Indian Appropriations Act. Locally, the United States, governed Indian peoples through agents of the Bureau of Indian Affairs (BIA), established in 1824 as the oldest bureau of the U.S. Department of the Interior. In 1899, anthropologist and founder of the Audubon Society, George Bird Grinnell, summed up the situation when he wrote, "An Indian agent has absolute control of affairs on his reservation … more nearly absolute than anything else that we in this country know of. The courts protect citizens, but the Indian is not a citizen, and nothing protects him. Congress has the sole power to order how he shall live, and where." What exactly would this mean for American Indians?

Unfortunately, influential Americans' belief in their latent potential for "civilization" translated into a legislative program of cultural annihilation for those American Indians who survived the decimation of their populations through warfare (Thornton 1987). From the late 19th through the early 20th centuries, the BIA implemented a series of policies designed to force Indian assimilation of "Anglo-American culture," for example, by transferring Indian children from their reservation homes to boarding schools for instruction by white teachers. The ultimate goal of these "vanishing policies" – ostensibly measures to promote Indian welfare – was the total erasure of Indian cultural practices. Beginning in the 1930s, legislators would reverse course and enact new federal policies designed to preserve Indian cultures. This change mirrored and reflected anthropologists' own turn from the paradigm of *cultural evolution* and ranking. According to anthropologist Lee Baker (2010), ethnologists' essentialist understandings of culture – honed primarily through constructing "the Indian" – would form the basis of an emerging race concept later applied in anthropological studies of African Americans.

Throughout the 19th century, aggressive westward expansion through warfare and acquisition and increased non-European immigration expanded significantly the nation's size and population, which increased six-fold from 1800 to 1860 alone. As U.S. lawmakers and other leaders of the time acknowledged, such growth brought new racial domains and challenges that extended beyond yet linked inextricably to problems posed by "black" and "red" peoples. Take, for example, the case of Texas, which under Mexican rule had been a refuge for runaways. The fact that Texas and most other Mexican territories were inhabited was incidental to U.S. settlers who believed themselves more capable of governing those territories than American Indians or Catholic, Spanish-speaking Mexicans. The settlers clashed with the Mexican government over attempts on the part of the United States at annexation, tariffs, and slavery (outlawed by Mexico in 1829 but practiced under a provincial law permitting "permanent indentured servitude") (American Social History Project 1989). Years of hostilities erupted in rebellion in 1835, and the victorious settlers established the independent slaveholding Republic of Texas the following year. The United States annexed Texas as a slave state in 1845.

Tensions between the United States and Mexico escalated during the near-decade required for Texas to gain admission to the Union (due to northern resistance to its extension of southern "slave power" in the Senate). Following two failed attempts to purchase New Mexico and California from the Mexican government, the United States initiated the Mexican–American War (1846–48), which ended with a peace treaty transferring both territories to the United States and extending the Texas border southward. In total, the United States claimed half of Mexico's national territory – almost 1.2 million square miles of land – and nearly 80,000 Spanish-speaking people. Most were people of Spanish and American Indian descent who would perform the difficult, low-paying labor necessary to make agriculture, ranching, mining, and industry profitable (American Social History Project 1989). A half-century later, U.S. military engagement would again play a significant role in expanding the country's Latino presence. In 1898, the United States added Puerto Ricans and other Caribbean island natives (e.g., Cubans and Dominicans) to its population as a result of the Spanish–American War.

This same period was one of intense racial strife and violence in California linked to carpenter James Marshall's 1848 discovery of gold at a lumber mill on the American River. Marshall's discovery led to the California Gold Rush, which helped sustain the national economy and brought hundreds of thousands of prospectors to the state, including immigrants from all over the world. This population boom eventually stripped the land of natural food sources relied upon by California Indians. When the Indians took to raiding mining towns and white settlements for food the California legislature retaliated by passing the misleadingly named Indenture Act of 1850. In reality, this act authorized the virtual enslavement of Indian peoples by white settlers, a practice that became common and included the kidnapping and sale of Indian children. In 1853, settlers began confining the remaining Indian population to military reservations. Prior to 1849, some 150,000 Indians lived in California. By 1870, less than 30,000 remained.

Among the many gold prospectors were tens of thousands of Chinese immigrant laborers who met with widespread and intense prejudice in San Francisco and other areas. Some Chinese miners, for example, were allowed to work only on sites abandoned by white miners. Fueled by the belief that Chinese workers took jobs away from whites, anti-Chinese sentiment grew over the coming decades, leading to violent mob attempts to clear western cities of any Chinese presence. As noted in chapter 4, depictions of the Asian political menace or the "yellow peril" drew inspiration from scientific and medical pronouncements of "Chinese contagion," the threat to Americans' physical and mental health allegedly posed by the mere presence of Chinese laborers. Eventually, the U.S. Congress enacted the Chinese Exclusion Act of 1882, prohibiting further immigration of Chinese laborers as well as naturalization of Chinese immigrants already living in the United States for ten years. Two years later, Congress expanded the act to bar all Chinese immigration. Widespread anti-Chinese violence persisted into the early 1900s, including lynchings by vigilante groups similar to those perpetrated against blacks (as well as Jews and Italian Americans) primarily in the South.

Thus, while current debate and conflict over immigration centers largely on Latinos, a century ago Asian immigrants received a great deal of critical attention from U.S. lawmakers. Historians and legal scholars regularly use the following two U.S. Supreme Court cases to illustrate the futility and risk inherent in their appeals to gain citizenship. In October of 1922,

Japanese businessman Takao Ozawa filed for U.S. citizenship under the Naturalization Act of 1906, which limited eligibility to white persons and persons of African birth or descent. Ozawa did not challenge the act's racial requirements but he did call into question the boundaries of the white racial category. He argued that people of Japanese descent should be classified as white, and thus eligible to become naturalized citizens. His case was unsuccessful. In a unanimous decision handed down by Associate Justice George Sutherland, the Court ruled instead that the Japanese were not commonly considered "Caucasian" and, therefore, were not white. Rather, the Japanese represented an "unassimilable race" uncovered by any Naturalization Act. Two decades later, during World War II, 120,000 people of Japanese ancestry were forced into "war relocation" or internment camps under President Franklin Roosevelt's Executive Order 9066. Most were U.S. citizens.

Three months after *Ozawa v. United States*, Associate Justice Sutherland issued a ruling on *United States v. Bhagat Singh Thind*. In this case, Thind, an Indian-born Hindu, sought U.S. citizenship based on contemporary anthropological classification of south Asian Indians as "Caucasian." He, too, was unsuccessful as the Court rejected his argument on grounds that his inclusion as a Caucasian represented "scientific manipulation" and did not conform to the "understanding of the common man" (Haney López 1996). The *Thind* decision classified south Asian Indians as "Asian" for the first time. It was a blow against not only immigrants seeking naturalization, but against previously naturalized Asian Indians as well, many of whom subsequently found their status as citizens voided. Once stripped of their citizenship, Asian Indians became subject to the California Alien Land Law, which prohibited people ineligible for citizenship from owning land, and other legal deprivations targeting immigrants. With the creation of the "Asiatic Barred Zone" in 1917 preventing any further immigration from Asia to bolster their communities, most Asian Indians left the country so that by 1940 their population was reduced by half, to 2,405. From its first deliberations of citizenship in 1790 until 1952, Congress restricted naturalization to "white persons" — and did not significantly dismantle racial restrictions on immigration until 1965 (Haney López 1996).

Racially exclusionary provisions are a hallmark of federal immigration legislation; only the targets change (Ngai 2004).

This brings us to the mid-20th century and to the interpretive challenge of racial justice since the U.S. Supreme Court decided *Brown v. Board of Education of Topeka* in 1954. Famously, the *Brown* decision overturned the doctrine of "separate but equal" established by *Plessy v. Ferguson* in 1896 (see the time line in this chapter) and authorized the legal desegregation of all public schools in the United States. Sure enough, since then we have witnessed many significant political, social, and cultural developments indicating ours is an increasingly inclusive society.

For many, individuals like Barack Obama and Sonia Sotomayor immediately come to mind, and appropriately so. As the nation's first African American president and Latino Supreme Court justice, respectively, Obama and Sotomayor represent social change almost unimaginable to previous generations. Their accomplishments matter and reflect underlying cultural and demographic changes that both reflect and expand our racial imaginations and perceptions of diversity. Along these lines, a growing population of multiracial Americans warrants mention, representing the upward trend of interracial marriages coupled with changes in U.S. census data collection methods (see Chapter 13). Of course, multiracial America is nothing new. As Painter (2010:385) notes, "Americans' disorderly sexual habits have always overflowed neat racial lines and driven race thinkers crazy." Still, this population's current prominence blatantly undermines bio-racial categories and purity myths, however defined, and pushes us to reevaluate critically our various social realities of race and racism (see chapter 13).

So, given this undeniable progress, where *do* we as a nation stand on issues of socio-racial equality?

- Today, the U.S. federal government technically recognizes American Indian tribal sovereignty. In practice, however, many tribes must function akin to special interest lobbying entities. They must secure annual federal appropriations needed for educational, health, and other services once overseen by the BIA. What do we make of this "nations-within-a-nation" model of sovereignty from a racial justice perspective? What alternatives exist?

- As noted above, current debate around immigration and naturalization policy focuses largely on Latino populations. Unfortunately, discourse on the matter frequently maligns non-U.S. citizens and obscures the legal citizenship status of immigrants and their children and of those from U.S. territories such as Puerto Rico. Would not debate be much more productive without an "illegal alien" trope that tends to homogenize and disparage Latinos racially along lines of language and color?

- As global economic competition increases between the United States and countries like China and India, should we be concerned about the return of "yellow peril" or other forms of nativist or xenophobic rhetoric similar to that targeting Arab Americans during the "war on terror"?

- Some scholars argue that, for many, whiteness and blackness continue to represent extremes of a spectrum of racial *and multiracial* possibilities. As such, the pursuit of whiteness and denigration (or strategic appropriation) of blackness delimit the prospect of a fully integrated America. Are they correct, and if so, how do we break the ideological commitment to this especially entrenched strand of racism?

Clearly, we have made great strides on the racial justice front. We would caution, however, against the belief that the United States is a racially egalitarian society or that it ever will become one without continued vigilance and work. As we have seen, socio-racial equality is a dynamic process and an elusive goal. Without a clear roadmap, the pursuit of equality has not followed a linear path or advanced unimpeded. Rather, the progress we observe and celebrate today came in fits and starts, and despite more than a few retreats from justice. It represents great sacrifice and political struggle on the parts of people of color *and* their white allies. And we know that significant challenges remain in the form of still-pervasive illogics of racial difference and structural inequalities in health, wealth, and educational opportunity. We explore these challenges in part 3.

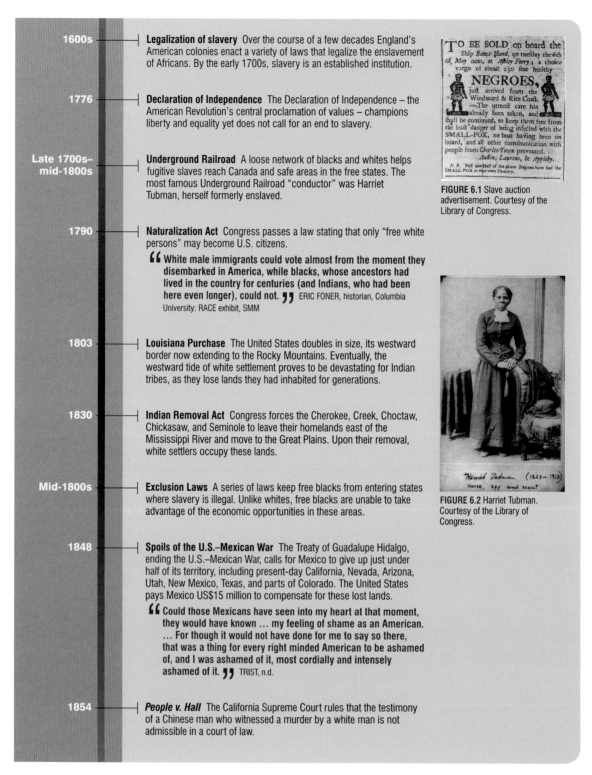

1600s — **Legalization of slavery** Over the course of a few decades England's American colonies enact a variety of laws that legalize the enslavement of Africans. By the early 1700s, slavery is an established institution.

1776 — **Declaration of Independence** The Declaration of Independence – the American Revolution's central proclamation of values – champions liberty and equality yet does not call for an end to slavery.

Late 1700s– mid-1800s — **Underground Railroad** A loose network of blacks and whites helps fugitive slaves reach Canada and safe areas in the free states. The most famous Underground Railroad "conductor" was Harriet Tubman, herself formerly enslaved.

FIGURE 6.1 Slave auction advertisement. Courtesy of the Library of Congress.

1790 — **Naturalization Act** Congress passes a law stating that only "free white persons" may become U.S. citizens.

❝ White male immigrants could vote almost from the moment they disembarked in America, while blacks, whose ancestors had lived in the country for centuries (and Indians, who had been here even longer), could not. ❞ ERIC FONER, historian, Columbia University: RACE exhibit, SMM

1803 — **Louisiana Purchase** The United States doubles in size, its westward border now extending to the Rocky Mountains. Eventually, the westward tide of white settlement proves to be devastating for Indian tribes, as they lose lands they had inhabited for generations.

1830 — **Indian Removal Act** Congress forces the Cherokee, Creek, Choctaw, Chickasaw, and Seminole to leave their homelands east of the Mississippi River and move to the Great Plains. Upon their removal, white settlers occupy these lands.

Mid-1800s — **Exclusion Laws** A series of laws keep free blacks from entering states where slavery is illegal. Unlike whites, free blacks are unable to take advantage of the economic opportunities in these areas.

FIGURE 6.2 Harriet Tubman. Courtesy of the Library of Congress.

1848 — **Spoils of the U.S.–Mexican War** The Treaty of Guadalupe Hidalgo, ending the U.S.–Mexican War, calls for Mexico to give up just under half of its territory, including present-day California, Nevada, Arizona, Utah, New Mexico, Texas, and parts of Colorado. The United States pays Mexico US$15 million to compensate for these lost lands.

❝ Could those Mexicans have seen into my heart at that moment, they would have known … my feeling of shame as an American. … For though it would not have done for me to say so there, that was a thing for every right minded American to be ashamed of, and I was ashamed of it, most cordially and intensely ashamed of it. ❞ TRIST, n.d.

1854 — **People v. Hall** The California Supreme Court rules that the testimony of a Chinese man who witnessed a murder by a white man is not admissible in a court of law.

❝ The same rule which would admit them to testify, would admit them to all the equal rights of citizenship, and we might soon see them at the polls, in the jury box, upon the bench, and in our legislative halls. ❞ CALIFORNIA CHIEF JUSTICE HUGH C. MURRAY, majority opinion, 1854: RACE exhibit, SMM

1857   *Scott v. Sandford* Dred Scott, a fugitive slave, sues for his freedom on the grounds that he has lived in a territory where slavery was illegal. The U.S. Supreme Court rules against him, asserting that blacks have no rights as American citizens and therefore no standing in court.

❝ We think they [blacks] are not … included, and were not intended to be included, under the word "citizens" in the Constitution, and can therefore claim none of the rights and privileges which that instrument provides. ❞ CHIEF JUSTICE ROGER B. TANEY, majority opinion, 1857: RACE exhibit, SMM

1861–65   **The Civil War** Among the causes of the Civil War is the belief in the South that the states – not the federal government – have the right to make their own laws about matters such as slavery.

FIGURE 6.3 Dred Scott. Courtesy of the Library of Congress.

1862   **Homestead Act** The Homestead Act, which grants 160-acre portions of public land to settlers, will lead thousands of white Americans to occupy Indian lands in the Midwest.

1865   **Slavery ends** The Thirteenth Amendment to the U.S. Constitution is formally ratified, outlawing slavery and involuntary servitude "except as a punishment for crime [of which] the party shall have been duly convicted."

1866   **Civil Rights Act** Citizenship is granted to all people born in the United States, regardless of race, color, or previous status. Chiefly aimed at African Americans, the law includes the rights to make contracts, to buy and sell land, to give evidence in court and to sue and be sued. But it does not include the right to vote.

❝ Slavery is not abolished until the black man has the ballot. ❞ DOUGLASS 1865:578

FIGURE 6.4 During the mid-19th century, advertisements like this one encouraged westward migration. Courtesy of An American Time Capsule: Three Centuries of Broadsides and Other Printed Ephemera, American Memory Collections, Library of Congress.

1868   **Fourteenth Amendment** The Fourteenth Amendment to the U.S. Constitution demands that states must not deprive "any person of life, liberty, or property, without due process of law; nor deny to any person within its jurisdiction the equal protection of the laws."

1870   **Fifteenth Amendment** African American men receive the right to vote. But poll taxes, literacy tests, and threats of violence, including lynching, keep many away from the ballot box until the mid-20th century.

1875   **Civil Rights Act** This law gives African Americans equal rights in public places and bans their exclusion from juries. Only eight years later, it will be struck down by the U.S. Supreme Court.

1880s–1960s

Jim Crow laws Many states and cities enforce segregation through so-called Jim Crow laws. Jim Crow was a character in popular minstrel shows: white performers would rub their faces with charcoal or burnt cork and sing and dance in caricatured impersonations of black men.

1882

Chinese Exclusion Act Chinese laborers are barred from entering the United States, and Chinese are excluded from citizenship. This act was not repealed until 1943.

❝ You are continually objecting to [the] morality [of the Chinese]. Your travelers say he is depraved; your missioners call him ungodly; your commissioners call him uncleanly. ... Yet your housewives permit him to wait upon them at table; they admit him to their bed-chambers; they confide to him their garments and jewels; and even trust their lives to him by awarding him supreme control over their kitchens and the preparation of their food. There is a glaring contradiction here. ❞ KWANG CHANG LING 1878

1883

States' rights The U.S. Supreme Court rules the Civil Rights Act of 1875 unconstitutional on the grounds that Congress exceeded its authority in an area where states alone had the right to make laws. This decision opens the door to legalized racial segregation.

❝ The world has never witnessed such barbarous laws entailed upon a free people. ... For that decision alone authorized and now sustains all the unjust discriminations, proscriptions and robberies perpetrated by public carriers upon millions of the nation's most loyal defenders. ❞ TURNER, 1883:228

SOME REASONS
FOR
CHINESE EXCLUSION
MEAT vs. RICE.
AMERICAN MANHOOD
against
ASIATIC COOLIEISM
WHICH SHALL SURVIVE?
PUBLISHED BY THE AMERICAN FEDERATION OF LABOR.

FIGURE 6.5 "Some reasons for Chinese exclusion," a 1902 American Federation of Labor pamphlet warning against Chinese laborers' "invasion" of "one [American] industry after another ..." Courtesy of The Bancroft Library, University of California, Berkeley F870.C5.C51 v.1:1.

FIGURE 6.6 Copy of a composite photograph of the heads of justices from various years, using as a background the photograph of the 1898 Fuller Court; portrait etchings are by Max and Albert Rosenthal. (This group of justices never actually sat together.) Front row, left to right: Justice Levi Woodbury, Justice Philip Barbour, Chief Justice Roger Brooke Taney, Justice Peter Vivian Daniel, and Justice Samuel Nelson. Back row, left to right: Justice Robert Cooper Grier, Justice Benjamin Curtis, Justice John Campbell, and Justice John McKinley. Courtesy of the Collection of the Supreme Court of the United States.

1884

Elk v. Wilkins John Elk, a Native American, sues Charles Wilkins for refusing to let him register to vote in Omaha. Elk argues that his U.S. birth and severed ties with his tribe render him an American citizen and entitle him to protection under the Fourteenth Amendment. The U.S.

Supreme Court rules against him, stating that Native Americans are not citizens because they come under the jurisdiction of, and owe allegiance to, their tribes.

> The Fourteenth Amendment has wholly failed to accomplish, in respect of the Indian race, what, we think, was intended by it; and there is still in this country a despised and rejected class of persons [who] … are yet not members of any political community, nor entitled to any of the rights, privileges, or immunities of citizens of the United States. ⟫ JUSTICE JOHN MARSHALL HARLAN, dissenting opinion, 1884: RACE exhibit, SMM

1887 **The Dawes Severalty Act** Under this law, Indian reservation land is divided into parcels (called "allotments") and a system of private land ownership is imposed on tribes. Proponents say the law will encourage Indians to become independent farmers. But allotment creates opportunities for white settlers and the U.S. government to buy Indians' land, often fraudulently. When the allotment system finally ends in 1934, their landholdings have been reduced from 138 million to 48 million acres.

1896 ***Plessy v. Ferguson*** Homer A. Plessy, an African American, is arrested when he boards a "Whites Only" train car in an effort to challenge segregation laws. The U.S. Supreme Court decides against Plessy, ruling that states may provide blacks with "separate but equal" facilities for transportation, education, and public accommodations.

1898 ***United States v. Wong Kim Ark*** The federal government claims that although Wong Kim Ark was born in California and has spent his life there, he is not a U.S. citizen and cannot return to California after a visit to China. The U.S. Supreme Court rules otherwise, stating that the Fourteenth Amendment guarantees the right of citizenship to all born in the U.S., not simply those of certain races.

> If [Chinese can become citizens], then verily there has been a most degenerate departure from the patriotic ideals of our forefathers; and surely in that case American citizenship is not worth having. ⟫ SOLICITOR GENERAL HOLMES CONRAD, counsel for the U.S. government, 1898: RACE exhibit, SMM

FIGURE 6.7 Wong Kim Ark. Courtesy of the National Archives and Records Administration, ARC # 296479.

1908 **Thurgood Marshall born** Marshall will serve as lead attorney for the National Association for the Advancement of Colored People (NAACP) in the landmark 1954 Brown v. Board of Education case, in which the U.S. Supreme Court will declare segregated schools to be inherently unequal. In 1967 he will become the first African American appointed to that court.

1913 **Alien Land law** California prohibits "aliens ineligible for citizenship" (meaning Asians) from owning property in the state. Similar laws are adopted in other states.

1924 **Johnson–Reed Immigration Act** Congress sets quotas for immigration that favor northern and western Europeans over people from eastern and southern Europe. It also completely excludes Japanese but places no limits on immigration from Canada or Latin America.

FIGURE 6.8 Thurgood Marshall. Courtesy of the Collection of the Supreme Court of the United States.

1924 — **Indian Citizenship Act** Native Americans are granted U.S. citizenship.

1926 — ***Corrigan v. Buckley*** Washington, D.C., resident John J. Buckley sues his neighbor, Irene Corrigan, arguing that a restrictive covenant prevents her from selling her house to a black woman, Helen Curtis. The U.S. Supreme Court agrees, and the sale is blocked.

> **No part of said premises shall be sold, given, conveyed or leased to any negro or negroes, and no permission or license to use or occupy any part thereof shall be given to any negro except house servants or janitors or chauffeurs employed thereon as aforesaid.** Standard Form, Restrictive Covenant, drafted for Chicago Real Estate Board, 1927

1929 — **Martin Luther King, Jr., born** As a child, King attends segregated schools in Georgia. Later, he becomes a leader of the U.S. Civil Rights Movement. His work, characterized by nonviolent protests for justice and equality, earns him the Nobel Peace Prize and makes him a national hero.

> **I submit that an individual who breaks a law that conscience tells him is unjust, and who willingly accepts the penalty of imprisonment in order to arouse the conscience of the community over its injustice, is in reality expressing the highest respect for law.** KING 1963:86

1935 — **Social Security Act** The act creates a system of monthly income, as well as disability, unemployment, and survivor benefits, for most Americans aged 65 and older. But it specifically excludes two occupations, agricultural workers and domestic servants – jobs held mainly by African Americans, Mexicans, and Asians at this time.

1942 — **Japanese Internment** Following Japan's December 7, 1941, attack on Pearl Harbor, the federal government declares that no one of Japanese ancestry may live on the West Coast. Nearly 120,000 people are forced to leave their homes and are moved into internment camps. Many families lose their homes and businesses. In 1988 the U.S. government officially apologizes for these actions and offers a US$20,000 per-internee reparations payment.

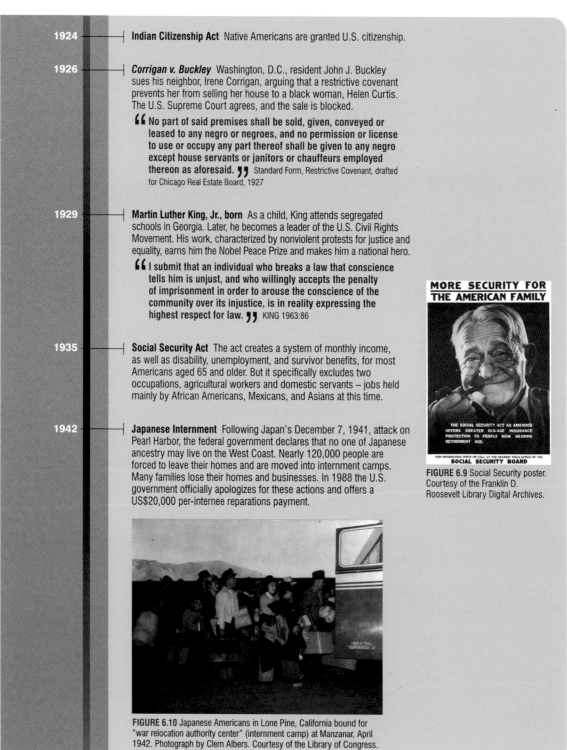

MORE SECURITY FOR THE AMERICAN FAMILY

THE SOCIAL SECURITY ACT AS AMENDED OFFERS GREATER OLD-AGE INSURANCE PROTECTION TO PEOPLE NOW NEARING RETIREMENT AGE.

FOR INFORMATION WRITE OR CALL AT THE NEAREST FIELD OFFICE OF THE **SOCIAL SECURITY BOARD**

FIGURE 6.9 Social Security poster. Courtesy of the Franklin D. Roosevelt Library Digital Archives.

FIGURE 6.10 Japanese Americans in Lone Pine, California bound for "war relocation authority center" (internment camp) at Manzanar, April 1942. Photograph by Clem Albers. Courtesy of the Library of Congress.

1944 — ***Korematsu v. United States*** Fred Korematsu, like everyone of Japanese ancestry on the West Coast in 1942, is ordered to be relocated to an internment camp. He evades internment, is arrested and convicted and then sues, arguing that his constitutional rights have been violated. The case goes to the U.S. Supreme Court, which rules against him.

> **❝ If any fundamental assumption underlies our system, it is that guilt is personal and not inheritable. ❞** Justice Robert H. Jackson, dissenting opinion, Korematsu v. U.S., 1944

1944 — **GI Bill of Rights** This bill creates a program providing federal aid to U.S. war veterans who want to purchase homes and businesses and attend college. This economic boost will be key in creating the country's post–World War II white middle class. Although racial minorities are not formally excluded from the program, practices maintaining segregated neighborhoods and schools, and systematic discrimination in many state policies, will make it very hard for them to take advantage of it.

1946 — ***Mendez v. Westminster*** In 1944 Gonzalo Mendez tries to enroll his children at a Westminster, California, elementary school, but he is refused and told they must attend a nearby "Mexican" school. Mendez, with other Mexican-American families and the NAACP, sues several boards of education in California on behalf of 5,000 Mexican-American children attending segregated schools. The U.S. District Court rules in Mendez's favor. This decision will lead to the repeal of all California school segregation laws and pave the way for the 1954 Brown v. *Board of Education* decision, which will make school segregation unconstitutional throughout the United States.

1950 — ***McLaurin v. Oklahoma State Regents*** George McLaurin, a black student, is allowed to attend the University of Oklahoma after proving that a "separate but equal" school is not available to him. However, he must sit at a separate desk in the library, a separate table in the cafeteria and in his own row in classrooms. The U.S. Supreme Court invalidates this arrangement, ruling it interferes with his "ability to study, to engage in discussions, and exchange views with other students, and, in general, to learn his profession."

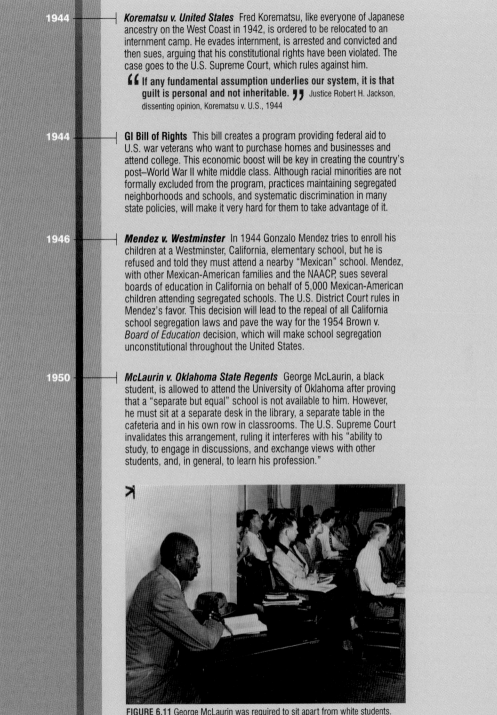

FIGURE 6.11 George McLaurin was required to sit apart from white students. Courtesy of the Library of Congress.

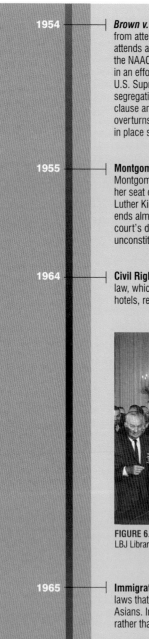

1954 — ***Brown v. Board of Education*** Eight-year-old Linda Brown, barred from attending a white school near her home in Topeka, Kansas, attends a black school several miles away. Her father, along with the NAACP and plaintiffs in similar cases nationwide, files suit in an effort to test segregation laws. The case reaches the U.S. Supreme Court, which rules unanimously that school segregation violates the Fourteenth Amendment's equal protection clause and should be ended "with all deliberate speed." This overturns the "separate but equal" Plessy v. Ferguson decision in place since 1896.

1955 — **Montgomery bus boycott** Rosa Parks is arrested after violating a Montgomery, Alabama, segregation ordinance by refusing to give up her seat on a bus to a white man. Black leaders, including Martin Luther King, Jr., organize a boycott of the bus company. The boycott ends almost a year later when the U.S. Supreme Court upholds a lower court's decision declaring Montgomery's segregated bus seating unconstitutional.

FIGURE 6.12 Rosa Parks was arrested for violating segregation law. Courtesy of the Library of Congress.

1964 — **Civil Rights Act** President Lyndon B. Johnson signs this sweeping law, which prohibits racial discrimination in public facilities (including hotels, restaurants, and theaters), schools, and employment.

FIGURE 6.13 President Johnson signs Civil Rights Act into law, July 2, 1964. LBJ Library photograph by Cecil Stoughton.

1965 — **Immigration Act** This act eliminates quotas established by previous laws that restricted the immigration of various groups, especially Asians. Immigrants are now to be admitted according to their skills rather than their nationality.

2006 — **Voting Rights Act renewed** The Voting Rights Act of 1965 was designed to address discrimination based on race at the polls. Renewing the act kept legislation in place that prevents communities from adopting changes in electoral practices that might weaken the voting strength of minority voters.

2010

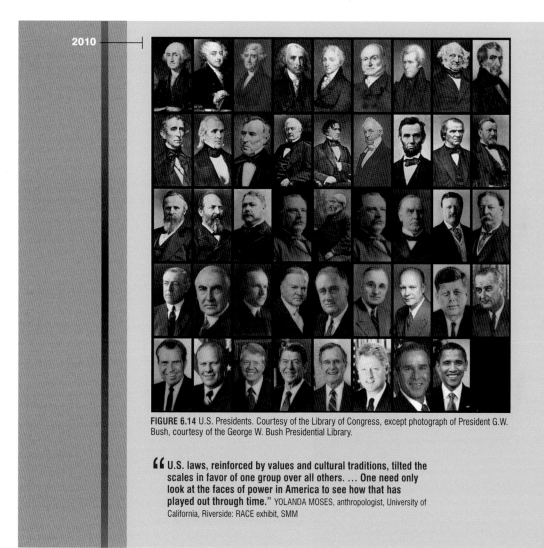

FIGURE 6.14 U.S. Presidents. Courtesy of the Library of Congress, except photograph of President G.W. Bush, courtesy of the George W. Bush Presidential Library.

❝ U.S. laws, reinforced by values and cultural traditions, tilted the scales in favor of one group over all others. ... One need only look at the faces of power in America to see how that has played out through time.❞ YOLANDA MOSES, anthropologist, University of California, Riverside: RACE exhibit, SMM

Jim Crow Laws

This small sampling of such laws reflects how they affected virtually every aspect of life.

"It shall be unlawful for a negro and white person to play together or in company with each other in any game of cards or dice, dominoes or checkers" (Birmingham, Alabama, 1930).

"Marriages are void when one party is a white person and the other is possessed of one-eighth or more negro, Japanese, or Chinese blood" (Nebraska, 1911).

"Separate free schools shall be established for the education of children of African descent; and it shall be unlawful for any colored child to attend any white school, or any white child to attend a colored school" (Missouri, 1929).

"All railroads carrying passengers in the state (other than street railroads) shall provide equal but separate accommodations for the white and colored races, by providing two or more passenger cars for each passenger train, or by dividing the cars by a partition, so as to secure separate accommodations" (Tennessee, 1891).

"It shall be unlawful for any white prisoner to be handcuffed or otherwise chained or tied to a negro prisoner" (Arkansas, 1903).

"No colored barber shall serve as a barber to white women or girls" (Atlanta, Georgia, 1926).

"Any person ... presenting for public acceptance or general information, arguments or suggestions in favor of social equality or of intermarriage between whites and negroes, shall be guilty of a misdemeanor and subject to a fine not exceeding five hundred dollars or imprisonment not exceeding six months or both fine and imprisonment in the discretion of the court" (Mississippi, 1920).

"Any white woman who shall suffer or permit herself to be got with child by a negro or mulatto ... shall be sentenced to the penitentiary for not less than eighteen months" (Maryland, 1924).

"The Corporate Commission is hereby vested with power to require telephone companies in the State of Oklahoma to maintain separate booths for white and colored patrons when there is a demand for such separate booths" (Oklahoma, 1915).

JONATHON ODELL
Learning Jim Crow

Jonathan Odell is the author of the acclaimed novel The View from Delphi *and, most recently,* The Healing, *which earned a Starred Review by the Library Journal. Throughout the United States, his novels and essays serve as the foundation for "authentic dialogue" across racial divides. In the following passage, Odell recalls a long-buried memory of his youthful initiation into 1950s' Jim Crow culture. Jonathan Odell. Photograph courtesy of Jonathan Odell.*

I was raised in the Deep South. I was born in 1951 in Jim Crow Mississippi in a little town called Laurel, Mississippi.

I was sitting in the backyard when I was six years old. And my neighbor was "Miss Helen," we'll call her, she

was the typical kind of Southern older woman, who had *carte blanche* with any white child to train them in how to be a young gentleman. I mean, that was what you needed to be in the South was to be a young gentleman, to be respectful of your elders. So she always taught me the rules about when to say "Mr.," and when to say "Mrs.," and when not to say "ain't," and how not to talk with my mouth full, and keep my elbows off the table and I loved this woman very much.

So I was sitting in my backyard watching this black man who was working in her backyard raking straw, this elderly black man. I don't know, he was probably 70 years old. And as I watched him, I became curious because it was a very hot day in the Mississippi summer – probably 80, 90, 100 degrees ... I don't know ... and he was wearing a long-sleeved shirt. And I was curious, why was he wearing something like that on a hot day like that? So I decided I'd go over and ask him. I said, "Why are you wearing a shirt like that? Aren't you sweating?" He told me, he said, "Well," he said, "I wear it because it makes me sweat, and when you sweat like this and a nice breeze comes along, it's like having air conditioning. It keeps you cool."

So I thought this was the wisdom of the ages. So we're talking, and Miss Helen this wonderful, esteemed, cultured white lady comes back and she says, "What are y'all talking about?" And I went into my manners. There's a certain nomenclature in the South at least when I was being raised about what you call people, what we call adults, if people are like my parents age you call them "Mr. Johnson" or "Mrs. Smith." If they get a little older, then you call them "Mr. & Mrs.," but you use their first name. It's a form of respect. So Mr. Joe or Mrs. … So I had found out his name was Joe, so she said, "Who are you talking to, and what are you doing?" and I said, "I'm just talking to Mr. Joe," wanting to impress Miss Helen. And she looked at me and she kind of screwed up her face and said "Oh no, honey! Joe's not a 'Mr.', Joe's a —," and then she used the N-word.

Now that was an extremely important moment in my life, and I didn't remember this moment until I was 30, 40 years old, which is true for most of these formative moments, things, walls have to fall before you can see back into your past and reinterpret it.

But I remember that moment now looking back on it, I knew something important had happened, and I looked at Miss Helen's face and it was the same Christian, loving face that I'd have remembered. She was a nice woman, and she looked at Joe in a very loving way. And then I looked at Joe to see if anything was the matter, and Joe was just nodding his head and smiling. So in my six-year-old world, I said, "Oh, this is normal, whiteness is normal, and I don't have to treat this man like a fellow human being." At that moment Joe no longer became a human being, he became Miss Helen's yardman.

And his moment of silence bestowed upon me a feeling of superiority. And what I have to understand [about] my own whiteness, what I have to realize is, I liked it. It wasn't something that made me embarrassed. It made me comfortable, because in that moment I understood the world. I understood why I drank out of separate water fountains. I understood in that moment why I went to a separate school, and why the black schools were falling down and rickety. I understood why I got a nice school bus, and I passed the blacks walking on foot to their schools. Everything made sense! I was like, "Oh, it's different!" And what was best – it was okay with everybody.

I became extremely successful. In 1986, I started my own company. Also, what was happening, at that same time I had come to the pinnacle of the white man's success. I had money. I had prestige. I had power. I had a beautiful home. I had big company cars. And I was dying inside. There was something that was broken and I didn't know what it was.

So what happened was [that] in 1988, I was sitting in front of the TV, and it was the 20th anniversary of the assassination of Dr. Martin Luther King. And as TV stations do, and newspapers do, they always go back and do some kind of retrospective showing all of these films of my formative years of Dr. King walking through these small, dusty Mississippi towns.

So I watched, and for the first time I looked and studied the people, not marching, but the people on the side of the road, the ones throwing the rocks, waving their Confederate flags, shouting in profanities, the "rednecks" – and then it hit me. I said, "Oh my God! Those are my people – that's my father, that's my mother, that's me." This is not black history. This is *my* history. This is what formed who I am.

I knew I had to do something … that I had to find out who I was. I didn't know exactly how to go about doing that, but I knew the experience that came up immediately was that lawn experience in the South with Joe. And I realized the world happened in that moment, and I missed it. And it was something about his silence that I had to find out about, and it's a silence and the invisibility of black people in America today, and how that gives us white people our privilege. It's the silence.

IAN F. HANEY LÓPEZ
Colorblindness

Ian F. Haney López *is John H. Boalt Professor of Law, University of California, Berkeley, where he teaches in the areas of race and constitutional law. He has published ground breaking books on the social, and specifically legal, construction of race and racial identities. His numerous articles have appeared in, among others, the* Stanford Law Review, Yale Law Journal, California Law Review, *and* Pennsylvania Law Review *and he has published opinion pieces in the* New York Times *and the* Los Angeles Times. *In this essay, he examines the emergence and operation of colorblindness in U.S. constitutional law as a harbinger of a new racial ideology aimed at legitimating and preserving the racial status quo.* Photograph courtesy of Ian Haney López.

Despite defeat in the Civil War, the South looked for ways to continue a culture and an economic system predicated on the exploitation of African Americans. Seeking to end persistent depredations, the nation passed the Fourteenth Amendment to the Constitution, mandating the "equal protection of the laws." We have been debating what this amorphous terms means ever since. Today, the predominant interpretation is that the equal protection clause strongly disfavors any governmental use of race. This stance is often referred to in short hand as "colorblindness," a phrase that harks back to Justice John Marshall Harlan's famous dissent in *Plessy v. Ferguson.* In *Plessy,* an 1896 decision, the majority announced the "separate but equal" standard that facilitated decades of Jim Crow racial oppression.[1] Harlan declared – in what amounted to aspiration rather than description – that "our constitution is colorblind, and neither knows nor tolerates classes

[1] This discussion draws on Haney López (2007).

among citizens."[2] Given the long, sorry history of racial subordination in the United States, there is tremendous rhetorical appeal to this utopian vision of a future society in which race no longer correlates with privilege or disadvantage. Yet a sharp distinction must be made between colorblindness as an ideal and as a current practice. To see this, consider colorblindness in historical perspective, in terms of democratic theory, and as a cultural phenomenon.

From emancipatory to reactionary

Over the twentieth century, colorblindness shifted from a progressive demand to a reactionary one. This metamorphosis finds reflection in the arguments made by Thurgood Marshall the lawyer and Thurgood Marshall the Supreme Court Justice. As counsel for the National Association for the Advancement of Colored People (NAACP) in the late 1940s and early 1950s, Marshall repeatedly encouraged his colleagues to cite Harlan's famous injunction to argue that, as Marshall put it in a 1947 brief to the Supreme Court, "classifications and distinctions based on race or color have no moral or legal validity in our society. They are contrary to our constitution and laws."[3] Marshall sought to harness colorblindness to attack the racial degradation given constitutional sanction by *Plessy.* He did so recognizing that racial subordination relies upon racial distinctions. The use of race, Marshall argued, lacked moral and legal validity precisely when deployed to oppress.

Rather than adopt a colorblind rule proscribing every use of race, the Supreme Court opted to dismantle Jim Crow "with all deliberate speed."[4] Initially, this reflected a decision to temporize: the Court feared taking on too much too rapidly, and particularly sought to avoid abruptly declaring unconstitutional – and implicitly immoral – the emotional core of white supremacy, the ban on interracial marriage. Over time, however, the decision not to flatly prohibit governmental distinctions based on race came to seem wise. By the mid-1960s, a simple truth became

[2] *Plessy v. Ferguson,* 163 U.S. 537, 559 [1896] (Harlan, J., dissenting).
[3] Brief for Petitioner, *Sipuel v. Bd. of Regents of the Univ. of Okla.,* 332 U.S. 631 [1948] (No. 369), at 27.
[4] *Brown v. Bd. of Educ. (Brown II),* 349 U.S. 294, 301 [1955].

increasingly apparent to the friends and foes of racial emancipation alike: segregation readily continued in the presence of formal racial neutrality. As late as 1965, less than one in one hundred black children in the South attended schools with whites, and the number of whites in predominantly black schools was infinitesimal. Civil rights lawyers dropped their demands for colorblindness and began to stress the necessity of race-conscious remedies to achieve integration and substantive equality, winning support from the Court in a series of decisions spanning the late 1960s and early 1970s.

Meanwhile, the opponents of integration became the new patrons of colorblindness. Thurgood Marshall himself had recognized that while colorblindness posed a radical demand as a right to be immediately free from all Jim Crow oppressions, colorblindness as a remedy promised tepid change, for it required only an end to explicitly segregationist laws, not actual remediation of the harms wrought by racial oppression (Schmidt 2008). This insight was scarcely lost on integration's opponents. A South Carolina district court articulated the colorblind counterargument to integration as early as 1955: "The Constitution … does not require integration. It merely forbids discrimination. It does not forbid such segregation as occurs as the result of voluntary action. It merely forbids the use of governmental power to enforce segregation."[5] From here, it was but a short step to the contention that colorblindness affirmatively *prohibited* race-conscious integration measures. North Carolina grasped this in 1969, passing a law that "no student shall be assigned or compelled to attend any school on account of race, creed, color or national origin."[6] In 1971, the Supreme Court unanimously struck this law down, declaring unequivocally that rigid limitations on government efforts to use race in a remedial fashion had no place under the Fourteenth Amendment. Seeing through North Carolina's stratagem, the Court recognized that "the statute exploits an apparently neutral form to control school assignment plans by directing that they be 'color blind'; that requirement, against the background of segregation, would render illusory the promise of *Brown v. Board of Education*." The Court continued,

> just as the race of students must be considered in determining whether a constitutional violation has occurred, so also must race be considered in formulating a remedy. To forbid, at this stage, all assignments made on the basis of race would deprive school authorities of the one tool absolutely essential to fulfillment of their constitutional obligation to eliminate existing dual school systems.[7]

As the civil rights era drew to a close, colorblindness had shifted valence, from emancipatory to reactionary.

Although initially rejected by the Court, as its composition changed, so too did its stance toward reactionary colorblindness. By the end of the 1970s, the rhetoric of colorblindness had been repurposed as an attack on affirmative action. In 1978, Justice Marshall found himself urging the Court in its first full affirmative action case to reject colorblindness: "It is because of a legacy of unequal treatment that we now must permit the institutions of this society to give consideration to race in making decisions about who will hold the positions of influence, affluence, and prestige in America."[8] Marshall did not prevail, either for colorblindness as a lawyer or against it as a justice. Today, colorblindness as a presumptive bar on affirmative action has been firmly read into the Constitution (Klarman 2010).

Colorblindness and courts in a democratic system

After the civil rights lions William Brennan and Thurgood Marshall retired from the Court in the early 1990s, the Supreme Court in race cases came under the rule of a solid block of five conservative justices. With rare exceptions, this coterie declared virtually all race-conscious remedial efforts unconstitutional. Relying on colorblind logic, the Court invalidated both state and federal efforts to increase the representation of minority owned businesses

---

[5] *Briggs v. Elliott*, 132 F. Supp. 776, 777 [E.D.S.C. 1955].
[6] N.C.Gen.Stat. § 115–176.1 (Supp.1969), quoted in *N.C. State Bd. of Educ. v. Swann*, 402 U.S. 43, 44 n.1 [1971].

[7] *Swann*, at 45–46.
[8] *Regents of the Univ. of Cal. v. Bakke*, 438 U.S. 265, 402 (Marshall, J., concurring in part, dissenting in part).

among those receiving government contracts, severely limited integration measures in government employment practices, and struck down numerous efforts to create voting districts in which nonwhites comprised a majority. In a rare exception to this trend, in 2003 the Court upheld a limited form of affirmative action in higher education in the *Grutter* case. This decision, however, reflected the defection from the conservative bloc of a justice who has since retired from the Court. Under the current chief justice, John Roberts, the Court has become even more aggressive in attacking racial remedies. In 2007, the Court used colorblindness to prohibit school district efforts to maintain integrated student bodies. Seattle and Louisville used race as a modest tiebreaker in pupil assignments in order to preserve hard-won gains in integrating their school districts. Roberts' opinion described this as "discrimination" and struck it down. The muscular language used by that decision will spur renewed challenges to *Grutter*. Indeed, it seems likely to invite lawsuits over the consideration of race in general governmental policymaking, for instance in decisions on where to locate schools or in census data collection, areas never before thought subject to colorblind attack.

Colorblindness is most renowned for its unyielding opposition to affirmative action. Yet there is another side to colorblindness that has probably done more to limit racial progress. In defining as "racism" as any use of race, colorblindness simultaneously defines what counts as "not-racism": all government action not expressly predicated on race, no matter how closely correlated with racial hierarchy or how disproportionate the harm to nonwhites. A 1987 Supreme Court decision, *McCleskey v. Kemp*, epitomizes this flip side.[9] The Court there famously shrugged off the most sophisticated and exhaustive survey of capital sentencing thus far undertaken when it rejected the claim that racism tainted Georgia's death penalty machinery. Though it accepted that Georgia sentenced to die blacks who murdered whites at *twenty-two times* the rate for blacks who killed blacks, the Court nonetheless opined that these statistics proved "at most … a discrepancy that appears to correlate with race." *McCleskey*'s dismissal of the evidence rested on a particular conception of racism as the episodic expression of individual malice. Neither Georgia's history of

discrimination in criminal law enforcement stretching back to slavery, nor the undeniable correlation between the excessive punishment of blacks and the persistence of a white–black hierarchy, mattered to the majority. Ensconced behind colorblindness, the Court reasoned as if racial discrimination did not exist unless the record included a racial epithet or a confession of evil intent. Most critiques of colorblindness focus on its role as a sword against affirmative action. But regarding government practices that discriminate against nonwhites, colorblindness also serves as a shield.

Supporters of colorblindness argue that affirmative action should be forbidden because it encourages racial factions, invites reliance on stereotypes, and stigmatizes its supposed beneficiaries. Opponents say that the real source of factions, stereotypes, and stigma in society is continued and even resurgent segregation and that race-targeted approaches offer the only feasible solution. Regarding the Court's narrow definition of discrimination, its defenders say remedying anything more than direct bigotry would have the courts second-guessing government officials and responding to embedded disadvantage. Critics say government officials, like other bigots, have learned not to announce their discriminatory motives, so that meaningful protection from discrimination requires looking beyond the words of state actors to the impact of their actions, to historical patterns, and to the larger context. In addition, these critics point out that today much of the harm done to nonwhites occurs through embedded disadvantage, which is to say, through the inertia of past injuries, and government has an obligation to at least not make things worse.

Framed in this way, colorblindness seems like a policy debate, with arguments for and against. These policy arguments, however, neglect to take into account the special role of courts in a constitutional democracy. Courts have the power to overturn the will of the electorate. When the Court does declare an act unconstitutional, it asserts that the basic law of the country forbids what the majority seeks. On one cut, this is anti-democratic, for it involves a small unelected body overturning the will of the voters. On the other, it is democracy-perfecting: it gives expression to the nation's deepest democratic values in moments when voters seek to use the power of numbers against vulnerable groups or disfavored ideas. Put in epigrammatic form, courts protect democracy by

---

[9]   *McCleskey v. Kemp*, 481 U.S. 279 [1987].

guarding against the tyranny of the majority. Colorblindness as an interpretation of the Constitution must be evaluated in this light, not simply as a policy argument against the use of race.

How does colorblindness fare when evaluated as an interpretation of the Constitution? Recall the 2007 school case, where the Court forbade Louisville to continue its efforts to maintain integrated schools. Louisville's policy was hotly debated locally, and indeed a slate of candidates ran for the school board promising to end the use of race. They lost the election. And then sued, eventually winning in the Supreme Court. Or reconsider *McCleskey*, the Georgia death penalty case. The Georgia legislature knew to a certainty that its capital sentencing system sent African American men to die in grossly disproportionate numbers, and it refused to do anything about it. Yet when blacks looked for legal succor, the Court said no, leaving them to the mercy of the political system. Colorblindness is perverse in striking down affirmative action while doing nothing about continued mistreatment. It is doubly perverse as a constitutional doctrine. When local majorities struggle through the difficult issues surrounding racial segregation and opt to take modest action, the Court upends democracy and forbids their efforts. But when local majorities refuse to correct practices that victimize and even murder a historically vulnerable group – indeed the group that the Fourteenth Amendment was originally adopted to protect – the Court shrugs and walks away.

The cultural politics of colorblindness

Colorblindness now permeates American society. It is perhaps the predominant way of conceptualizing race and racism, and examples of colorblind reasoning are omnipresent in politics and culture. In this context, reconsider colorblindness as a cultural framework that seeks to answer the following questions: (1) What is – and is not – race? (2) What is – and is not – racism? and (3) What is the relationship between race, racism, and inequality, and by implication, what is required of society?

To begin, colorblindness understands race as little more than skin color. This sense that race reduces to integument has a long and indeed progressive history, perhaps best summed up by the expression "everyone is the same under the skin." This injunction, common during the civil rights era, was not a sociological claim but a moral demand: it might have been more accurately expressed as "stop treating folks better or worse depending on their race and instead treat everyone as if they are the same under the skin." Today, though, this notion of race as epidermis serves as an ostensible description of social dynamics. Under this vision, racial groups exist only as individuals irrationally lumped together on the basis of arbitrary differences in physical appearance. They are *not* groups constructed through a history of subordination and exploitation, and as such differentially situated even today. Rather, since race is only color, race says nothing about individual or group position in society.

Stripped of history and context, this superficial definition of race in turn undergirds the colorblind understanding of racism as every advertence to race. Because race by definitional fiat lacks all social meaning, colorblindness is able to present every use of race as equally without justification. To take cognizance of race, whether to segregate or to integrate, is ostensibly to treat people differently on the basis of an arbitrary characteristic that lacks social relevance and over which individuals have no control. Notice that this vision comprehends racism in individual and symmetrical terms: individual, in that racism harms the person classified by race, and symmetrical in that nothing distinguishes the group positions of whites and nonwhites. Thus, affirmative action becomes reverse discrimination: the exclusion of nonwhites under white supremacy differs not at all from the preference given them in furtherance of social repair. In the words of Clarence Thomas, "government-sponsored racial discrimination based on benign prejudice is just as noxious as discrimination inspired by malicious prejudice. In each instance, it is racial discrimination pure and simple."[10] Who, under this understanding, is the racist? It is the first person in the room to actually use the word "race." Often, this will be the person decrying the persistence of discrimination or advocating for racial repair. Witness the vitriolic charges of racism repeatedly levied against President Obama whenever he refers, however obliquely, to the continued astringent of race in our society.

What, then, of the relationship between race, racism, and inequality? Having stripped race and racism of almost all content, colorblindness would seem

[10]   *Adarand v. Pena*, 515 U.S. 200, 240-41 n.1 [1995].

unable to explain the continued correlation between race and inequality in the United States. Yet this correlation is undeniable and readily observable to all. To give but one example, black median wealth dramatically lags that of whites, even as African Americans have suffered disproportionately in the current recession. According to the *New York Times*, "As of December 2009, median white wealth dipped 34 percent, to $94,600; median black wealth dropped 77 percent, to $2,100" (Powell 2010) How can colorblindness account for this?

Recall that colorblindness defines racism as only the mention of race. The flip side of this is that any reference to group culture is treated as if it is "not racism." Eduardo Bonilla-Silva (2003:28) identifies "cultural racism" as a key feature of what he terms "colorblind racism": "*Cultural racism* is a frame that relies on culturally based arguments such as 'Mexicans do not put much emphasis on education' or 'blacks have too many babies' to explain the standing of minorities in society." Under the semiotics of colorblindness, only open references to skin color or the use of explicitly derogatory racial epithets count as racism. In contrast, alarmism about the cultural or behavioral deficiencies of nonwhites ostensibly bears no relation to racism and xenophobia. Recall the evolving vocabularies of the 1980s and 1990s: super-predators, gang bangers, and welfare queens. Or reflect on our current racial boogeymen, Mexican illegal immigrants and Muslim terrorists. No matter how hysterical the commentary or how outrageously punitive the government's actions, colorblindness insists race is not involved so long as the focus is on failed cultures or bad behavior, even when attributed to whole groups in ways that

bear uncanny resemblances to the racial stereotypes of yore. Thus colorblindness answers the question of continued group inequality: groups have earned their relative advantage, or deserve their relative disadvantage, because of choices, values, and abilities inherent in the groups themselves. It follows that, to seek to alter the maldistribution of privilege and hardship is to engage in illegitimate "social engineering," taking from those who value hard work to reward those with an entitlement mentality. In the face of inequality rationalized as legitimate, warranted, earned, and deserved, colorblindness tells us society is morally forbidden to do anything.

Quite frankly, the present incarnation of colorblindness seems geared to preserving the racial status quo. The great triumph of the civil rights era lies in the defeat of white supremacy, not only as a set of ideas but in its most egregious practices. This tradition of struggle against racial injustice continues, even as discrimination has evolved and remains stubbornly entrenched and even sometimes actively pursued. Colorblindness originally boldly demanded that Jim Crow be dismantled. Contemporary colorblind partisans wrap themselves in the moral legitimacy of this history, loudly trumpeting their opposition to already defeated practices and seeking to arrogate to their use the heroes and slogans of the civil rights era. But in practice they defend continued inequality. Using the rhetoric of colorblindness, they oppose affirmative action, refuse to look critically at discriminatory practices, attack as racists all those who speak forthrightly about continuing racial problems, and tolerate and even promote rank stereotypes so long as masked in cultural and behavioral terms.

Separate and Unequal

A Conversation

We hear once again from a group of experts who summarize for us the main ideas and themes of this chapter and section of the book. **Mia Bay** *is Professor of History and*

Associate Director of the Center for Race and Ethnicity at Rutgers University. **Joseph Graves** *is Dean of University Studies and Professor of Biological Studies at the University of North Carolina Agricultural and Technical State University.* **James Horton** *is Benjamin Banneker Professor of American Studies and History at George Washington University and Historian Emeritus of the Smithsonian Institution's National Museum of American*

History. **Robin Kelley** *is Professor of American Studies and Ethnicity at the University of Southern California.* **Mae Ngai** *is Lung Family Professor of Asian American Studies and Professor of History at Columbia University.* **Pilar Ossorio** *is Associate Professor of Law and Bioethics at the University of Wisconsin at Madison.* **john a. powell** *is Executive Director of the Kirwan Institute for the Study of Race and Ethnicity at The Ohio State University.*

ROBIN KELLEY: Racism, in some ways, is a very complicated system of knowledge, of where science, religion, philosophy, are used to justify inequality and hierarchy. That's foundational.

Racism is not simply a kind of visceral feeling you have when you see someone who is different from you. Because, in fact, if you look at the history of the world, there are many people who look different who are seen as both attractive and unattractive. You know, it's not even about how you look. It's about how people assign meaning to how you look. And that's learned. That's learned behavior, you see.

JOSEPH GRAVES: America created our socially defined races in conjunction with its history of colonialism against the American Indians and the enslavement of African Americans. In a social system where the right to take one's land or to take one's life was defined by your racial characteristic, it was important to come up with rules to identify who was who.

JAMES HORTON: But the thing that makes American slavery so distinctive is it's based on race. That America's slavery is a kind of slavery that is justified not, for example, as West African slavery is justified. That is, people were captured in battle, and therefore, they are now held in a kind of captivity. Think about that for a second. Any of us could have lost that battle. Any of us could have been held in captivity. Any of us could have been a slave. But when you base slavery on the question of race, well if one of us is black, and one of us is white, and slavery is linked to blackness, one of us could never have been a slave.

MIA BAY: Well, a lot of people don't like to think that there is a natural link between democracy and slavery, but you cannot get around the fact that they grew up together in this country. The south, which produced our great democratic thinkers, Jefferson, the revolutionary leaders, you know, it was a slave society.

Reproduced courtesy of California Newsreel.

JOHN A. POWELL: And a lot of white people say, "Well, you know, I don't want to hear about slavery, you know. I had nothing to do with that, and my parents came much later." They don't realize that even for them to be able to come was part of the racialized system. That the fact that they could come to the United States was already a benefit of being white, because if you're Chinese or if you're black, you couldn't come.

ROBIN KELLEY: Race was never just a matter of categories. But it was a matter of creating hierarchies. Race was about racial supremacy or a racist system of supremacy in which one group dominates the other.

JAMES HORTON: And here is where it really gets interesting. You got some places, for example, Virginia: Virginia law defined a black person as a person with one-sixteenth African ancestry. Now Florida defined a black person as a person with one-eighth African ancestry. Alabama said, "You're black if you got any black ancestry, any African ancestry at all." But you know what this means? You can walk across a state line and literally legally change race. Now what does race mean under those circumstances? You give me the power, I can make you any race I want you to be, because it is a social, political construction. It is not a matter of biology.

PILAR OSSORIO: Actually, if you read the law on race, right, there was a whole history where, in order to be a naturalized citizen in this country, as an immigrant, you had to be categorized as white or black. And almost everybody who tried to naturalize, all but I think one case that went to the Supreme Court, all of them were people trying to be categorized as white. So the court had to make decisions about who was white and who was not, and is an Armenian person white? Or is ... there were a number of cases dealing with Asian people, and are they white or not white? And so one of the things that would happen is the person would come into court and they would say, "Look, my skin color is as white as anybody else's skin color in here who is categorized as white."

And, you know, it's very interesting to read these decisions and opinions and have the court say, "Well, it's ... but race is not only about the color of your skin. It's about other things too, like your attitudes about family, your attitudes about politics." Right? And whether or not somebody ... the court often decided who was white and who wasn't based on whether they just felt that the person would politically fit well into the kind of society we were trying to build. And sometimes it was pretty explicit that this was what the court was doing, right?

MAE NGAI: So there's this idea that Asians are not only so different that they can never become like other Americans, there's also an idea because that there's so many people in Asia, that this yellow peril is envisioned as a horde of millions and millions of yellow people who will just overrun the country.

PILAR OSSARIO: Race, as we understand it as a social construct, has a lot to do with where somebody will live, what schools they will go to, what jobs they will get, whether or not they will have health insurance. So race does play a very important role in our lives.

References

American Social History Project
1989   Who Built America? Working People and the Nation's Economics, Politics, Culture, and Society, vol. 1: From Conquest and Colonization through Reconstruction and the Great Uprising of 1877. New York: Pantheon Books.

Baker, Lee D.
2010   Anthropology and the Racial Politics of Culture. Durham, NC: Duke University Press.

Blackmon, Douglas A.
2008   Slavery by Another Name: The Re-enslavement of Black Americans from the Civil War to World War II. New York: Doubleday.

Borden, Philip
1970   Found Cumbering the Soil: Manifest Destiny and the Indian in the Nineteenth Century. In The Great Fear: Race in the Mind of America. Gary Nash and Richard Weiss, eds. pp. 71–97. New York: Holt, Rinehart and Winston, Inc.

Fields, Barbara J.
2001   Whiteness, Racism, and Identity. International Labor and Working-Class History 60:48–56.

Haney López, Ian F.
1996   White by Law: The Legal Construction of Race. New York: New York University Press.

Higginbotham, A. Leon, Jr.
1978   In the Matter of Color: Race and the American Legal Process: The Colonial Period. New York: Oxford University Press.

Jaynes, Gerald D.
1986   Branches without Roots: Genesis of the Black Working Class in the American South, 1862–1882. New York: Oxford University Press.

Ngai, Mae M.
2004   Impossible Subjects: Illegal Aliens and the Making of Modern America. Princeton: Princeton University Press.

Painter, Nell Irvin
2010   The History of White People. New York: W. W. Norton and Company.

Patterson, Thomas C.
1997   Inventing Western Civilization. New York: Monthly Review Press.

Roediger, David R.
2008   How Race Survived U.S. History: From Settlement and Slavery to the Obama Phenomenon. London: Verso.

Thornton, Russell
1987   American Indian Holocaust and Survival: A Population History since 1492. Norman: University of Oklahoma Press.

Ian F. Haney López, Colorblindness

Bonilla-Silva, Eduardo
2003   Racism without Racists: Color-Blind Racism and the Persistence of Racial Inequality in the United States. Lanham, MD: Rowman and Littlefield.

Haney López, Ian
2007   A Nation of Minorities: Race, Ethnicity, and Reactionary Colorblindness, Stanford Law Review 59:985.

Klarman, Michael J.
2010   Has the Supreme Court Been Mainly a Friend or a Foe to African Americans? SCOTUS Blog, February 1. http://www.scotusblog.com/2010/02/has-the-supreme-court-been-mainly-a-friend-or-a-foe-to-african-americans, accessed November 23, 2011.

Powell, Michael
2010   Blacks in Memphis Lose Decades of Economic Gains. New York Times, May 30.

Schmidt, Christopher W.
2008   Brown and the Colorblind Constitution, Cornell Law Review 94:203, 234.

Separate And Unequal, 1650–2000

Douglass, Frederick
1865 [1999] The Need for Continuing Anti-Slavery Work, speech at Thirty-second Annual Meeting of the American Anti-Slavery Society (May 10, 1865). *Cited in* Frederick Douglass: Selected Speeches and Writings. Philip S. Foner, ed. Adapted by Yuval Taylor. Chicago: Lawrence Hill Books.

King, Martin Luther, Jr.
1963 [1964] Letter from Birmingham Jail. *Cited in* Why We Can't Wait. Martin Luther King, Jr. New York: Harper and Row Publishers.

Kwang Chang Ling [pseud.]
1878 Why Should the Chinese Go? A Pertinent Inquiry from A Mandarin High in Authority. *In* Alexander Del Mar, Letters of Kwang Chang Ling: The Chinese Side of the Chinese Question, By a Chinese Literate of the First Class, Communicated to the San Francisco Argonaut. p. 8. See http://content.cdlib.org/ark:/13030/hb3m3n99bq/?order=1&brand=calisphere], accessed January 29, 2012.

Trist, Nicholas P.
N.d. U.S. negotiator of the Treaty of Guadalupe Hidalgo, 1848, as reported by his wife, Virginia Trist. Trist Papers, University of North Carolina.

Turner, Henry McNeal
1883 [1967] *Cited in* The Burden of Race: A Documentary History of Negro–White Relations in America. Gilbert Ofosky. New York: Harper and Row.

PART 2

WHY HUMAN VARIATION IS *NOT* RACIAL

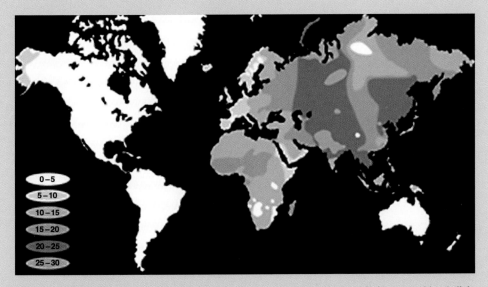

Race is not "in the blood." This map shows the percentages of individuals with the B type blood allele within indigenous human populations. Scientists once thought the ABO blood system apportions by race. However, the generally east–west distribution observed here – with high concentrations in Central Asia and low concentrations throughout Australia and the Americas – is not seen for the A or O blood alleles. The distributions of A, B, and O blood types are continuous or clinally distributed. Courtesy of Dennis O'Neil, modified from A.E. Mourant et al. (1976), *Distribution of the Human Blood Groups and Other Polymorphisms*, 2nd edition, © 1976 by Oxford University Press.

7

Introduction

Race ≠ Human Biological Variation

Isn't Race Biologically Obvious?

You have probably heard it said that race is genetic, or biological, or physical. Most Americans assume that there is an unassailably tangible reality to race and that race has a clear inherent basis. Race is in our genes. Race seems to be obvious: certain and scientific. Race is universal. Race is a truth. Without thinking much, you have probably taken the fact that race is biologically real and a scientific universal to be unquestionably true. A fact! Like the air we breathe, race is just there.

But the facts are different from what our eyes tell us.

Simply put, people are different. We see this difference, first with our eyes and later on by measuring and by microscopes.

However, this does not mean that races are real. Human variation is real. Race is an explanation for that variation. We have better explanations. Evolution is a much more dynamic and fitting explanation. Our culture still retains the idea that race explains variation as a remnant from a time, not so long ago, when we thought that what was today, was always. The world did not change. But it evolves and that evolutionary process explains the variations and similarities among us. Race, on the other hand, does not.

In part 2 we explore human variation, patterns of differences and similarities from one person to another and one group to another. We describe the patterns we observe over space and time as well as other ways

to look at variation. Our question is, How did the structure of human variation, the patterns we see, come to be? In some cases, specifically for skin color and sickle cell, we use scientific detective work to make a case for how specifics of evolution and history lead to these well-known variations. We then explore why race is a faulty and even harmful explanation.

You might marvel at the many, many physical differences, or what biologists call outward phenotypic differences, among us. People come in different sizes and shapes. Skin colors are different. So too are eye colors. Hair varies in color and texture. Our eyes see lots and lots of difference. Below these visible differences are even more variations from the size, shape, and function of internal organs to single changes in the chemical structures of molecules such as proteins and DNA. *Vive la différence!*

But these differences are not RACE.

Some of you might remember a widely used American Express Commercial featuring Wilt Chamberlain, the retired basketball player, and the retired jockey, Willie Shoemaker. They are similarly attired in white formal wear against a blue sky. Among their many differences are skin color and height: Willie is rather short and light skinned Wilt is rather tall and darker skinned. Figure 7.1 also foregrounds two famous personalities from the world of basketball. Jeff Van Gundy, a coach, is in the suit and Yao Ming, the basketball player is in the red and white uniform.

Figure 7.1 Jeff Van Gundy and Yao Ming. Courtesy of Sports Illustrated.

Take a moment to look at them and think about all the ways they are the same and all the ways they are different. John Barlow Reid, a geologist and former professor at Hampshire College, calls this exercise "page 1." On page one, students try to describe what they see as best they can without yet theorizing the explanation for the facts that they are describing. It's often not easy to "see" without trying to "explain."

There are many similarities such as in attire, number of arms and legs, and stuff like that that we take for granted. The most obvious difference is probably size, and particularly stature. Jeff is short and Yao is very, very tall: over seven feet tall. Jeff and Yao also differ in hair texture and hair and skin color. These latter differences are, in the American system of racial classification, signs of race. As we previously noted, these biological signs have been imbued with deeper meaning because they are looped into a cycle of racial thinking, a cycle that is flawed. Jeff and Yao are classified as different races in the United States because of these differences.

But race does not explain all the marvelous differences between them. Race certainly would not seem to explain why one is good at coaching and the other is good at playing basketball. Size explains some of that but not all. Those so-called racial traits, like skin color and hair texture, are also just parts of the

wonderful spectrum of human variation. How they came about – through marvelous stories of evolution and history – have nothing to do with the human invention of racial types. In the following chapters we tell the story of two of these traits, skin color and sickle cell, which are not indicators of race, but rather, marvels of evolution.

What do we mean – *and not mean* – by that short declarative sentence that race does not explain human variation? In this section we will work through the following propositions:

- The idea of race is real. Like all ideas, it is "real" in the sense that it influences thoughts and actions. We do not see everything without beginning to classify and otherwise make sense. Race was a category that once made sense. Ideas such as "democracy" and "superiority" are powerful, and race is among the most powerful of ideas.
- Humans vary biologically, as our eyes and our scientific instruments make clear. Variation is also real. We will explore this variation at the visible (phenotypic) level and also at the genetic level, with surprising results.
- Human variation is real, BUT the idea of race, as a way to describe and studying biological variation, is factually and theoretically inaccurate and outmoded. As the title of this section declares, *Race ≠ human biological variation*. The main point of this section is to demonstrate this "reality."
- Furthermore, we would be better off both scientifically and socially if were we to stop using race as a proxy for human biological variation and used it solely as a socio-cultural designation. Separating the reality of human variation from the idea of race is both scientifically correct and a matter of social justice.

In other words, race and human biological variation are each real – but in different ways. One cannot be reduced into another. The biological and the social have been linked. However, our studies show us that the way they are linked, primarily that the biological explains the social, is wrong. As we will later see, the social idea of race has biological costs in terms of health. However, for now we might argue that human biological variation and social ideas of race are better off with a complete divorce.

In part 1 of this book we told the story of how the idea of race was invented and became real (the first of the points in the bullet-point list in this chapter). In this section we focus on the next two bullets, showing that human biological variation is real, but that it is not race. In this sense, we are granting a divorce for irreconcilable differences between the idea of race and the reality of human biological variation. Their passion for each other was an adolescent flirtation, and as they lived together, their lives became almost completely entangled and enmeshed. However, as mature adults, they have grown irreconcilably apart. It is time to cut the ideological cord.

So, why do we think this is a critical distinction? Why such a cold divorce?

A fundamental lesson from the study of both science (which is a sort of culture) and society is that ideas are powerful. And, of course, race is among the most powerful ideas of all time. Here, thinking that race and human biological variation are much the same is part of the deep and persistently wounding history of race and racism.

This conflation of race and human biological variation is no less than the chief weapon of racists. How this conflation came about is doubtlessly intentional in part and serendipitous in other parts. Once the conflation was fixed, it could be used by deeply intentional racist scientists and others to support slavery and other race-based institutions. More important still, the racial smog caused many to see racist institutions as natural, and instead of fighting racism, we aided and abetted racism. It is time to disarm.

We are not so naive as to think that we will end all of racism by divorcing the idea of race from human biological variation. However, ideas are powerful. By showing that race is not the same as human biological variation we undermine one of racism's chief ideological tennets.

Think of ideology as a loaded gun. It is time to take the bullets out, one by one.

In this introduction to part 2 we are going to outline two bottom-line points: (1) that humans do vary biologically and (2) that this variation is explained by evolution (and not by race). Then, in the following three chapters of part 2, we will fill in the details to

Figure 7.2 Race is like a gun. One could say it is not the gun that maims and kills, but the gun is a powerful ideological tool; it is a threat of violence and control. Like a gun in the hands of an angry man, race in the hands of a racist does harm. *Discovery of Nat Turner* by William Henry Shelton. Courtesy of Encyclopedia Virginia.

understand more completely the key differences between race *as an idea* and human biological variation as a measurable set of attributes that are amenable to scientific investigation.

Humans Do Vary Biologically

Consider this thought experiment. You are sitting comfortably in a room. It is a large room such as a gymnasium. Two hundred fellow members of your species, *Homo sapiens*, otherwise known as humans, parade in, one by one. One hundred of them are from Nairobi, Kenya, and the other one hundred hail from Oslo, Norway, some 7,109 kilometers away. Once in the room, they line up along the walls and you can move them and sort them around the room in any way you choose. Your task is a simple one: to make an educated guess at who is from Nairobi and who is from Oslo.

You quickly notice that individuals vary in skin color, as well as eye color and hair color. In fact, you sense that there are two clusters of individuals, one with light, pale skin and light, straight hair and the other with dark, brownish skin and dark and curly hair. You also notice a wide variety of sizes and shapes: tall and short; thin and thick. But these size differences don't seem to relate to the color differences and you

Figure 7.3 Kenyan children. Photograph courtesy of Jeremy Wilburn.

Figure 7.4 Girls from Oslo. Photograph courtesy of Ilan Kelman (http://www.ilankelman.org).

stop focusing on them. Of course, you guess that those with lighter skin and hair are from Oslo and those with darker skin and hair tones are from Nairobi. You are almost certainly right. The pictures above show clear differences, in gender, dress, and physical appearance. In fact, you may be perfectly right. Everyone fits into a box, correctly classified.

What did this prove? Proof only comes with repeated confirmation of results. So, technically this doesn't prove much, except that on this day you did a good job of separating out individuals from two locations that are thousands of miles apart. That said, most would agree that it shows that human phenotypes seem to vary geographically. Phenotypes, defined as

the measurable result of the interaction of genes and environment, tend to vary by location. In fact genotypes, the differences in alleles and at the level of the genome, as we will see, also vary by location. But here it is particularly interesting that some aspects of phenotype, most notably skin color, that we very visual humans can all see, seems to particularly change with geography.

If you have ever bought a house, you have doubtlessly noticed that some houses cost more than others. Size matters as does the quality of the home. But those in the real estate business have another saying. When it comes to price, real estate agents are fond of saying, "Location, location, location." The three most important determinants for housing costs are location (and location and location).

The same is true for human biological variation. Location determines variation. In chapters 10 and 11 we will focus on how evolutionary forces vary by geography and are the driving force behind the geographic variation we see.

Variation ≠ Race

If you lived during the 18th or 19th century, you'd have virtually no cognitive alternative, no conceptual framework, but to think that the biological variation you observed on the street, in your medical practice, or even studied in your laboratory was the same as race. Human variation was race. Race was your only tool to describe and explain differences. So, naturally, to use the tool metaphor again, one would use the hammer of race to pound the nail of difference. You did your best with that one tool. Where the hammer didn't work, perhaps bending the nail, you just got by and sort of ignored that it wasn't working, and grabbed another nail. This natural inclination is not unlike ignoring size variation because it does not help to figure out who was from Oslo. The idea of race became reified and transformed into a unity with the reality of biological variation. We do not want to suggest that doing so was a planned conspiracy, but it is clear that doing so helped justify systems of inequality such as slavery and even contemporary differences in wealth. Basing such differences on a faulty belief in biological inferiorities and superiorities helped make them seem less unjust.

Many scientists and most non-scientists (politicians, teachers, garbage collectors, whatever) still think this way. Biological anthropologist Alice Brues told *Newsweek*, "If I parachute into Nairobi, I know I'm not in Oslo." Another biological anthropologist, Vincent Sarich, would say that the experiment in which you separated Norwegians from Kenyans proves that race is real.

However, the variation we have just noticed – that was knocked-us-over-the head obvious – is NOT race. Why not? The short answer is that the idea of race inadequately describes and explains human biological variation. Below are five key reasons why race ≠ human variation.

1   *Evolution, rather than race, explains human biological variation.* Race-as-biology is based on the false idea of fixed, ideal and unchanging types. Race categories were first a European folk idea from an era in which the world was seen as fixed and unchanging. As is outlined in the history of mismeasurement (chapter 4) European scientists once thought the world was fixed and static. All of that changed with evolutionary theory. The illusion of unchanging racial types is completely incompatible with evolutionary theory.

2   *Human variation is continuous.* Allele frequencies, or variations in DNA, tend to vary gradually. Therefore, *there is no clear place to designate where one race begins and another ends.* Skin color, for example, the physical characteristic we most often use to distinguish "races," slowly changes from place to place and person to person.

If one were to take a walk from Norway to Nigeria one would encounter slow and gradual changes in skin color. There is no place to unambiguously say where dark skin ends and lighter tones begin. Variation is continuous.

The same that is true about the average variation among groups is also true of variation within groups. Line a group of individuals up by height and one can see that variation in height is continuous. Continuous variation in height is further illustrated in the boxed text.

3   *Human biological variation involves many traits that typically vary independently.* Skin color, for example, is only correlated with a few other traits such as hair and eye color, leaving unpredictable the huge number of other traits. While we might be able to predict that someone with light skin is more likely to have light hair, we are unable to predict virtually any other traits. Thus, it is a truism that "race is only skin deep."

Figure 7.5 is a visual representation of this phenomena of trait independence originally developed by Paul Ehrlich and Richard Holm (1964). Imagine that there are four traits represented by four layers. In this case, suppose that skin color is on top, followed by eye and hair color and hair form. However, they could be most any trait, and of course there are thousands to choose from, from simple to complex. Think of the four "cores" as either individuals or groups. The two to the right both have light skin color, but then they differ in the other traits. This is because the top layer, skin color, does not predict the variation in the other traits/layers. Skin color is independent of most other traits.

4   *Genetic variation* within *so-called races is much greater than the variation* among *them.* One might assume that genetic variation among races is great; however, there is actually little genetic variation among the groups we have come to call races. For example, two individuals who might identify as "white" might well be far more genetically different from one another than from someone self-identified as "black." Moreover, rather than seeing Europeans and Asians as "races," they may be more accurately seen as different-looking subsets of Africans, since the human population descended from human beings living on that continent. Given these genetic realities, race simply fails to account for the genetic variation among us. This phenomenon is explained in detail in subsequent chapters.

5   *There is no way to consistently classify human beings by race.* Race groups are impossible to define in a stable and universal way, and if one cannot define groups one cannot make scientific generalizations about them. Race groups are unstable primarily because the socially determined color line changes over time and place. Someone considered "white" in Brazil can be considered "black" in the United States; someone who lives as "white" in the United States today might have been considered "Mexican" a generation earlier.

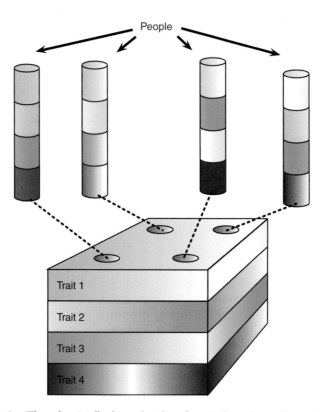

Figure 7.5   Cube of variation. The cube visually shows the idea of trait independence. Illustration by R. Boehm. (Redrawn from Ehrlich, 1964). Modified from Michael Alan Park, Biological Anthropology, 2nd edn, © McGraw-Hill Companies, Inc.

Roma and other "dark" babies in Romania are classified as inferior, and even "black" and were often put up for adoption at the fall of the Communist regime. In the United States, where white couples clamored to adopt them, these children were seen as "white." Their racial classification was totally nationally dependent. Since there is no consistent way to classify human biological diversity using race categories, we cannot use these categories to say anything scientific about human biological diversity.

Summary

A number of linked reasons lead us to strongly urge the reader to rethink the relationship between the idea of race and the structure of human variation. For theoretical reasons, for practical reasons, and for scientific reasons, race fails to explain or describe human variation. The result of using race ambiguously is that individuals often go to a default position of accepting that race has something to do with genetics and evolution, and thus, that inequalities in health and others aspects of life could be explained based on racial genetics. But this is conceptually and factually incorrect. It now appears that the increased blood pressure of African diasporic groups, for example (see chapter 16) has more to do with perceptions of difference and the social dynamics of skin color than it does with underlying biology. And of course, skin color is not race. Moreover, a focus on race-as-genetic has inhibited a full exploration of the consequences of racial thinking and racism.

In the chapters of part 2 we explore the details of how variation in sickle cell and skin color came about, and what the world geographic distributions of these traits means. We will then explore in detail the underlying structure of human genetic variation, with some surprising results.

Height, History, and Human Variation

Figure 7.6 "The Tall and Short of It." Photograph # NH 45759. Courtesy of Naval History and Heritage Command.

Not all variation is associated with race. Some variation, such as height, does differ by group; however, what is remarkable is the degree of variation in height and other size variables within groups. Archaeologists and historians have also found that height also varies over decades, centuries, and millennia. Not surprisingly, they find that as nutrition, health, and other living conditions wax and wane, heights change. They are a sort of biological barometer of the quality of life. Height is an example of a complex trait that has multiple genetic and environmental causes.

Humans come in all sizes. Historically, we have changed heights based on living conditions. And it is also clear that there is a great deal of variation within any human group.

Height is one aspect of variation that clearly displays the notion that variation is continuous. Figure 7.7 shows three ways to look at height variation. In Figure 7.7a, three individuals are displayed in profile. One could clearly distinguish the short from the medium and tall individual. However, as individuals are added, in Figure 7.7b and Figure 7.7c, where one draws the line becomes increasingly difficult. Height changes from a discrete trait with clear differences among

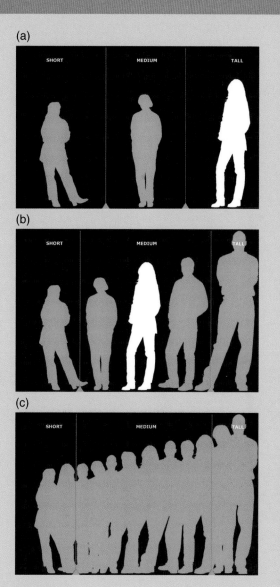

Figure 7.7 Drawing of silhouettes of individuals from short to tall. Courtesy of S2N Media, Inc.

the groups, to a continuous trait. In the latter case it becomes difficult to objectively decide where to draw the line between short and tall.

Conclusions

Variation is marvelous. However, it does not conform to the idea of race. Variation, as we have noted, is continuous with no clear breaks. And the pattern of variation in one trait is invariably a poor predictor of the variation in another. Thus, we are truly complex creations. You cannot tell much from any one trait.

References

Ehrlich, Paul, and Richard Holm
1964   A Biological View of Race. *In* The Concept of Race. Ashley Montagu, ed. pp. 153–179. New York: Free Press of Glencoe.

Further Resources

American Anthropological Association
1998   AAA statement on race. Anthropology Newsletter, September. p. 3. (www.aaanet.org/stmts/racepp.htm.).

AAPA (American Association of Physical Anthropologists)
1996   AAPA Statement on Biological Aspects of Race. American Journal of Physical Anthropology 101: 569–570.

Brace, C. Loring
1964   A Nonracial Approach Towards the Understanding of Human Diversity. *In* The Concept of Race. Ashley Montagu, ed. pp. 103–152. New York: Free Press of Glencoe.

Diamond, Jared
1994   Race Without Color. Discover 15(11):82–89.

Goodman, Alan
1997   Bred in the Bone? Sciences 37(2):20–25.

Loveyoy, A. O.
1936   The Great Chain of Being. Cambridge, MA: Harvard University Press.

Marks, Jonathan
1995   Human Biodiversity: Genes, Race, and History. New York: Aldine de Gruyter.

Montagu, A.
1963   Race, Science and Humanity. New York: Van Nostrand.

Montagu, A.
1964   Man's Most Dangerous Myth: The Fallacy of Race. Meridian Books: New York.

8

Skin Deep?

Life Under the Sun: An Evolutionary Balance

Figure 8.1 Individuals as well as groups vary by skin color. "Rainbow of human skin colors." Courtesy of Sarah Leen/ National Geographic Stock.

Variations in skin colors from light to dark among neighboring populations as well as individuals appears to result from selection to life under the sun. It is a triumph of human evolution, and a story that is unfolding …

Adapted from RACE exhibit, SMM

Sun: The Motivator

The organic compound necessary for skeletal health, vitamin D, is unique in humans because as well as needing to absorb it directly from certain foodstuffs (from which necessity it derives its classification as a vitamin), it is a hormone-like compound that we

Figure 8.2 Life under the sun.
© iStockphoto.com/Michieldb.

Race: Are We So Different?, First Edition. Alan H. Goodman, Yolanda T. Moses, and Joseph L. Jones.
© 2012 American Anthropological Association. Published 2012 by Blackwell Publishing Ltd.

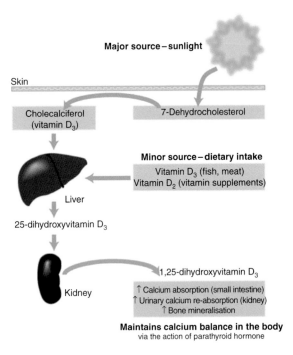

Figure 8.3 Vitamin D metabolism. Vitamin D can come from the sun, turning a precursor into vitamin D_3, or from a few select foods such as fish oils. Courtesy of Harriet Greenfield.

produce spontaneously. In the latter form it is largely inactive, but by exposure to ultraviolet radiation (UVR) in sunlight we synthesize it as vitamin D_3 and use it along with the vitamin D_3 we get from a few foods to regulate our absorption of calcium and to deposit it in our bones. Thus, sunlight is good – in this respect. Too much UVR, however, can also break down another vitamin, called folate (or folic acid), one of the B vitamins that is especially important for healthy development of fetuses. Like many things, you can have too much or too little of a good thing. Here, however, just the right balance depends on skin color.

Evolutionary anthropologist Nina Jablonski and others (see her essay in this chapter) theorizes that different skin colors evolved to balance the need for folate and vitamin D. Depending on the regions where people live, the amount of sunlight varies. Darker skin blocks more folate-destroying UVR. Lighter skin permits more UVR to be absorbed and allows you to make more vitamin D. According to Jablonksi's elegant theory, the skin color in any

population is a balance between the need to protect folate and the need to produce enough vitamin D to grow and maintain a healthy skeleton.

Early hominids (human ancestors) adapted to new selective pressures as they moved from forested to warmer savannah environments. For example, increased heat resulted in their losing much of their hair (except in certain areas like the top of the head) and gaining the ability to sweat. Soon after, they may have also evolved darker skin.

Fossil and genetic evidence suggests the earliest humans lived in Africa between 150,000 and 200,000 years ago. Most likely, their skin was darkly pigmented to protect against high-level UVR exposure. Populations that migrated away from the equator and settled at higher latitudes with less UVR exposure evolved lighter skin over tens of thousands of years. The gradual or clinal nature of change in skin color across neighboring geographic regions is an example of a continuous trait variation.

Skin Color

Human skin comes in a range of colors, although that range leaves out many interesting colors. We have lots of shades of brown and tans, but no blues and greens. There are not many creatures that have skin colors in the primary colors such as blue or red. The scale is pretty much shades of white, cream, black, and brown – but that doesn't inhibit our eyes from noticing it or our culture and brains from making a big deal of it.

Skin color variation has a rather simple biological cause: it is mainly related to the amount of *melanin* in the deeper layers of the skin. Through the course of evolution, humans probably increased their production of melanin to meet the new environmental demand of greater UVR exposure. This is likely to have been related to the loss of hair to better dissipate heat loss in the tropics. Melanin is produced by cells called *melanocytes* that are located in the bottom of the five layers of the epidermis (outer skin), known as the basal layer. Melanin is also found in the eyes (irises) and hair bulbs. The most common form (eumelanin), dark brown in color, is primarily responsible for much of the variation we see in skin color lightness and darkness.

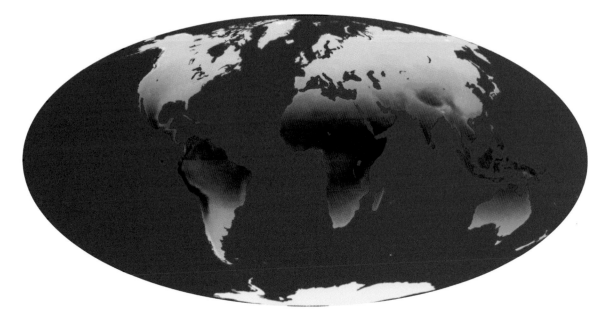

Figure 8.4   This map of predicted human skin colors is based on annual UVR exposure and other environmental factors. It is a good approximation of actual skin color variation among indigenous populations. © George Chaplin, reproduced by permission of Nina Jablonski.

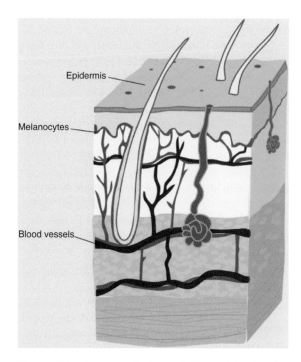

Figure 8.5   Cutaway of a layer of skin and the location of the melanin-producing melanocytes in the inner layers of the epidermis. Courtesy of the Science Museum of Minnesota/C. Johnson.

Skin Color, the Sun, and Evolution

All skin colors, whether dark or light, are due not to the static concept of race but to continually shifting adaptation to life under the sun.

RACE exhibit, SMM

Why is sunlight so important? As Jablonski outlines (see her essay in this chapter), researchers once hypothesized that skin color variation is a product of exposure to excessive heat and cold.

Darker skin has long been known to be associated with increased frostbite, and as serious as this might sound, it is not so likely to be a serious evolutionary pressure. After all, we have gloves and boots and Inuit, who are not particularly light skinned, live in some of the coldest environments. In fact, the Inuit provide an interesting piece of the evolutionary riddle of skin color. They live in one of the most northern of locations, yet their skin color is not as light as one would predict if temperature or latitude was the main cause of skin color variation. Let us save the answer to this riddle for a moment. As your dermatologist or mother may have warned you, light skin is prone to sunburn and skin cancer, melanoma. However severe this cancer is,

Figure 8.6 Inuit children. Their skin color (melanization) is relatively dark even though they live in one of the most northern areas and furthest from the equator. Part of their adaptation might be in their hands. Fish might provide a source of vitamin D. Courtesy of Eric Loring.

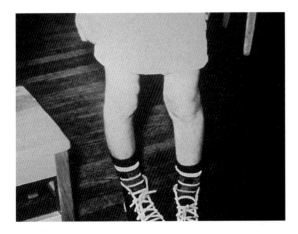

Figure 8.7 Example of childhood rickets. Note the bowing of the lower leg bones. Courtesy of U. S. Centers for Disease Control and Prevention, U.S. Department of Health and Human Services.

it is unlikely to kill you at an early age, and early age is when the evolutionary action is greatest.

That leads us to childhood nutritional problems. Lack of folate is one of the chief causes of birth defects in children today. Folate, as well as other B vitamins, is critical for the proper formation of the central nervous system. Thus, it is not unlikely that folate deficiency has been a strong selective force.

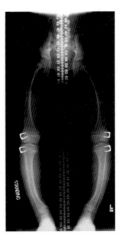

Figure 8.8 Radiograph of a child with rickets, a condition due to vitamin D deficiency. The long bones of the legs do not absorb sufficient calcium [and phosphate]. As a result, they cannot adequately support the full body weight and become bowed with time. The corresponding condition in adults is referred to as osteomalacia. Courtesy of Shriners Hospital for Children – Twin Cities.

Similarly, we know that lack of vitamin D causes the nutritional disease rickets in children (see Figure 8.7 and Figure 8.8). Rickets leads to a noticeable bowing of the legs and in severe form can lead to improper formation of the pelvis, causing serious difficulty for women with this condition in giving birth. The reproductive issues are clear. Moreover, rickets is a well known disease, seen, for example, among children of the poor in Victorian England who worked in shops and factories all day and had little exposure to sun light.

Why, then, are Inuit relatively dark? The answer, we think, is that they have sufficient exposure to solar radiation reflected from the snow to ward against rickets. They might also have an added benefit from eating fish with oils that contain vitamin D. Here is what Nina Jaklonski says:

> Native people of Alaska and Canada have darker skin than we might predict. This is for two reasons. First, in the summer they get high levels of UVR reflected from the surface of snow and ice, and their dark skin protects them from this reflected light. Second, although their darker skin slows down the process of making vitamin D in their skin, this problem is compensated for by their traditional diet, which consists mostly of vitamin D-rich foods such as seal, walrus and fish. (RACE exhibit, SMM)

Measuring Skin Color

Skin color is easy to observe. However, it is not all that easy to measure in a quantifiable and repeatable way. Humans vary by skin color in a seasonal way. Babies have lighter skin that gets darker with aging. And certain parts of the body, like the palms, have lighter skin than other parts of the body.

Until the middle of the twentieth century, there wasn't a widely agreed upon way to measure skin color, and most anthropologists simply classified groups in rough skin-color categories, not unlike the rough racial categories: light, brown, black, etc. At some point, it was decided to use the inner arm as a standard place for assessing skin color.

One effort to provide a more objective comparison was developed by Austrian anthropologist Felix Ritter von Luschan. Felix von Luschan developed a set of 36 color tiles, not unlike those used by painters and decorators today. An Individual's skin color could then be compared to the 36 tiles (see Figure 8.9). Go ahead and try it. Unfortunately,

as you may discover, most of the lighter colors look much the same and it is difficult to get the same measure each time you use the von Luschan chromatic scale.

Today, researchers can more accurately measure skin color by actually measuring the percentage of light reflected from the skin. This technique is called light reflectance spectrophotometry and is performed using a, you guessed it, reflectance spectrophotometer (Figure 8.10). Paler skin reflects more light. A great example of the use of this equipment is a study by Clarence Gravlee, a University of Florida anthropologist. Gravlee measured skin color in this way in Puerto Rico and then compared the "objective" measure of skin color to how individuals classified each other by the Spanish term "color." The two measures are of course correlated, but not perfectly. Interestingly, the social classification seems to have more to do with blood pressure variation than the objective classification (see chapter 16)

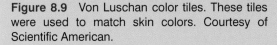

Figure 8.9 Von Luschan color tiles. These tiles were used to match skin colors. Courtesy of Scientific American.

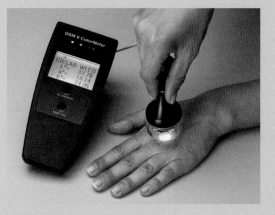

Figure 8.10 Example of use of a skin reflectance spectrophotometer. Courtesy of Cortex Technology.

NINA G. JABLONSKI

The Evolution and Meaning of Human Skin Color Variation

Nina G. Jablonski is Professor and Head of the Department of Anthropology at The Pennsylvania State University. Photograph by Dong Lin, courtesy of Nina Jablonski.

Human skin is mostly hairless and comes in a range of colors. Some people have very dark skin which is almost black, others have very pale skin which is nearly white. Most other people have skin that has a color somewhere in between. Skin color is remarkably variable in people from place to place, and differences in skin color started to be noticed thousands of years ago when people began traveling widely and engaging in long-distance trade. Observers noted that people who lived under intense sun close to the equator had dark skin and those who lived under weaker sun away from the equator had light skin. But why?

Many centuries ago, some early Greek and Roman philosophers speculated that skin color and other features were associated with climate. According to them, dark skin tones were produced by excessive heat and light tones by excessive cold. By the mid-1700s naturalists, including the American Samuel Stanhope Smith, observed that skin pigmentation showed a pronounced gradient according to latitude, from dark near the equator to light toward the poles. He related this mainly to differences in sunshine experienced by people at different latitudes: "This general uniformity in the effect," Smith wrote, "indicates an influence in climate, which under the same circumstances, will always operate in the same manner." But was it the heat caused by the sun or something else in the sunshine that skin was responding to?

By the middle of the 20th century, scientists such as Frederick Loomis determined that skin color was most strongly correlated with ultraviolet radiation (UVR) from the sun. In fact, my research shows that UVR accounts for over 87 percent of the variation in human skin color. So how can it be shown that human skin pigmentation is an actual evolutionary adaptation to UVR? In evolutionary terms, an adaptation is a characteristic of an organism that allows it to reproduce more successfully under certain environmental conditions than other organisms which don't have the characteristic. We first need to understand exactly what UVR is and what it does.

UVR is a highly energetic and invisible form of solar radiation, which is capable of causing a lot of damage to living organisms. Life on earth is mostly protected from damaging UV rays by our atmosphere, but some UVR still gets through and has powerful biological effects. UVR damages DNA, and this activity can eventually cause skin cancer. Skin cancer is bad, but it is rarely fatal and it mostly affects people after their child-bearing years. Other harmful effects of UVR have potentially much greater effects on reproductive success. Some wavelengths of UVR break down other important biological molecules, such as some forms of folate in the body. Folate is a B vitamin, which is needed to produce DNA and support cell metabolism. We normally get folate from green leafy vegetables, citrus fruits, and whole grains in our diet. Without adequate folate, we can't make sufficient amounts of DNA to maintain normal levels of cell division in our body. Cell division is needed to maintain the function of organs and tissues in our body, and is especially important in tissues with a high turnover, like the lining of the gut and the lining of the mouth. Cell division also occurs rapidly in the early embryo and in the production of sperm. During the first few weeks of embryonic development, rapid and precise cell division leads to the establishment of the basic body plan of the body, and the development of the early nervous system and circulation. If cell division is slowed or inhibited at this critical time, serious or even fatal birth defects can occur. Protection of the body's folate supplies is therefore important for successful reproduction. And successful reproduction is what evolution is all about. How then, was this insured?

When it comes to protection against harmful UVR, many biological systems have evolved natural sunscreens. Most natural sunscreens are special molecules which reduce UVR damage by absorbing or scattering UV rays. The pigment called melanin – and especially the most common type in human skin called eumelanin – is one of the most effective natural sunscreens. Eumelanin is intensely dark and has the ability to absorb potentially damaging UVR as well as neutralize harmful chemical byproducts caused by UVR exposure. Evolution often works by modifying biochemical pathways or structures that are already in existence. Ancestors of the human lineage had the ability to produce eumelanin in the naked skin on their faces and hands when they were exposed to UVR. When our ancestors lost most of their body hair, there was evolutionary pressure to protect exposed skin from the harmful effects of UVR. The solution to this problem was to make dark pigmentation permanent. This was accomplished by natural selection. Individuals who carried the genetic changes or mutations leading to the production of more protective eumelanin pigment left more offspring behind than those who didn't. Genetic studies have shown that some of the most important changes occurred in a gene called *MC1R*. This gene regulates the production of a protein called the melanocortin-1 receptor that plays an important role in normal pigmentation. All modern humans originated from darkly pigmented ancestors who evolved permanent eumelanin pigmentation in their skin to protect them from the UVR-rich sunshine of equatorial Africa.

When some of our modern human ancestors moved away from the most intensely sunny parts of Africa into southern Africa, Asia, and Europe, they encountered lower levels of UVR. This meant that they faced less potential damage to their bodies from harmful radiation, but there was also a downside. UVR is not a universally bad thing: the one important good thing it does is to initiate the process of making vitamin D in the skin. Vitamin D helps us to build and maintain a strong skeleton by regulating the absorption of calcium from the foods that we eat. Without enough vitamin D, bones don't develop properly and are weak. Vitamin D also helps to maintain the health of our immune systems. If we don't get enough vitamin D, our bodies can become physically weak and susceptible to disease. Only certain wavelengths of UVR are capable of starting the process of making vitamin D in the skin, and these are in the UVB range. The equator receives a lot of UVB throughout the year, but north and south of the tropics (23.5°N and 23.5°S) there is much less, and it falls in a highly seasonal pattern. And dark skin with lots of sun-protective melanin slows down the process of making vitamin D in the skin. So these circumstances posed another challenge to our ancestors. How could vitamin D production be main-

tained in people who were living under low UVB conditions? The answer is – with lighter skin.

Light skin is actually depigmented skin. When people started moving away from very sunny places with high levels of UVB to less sunny places with lower levels of UVB, those individuals who had lighter skin were able to stay healthier and leave more offspring. Evolution was at work again. The individuals with lighter skin had specific genetic mutations that resulted in their producing less eumelanin and so having less natural sunscreen in their skin. These new patterns of genetic variation were very successful. We see evidence, in fact, that "selective sweeps" – greatly accelerated periods of evolution by natural selection – led to genes for lighter skin becoming widespread over the course of just a few thousand years.

One of the most interesting and important things about the depigmentation process is that it didn't happen just once. Genetic evidence shows that that the ancestors of modern western Europeans and the ancestors of modern eastern Asians underwent independent genetic changes leading to the evolution of lighter skin. These changes involved different genetic mutations, which then were favored by natural selection. In other words, depigmentation evolved independently in both of the lineages of modern humans that began to inhabit higher latitudes of the northern hemisphere. We also know from the examination of ancient DNA that loss of skin pigmentation as a result of natural selection occurred in our distant, extinct cousins, the Neanderthals (*Homo neanderthalensis*), who inhabited much of eastern Europe and the region around the Mediterranean during the last ice age.

As modern humans moved around the world in greater numbers and over longer distances in the time between 50,000 and 10,000 years ago, a lot of "fine tuning" occurred in the evolution of skin pigmentation. As populations moved to parts of the world with different UVR levels, they underwent genetic changes that modified their skin pigmentation. As people moved into the Americas from Asia, for instance, we see evidence that some populations entering high UVR environments underwent genetic changes which made it possible for them to tan easily. Tanning is the ability to develop temporary melanin pigmentation in the skin in response to UVR, and has evolved numerous times in peoples living under highly seasonal patterns of sunshine.

In the last 10,000 years, we have become better and better at protecting ourselves against the extremes of UVR by cultural means. Sewn clothing and constructed shelters now protect us from strong sunlight, and augment the protection afforded by natural melanin pigmentation. In far northern environments, diets composed of vitamin D-rich foods like oily fish and marine mammals supplement the vitamin D we can make in our skin under low UVR conditions. The major problem we face today is that we are able to travel so far so fast. Many people today live or take vacations far away from the lands of their ancestors. This means that, often, our skin color is mismatched to the UVR levels we are experiencing. Darkly pigmented people living in low UVR environments, and people working indoors all of the time, are at high risk of developing vitamin D deficiencies.

Lightly pigmented people living in high UVR environments are at high risk of developing skin cancers. We must recognize these issues in order to avoid major health problems.

Skin pigmentation provides one of the best examples of evolution by natural selection acting on the human body. The fact that skin color has been so responsive to evolutionary forces is fascinating and it is important for modern human societies. Similar skin colors – both dark and light – have evolved independently multiple times in human history. When we think of how races have been defined in the past using skin color, we can immediately see the problem. When the same skin color has evolved many times independently in different places, its value as a unique marker of identity is eliminated and the race so defined is rendered nonsensical. Just enjoy being a "hue-man"!

Skin Color Does Not Explain Deeper Traits

Pictures and the television camera tell us that the people of Oslo in Norway, Cairo in Egypt, and Nairobi and Kenya look very different. And when we actually meet people from these separate places, we can see representations of those differences at first hand. But if one were to walk along the Nile from Cairo to Khartoum in the Sudan and on to Nairobi, there would be no visible boundary between one people and another. The same thing would be true if one were walk north from Cairo up into Russia, eventually swinging west to Scandinavia. The people at any adjacent stops along the way look like one another more than they look like anyone else since, after all, they are related to one another. As a rule, the boy marries the girl next door throughout the whole world, but next door goes on without stop from one region to another. (C. Loring Brace, anthropologist, University of Michigan: RACE exhibit, SMM)

Skin color, of course, often serves as the primary racial "marker" in the United States and elsewhere. Yet it is actually one of the most useful *phenotypic* traits for demonstrating the explanatory limits of biological race. This is because assumptions behind traditional

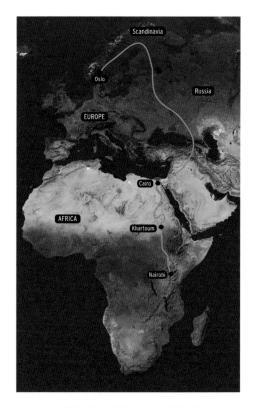

Figure 8.11 Walk from Nairobi to Oslo. Courtesy of the Science Museum of Minnesota/Roger Boehm.

race-based classifications contradict two concepts that relate to human biological variation.

Skin color has nothing scientifically to do with race. As we have shown in the above, skin color has a different explanation – evolution. Specifically, skin color varies as a result of selection for ability to process vitamin D versus protect against the degradation of folate. Furthermore, many dark-skinned individuals – from southern India and Sri Lanka, from Central Africa and from the Pacific Islands, vary greatly in other traits, and have evolved separately. In folk terms, we would classify them as being from different races, even though their skin tones are very similar.

The first concept that is exemplified in the distribution of skin color is *continuous variation*. Once again, the geographic distribution of skin color is shown in Figure 8.4. Notice that the gradual blending of skin colors into one another across clines and populations is a function of geographic distance and simply does not lend itself to any clear separation. As a result, racial distinctions based on skin color (and other continuous traits) are arbitrary – or at least unempirical.

The last important lesson is that skin color does not explain many other variations. Recall the cube with four layers (see Figure 7.5, the cube of variation) and each layer represents the distribution of a different trait. In this example, the top layer is skin color, then eye color, hair color, and hair form. We could imagine other traits like height and weight or genetic traits. Now we have drilled four cores, to expose the four layers. Each core could be an individual or a group. The two cores on the right have the same skin color. But now notice that the deeper layers are different. In other words, the top layer did not predict for the deeper layers.

This is because skin color is only weakly correlated with most other human traits. Skin color cannot predict other traits. The same is true, interestingly, for all human traits. Traits having to do with color are slightly correlated with each other as are traits having to do with size. But the size traits are not correlated with the color traits, and neither size or color traits are correlated in any strong and meaningful way with other genetic traits or complex traits. This is called nonconcordance or trait independence. What it means is

that evolution tends to select a few traits together, but not large clusters. It also means that if race is skin color, then it is only skin deep.

Conclusions

How will skin color variation, race, and racism continue to coevolve in the United States? This is not easy to predict. Skin color variation is an important and fascinating aspect of human history and health. Indeed, an ecological understanding of skin color is vital for protecting DNA and maintaining healthy vitamin D and folate levels, which are critical to skeletal growth and development and reproductive health.

Some suggest that as we become more at ease with our nation's multiracial legacy, racial classifications and identities will become more fluid. Yet, even in parts of the world where racial identities are already more complex than those traditionally employed in the United States, skin color discrimination persists. This underscores the need to abandon the very idea of human biological races. As we hope is now clear, this is not tantamount to arguing against the existence of biological differences between human populations. Rather, it is a vital step towards understanding which of those differences are important and why we should explore and, ultimately, celebrate them.

As noted anthropologist C. Loring Brace explains, variation is continuously graded. That is one of the clear lessons of skin color. Another deeper lesson is that evolution rather than race explains the remarkable variation. As we will explain in chapter 9, life is a remarkable balance.

Additional Resources

Blum, H. F.
1961   Does the Melanin Pigment of Human Skin Have Adaptive Value? Quarterly Review of Biology 3:50–63.
Brace, C. Loring
2005   "Race" Is a Four Letter Word: The Genesis of the Concept. Oxford University Press, New York.
http://www.understandingRACE.org/humvar/index.html
Jablonski, Nina G.
2006   Skin: A Natural History. Berkeley: University of California Press.

Jablonski, Nina G., and George Chaplin
2000   The Evolution of Human Skin Coloration. Journal of Human Evolution 39(1):57–106.

Loomis, W. F.
1967   Skin-Pigment Regulation of Vitamin-D Biosynthesis in Man. Science 157:501–506.

Relethford, J. H.
2000   Human Skin Color Diversity is Highest in Sub-Saharan African Populations. Human Biology; An International Record of Research 72(5):773–780. PMID 11126724.

Roberts, D. F.
1977   Human Pigmentation: Its Geographical and Racial Distribution And Biological Significance. Journal of the Society of Cosmetic Chemists 28:329–342.

9

Sickle Cell Disease

Not for Blacks Only

Although sickle cell anemia is viewed as a "black" disease in the United States, the gene variation that causes it is common in parts of Africa, the Middle East, southern Europe and South Asia. It is widely thought that the sickling of the red blood cells originally arose through natural selection as a protective response to malaria. People who are "sicklers" are less likely to die from malaria.

Cathy J. Tashiro, Professor of Nursing, University of Washington: RACE exhibit, SMM

The genetic variant called sickle cell provides a breathtaking example of how human evolution shapes variation. Sickle cell disease, and the human genetic variant called sickle cell trait (one copy of the sickle cell allele compared to two in sickle cell disease) are the results, like skin color, of the biocultural processes of evolution and human history. In this case, the evolutionary stressor is singular and clear: malaria. Ever since humans came into contact with the malaria parasite, carried by mosquitoes, humans have suffered and died in the millions. Malaria has resisted eradication and continues to kills thousands and millions of individuals each year. Sickle cell trait, however, a single copy of the genetic variation, appears to be an efficient genetic compromise between malaria and sickle cell disease. Sickle cell trait confers resistance to malaria without the detriments of sickle cell disease.

Yet, another interesting aspect of sickle cell is how a trait became so fixed in our culture as a disease of blacks, of Africans, whereas the association with Africa is non-causal.

(a)   (b)

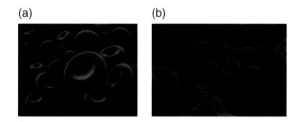

Figure 9.1 Normal red blood cells (a) and sickled red blood cells (b). Rich in oxygen-carrying hemoglobin, healthy red blood cells are flexible disks that move easily though the small blood vessels. On the other hand, the crescent-shaped red blood cells can coagulate and get stuck in small blood vessels, causing an anemic crisis. Courtesy of (a) Omikron/Photo Researchers, Inc. and (b) © iStockphoto.com/adventtr.

Race: Are We So Different?, First Edition. Alan H. Goodman, Yolanda T. Moses, and Joseph L. Jones.
© 2012 American Anthropological Association. Published 2012 by Blackwell Publishing Ltd.

Medical History: The Discovery of Strangely Shaped Red Blood Cells

"Sickling" of red blood cells was initially discovered by medical doctors in the United States and Europe. It was found in individuals of African descent. The first discovery of sickle-shaped cells was published around a century ago. This was a time when diseases were often viewed as "racial" and sickle cell fell into this classificatory scheme as a disease of "negro blood." Sickling was quickly and firmly framed in the medical literature as a condition distinct to the so-called Negro type. At this time a wide variety of diseases from heart disease to ovarian cysts were cast in this racial framework. In retrospect, the classifications often made little medical or biological sense. However, at the time a prevailing medical thought was that Europeans (whites) were indeed more susceptible to so-called diseases of civilization (another odd classification) whereas blacks were not. Of course, today we know that these "diseases of civilization," such as cancer and heart disease, are even more deadly to African Americans than they are to white Americans.

Once sickle cell was first associated with African descent it was hard to break the association. Medical knowledge that is assumed to be true is easily handed down from teacher to students and from one edition of a textbook to another. Indeed, this association of sickle cell with African descent remains today, at least in popular culture. It is of course true that, if one is of African heritage, especially from West Africa, where the frequency of the trait is highest, one is more likely to have sickle cell, but as we shall see, it is not "inherent" to black blood as explained by race.

With the development and increased use of the microscope in medicine and the birth of the medical specialty of hematology, the study of blood and its disorders, it did not take long to discover that not all red blood cells are similarly perfectly shaped. In his writing on the fourth published case of sickle cell in 1922, Vernon Mason writes: "It is of particular interest that up to the present the malady has been seen only in the negro" (1922:1320). A few years later the influential hematologist Thomas B. Cooley concurs that "sickle cell anemia is distinctly racial" (1928:1258).

The paradigm of a distinctly racial disease challenged the diagnosis of sickle cell anemia in a European. Physicians who discovered sickle cells in a presumably European patient first searched for evidence of African admixture rather than challenge the racial distinctiveness of the variant (Tapper 1995). For example, T. S. Lawrence, an American physician, states of a possible case of sickle cell in a European, "Special attention was paid to the question of racial admixture of negro blood in the family but no evidence could be obtained. ... There must be some caution in calling this sickle cell anemia because no evidence of negro blood could be found" (Lawrence 1927:44).

The linking of races as distinct types with distinct diseases blinded physicians to the possibility that sickle cell was not purely a disease of blacks. Today, it is still widely accepted that sickle cell is somehow associated with blackness. Here, we will first explain what sickle cell is, how it evolved, and why sickle cell is an example of selection, evolution, and history, rather than race.

What is Sickle Cell? Genetics and Physiological Consequences

Sickle cell is a variant of the red blood cell (see Figure 9.1). It is a phenotypic variant that can be seen by examining blood cells under a microscope. This phenotypic variant was discovered about a century ago. The question of what causes it and why is medically significant.

Most phenotypic variations, such as skin color or the risk of heart disease, are remarkably complex. They are not only the result of mixtures of multiple genes and environmental conditions, but the mix changes from person to person and even over the lifetime of a person. So, one cannot easily pinpoint single causes or sometimes say that x is the cause of y percent of the condition. If we could do that, we would do much better in preventing and curing diseases and, we would imagine, in solving lots of problems.

As in life, variations tend to be complex. Two siblings grow up in the same house and have much the same alleles, they share lots of their environment and genetics, but can be remarkably different in significant ways. Most phenotypes are complex riddles.

Sickle cell is thankfully about as simple as you get. It is classified as a simple genetic condition (one could say disease or disorder but these sound judgmental even if they are not meant to be). A simple genetic condition is one that is caused by a change in a single gene and is clearly expressed phenotypically. We can see the result of that change and there are not a lot of gradations in between. That is, there is little variation in the phenotypic result. The allele show through. This is called penetrance.

With the exception of genes on the X and Y chromosomes in males, an individual receives two copies of each gene, and thus two chances to turn the gene into action and make the gene product. In the well known case of sickle cell, the gene codes for part of the hemoglobin molecule. What this all boils down to is that the gene is on chromosome 11. It makes what is called the beta chain or beta globin molecule, a string of 146 amino acids that is essential to the shape of the hemoglobin molecule. At the sixth position a simple point mutation occurred and changed a letter A to a G that changed the amino acid from a guanine to a valine. Like that, the beta chain wraps differently. Getting one or two of the sickle cell alleles makes a big difference. One copy = sickle cell trait; two copies = sickle cell disease.

Hemoglobin is a remarkable molecule. It is a protein with four amino acid arms (or chains) and an iron molecule attached (see Figure 9.2). The remarkable design has consequence for the shape of the red blood cells. However, its main function in life is to allow red blood cells to transport oxygen from the lungs to the cells, where it is used. The red color of blood comes from a change in the hemoglobin molecule when oxygen is attached to the iron molecule. The redder the better.

Going deeper, we have long known that a gene codes for the amino acid sequence of the chains of the hemoglobin molecule. There are a number of known variations in the gene for hemoglobin that result in different amino acid sequences. The sickle cell variation is the result of a single substitution of one amino acid for another. The result changes the shape of the molecule and subsequently leads to red blood cells that are rigid, sticky, and shaped like a crescent, or sickle. Normally, red blood cells look like discs. The sickled cells do not carry oxygen as effectively and

Figure 9.2 The structure of hemoglobin. Adult human hemoglobin molecules consist of four chains of amino acids (or polypeptide chains) and four heme groups. In this "ribbon model," the alpha (α) chains are red and the beta (β) chains are blue. Each chain carries a heme group, a nonprotein molecule that contains an iron atom that in turn can carry a molecule of oxygen. Here, the heme groups are designated in green. This image was created from the Research Collaboratory for Structural Bioinformatics Protein Data Bank ID 1GZX using PyMOL. Courtesy of Richard Wheeler.

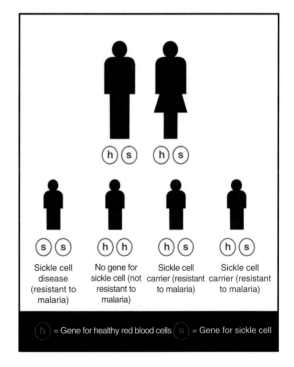

Figure 9.3 How individuals might inherit sickle cell disease and sickle cell trait. In this example, two individuals who both have sickle cell trait have children. Courtesy of the Science Museum of Minnesota/C. Johnson.

may get stuck in small vessels, blocking the flow of blood, causing anemia, joint pain, and damaging the bones, lungs, kidneys, eyes, and other organs. Each of us receives two copies of every gene – one from each parent. If both parents have one copy of the sickle cell gene, each of their children has a one-in-four chance of having sickle cell disease. But children who inherit just one copy of the sickle cell gene do not have sickle cell disease and also have added resistance to malaria.

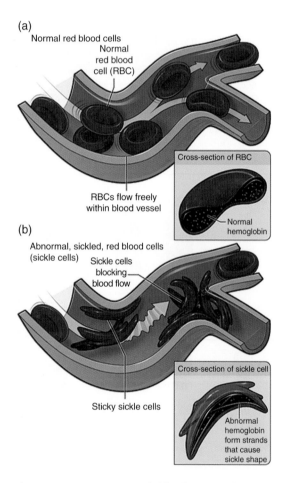

Figure 9.4 Cross section of a blood vessel with normally shaped red blood cells (a) and sickled red blood cells (b). The sickled cells can coagulate and have a much harder time carrying oxygen. Courtesy of the National Heart, Lung, and Blood Institute, National Institutes of Health, U.S. Department of Health and Human Services.

The question that evolutionary anthropologists think they have answered is why such a variant that could lead to a disease, sickle cell, could become so common. The answer to the riddle is this resistance to malaria. The details are fascinating.

The Sickle Cell Story: Unnatural History of the Mosquito, Humans, and Malaria

Malaria is a debilitating parasitic disease. It is transmitted to humans by the bite of a mosquito carrying the malaria parasite. The parasite, once transmitted, can multiply inside red blood cells, which then rupture and infect other red blood cells. Malaria symptoms typically begin between ten days and a few weeks after the initial bite. One consequence of the infection is anemia, resulting from the destruction of the red blood cells.

Malaria is a major health threat. The Center for Disease Control has estimated that there are as many as 500 million cases of malaria each year, and more than one million people die annually. Malaria remains the leading cause of death in Africa for children under five years of age. Malaria persists in part

Figure 9.5 Farming in humid climates that results in pools of stagnant water is part of the cause of malaria. The same gene mutation that causes sickle cell disease also provides protection from malaria. People whose ancestors were from areas where malaria was common are more likely to carry the sickle cell gene variation. History and evolution explain sickle cell. © iStockphoto.com/dannyzhan.

because the conditions that have always led to infected mosquitoes coming into contact with humans – stagnant waters in hot, humid climates – persist. Furthermore, the mosquitoes that carry

Figure 9.6 *Anopheles minimus.* In order to contract malaria, humans must come into contact with mosquitoes. Courtesy of U.S. Centers for Disease Control and Prevention, U.S. Department of Health and Human Services.

malaria, in particular *Anopheles*, develop resistance to insecticides, and the parasite itself can develop resistance to antibiotics.

One of the best ways to resist malaria is one of the oldest – a genetic adaptation. The sickle cell story was uncovered by some serious scientific detective work by anthropologist Frank Livingstone and others working at about the same time. The group that happened on the mysterious evolution of sickle cell also includes the Nobel Prize winner Linus Pauling. Pauling helped to discover that sickle cell anemia is caused by an alteration in the hemoglobin protein's molecular structure. His paper reporting this discovery, "Sickle Cell Anemia, a Molecular Disease," was published in *Science* in 1949 and later led geneticists and anthropologists to further unravel the evolution of sickle cell.

Sometime around five to eight thousand years ago agriculture began to take hold in semitropical and tropical areas including West Africa, the

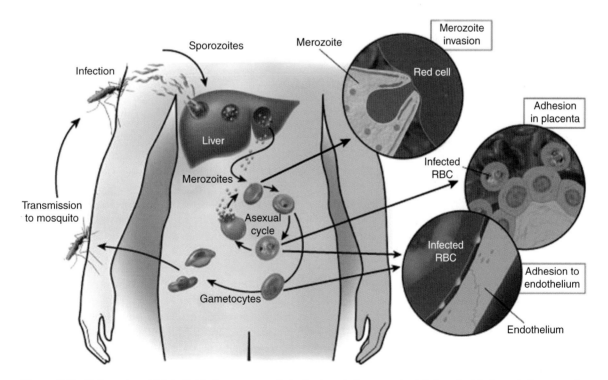

Figure 9.7 Pathway by which individuals contract malaria. An Anopheles mosquito is infected with the malaria sporozoite in its gut. The mosquito bites a human and the sporozoite gets to the human, transforms, multiplies, and invades red blood cells. Reprinted by permission from Macmillan Publishers Ltd: Nature, The Pathogenic Basis of Malaria by Louis Miller, Dror Baruch, Kevin Marsh and Ogobara Doumbo, © 2002, Nature Publishing Group.

Figure 9.8 Distribution of malaria. This map represents the distribution of malaria prior to the widespread use of pesticides that reduced the mosquito populations transmitting the disease. Courtesy of the Science Museum of Minnesota/Paul Morin.

Mediterranean, southern India, and the Arabian Peninsula: areas that were also inhabited by mosquitos. With agriculture came a growth in the human population, increasing the potential for human contact with malaria-carrying mosquitoes. As well, it is likely that the slow-moving breeding ponds for mosquitoes were increased by land clearance: the density of humans and mosquitoes increased at the same time and in the same place.

As is clear, malaria is among the most debilitating and deadly illnesses, so if ever there was one for which a genetic adaptation would be worth a cost, it is the adaptation to malaria. Indeed, there are a variety of different sequences to the hemoglobin molecule,

some of which appear to make it more difficult for the malaria parasite to wreak its havoc. Sickle cell is one of those. It appears to be a balanced polymorphism, a genetic condition in which the heterozygote is selected for over either homozygotic condition. The balance is a trickly one between the selective disadvantages of either having a double dose of sickle cell or decreased resistance to malaria. One copy provides the optimal advantage between malaria on the one hand and sickle cell disease on the other.

All of this is speculative. However, if there is a smoking gun in this detective story it is the map of the distribution of the frequency of the sickle cell allele compared to a map of areas of high human

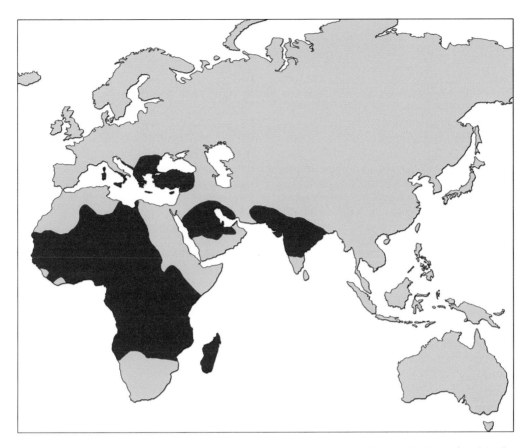

Figure 9.9 Distribution of the genetic variation that causes sickle cell disease. The trait has been found in those with Middle Eastern, Indian, Mediterranean, and African heritage. Millions worldwide suffer complications of sickle cell disease. Sickle cell is found in high frequencies in areas that experienced endemic malaria because of the clearing of forests for agricultural lands. Courtesy of the Science Museum of Minnesota/Paul Morin.

habitation, agriculture, and especially zones in which the anopheles mosquito is found. Sickle cell trait is clearly highest in places such as West Africa where all the preconditions are met. In fact, there appear to be four places where sickle cell trait peaks, and it is quite possible that selection favored this trait and it spread independently in four areas.

Race and Sickle Cell

In conclusion, sickle cell appears to be the result of human history and evolution. Race has nothing to do with the genetic adaptation. This is true on a conceptual level. The above explanation does not mention race and there is no need to invoke race in any of the explanation. Thus, the early association of sickle cell as a "disease of negro blood" is profoundly in error. We can also see from the maps of distribution of sickle cell that it is not uncommon for individuals who are not "black" to have the sickle cell trait and the reverse is also true. Many "blacks," such as those from northern and southern Africa, are unlikely to have sickle cell.

Standards and Race: Iron Deficiency

There are at least two ways that race gets into medicine. On one extreme is informal and individually held knowledge. Medical personnel may see patients as members of a certain race. They then interact and act based on what they think they know about individuals of that race. Do they complain at the slightest ache? If they are asked to take a medication, will they? Will they understand instructions? Are they susceptible to a particular illness? In the face of little formal information on racial differences, these individual impressions and stereotypes do a great deal of work.

But science likes to set up categories and make things more formal. Do we need separate formulae to estimate the stature of a Mexican (see "Height, History, and Human Variation" in chapter 7)? Do we give a separate dose of a drug to Chinese women? Do we change the settings on an x-ray machine with a black patient? Do we diagnose a nutritional deficiency differently in black and white children?

Research on race and anemia provides a useful example of the extreme public health implication of assuming group differences are real and pan-racial. In the 1970s Stanley Garn and colleagues presented data on the distribution of hemoglobin levels in blacks and whites in the United States. Garn was a graduate of the Harvard University anthropology program. He coauthored Races with Coon in 1950 and went on to a record setting career as a physical anthropologist at University of Michigan (Coon et al. 1950).

Garn and his colleagues reported an approximate 1.0 g/dl mean difference in hemoglobin volume (blacks less than whites; Garn et al., 1974; 1975; Garn 1976). Following this work the suggestion was made to institute separate cut-offs for anemia for blacks and whites, a suggestion that is still widely supported (Pan and Habicht 1991).

Robert Jackson (1990; 1992; 1993; R. Jackson and F. L. C. Jackson, 1991) has reexamined some of these same data and has introduced new data. He has endeavored to control, as much as is possible, for obvious environmental factors such as iron intake, and to eliminate from analysis low hemoglobin values that may be related to genetic anemias. What Jackson and Jackson find is that the mean hemoglobin difference between blacks and whites is reduced to the 0.2–0.3 g/dl range when these obvious environmental factors and hemoglobin variants are controlled for. Furthermore, inconsistent variation between black and white infants, for example, where black infants had higher hemoglobin values before six months and white infants higher values after six months, does not suggest genetic etiology (Jackson 1993).

Despite these data, even very knowledgeable researchers such as Pan and Habicht (1991) continue to call for separate hemoglobin cut-offs for classification of anemia in blacks and whites. What are the policy implications of separate cut-offs? If the black cut-off is reduced just 0.5 g/dl, from 12.0 g/dl to 11.5 g/dl, half the difference proposed by Garn et al. (1974), the prevalence of anemia in nonpregnant, nonlactating black women (18–44 yrs) is estimated to be reduced "on paper" from 20 to 10 percent (Pan and Habicht 1991). The result is thousands and even millions of cases of under-treated anemia.

Yet still, separate cut-offs are supported despite the fact that the purported "race" difference in iron metabolism has no known genetic basis, especially one that suggests that blacks are uniformly more efficient than whites in their metabolism of iron, or that they somehow do just as well on 0.5 g/dl less hemoglobin. Nor has it been proven that the difference is pan-racial, Moreover, the issue is more than a theoretical one: separate cut-offs lead to profound health implications when one considers some of the functional consequences (in learning, work, and immunological capacity) of low hemoglobin values in ranges near anemia cut-off values (Scrimshaw 1991).

I Have Sickle Cell

When I was born in 1976, my doctors took vial after vial of blood from my foot but never told my mom why. There was obviously something different about me, but they could not figure it out. It turns out that I have sickle cell, but they never tested me for that because I am white. My mother is a first generation American from Italy, and my father was born in Sicily. I even had some of the common side effects of the disease, such as an enlarged spleen. But they still did not think to test me for it.

In 1986, after 10 years of extreme joint pain, confusion, and frustration, I was diagnosed with a form of sickle cell disease. Finally, there was a name for the pain and a way to treat it! However, most people still do not believe me, and even new doctors have a hard time seeing past my color to help treat me. Because of my limitations, I have to explain my disease to doctors, dentists, employers, and peers.

In 2004 my wife gave birth to our daughter, Angelina, and her newborn screening test was abnormal for sickle cell. When my family had her tested to determine exactly what she carried, every doctor there assumed there was some mistake. Much to their surprise, our little light-haired, green-eyed daughter in fact does carry the sickle cell trait!

We are lucky to live a normal life, and I have learned how to limit and control my sickle attacks. However, people continue to assume that sickle cell is a disease that only affects people of African ancestry. (Frank Giacomazza)

Figure 9.10 Frank Giacomazza and his daughter, Angelina. Courtesy of Vickie Giacomazza.

Race and Athletic Performance

An Interview with Joseph Graves

Joseph L. Graves, Jr. is Associate Dean for Research and Professor of Biological Studies at the Joint School for Nanoscience and Nanoengineering, jointly administered by North Carolina Agricultural and Technical State University and UNC Greensboro. Using his background in evolutionary biology, he has also written extensively on myths and theories of race in American society and particularly on race and athletic performance.

Is There Any Link between Race, Genes, and Athletics?

I'm going to start with the idea that many people hold that there is some special athletic prowess held by people of African descent in America. Most people sort of believe that African Americans are genetically predisposed to being faster runners or better basketball players or for being better cornerbacks in the National Football League. And there's also now some scientific studies which are attempting to look at population-based differences in genes that have to do with various aspects of physiological performance related to athletic ability.

Now, at some level, when we look at human physical variation, there are some differences between human populations that could possibly relate to athletic performance. For example, if we were to look at people from northern climates, who were indigenous residents of northern climates, they tend to be short and stout instead of long or tall and lean. And there are good physical reasons for that. If you evolved in northern climates, like the Aleut or the Eskimo populations did, heat retention is facilitated by being short and stout. If you evolved in the tropics, where the environment is very hot, then heat loss is facilitated by being long and lean. So you're going to see differences in body proportions on that kind of scale.

Now, if you were to ask yourself, "Is it likely that an Alaskan Eskimo is going to become a center in the NBA?" well, probably not, because height has something to do with your performance at that position in the NBA. So, we can see that in the gross scale it's likely that physical differences may have something to do with various forms of athletic performance.

But when we talk about subtle things like, for example, whether a given population is going to be fastest in sprinting, then it's not so simple. The fact is that most of the world record holders in the 100-meter dash are of Western African descent, but they also tend to be African Americans who have mixed with Europeans and American Indians. So it's not easy for us to determine whether it's being African that might have something to do with them being so fast, or whether it's the fact that they have European and American Indian ancestry that might have helped them be so fast.

And all of those genetic factors have to be tempered in terms of the environment in which individuals train. For example, if you look at those sprinters of Western African ancestry, they all got their records because they trained in the United States, Canada, Great Britain, or even in the Caribbean. If you look at the Western African countries where those sprinters' ancestors supposedly came from, none of those countries have ever produced any world record holders in the sprint events.

So if it was something uniquely about being African that makes you a fast sprinter, then you'd expect that Western African countries would be holding all these records too, but in fact they don't. It has something to do with genetic predisposition, it has something to do with environment, it has something to do with

training regimes, and particularly at the level of world-class athletic performance.

One of the factors that shows how the situation of populations in different geographical regions influences predisposition for sport is altitude. The Kenyan success in long-distance running may have something to do with the fact that the Kalenjin Kenyans come from a high-altitude region in Kenya. But, Kenyans from low altitudes don't do well in long-distance running, so it's not something special about being a Kenyan, it's something special about living at those high altitudes.

Now, in the last Boston Marathon, which [laughter] someone predicted would be won by a Kalenjin Kenyan, it was in fact won by a South Korean. Now, Korea is also a mountainous country, and so it's entirely possible that this individual at least trained at high altitude. Second place was won by an Ecuadorian, which also is a mountainous country, and they also probably trained at a high altitude.

So we have both short-term physiological adaptation that occurs from training in high altitude, and also long-term genetic adaptations for living at high altitude that might come from populations who live in those regions. And again, none of these things are consistent with our 19th century notions of race, because within the same country low-altitude Kenyans don't do well at long-distance running whereas high-altitude Kenyans do.

So we can't come to any fast, hard rule about how genetic ancestry is going to influence the ability of an individual to perform an athletic event. I think that the simplest thing is to look at the individual's history, how hard they trained, where they got their training, what kinds of resources were put into getting them to be able to participate in world-class athletics, that it's a combination of all these things and that we'll never have a simple genetic answer that says, "Because you came from this region of the world, you're going to dominate in swimming or long-distance running." I don't think we're ever going to have that.

Do Discussions of Superior Athletic Ability Always Imply Inferiority In Other Areas, Like Intellect?

American society has created a mythology about the African American male in particular. If an African

American male is walking on a major college campus, they are more likely to be thought of as an athlete or a coach of an athletic team than as a faculty member. On my own campus, when I walk to classes, students often come up to me and ask me if I'm the football coach or the basketball coach. And I tell them, "No, I'm a professor in the department of life sciences." And when I come in to teach genetics in the fall, 99% of the Euro-American students in my class have never seen an African American professor teach a science class in the time that they've been enrolled in science courses.

So we have a social history of believing that African Americans cannot perform intellectually. When most Americans see African Americans it's in the context of sports and entertainment. If you look at television shows and the television coverage of African Americans, what most Americans see on the news at night, is African Americans in sports – and unfortunately recently it's been African American sports figures in trouble with the law – and it's been African Americans in entertainment or it's been African Americans in comedy. So we sort of go back to the history of the minstrel show, in terms of the way that the African American is treated in American social life.

How Have the Groups that Dominate Certain Sports Changed over Time?

One of the funny things about athleticism and sports is how the expectations of athletic performance change through the years. For example, in the sixties everyone thought that Africans were fast, and so they expected African Americans to win sprint events, but that the long-distance events were all going to be won by Europeans or Middle Easterners. Then the Kenyans came along and began to dominate long-distance track and field.

When professional basketball first began, one of the best teams was made up of mainly Eastern European Jews, and it was said that the reason why they were so good at basketball was because the "artful dodger" characteristic of the Jewish culture made them good at this sport.

There were also, in boxing, at the turn of the century, a lot of European immigrant groups, particularly Irish, who were important in boxing [as well as Jews].

And that has changed. In sprinting, track and field events, it was said that Africans and African Americans were fast and so they could run the short distances but the long distances belonged to Europeans. But then again, the Kenyans came along and blew that theory out of the water.

And so we even see today sports that have been traditionally dominated by people of upper-middle-class backgrounds, like tennis and golf – the arrival of the Williams sisters in tennis and Tiger Woods in golf – has made some people think that there's something general about being African or African American descent that makes you excellent in athletics.

But I think the history shows us that as opportunities change in society, different groups get drawn into sporting arenas and depending upon, again, opportunity and training, along with individual motivation, that determines who becomes the champion. I don't think it's so much genetic predisposition from some particular region of the world, and certainly it's not race, because as we pointed out in this program that [sic] there are no biological races in the human species.

So we have seen, particularly in professional athletics over the last couple of decades, a change in its composition. In the 1950s, social discrimination barred African American athletes from pursuing a career in baseball, in football, in basketball. And now that discrimination has been removed and people with athletic ability of all ethnicities have had a chance to enter sports, and in that time period African Americans now have excelled. Some people argue that this is necessarily a result of the genetic superiority of the African American athlete.

I argue that we don't know this, and, in fact, again, it would be difficult to make that claim based upon all of the things that are required for someone to excel in a given sport. Also, football, basketball, and baseball, are not the only sports in America. If we look at other sports, such as, for example, soccer or lacrosse or volleyball, we don't see African Americans dominating those sports. It takes just as much athletic ability to do well in those sports as in baseball, basketball, and football.

So there are strong cultural aspects of what sports individuals choose to play, along with access and training that have something to do with one's performance.

So I don't think we're ever going to be able to isolate the African American gene for athletic performance. I don't think such a gene exists. Given what we know about the overlap of populations and genetic composition, I think it's highly unlikely that alone would [explain] differences in sports prowess.

It has to do with the interaction of individual genetic background, of opportunity, and training, and I think we should get used to the idea that that's what we're going to know, and we shouldn't be worried about the fact that we can't locate the athletic gene.

Conclusions

Sickle cell shows us how we want to put traits into boxes. We then seem to want to hit them with the same crude hammer until they explain something. But they often break instead of revealing something useful and true. Worse, we have spent some much time using the wrong concept, the wrong tool, that we forget the original question. How does variation come about? Why? Now go explain sickle cell to a friend or family member. Try it.

References

Ashley-Koch, A. Q. Yang, and R. S. Olney
1998   Hemoglobin S Allele and Sickle Cell Disease. American Journal of Epidemiology 151(9):839–45. http://www.cdc.gov/genomics/hugenet/reviews/sickle.htm, accessed September 2003.

Cooley, Thomas B.
1928   Likenesses and Contrasts in the Hemolytic Anemias of Childhood. American Journal of Diseases of Childhood 36(6):1257–1262.

Garn, S. M., N. J. Smith, and D. C. Clark
1974   Race Differences in Hemoglobin Levels. Ecology of Food & Nutrition 3:299–301.

Garn, S. M., A. S. Ryan, G. M. Owen et al.
1975   Income Matched Blackwhite Differences in Hemoglobin Levels after Correction for Low Transferrin Saturations. American Journal of Clinical Nutrition 28:563–568.

Garn, S. M.
1976   Problems in the Nutritional Assessment of Black Individuals. American Journal of Public Health 66:262–267.

Jackson, R. T.
1992   Hemoglobin Comparisons between African American and European American Males with Hemoglobin Values in the Normal Range. Journal of Human Biology 4:313–318.

Jackson, R. T., and F. L. C. Jackson
1991   Reassessing hereditary interethnic differences in anemia status. Ethnicity and Disease 1:27–41.

Johns Hopkins University, Baltimore, MD
N.d.   Mendelian Inheritance in Man, Online Mendelian Inheritance in Man (TM). MIM No.141900. http://www.ncbi.nlm.nih.gov/entrez/query.fcgi?db=OMIM, accessed September 2003.

Joint Center for Sickle Cell and Thalassemic Disorders
N.d.   How Does Sickle Cell Cause Disease? http://sickle.bwh.harvard.edu/scd_background.html, accessed September 2003.

Lawrence, J. S.
1927   Elliptical and Sickle-Shaped Erythrocytes in the Circulating Blood of White Persons. Journal of Clinical Investigations 5(1):31–49.

Mason, V. R.
1922   Sickle Cell Anemia. Journal of the American Medical Association 79(16):1318–1320.

Pan, W. H., and J. P. Habicht
1991   The Non-iron-deficiency-related Differences in Hemoglobin Concentration Distribution between Blacks and Whites and between Men and Women. American Journal of Epidemiology 134:1410–16.

Scrimshaw, Nevin
1991   Iron Deficiency. Scientific American (October), 46–62.

Tapper, Melbourne
1995   Interrogating Bodies: Medico-Racial Knowledge, Politics, and the Study of a Disease. Comparative Studies of Society and History 37:76–93.

Additional Resources

- CDC resources on Sickle Cell Disease: http://www.cdc.gov/ncbddd/sicklecell/resources.htm.
- http://raceproject.org
- Sickle cell foundation of Oregon. http://dev.yellowsolutions.ro/sicklecell/about_sickle_cell.html.

10

The Apportionment of Variation, *or ...*
Why We Are All Africans Under the Skin

Introduction

The key question we are grappling with in this chapter concerns the very structure of human genetic and phenotypic variation. Some of what we have explained in the introduction and in previous chapters is that variation tends to be continuous and that the geographic variation in one trait is structured or patterned differently from that in another trait. As we have seen, the above rule applies to skin color and sickle cell anemia.

Here, we delve into the heart of the matter: whether genetic variation is apportioned along racial lines. Said another way, Does race explain the structure of human variation? Along the way you will be introduced to the history of the study of the apportionment of human variation and then forces of evolution that shaped the current distribution, and finally a surprising recent find on the preponderance of variation in Africa.

Ashley Montagu and the Myth of Race

In the 1940s, the renegade British-born and US-trained anthropologist Ashley Montagu wrote a brilliant book called *The Myth of Race*. Coming off

the horrors of World War II and continued racism and segregation in the United States, Montagu followed in the intellectual footsteps of W. E. B. DuBois and his mentor at Columbia, Franz Boas, in showing that the idea of human races was, at best, a biocultural classification. As a classification, it was cultural rather than based on universal facts. It had no evolutionary basis and it invoked a static view of diversity. He considered individuals who used this scheme to be non-evolutionary and old in their thinking. Certainly, Montagu argued, race failed to explain difference.

As well, the ideal type left little room for differences that were the result of environment. Boas, a German Jew, showed in the earlier part of the century that head form, then a marker of European racial types, could vary quite widely depending on nutrition, immigration, and other environmental factors.

Montagu, in writing a complete book about the myth of race, meant to overturn centuries of belief that races were biologically real. Indeed, many books and articles both before and after him made this point. And in the America of the 1940s it must have seemed crazy to think otherwise. Race was so real in the days of segregation. The Jews and the Irish were thought to be distinct racial types. In addition to arguing against the notion of racial types and the fixity of these types, Montagu demonstrated that variation in one trait did not correspond to variation in another, as we

Race: Are We So Different?, First Edition. Alan H. Goodman, Yolanda T. Moses, and Joseph L. Jones.
© 2012 American Anthropological Association. Published 2012 by Blackwell Publishing Ltd.

showed previously, and that traits are continuous and do not follow racial lines. Montagu did not yet have modern population genetics to back up his claims. He also made the mistake of continuing to mix race as a cultural concept with race as a biological concept. Thus, he advocated throwing out the baby of race as a cultural construct with the bathwater of race as a biological concept. Subsequent social scholars disagreed with this aspect of his argument, as do we.

Montagu influenced a generation of anthropologists. For example, C. Loring Brace, who then took up the mantle against race as biology, although his biological explanations were not complete either. Despite their pioneering work, it appears that neither scientists nor most other members of the dominant culture were ready for the paradigm shift.

Richard Lewontin and the Apportionment of Variation

Enter the young population geneticist Richard Lewontin. In the 1950s, scientists began to collect data on the world distribution of simple Mendelian traits such as sickle cell. As these data accumulated, they led to some interesting discoveries, such as that blood polymorphisms like sickle cell did not necessarily cluster in Africa. Lewontin, an evolutionary geneticist, was interested in the overall pattern of human variation. Specifically he wanted to test out how much of the variation was explained statistically by race, and conversely how much was explained at two other levels – among individuals within a group or population and between groups within a so-called race. In short, his statistical analysis, using a recently developed technique, estimated the average amount of variation at three levels: within local groups, among groups within races, and among races.

His results were published in a famous 1972 paper titled "The Apportionment of Human Variation." The astonishing result was that, of the blood polymorphisms he studied, the average variation was almost entirely local – that is, most variation occurs within a local group, then some occurs between groups but still within the race, and then a small percentage, certainly less than 10 percent and probably

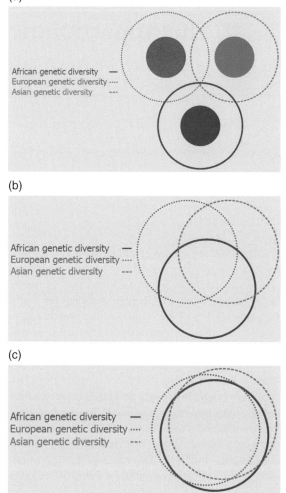

Figure 10.1 These Venn diagrams represent three views of human genetic variation. (a) Essentialist model; (b) Population model; (c) Lewontin 1972. Courtesy of the American Anthropological Association, illustration by Mark Booker.

more like 6 percent occurs among races. These results have been repeated over and over again.

Figure 10.1 illustrates a way to think about the different worldviews of race. Figure 10.1 shows just how revolutionary Lewontin's results proved to be. The first Venn diagram (Figure 10.1a), with separate, slightly overlapping circles or orbs of variation, represents a typological view of distinct racial types. Each race has a center and some variation around it, represented by the size of the circle. However, there is a clear center and no overlapping variation. The borders are clear and unambiguous.

The middle diagram, Figure 10.1b shows some overlap. When we have queried classes and other groups, they often think that this one makes the most sense – that it best describes the structure of human genetic variation. It makes sense, for example, because we can see some racial ambiguities, some overlap in skin color and hair texture, for example. There are still pretty distinct differences, however, in the center points. And one might think from this diagram that race, though it contains some ambiguities at the fringes, is basically true and useful.

The last diagram, Figure 10.1c, is a visual representation of Lewontin's actual results in 1972, some forty years ago. He found that the rule was incredibly strong overlap among the races, and that the center of variation in one race was very near the center of variation in another. Each population group actually displayed a remarkable degree of variation.

Given Lewontin's results, it is simply hard to think that race is very important. Moreover, we see confirmation of these results when one looks at the distribution of complex traits such as running. As well, the sickle cell example tells us that a trait might be high in one part of a continent but nonexistent in another. This is an example of great variation within a race. So, while race is real culturally, it is of little use genetically.

An Interview with Richard Lewontin

Richard Lewontin, Alexander Agassiz Professor Emeritus of Zoology at Harvard University, is one of the world's most eminent authorities on human diversity. He has written many celebrated books on evolution and human variation including Human Diversity, Not in Our Genes, *and* The Triple Helix. *Photograph courtesy of Richard Lewontin.*

Does racial difference exist on a genetic level?
Peoples who have occupied major geographical areas for much of the recent evolution of humans look different from one another. Sub-Saharan Africans have dark skin and people who live in East Asia tend to have a light tan skin and an eye color and eye shape and hair that is different than Europeans. So there is this kind of genetic – it is genetic – differentiation of some features of the body between people who live in

Reproduced courtesy of California Newsreel.

Central Asia, Africa, Europe, North America, and South America.

And those features, which are geographically determined, were used to erect notions of different races. There's the African race, the Black race, the Yellow race, the Red race, the Brown race, and the White race. And it's mostly skin color plus hair shape and eye shape and so on. That's the everyday observation, that "they" all look alike – and we all look different.

The real question is not whether those differences in skin color and hair form are genetic, because they are. We know that because the children of black slaves brought to North America were the same color as their parents were. The question is what else does that tell us about biological differences? How much difference in other genes beside the genes that are relevant to skin color is there between these major geographical groups?

If we want to use the notion of race in a sensible, biological way, we could only do that if there really were a lot of genetic difference between those groups aside from the superficial differences that we can see. And that's an important issue which we now understand. We understand it because over the years a lot of data were gathered by anthropologists and geneticists looking at blood group genes and protein genes and other kinds of genes from all over the world. Anthropologists just went around taking blood out of everybody.

I must say, if I were a South American Indian, I wouldn't have let them take my blood, but they did. And one of the consequences of that is by the early 1970s we had a huge amount of information about the different genetic forms all over the world for a large number of genes that had no relevance to those outward manifestations like skin color, but had to do with blood type and proteins.

And when you brought all that together, it became pretty clear that there really were minor differences in the frequencies of the different gene forms between the major geographical so-called races.

Since the 20th century, it's been recognized that there's what's called polymorphism of blood type. There are type As and type Bs and type Os and Rh-positive and Rh-negative and so on in every group in the world. But the assumption was that people in Africa would have a very different relative frequency of A and B and O than people would in North America or in Europe and in Asia.

And what all these studies showed was that that wasn't true. That you couldn't really tell the difference between an African population and a European population and an Asian population by looking at the frequency, the relative proportions of the different blood types. They were essentially the same in all these groups.

That isn't true for every blood type. There are occasional types which are strongly differentiated between populations. There's one blood type called the Duffy blood type and that's very different between Asians, Africans, and Europeans. But that's an exception rather than a rule.

For almost every gene we know, either everybody in the world has the same form of the gene, in which case all human beings are the same, or if there's variation, the frequencies of the different variants are the same relatively speaking, close to the same, in Africans, Asians, North Americans, Austro-Asians, and so on. And only about – well, I estimated 7% of all of human genetic variation could be ascribed to differences between groups, between major races. Anyway, about 75% of all the genes [come in only one form and] are identical in everybody. So there's very little differentiation.

How do you measure human genetic variation?
The way we measure human variation genetically is to look and find all the different forms of a particular

gene, the alternative forms of a gene, and then see what percentage of the population has form one, form two, form three, form four, form five, and so on. Now if 99% of the population has one form and only 1% has another then there isn't much genetic variation in the population for that. And if different populations all have 99% of form one and 1% of form two, then there's no differentiation between populations because they have all the same percentages.

If on the other hand one population had 99% of form one and 1% of form two but some other population had 99% of form two and only 1% of form one, then even though within the population almost everybody is the same, between the populations there'd be a big difference.

So that's the way you characterize it. You see the percentages of the different forms in different populations and you ask – If I take a sample from one population, are proportions of the different forms similar whether it's an African population or an Asian population or a European population? If so, there's no difference BETWEEN populations, and all the difference is found WITHIN populations.

So what did you discover about population differences?
Well, the problem back then for evolutionists and population geneticists was always to try to actually characterize how much genetic variation there was between individuals and groups and so on. And nobody knew how to do that because you had to connect genes with some outward manifestation that you could actually observe, and most genes don't have an outward manifestation in their variation.

So people didn't really know whether individuals varied genetically a lot from one another or only a little bit. They could see variation between individuals but they didn't know how much of all the genes that variation represented. And for a very long time, nobody had the faintest idea how genetically variable our species was from individual to individual.

And I spent a lot of time worrying about that like other people in my profession. And then I met a guy who had an experimental gimmick and he didn't know what to do with it, but I knew what to do with it. So I was sort of a person with a problem without a method and he was a guy with a method without a problem and we got together.

And that method was essentially to extract proteins from individuals and to run them in an electric field and to see whether the proteins moved at different rates in an electric field. If there were alternative forms of the genes that were for that protein, then the proteins would move at a different rate in the electric field, and you could visually identify the proteins by staining them.

So what you did is you ground up a fruit fly, you stuck it in a slab of jello, you turned on the current, all the proteins moved in the jello, and you turned off the current. You stained it, and sure enough you would see that different individuals had the same protein moving different distances. And that would be because they had a different form of the same gene.

And that method, which is called gel electrophoresis, a very fancy name, we were able to use it on any organism at all. If you could grind it up, you could do it, and that included people. You didn't have to grind up the whole person, but you could take a little bit of tissue or blood; you could do it on flies, on mice, on plants, on bacteria, anything. And the result was for 20 years people interested in this question of genetic variation were grinding up organisms and measuring the genetic variation.

And what they discovered was that organisms within a species were tremendously genetically different one from another. Many people had said, "No, they're all the same because any genetic differences are mutations and they will be selected out by natural selection. And except for a few superficial differences, everybody in a species is the same."

But that's not true. It turns out that between 25–33% of genes within a species are of the variable kind. They differ from one individual to another. And that's what that method discovered, that something around a quarter or a third of all your genes – not your genes, but genes of any organism – are variable between individuals of the species. So that gave us a different view of the possibility of evolution. And I thought, "Well, this raises the possibility that we could ask how much genetic differentiation there is between humans in different population groups."

It had already been established by a guy named Harry Harris that there was a lot of this genetic variation in humans, the kind that we have found in fruit flies, that people have found in plants. He used the same technique and showed that humans are genetically variable. But what he didn't know was how much difference

there was between Africans and Asians and Europeans and so on. But a certain amount of that data began to accumulate, and by 1972 a lot of those data existed.

We could then tell from older data on human blood groups, which were known for a long time, and from this more recent data on their proteins which we could visualize in these gels, how much difference there was between any two individuals genetically and between a collection of individuals from France and a collection of individuals from French Equatorial Africa, and from Asia. And that collection of data is now huge, I mean, we know an immense amount about that kind of protein variation in humans. That was before people were sequencing DNA. That's when we were just looking at people's proteins.

And so I thought, "Well, we've got enough of this data, let's see what it tells us about the differences between human groups." And so I just looked into the literature, and that literature was in books and so on. And so one day I was going to give a lecture, I think it was in Carbondale, Illinois, or somewhere south. I was working in Chicago at the time. So I took a couple of these books with me and a pad of paper, and a table of logarithms which I needed for this purpose, and a little hand calculator, and I sat on this bus trip for three or four hours looking at the books, picking out the data, looking it up in the table of logarithms, doing a calculation, and writing it down in tables. And when I got back after the round trip I had all the data I needed to write the paper about how much human genetic variation there was, and so I did it. And that's been repeated in recent years using DNA and so on. You always get the same result. Shows you it's worthwhile being afraid to fly, by the way, because you have lots of time on a bus to work.

So how much difference is there between human groups?

And the numbers come out as follows:

Roughly speaking for human beings, for about three-quarters of all our genes, everybody in the world, except a rare individual, has only one form of the gene. So all human beings share that form. For the 25%–33% or so of those genes for which there is some variation – 99 to one or 50/50 or 75/25 of different forms – for almost all of those genes, it doesn't matter from which population you take the sample; they have the same proportions. That is to say, if it's 75% of form one and 25% of form two in Europeans, it's 70% of form one and 30% of form two in Africans and 73% of form one and 27% of form two in Asians, and so on. Most genes are like that.

But there are a very few genes, like the Duffy blood group, in which in Asian populations there is one very common form, in African populations there are two forms, but they're not the same as the common one in Asians, and in Europeans there's another different ratio. So for that gene, there's a big difference in the frequencies, but that's rare.

And if you put it all together – and we've now done that for proteins, for blood groups, and now with DNA sequencing, we have it for DNA sequence differences – it always comes out the same: 85% of all the variation among human beings is between any two individuals WITHIN any local population, 85% of all the variation; please remember that 75% of all genes are identical for everybody. But of the variation there is, 85% of that is between individuals within Sweden or within Denmark or within the Ewe or the Ki-kuyu or the Chinese or something.

Of the remaining 15% of human variation, it's roughly a 50/50 split of the variation between nationalities within what used to be called a major race, between Swedes, Italians, French, and so on, or between Ewe and Ki-kuyu and Zulu or something. And the other remaining 7% or so is between those major groups – the blacks, browns, yellows, red, and whites.

What does that tell us about race?
Well, it might have turned out that there were big genetic differences between groups, and that most genes were highly differentiated between the major races. Now, if that turned out to be true, then at least it would be a possibility, although not demonstrated, that there might be, as some like to dream, high differentiations between groups in their mental abilities or in their temperaments or anything like that. Although nobody knew about any genes for those things, at least it was a living possibility.

But when we found that there were practically no genetic differences between groups except skin color and body form and a few things like that, it became a great deal less likely and less interesting to talk about genetic differences between groups. And the consequence is that from the biological standpoint those

major so-called races – black, brown, yellow, white, and red – were not biologically interesting.

And that in turn meant that the differences that people were constantly emphasizing for social purposes were social constructs which almost certainly didn't have any biological basis. And therefore we should stop talking about major races because to talk about major races gave the impression that there were big differences between these groups in things that mattered – I mean, skin color, after all, doesn't matter except in some vague aesthetic sense – but things that really mattered: people's characters, their intelligence, their behavior, whether they're going to compete with other people or not and so on. The evidence then became that there weren't any interesting differences in such things, and so we should stop talking about race.

Why do people still hold on to biological explanations of difference?
Well, first of all, race is a social reality. I mean, there are people who are dark skinned and they are called black, and that's a social reality. You can't deny that. The question is why people hold onto that social reality. There are two reasons, one optimistic one, mainly that just because an idea changes or is seen to be without a basis, it doesn't go away right away. It takes time as human generations go on.

But more than that, race and racial categorizations serve a very important social function, namely, they justify the inequalities that exist in a society which is said to be based on equality. Why is it that if all men are created equal – not women, notice, but men – if all men are created equal, then why is there a much greater proportion of black people in jail than white people?

Is it possible that people are not treating them fairly? "No," you say, "that can't be, because we live in a society of equality." So the easy answer is, "Well, they're in jail because more black people ought to be in jail because black people have genes that make them criminals." And the beauty of that ideology [is] that it justifies what is the greatest social agony of American life, certainly, and partly, European life – namely, the huge social inequalities between groups in a society which claims to be a society of equality.

And you have to cope with that, you have to somehow become at ease with it, because the alternative is to demand a real revolution in social relations, and that's not easy to do.

What is the relationship between your DNA and how you turn out as a person?

The word that geneticists use for a description of your outward manifestations and your physiology and your metabolism and your anatomy and so on, including your behavior, is phenotype – literally, "what appears," from the notion of *pheno*, to appear. And in theory that's supposed to be the result of the genes that you have, which are called the genotype.

The question that geneticists have been struggling with for a very long time is, What's the relationship between those elements in the genotype, the DNA, and what comes out at the end of the developmental process, the phenotype?

You have to remember, we start as a fertilized egg, and that egg goes through cell divisions and becomes a whole organism, and that organism develops throughout its entire life. We are all developing continuously. We get taller and then we get shorter. We get smarter and then we get dumber. That happens continuously.

So the question is, What's the relationship between those inner elements, those genes, the genotype, and the phenotype. And the answer that we know from years of experimental study and ordinary observation is that there's no simple one-to-one relationship between the genotype and the phenotype. The organism is certainly influenced in powerful ways by the genes – there is no chimpanzee that will be interviewed on television and say the things I'm saying now, because chimpanzees don't have the genes to enable them to speak, to form these abstract ideas, because their brains are not the right shape and so on.

So clearly differences between the species are, in some sense, in the genes. But at the same time it's not the case that every aspect of the phenotype is determined by the genes, because the environment in which you develop, both within the womb and after you're born, your whole psychic environment, your education, what comes in on you, the food you eat, the society you live in – all that goes to form the phenotype.

That phenotype can't be anything in the world. As I said, no matter what environment a chimpanzee lives in it'll never be a professor, although some professors might be sort of like chimpanzees. No matter what environment we live in, I think it's extremely unlikely that human beings will live to be 200 years old, for example, because of our genes.

Now, what's interesting about our phenotypes, about the variation of phenotypes between individuals, is that they sort of vary continuously – like heights or shapes or colors – there's not just three different colors or four different heights, yet the genes exist as discrete objects which have particular different forms. You can have form one of the gene or form two of the gene or form three. So you have these discreet differences at the genotypic level, which are somehow converted into continuous variation between individuals and their behavior and their morphology and their physiology, and it's kind of like a pointillist painting, in which, if you stand back from the painting, you see continuous figures, but when you go up close to them you see that they're made by tiny little dots of paint which fuse together in your eyes and in your brain from a distance, but are discreet and individual.

And the observer who observers a pointillist painting is performing an action, is making the phenotype out of that underlying genotype, so to speak, by the intervention of their eyes and their central nervous systems. In the same way, our genotype is converted into a phenotype through the developmental process which is occurring in a particular environment. And every environment is different, and environments are changing all the time.

So there's a very complicated relationship between genotype and phenotype. People who say, "Well, if only I knew all your genes I'd know exactly all about you," are wrong. Indeed, the notion that if I cloned an individual by reproducing that person's genes in another individual, that the cloned individual would be identical with the ones from which the genes came, is wrong. When I was a child, the most famous people in the world were the Dionne Quintuplets. The Quintuplets were five girls born in rural Quebec, all identical quintuplets. And they were dressed alike and they had their hair done alike and they looked alike, and they were put into a kind of zoo by their parents and by the doctor who delivered them and by the province of Ontario. And everybody looked at them and they were made as alike as they could be so they'd be the wonder of the modern age. They were clones of each other.

But in fact, when they got older, when they left this artificial environment, they became quite different from each other. A couple became nuns, some were married and some not, two died and three are still alive – I think a third one died recently. One was schizophrenic, the others weren't. They were as different from each other as any five girls could be, although they still looked pretty much alike.

And that's the important point: that although a lot of our morphology, a lot of our facial features appear not to be greatly influenced by environmental variation, our personalities clearly are tremendously influenced by it, and our abilities. And the Dionne quintuplets are a wonderful example.

Aren't groups like Icelanders genetically distinct because they've been more isolated?

Iceland has been in the news a lot recently because the Icelandic government has awarded the entire Icelandic genome to a private company to exploit. The claim of this company is that the reason why they want to have the genotypes of all Icelanders is because Icelanders are uniquely homogenous people. And why are they uniquely homogenous? Because, the story is, Iceland was founded in the 9th century by people who came from Norway – a very small number of people who came from Norway, just these immigrants. There was nobody in Iceland when they arrived – that's true – and all Icelanders at the present time are descended from those few immigrants at the very beginning, and therefore Icelanders are all related to each other very closely, and therefore if somehow we could study their genes we could find the genes for disease and other things because everybody's related to everybody, and we could carry out the pedigree.

And so the whole thing is based on the claim that Iceland is extremely homogenous, genetically. Now, that's bolstered by the fact that Icelanders speak a language which elsewhere has been dead for 1500 years; that is to say, they speak a form of Old Norse which is related to Norwegian and Swedish but very different. And also they are claimed all to look alike – they're all sort of reddish-haired or blond and so on – and they're isolated and they all know each other; it's a very small country, only a couple hundred thousand people.

So all of that comes together, this notion that Iceland is a genetic isolate, a few people came there, they've been genetically isolated from everybody ever since, and that's why they speak this crazy language and everything is homogenous.

Now, the trouble is that we know that that's not true, and we know it from a source which is in one sense the source of Icelandic national pride, which is the Icelandic Sagas. The Icelandic Sagas, which were composed or spoken verbally during the Middle Ages by a variety of Icelandic authors and eventually written down, tell us the story of the founding of Iceland, of the wars that the Icelanders, the Vikings, engaged in.

And they give this impression at first that it's a very homogenous society. But when you begin to read the sagas, what you discover is that those early Icelanders, those Vikings, were in fact making a living doing exactly the same thing that the Ancient Greeks were doing: namely, half the time they spent farming, and then half the time they were pirates. They got in their boats, and they went around raping and pillaging and taking slaves and just warring everywhere, and that's what Vikings were. Vikings were pirates. And they didn't try to excuse it; that was the way of life the Sagas described.

And in the process of that piratical existence, they took slaves, they brought people back to Iceland from other countries. There's a wonderful place in I think it's Egil's Saga, which is a story of a guy who wants to buy a concubine. So he goes to Russia and he deals with a Russian trader, and the Russian trader asks him a certain price for this concubine. He said he had a dozen of these women in his hut. And the Icelander says, "Wait a minute, I'm not going to pay that. That's much more than the usual price for a woman slave."

So there was a usual price, which meant that Icelanders were doing this all the time. They were getting women and bringing them back. If you look around northern Scotland, you see lots of town names – this "ness" and that "ness" – Loch Ness, Inverness, so on. Ness is an Iceland word; it means cape. Those are all the places the Icelanders landed and took their slaves. One of the sagas is all about the fighting in the Orkney Islands and how the Icelanders landed in the Orkneys and established their position there and so on.

So Iceland, in fact, is a place made up, yes, partly of descendants of those early Viking ancestors who fled from Norway to escape the king, but in large part also from slaves they took, from people they brought from all over, and became part of the Icelandic genetic pool. So Iceland turns out, in fact, when you look at Icelanders, when you look at their proteins, you look at their DNA, they turn out to be not any more genetically homogenous than Swedes, Germans, English, French, all of Northern Europe. They look like a typical Northern European country.

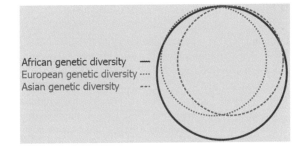

African genetic diversity —
European genetic diversity ····
Asian genetic diversity ---

Figure 10.2 Venn diagram of human genetic diversity based on data from Yu et al. (2002). Diagram by Jeffrey C. Long, illustration by Mark Booker. Courtesy of the American Anthropological Association.

Updating Lewontin: The Structure of Genetic Variation Today

Lewontin had it mostly right. However, if he made one error it was in not being able to consider that one group might actually vary more than another. Lewontin surely knew this. Increasingly researchers had observed that Africans were very much more variable than the rest of us. However, his statistical procedure did not take into account this fact. Besides, he was measuring blood group polymorphisms and not directly measuring human genetic variation.

To end this story, let's turn to the work of Yu and colleagues. With the advent of modern genetic technologies it has become possible to read a long portion of the genetic code of an individual. Yu and colleagues did this and published their results in a 2002 paper, three decades after Lewontin.

They compared a long sequence of DNA of individuals who were identified as "European," "Asian," and "African." The DNA section sampled consisted of 25,000 single nucleotide polymorphisms. They then tabulated the number of differences between any two individuals of the total of 30, ten from each so-called race.

What they found is that the average difference between any two Europeans and any two Asians was slightly greater than 0.6/1000 or about 15 in total. This

is not so surprisingly low as it has been crudely estimated that about 99.9 percent of single nucleotide polymorphisms are identical between any two individuals. They then found very little difference between an Asian and a European. Thinking about that, this makes sense as the dividing line between these continents is permeable and rather arbitrary. More variation was found between an African, on the one hand, and either a European or Asian on the other hand, right about one variation per thousand. The shocker comes next. However, the greatest variation was found between two Africans, about 1.2 variations per thousand. Said slightly differently, there is more variation among Africans than between Africans and non-Africans.

This is illustrated by Figure 10.2. The new Venn diagram differs from those in Figure 10.1 in one simple way: the "race circles" differ in size. The African genetic diversity circle is the largest and pretty much incorporates the diversity of the other groups. In a sense, Europeans and Asians are a subset of Africans. This is why we are all Africans under the skin. Strange as this may sound, the next chapter will show how this came about evolutionarily.

Conclusions

The most remarkable fact we know about human variation is that it is local. Nearly all variation is found within any one group. The second most remarkable fact, perhaps even more remarkable

from a biocultural perspective, is that is that most variation occurs in Africa and non-Africans are a subset of Africans. If we were to assign races objectively, most of them would be Africans.

In the next chapter we see how this variation came about.

References

Lewontin, R.
1972 The Apportionment of Human Diversity. Evolutionary Biology 6:381–398.
Long, J. C.
2004 Human Genetic Variation: The Mechanisms and Results of Microevolution. American Anthropological Association. Published on line at: http://understandingrace. org/resources/pdf/myth_reality/long.pdf.
Montague, A.
1942 Man's Most Dangerous Myth: The Fallacy of Race. New York: Columbia University Press.
Yu N., F. C. Chen, S. Ota, L. B. Jorde, P. Pamilo et al.
2002 Larger Genetic Differences within Africans than between Africans and Eurasians. Genetics 161:269–274.

Further Reading

Brown R. A., and G. J. Armelagos
2001 *Review of* Apportionment of Racial Diversity. Evolutionary Anthropology 10:34–40.

Mielke, J. H., L. W. Konigsberg, and J. H. Relethford
2006 Human Biological Variation. New York: Oxford University Press.
Serre D., and S. Pääbo
2004 Evidence for Gradients of Human Genetic Diversity within and among Continents. Genome Research 14:1679–1685.
Templeton, A. R.
2003 Human Races in the Context of Recent Human Evolution: A Molecular Genetic Perspective. *In* Genetic Nature/Culture: Anthropology and Science beyond the Two-Culture Divide. A. H. Goodman, D. Heath, M. S. Lindee, eds. Berkeley: University of California Press, 234–257.
Tishkoff, S. A., and K. K. Kidd
2004 Implications of Biogeography of Human Populations for "race" and Medicine. Nature Genetics 36:S21–S27.
Weiss, K. M.
1998 Coming to Terms with Human Variation. Annual Review of Anthropology 27:273–300.

11

The Evolution of Variation

Figure 11.1 "21 A Bus" (part of Lake Street USA series, 1997–2000). Courtesy of Wing Young Huie.

> *Our studies of genetic diversity give us an even greater under-*
> *standing of how similar we all are in our marvelous variation.*
> *The variation that makes each of us genetically unique repre-*
> *sents a fraction of 1% of what makes all of us the same.*
>
> Kenneth Kidd, geneticist, Yale University:
> RACE exhibit, SMM

Race: Are We So Different?, First Edition. Alan H. Goodman, Yolanda T. Moses, and Joseph L. Jones.
© 2012 American Anthropological Association. Published 2012 by Blackwell Publishing Ltd.

A History of Moving and Mixing

Human genetic variation is the consequence of a long history of migration, of cross mating, of piracy, of slave taking … mixing things up, leaving behind some variation.

Richard Lewontin, evolutionary
biologist and geneticist, Harvard
University: RACE
exhibit, SMM

The sharp lines of physical difference implied by race disappear on closer examination. To be sure, people from two distant points on the globe tend to look quite different. But to a traveler walking between those points, the

Figure 11.2 Dominos provide a visual metaphor for the spread of genetic variation. The first domino has no contact with the last. However, its motion connects with the next and so on down the line. In the same way, alleles can spread through mating. Courtesy of City's Best Marketing, www.c-b-m.com.

people encountered at any point along the way would look pretty much like those nearby. There are a million shades of human skin color – not four or five – and no geographical boundary that separates those with straight hair from those with curls. The features that make people in one part of the world look different from those in another blend and mix in ways that defy easy categorization. The complex patterns of human variation reflect a history of human movement and mixing that has gone on since our origins in Africa hundreds of thousands of years ago. Recent history has only accelerated, not begun, a long pattern of moving and mixing, one that began with bands of hunters and gatherers and nomads in millennia past and has accelerated with travel by boat and the recent mass movements of individuals by plane.

The Evolution of Human Variation

Variation is greatest where humans have lived longest. People have lived in Africa far longer than anywhere else – evolutionary anthropologists such as Ken Kidd (featured in this chapter) estimate that the human lineage originated in African between 150,000 and 200,000 years ago. This time has allowed the population in Africa to accumulate more of the small mutations, or genetic changes, that are the source of our genetic variation. Because only part of the African population moved beyond Africa to begin colonizing the world, only part of Africa's genetic variation moved with them. For this reason, most genetic variation found in people living outside Africa is a subset of that found among Africans, and more variety remains with Africa even today.

KEN KIDD

The Evolutionary Dispersal of Human Variation

His current research focuses on human genome diversity: the patterns of normal genetic variation among populations from around the world, the variation in those patterns along the genome, and the inference of recent human evolutionary processes. Photograph courtesy of Kenneth Kidd.

Kenneth K. Kidd *is Professor of Genetics, of Ecology and Evolutionary Biology and of Psychiatry at Yale University.*

A little over a decade ago the majority of genetic data on the relationships of human populations consisted of mitochondrial DNA haplogroups with a beginning of Y chromosome (the non-recombining parts of the Y (NRY)) haplogroups. Because new mutations arose on those non-recombining molecules as human populations expanded, maps of the "migration" patterns were being developed. A difficulty with interpreting those maps with the broader patterns and pathways of human expansion was that each represented only one gene that had a sex-specific pattern of inheritance. For example, a powerful leader's wife brought back from a more distant region/population might have impact on the gene pool of the population through her sons who would inherit power (reproductive fitness) from their father. However, her mitochondrial DNA would be under-represented relative to her nuclear DNA. In the late 1980s and early 1990s we and others were accumulating autosomal polymorphism data on sites with low mutation rates, SNPs (single nucleotide polymorphisms), and were beginning to find that each independent polymorphism showed a different allele frequency pattern around the world. Some patterns were very similar but others were very different. The initial data being accumulated showed that most polymorphisms (SNPs, then generally called RFLPs) identified in people of European ancestry occurred throughout the world. However, as more individuals of African ancestry were studied, it became clear that polymorphisms with high heterozygosity existed in African populations but not in any non-African populations. At the same time, as more haplotypes (combinations of alleles at molecularly close polymorphisms) were being studied, many more combinations were found in African populations than non-African and the non-African populations had a subset of those in Africa. Thus, most haplotypes share with mitochondrial and Y chromosome DNA, a great reduction of variation outside of Africa relative to what remained (and still exists) in Africa. All of these data resulted in acceptance of the "Recent Out of Africa" model by almost all researchers.

The accumulated data for essentially all genetic markers argue strongly for the considerable loss of variation associated with the expansion out of Africa. That is the clearest aspect and has put to rest the notion of independent evolution to *Homo sapiens* in Africa, Europe, and East Asia that had been based on a few morphological similarities of modern populations to archaeological remains of pre-*Homo sapiens* fossils

in the same region. It is now accepted that the population that expanded out of Africa became the founder of all non-African human populations. Beyond that point there is relatively little certainty in the field of exact expansion pathways and time at which different regions of the world were initially occupied. The representation of human migration out of Africa and subsequent spread around the world is often depicted as a series of arrows with more or less implied precision but often referred to as migration routes. It is more accurate to refer to them, at least in terms of the original population of the world, in terms of expansion routes. Quite sophisticated models have been developed to show that genetic drift accumulates along expansion routes and that this accumulation is relevant to autosomal loci as well as mitochondrial DNA with mutations accruing along the expansion pathway. Drift will result in some variation being lost but also some new variation (e.g. a new mutation in mtDNA, NRY, or autosomal genes) reaching high frequency. While mtDNA and NRY show a single pattern each, as noted above, each different autosomal SNP showed a different pattern around the world.

What is clear is that modern humans expanded out of Africa within the last 100,000 years. Some timing estimates put that expansion from southwest Asia as recent as 50,000 years ago and there are many other estimates going back as far as 90,000 years ago. These various estimates are based on different data sets and different molecular clock models and estimation procedures; there is a dearth of hard archaeological evidence with good data supporting age.

Relevant results from our lab showed that populations in northeast Africa shared much more similarity to the non-Africans than did populations from west and central Africa. One explanation would be the relatively recent gene flow into northeast Africa from non-African populations. Conversely, it seemed logical to believe that it was populations from northeast Africa that expanded outside of Africa. A population from western or southern Africa would not have migrated across the already occupied intervening parts of Africa to found non-African populations. We were also finding that changes in allele frequencies were showing a pattern of continuous change across geographic regions outside Africa. The pointillist representations in Figure 11.3 are an attempt to

(a)

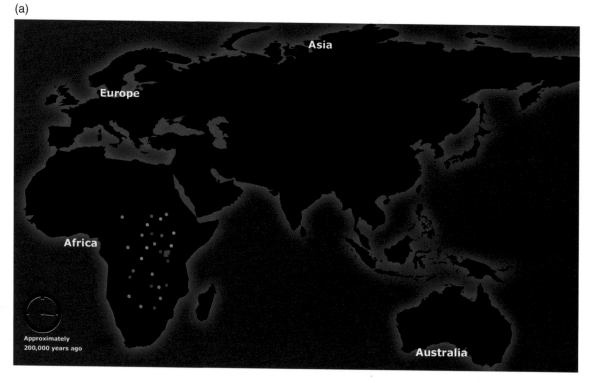

(b)

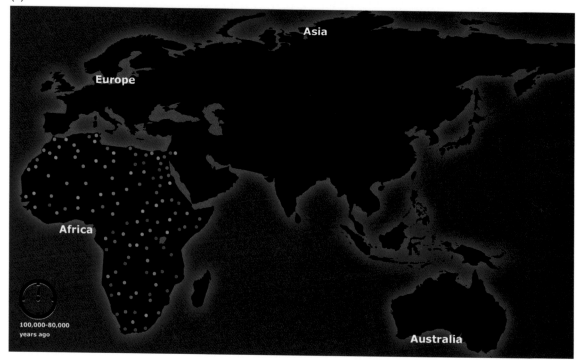

Figure 11.3   A pointillist view of human evolution and variation based on the work of Kenneth Kidd. Courtesy of S2N Media, Inc.

(c)

(d)

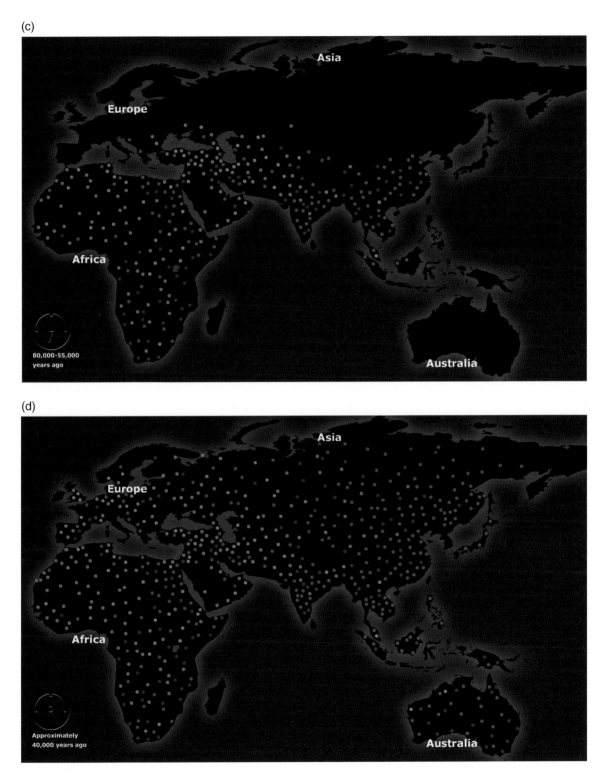

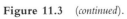

Figure 11.3 *(continued)*.

convey the complexities we were finding in the autosomal data in a simple and clear way.

Any widely distributed species will have some genetic variation across its range with the most distal and fringe populations tending to have more differences. Thus, one would expect populations at the edges of Africa to have allele frequency differences – alleles at some loci will have their highest frequencies in western Africa, alleles at other loci will have their highest frequencies in southern Africa, etc. Thus, by about 100,000 years ago there would have already been considerable genetic variation within and across Africa, represented abstractly in Figure 11.3a by the multiple dots. Note that individual dots do not specifically represent an individual or a population; rather, the diversity of colors in a region represent the amount and nature of genetic variation in that region. Slight differences in the numbers of colors in any region represent that geographic variation.

About 100,000 years ago, possibly later, some Africans walked out of Africa into southwest Asia, as depicted in Figure 11.3b. They carried with them the alleles that were already most common in northeast Africa. The evidence suggests that it was a fairly small number of individuals and/or the new population in southwest Asia remained small for a long time before expanding into the rest of Eurasia. As a result, there was considerable loss of the variation that still exists in eastern Africa. By no later than 40,000 years ago, that single founder population had expanded to occupy the habitable parts of Eurasia. Figure 11.3c shows that this expansion resulted in a subtle loss of variation in eastern Eurasia relative to western Eurasia. By about 20,000 years ago a population from central Asia had migrated into the Bering land bridge and then down into the rest of North and South America, with additional genetic drift establishing a genetic profile that is somewhat unique to the Native Americans.

Factors complicating the full reconstruction of the peopling of the world (including Africa) are subsequent migrations of peoples based on climatic and geologic phenomena. We do not know whether humans had already reached Southeast Asia by 75,000 years ago but it is very clear that the eruption of the Lake Toba super-volcano at that time would have had a lethal effect on populations from India through south China, the Philippines, and parts of what is today the Indonesian archipelago. (Did this help keep *Homo floriensis* isolated?) The ash and sulfur in the upper atmosphere resulting from that eruption would have led to global cooling for at least several years. This cooling of the entire earth would have affected plant and animal life everywhere and might have considerably reduced human population sizes, enhancing the effects of genetic drift and might possibly have resulted in selection affecting some alleles at some genes. Another major event was the advance and retreat of glaciers during the past 100,000 years. With the increase in glaciations, sea levels dropped. Most of what is now Indonesia would have been a single land mass 20,000 years ago. Thus, retreat from the north as glaciers advanced and subsequent re-expansion into those areas much more recently all complicate the modern picture. Nonetheless, the pointillist drawings of more than a decade ago provide a fair overview of modern human variation until the large-scale migrations of historic times.

In a very abstract and stylistic way Figure 11.3a represents the genetic variation that had already accumulated in anatomically modern humans in Africa at about 200,000 B.P.; that genetic variation is represented by the different colored dots. Notice that the colors are not evenly distributed across the continent as would be expected from an isolation by distance model. There is a bit more "red" in southern Africa; there is a bit more "blue" and "yellow" in northeast Africa.

About 100,000 years B.P. some peoples from northeast Africa migrated into southwest Asia as shown in Figure 11.3b. Since the people who migrated originated from the populations of northeast Africa, they sampled from that already partially diverged gene pool and this "sampling error" accentuated the loss of variation. Only a fraction of the genetic variation in Africa as a whole was represented in that initial "non-African" population. It was that population in southwest Asia that then increased in numbers and spread geographically to occupy all of Eurasia and Australo-Melanesia by about 55,000 years B.P., as shown in Figure 11.3c. There was not enough time for much new genetic variation to arise within the populations that eventually reached the east of Asia. On the other hand, some of the variation that had accrued in the southwest of Asia was lost.

Some time more recently than 40,000 years B.P. some of the populations from Siberia and the east coast of Asia migrated to the Americas and expanded to occupy both North and South America. Some additional variation was lost during that colonization but the effect was less than associated with the migration out of Africa.

Mixing and Moving

We came out of Africa and never stopped moving and mixing. Ain't no mountain high enough.

RACE exhibit, SMM

Although Ken Kidd would say that the routes of human migration are not as definite as in Figure 11.4, the map does give us a sense of the various main patterns of human migration. These may be reconstructed based on genetic variation and corroborated by archaeological evidence. We tend to think of North America of before European contact as a rather stable land of small, relatively isolated groups, such as Northeast, Plains, and Southwest Indians, who may have traded with each other in a local way (though, interestingly, objects found at the Middle Mississippian site of Dickson Mounds, Illinois, a poor hamlet inhabited a thousand years ago, can be traced to the corners of North America).

Figure 11.5, a map of trade routes, and Figures 11.6 and 11.7, which show archaeological items, are fascinating because they tell of movement across landscapes. What is made in one place is unearthed in another, perhaps a traded object. The same is true of genes. If we know that trade took place, it is also likely

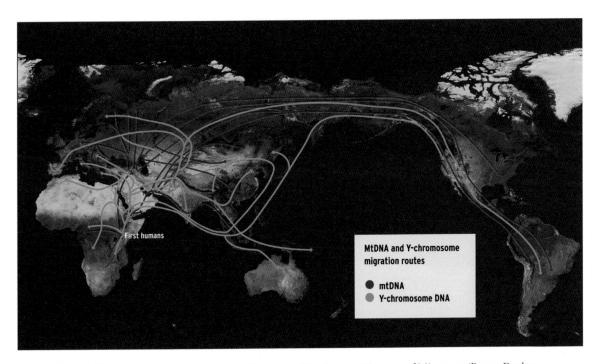

Figure 11.4   Major route of genetic migration. Courtesy of the Science Museum of Minnesota/Roger Boehm.

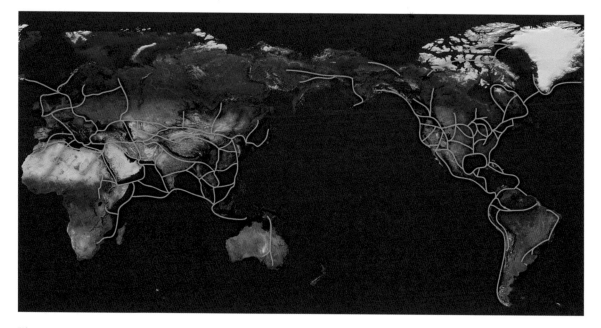

Figure 11.5 Map showing how objects developed in one area show up in another. Based on archaeological evidence, this map is a compilation of trade routes that existed about 800 to 1,000 years ago. It provides a snapshot of the dynamic system of trade that has linked people across great distances through history. African, Asian, and European routes adapted from Andrew Sherratt (2004) "Trade Routes: the Growth of Global Trade," ArchAtlas, February 2010, Edition 4, http://www.archatlas.org/Trade/Trade.php, accessed: January 6, 2012. North and South American routes compiled by Ed Fleming, archaeologist, Science Museum of Minnesota. Courtesy of the Science Museum of Minnesota/ Paul Morin.

Figure 11.7 Beginning around 2,600 years ago, jade ornaments such as this Costa Rican pendant became symbols of status throughout Central America. Mines in Guatemala are the region's only known source of this gemstone and may have provided jade that was traded throughout Central America and as far east as the West Indies. Courtesy of the Science Museum of Minnesota.

Figure 11.6 This ear ornament, made of seashell from the Gulf Coast, was produced sometime between 1150 and 1350 C.E. Found in Pierce County, Wisconsin. Ornaments with similar faces, made of copper, bone, and shell, have been unearthed throughout the South and Midwest. Courtesy of the Science Museum of Minnesota.

that mating did, too, and thus genetic transfers. People interact and so their ideas, objects, and genes travel the globe. There are virtually no reproductive isolates. We are one big breeding group.

Perspectives on Genetic Genealogy

We asked four scientists and a legal scholar about the use of genetics to reconstruct ancestry. We did not ask about race, but their answers would probably be consistent with the message of this book. However, genetics has moved to include an allure of stories about individual histories and ancestries. Genetics could be quite powerful in telling who one is genetically, and perhaps to extrapolate from the genetics to the cultural and social ancestries of individuals.

Genetic genealogy – what can it really tell us?

Genetic genealogy allows individuals to explore their own ancestry using commercial kits that test their DNA. Consumers can choose from three different tests to receive a report on the geographic ancestry of their DNA. One test examines mitochondrial DNA, which is passed from a mother to her children. Another examines Y-chromosome DNA, passed from a father to his sons. A third test looks for "Ancestry Informative Markers" in a person's DNA. What do the results of these tests really reveal about personal ancestry and identity?

Here are five perspectives.

The limits of genetic genealogy

Because genealogy based on mitochondrial DNA or Y-chromosome DNA follows only a single line of ancestry, it misses the great majority of a person's total number of ancestors. Going back ten generations, about three hundred years, an mtDNA or a Y-chromosome test reveals information about only 1 of 1,024 total ancestors in that generation. The tests miss all

the other ancestors. DNA tests such as these can tell you a lot about your ancestry, but you have to be aware of what they *can't* tell you. (Henry Greely, law professor, Stanford University: RACE exhibit, SMM)

Recovering the past

The importance of mtDNA and Y-chromosome-based genetic tests varies among groups. For African Americans, especially those who are avid genealogists, such tests are valued for supplying evidence that can be used to help reclaim history, culture, and knowledge that were long denied to them. The transatlantic African Slave Trade basically erased significant aspects of their ancestral stories. As a result, many African Americans are unable to trace their family histories back to Africa. Genetic information on maternal and paternal ancestry has proven to be an ideal resource to supplement historical documents and extend the recovery of their past. (Rick Kittles, geneticist, University of Illinois at Chicago, and scientific director, African Ancestry, Inc.: RACE exhibit, SMM)

Figure 11.9   Rick Kittles.

A matter of interpretation

I study how and why African Americans use genetic genealogy tests. Consumers of genetic genealogy often believe that they are being supplied with definitive scientific evidence of their ancestry. But I find that these same consumers may play a role in interpreting this data to fit their expectations. One woman in my

Figure 11.8   Henry Greely. Photograph by Steve Gladfelter.

study conducted conventional genealogical research that led her to believe her maternal ancestors came from southern Africa. But a mitochondrial DNA test of her maternal line inferred ancestral origins in western Africa. The woman reconciled these different ancestry accounts by weaving a story about the African migration of her ancestors from the west to the south. (Alondra Nelson, sociologist, Columbia University: RACE exhibit, SMM)

Figure 11.11 Kimberly TallBear. Photograph by Jun Kamata.

TallBear, Department of Environmental Science, Policy and Management, University of California, Berkeley: RACE exhibit, SMM)

Less than advertised

The results of Ancestry Informative Marker (AIMs) testing *look* far more clear-cut than they really are. At base, such tests operate on the likelihood that variations, commonly referred to as "markers," in a person's DNA are found among "Africans," "Europeans," "Asians," and "Native Americans." But these genetic variants aren't strictly limited to any particular population. For example, markers identified by the test as "Native American" are also found among people of Central Asian descent. So the results might read out "Native American" ancestry, when a person's heritage could, in fact, be Uzbek. These *Ancestry by DNA* types of tests can give some information about the genetic markers a person shares with people around the globe. This shared DNA substance is not necessarily from a shared ancestor, however, which is the misleading element

Figure 11.10 Alondra Nelson. Photograph by Laylah Amatullah Barrayn.

Claiming identity

Some people promote DNA analysis as a way to determine who is and who is not genetically "Native American." That approach implies that specific Native American identities, and even specific tribal affiliations, can be indicated in DNA. However, tribes are living entities that have repeatedly reconfigured their definitions of group belonging along complex and changing political and kinship lines. Genetics alone don't make a person Native American – it's a matter of culture and way of life. Also, Native American tribes assert governance rights based on their historical authority as sovereigns. I worry that DNA testing will encourage some people to claim tribal political authority based on a narrow form of genetic descent, thus undercutting tribal political and cultural sovereignties. (Kimberly

Figure 11.12 Duana Fullwiley.

here. In fact, many people around the world 'co-possess' markers of all sorts for lots of different ecological and evolutionary reasons. This sounds less exciting than direct, inherited ancestry from Africa, or wherever, but it is often more accurate. (Duana Fullwiley, anthropologist, Harvard University: RACE exhibit, SMM)

Conclusions

In this section we have followed the museum exhibit and website and further explained visually and in words why race does not explain human variation. At the same time, we hope we have supplemented some of the interesting history of the study of human variation. The adage that we see what our brain wants us to see appears to be correct. Perhaps most important, we have shown just how remarkable human variation is. Yet, how we vary: the structure of human variation is not at all what we thought it was.

Further Reading

Additional Resources

Davis, D. S.
2004 Genetic Research and Communal Narratives. Hastings Center Report 34(4):40–49.

Elliott C., and P. Brodwin
2002 Identity and Genetic Ancestry Tracing. British Medical Journal 325:1469–1471.

Kittles R. A., and K. M. Weiss
2003 Race, Ancestry, and Genes: Implications for Defining Disease Risk. Annual Review of Genomics and Human Genetics 4:33–67.

Lee, S., D. A. Bolnick, T. Duster, P. Ossorio, and K. TallBear
2009 The Illusive Gold Standard in Genetic Ancestry Testing. Science 325(5936):38–39.

Rosenberg, N. A., J. K. Pritchard, J. L. Weber, H. M. Cann, K. K. Kidd, L. A. Zhivotovsky, M. W. Feldman
2002 Genetic Structure of Human Populations. Science 298:2381–2385.

Templeton, A. R.
2003 Human Races in the Context of Recent Human Evolution: A Molecular Genetic Perspective. *In* Genetic Nature/Culture: Anthropology and Science beyond the Two-Culture Divide. A. H. Goodman, D. Heath, M. S. Lindee, eds. Berkeley: University of California Press, 234–257.

Tempelton, A. R.
2007 Genetics and Recent Human Evolution. Evolution 61(7):1507–1519.

PART 3

LIVING WITH RACE AND RACISM

In 2007, the Board of Trustees of the University of Illinois at Urbana-Champaign retired controversial school mascot, "Chief Illiniwek." Courtesy Illini Media.

12

Introduction

Living with Race and Racism

In this part of the book, we will be looking at the consequences of believing that there are biological races and the fact that in the United States there has developed a social, economic, and political system built on the belief that races are real, and that some races are more privileged than others; we will look, too, at the impact of treating the biological and historical myths of race as real. To do this, we will examine race through the institutional lenses of wealth accumulation, education, health, and how race is counted and used in the census. Finally we will look at the future of race in the United States by focusing on the timely issues of multiracial identity, intersectionality, immigration, and globalization.

But before that, we think it is important to take the current temperature of how race is being played out in popular culture in the United States as we write. Let's start first with the presidency of Barack Obama. The first African American President (his own choice of identity), took office of January 20, 2009, and many in the press and the media heralded this achievement as the end of racism in the United States. Soon after, many called the United States a colorblind society and the talk was about how far the United States had come to elect a black president, a man whose father was Kenyan and whose mother was Euro-American. That is the stuff of American dreams and achievement. His is the story of the child of an immigrant father and an American mother who makes good, right? His is the story of how hard work, dedication, and high educational achievement pays off in America, right? An African American

president, because of the uniqueness of his position, could finally be the personification of an authoritative voice to lead a national discussion on race relations. Perhaps he could even lead the discussions around understanding larger social issues such as the intractable problem of changing racialized institutions. Let's look more closely at what the media has done with the issue of race during the first year of the Obama administration. An analysis of African Americans in U.S. news coverage during the first year of President Obama's incumbency by the Pew Charitable Trust showed that as a group African Americans, or broad issues affecting African Americans, attracted very little attention in the U.S. mainstream media. (Pew Research Center 2010:1). As a matter of fact, what coverage there was tended to focus on specific episodes, like the arrest of black Harvard professor Dr. Henry Louis Gates or the death of Michael Jackson, the internationally iconic black pop star, and finally on the attempted Northwest Airlines attack by Umar Farouk Abdulmutallab rather than on the broader issues and themes that address the lives of African Americans and other people of color more generally. According to the Pew survey, those three incidences accounted for more than 46.4 percent of all coverage that had substantial mention of African Americans (Pew Research Center, 2010:1). The take-home message from this review is that the presidency of Barack Obama did not automatically lead to a broader and more inclusive conversation about race or about the plight of African Americans or other people of color. The June 30, 2010 issue of the *Chronicle of Higher*

Education featured an article by Kelly Troung called "Review of Harvard Scholar's Arrest Cites Failure to Communicate," in which the report of an independent panel in Cambridge, Massachusetts convened by the Cambridge Police Department said that the blame for the incident in July 2009 was because of "failed communications" between the police officer and the scholar. The panel, made up of experts in criminal justice, law, community relations, and conflict resolution did not blame the police officer or Dr. Gates, but left it very vague about what the underlying behaviors of the police officer suggested (Troung 2010). Nowhere in the report, for example, is there an analysis of how structural racism had played a role in the incident. That is, why would the police officer automatically assume that Dr. Gates was a burglar even after he told him who he was, and showed the officer his Harvard faculty identification card? The point here is that having a black man in the White House does not automatically change the structural nature of racism or of racially based assumptions in this society. According to the PEW study mentioned above, it was actually in the black press, and not in the main stream press, that those discussions of structural racism took place – as they have done in the past.

Several other recent media events illustrate the depths of structural racism still in our society. For example in the area of sports, Dr. Robin Lee Hughes reminds us in her recent article "Tennis Anyone? Race and Class still matter in Sports" that students of color are held to a double standard because the assumption in higher education is that because they are poor and "colored." As she says, that they cannot pursue both a professional career in say, basketball and football, and get an education. She says,

> I just read a newspaper article filled with the rhetoric about how young, elite athletes, those who play basketball and football, should care more about their education—assuming that they do not. I am still asking, who was concerned when Nancy Kerrigan decided to skate or when Michael Phelps decided to swim ... no one ever seems to question why sports such as golf and tennis allow you to turn pro while in school. Who makes that decision? Why can't you do both? (Hughes 2010:1)

She goes on to say that these pronouncements or double standards are really about the intersections of socioeconomic status (class) and race. If well-meaning liberal pundits are so concerned about the fate of all

athletes then include those at tennis clubs as well. She believes there is an assumption built into a sports metanarrative that those athletes who are in the middle and upper classes and who are white can do both; they can pursue professionalism *and* get a university or college degree. As a remedy she encourages colleges and universities to tackle the difficult discussion of structural racism that poor students have to deal with which perhaps underlie their choices to go professional:"Perhaps we should start looking at the structural or systemic issues that might push certain students in the direction of professional sports." She goes on to say that warning students of color and poor students away from professional sports is not the answer. "In fact," she says, "let's take a look at our meritocratic, caring college campuses. I think warning students away from careers like professional sports, in particular basketball and football, merely scratches the surface of a bigger discussion-called structural and institutional racism." (Hughes 2010:3) The conversation around structural racism is not taking place in the popular media, nor does it appear to be happening on college and university campuses, at least around the issue of sports and professionalism.

In our supposedly "colorblind "and "post-racial" world, some people, especially political conservatives, say that there is no more need for such programs as affirmative action. Some say that not only do we not need those kinds of programs anymore, but that those programs are actually discriminatory against white people (read white males). This has been the mantra since President Lyndon Johnson, using his executive authority, created an executive order that put the affirmative action policies in place in 1972. These programs have been bitterly contested over the years, both in and out of court, with several of the more notable cases making it to the Supreme Court, those cases being *Bakke v. the University of California*; *Grutter v. the University of Michigan*, and *Gratz v. the University of Michigan*.[1] But, more recently, people representing the conservative Right have co-opted or adopted and adapted the language of the civil rights movement to

---

[1]   Expert report of Patricia Gurin, *Gratz, et al. v. Bollinger, et al.*, No. 97-75321 (E.D. Mich.) *Grutter, et al. v. Bollinger, et al.*, No. 97-75928 (E.D. Mich.) at www.vpcomm.umich.edu/admissions/legal/expert/gurin, accessed November 15, 2011. Also see "*Regents of the University of California v. Bakke*" at www.infoplease.com/ce6/history/A0841421.html, accessed November 15, 2011.

shift the agenda to one that serves their needs. The theme of the mantra is asserting that they are being discriminated against. They are claiming that the laws, policies, and people on the Left (both white, but especially people of color) are actually racist and are discriminating against white people. The high-profile case that we want to mention is one that has been recently in the media, and that is the case of Shirley Sherrod. Shirley Sherrod, a Department of Agriculture official, was unceremoniously fired by the Obama administration in 2010 because she said in a taped speech that she discriminated against white people. She was subsequently reinstated, but only after it was shown that a right-wing blogger, Andrew Breitbart, had taken her statement out of context. Even though the entire incident has ended up with more media focus on race, the conversation does not tackle the deep structural issues of institutionalized racism in this example. The fact that a white, male, right-wing blogger could get a black woman fired so quickly by a white administrator in the cabinet of the first black president should give us all pause. While Ms. Sherrod has been reinstated, in part because of further investigation which showed that her statement made at the national convention of the NAACP had been taken out of context and manipulated by the blogger, and to public outcry from, among other groups, the Congressional Black Caucus of the United States House of Representatives, this does not bode well for a national willingness in the right-wing media to have an honest discussion about structural racism in the United States. Nor does it indicate an Obama administration that is comfortable with talking about race at a structural level. Some say that the Shirley Sherrod incident was a teachable moment in which the White House could take a leadership role, or in which the mainstream media could take on the press of the conservative Right to begin to provide an alternative metanarrative to educate a nation about how far we really do have to go to get to an honest conversation on the topic; never mind "post-racial" let's just get to "honest racial." It remains to be seen if it will happen on President Obama's watch.

Another example of the white backlash, or white conservatives co-opting and using the language of the victim or the underdog, is the case of U.S. Senator James Webb calling for the end of government-run diversity programs because they have "disadvantaged struggling Whites and hurt the cause of racial harmony."

(Lewis 2010:1) Webb wrote a column for the *Wall Street Journal* that said that he believed that affirmative action programs have lived past their usefulness and primarily benefit new immigrants over struggling white and even black Americans who, Webb claims, were the original beneficiaries of such programs. Webb has written two books, *Born Fighting* (2004) and *A Time to Fight* (2008), both published by Broadway Books, in which he develops these arguments more thoroughly. He has been criticized by such people as Douglas Wilder, and Senator Webb, former Governor of Virginia in the opinion column in the *Wall Street Journal*. Douglas, the nations' first elected black governor – who, incidentally, endorsed Webb in 2006 – said, according to Lewis, "if it were not for the civil rights movement and diversity programs, he would not be a United States citizen today." Wilder was referring to strong minority support that helped Webb to beat his opponent by only 9,000 votes. (2010:2) What is interesting about the opinion piece when you read it in its entirety is that Webb makes several major points, including: 1) poor Whites are disenfranchised; 2) Blacks are also not served well because the programs favor recent immigrants, many who are benefitting illegally. So, he is using a class argument to bolster his argument for whites (primarily white males) who are angry it seems at Obama, the economy, and the growing role of big government in their lives. At the same time, Webb is trying not to distance himself from black voters who put him in office and who have benefitted from diversity programs in the past. He is trying to paint the picture of recent immigrants, read "illegal immigrants," as the people who are currently benefitting the most from these programs. Yet, he does not produce any data to bolster that statement. It is another way to fan the flames of xenophobia that are rampant in the United States around SB 1070 (Arizona's controversial immigration enforcement law passed in 2010) and to create an enemy of the immigrant, the threat to both deserving struggling whites and blacks whom the government has let down in the past.

Speaking of U.S. history, it is interesting how race is seen or not seen through the prism of time. While we are all familiar with the controversies surrounding such symbols as the Confederate flag, and the playing of the song "Dixie" at formal governmental and university events in the South, a more recent take on this has been what happens when you have to remove an honor from someone because of their racist past. In the July 12, 2010 issue of *Inside Higher Education*, Scott Jaschik wrote in "Removing an Honor" about the controversies surrounding renaming the building named after long dead Klansmen. Apparently, in the not so distant past, it was not unusual for upstanding citizens in communities also to be members of the Klu Klux Klan. It was an organization that boasted stalwart citizens. It is only now that the history of race in this country is being scrutinized through the lens of structural racism that we see just how embedded was the acceptance of behaviors that segregated blacks and other people of color. This segregation was not only perceived as natural, but the borders of these behaviors were policed by upstanding citizens who were not ashamed to be known as members of the KKK, one of the most notorious racist organizations in the United States, responsible for some of the most heinous lynchings in the history of the country. Lest we think that members of the KKK only hailed from the deep South and from states like Texas, it is well to know that there is a California tradition as well. In the southern California community of Riverside, located in one of the most multiracial counties in California, research into the KKK shows that the national premiere of *Birth of a Nation* by the filmmaker D.W. Griffith debuted at the Grove theater in Riverside on April 10, 1913. Researcher Zita Worley noted that the KKK membership was so widespread in the community that the newspapers announced that the induction ceremony would take place in the gymnasium of Riverside polytechnic high school. (Worley 2010:7).

The question it seems to us is not whether we have contemporary conversations about the contradictions of a society that allowed stalwart citizens to be members of an organization that struck terror in the hearts of people of color, but *how* we have that contemporary conversation.

The information contained in this book, but especially in the chapters here in part 3, are another integral piece of a major national project designed to help the United States have those deep conversations about structural race and racism. The overall project of which this book is a part, was designed by members of the American Anthropological Association with a grant from the National Science Foundation and the Ford Foundation. The Race Project, consists of the national exhibit, Race: Are We So Different? three copies of which are touring the United States until at least 2014 (two of 5,000 square feet and one of 1,500 square feet); the website www.understandingrace.org; and materials and resources that can be freely downloaded from the website. Please see our resource list at the end of this introductory chapter for more books articles and resources that directly pertain to the topic of structural and institutionalized racism.

Since our overriding goal is to provide people with tools for better understanding and communicating around issues of race, in the first guest essay in the contemporary experience section of our book Bonnie Urciuoli reveals some of the important ways that we frame issues of identity, knowingly and unintentionally through race.

BONNIE URCIUOLI
Language and Race

"diversity" in U.S. higher education. Her book Exposing Prejudice: Puerto Rican Experiences of Language, Race, and Class was awarded the 1997 Gustavus Myers Center Award for the study of human rights in North America. Photograph courtesy of Bonnie Urciuoli.

Bonnie Urciuoli *is Professor of Anthropology at Hamilton College. Her areas of interest are linguistic and cultural anthropology, specializing in public discourses of race, class, and language, and the discursive construction of*

Race is not a thing that people "have." It is, like nationality, ethnicity, class, or gender, a social classification system. Systems consist of categories that exist all at once in relation to each other, and where people fit into a category depends on interpretations of how they look, act, talk, and so on. As a system, race is made up of categories such as white, black, Asian, and so forth in which skin tone, facial features, hair, language, etc. are assumed to be natural markers of origin. Such markers themselves are not race. Race is the idea that those markers signify an origin associated with certain inherent qualities, and people may be assigned to race categories based on assumptions about descent, yet have few or no perceptible markers. The notion of system is often hard to grasp because it is much harder to see a whole system from its inside than to see pieces of the system as if they are the reality. But change or remove any one category and the whole system changes. In race, as in other social classification systems, one category tends to dominate, taken for granted as normative or typical or most desirable, or as semioticians put it, *unmarked*. In race the unmarked category is white and the rest of the race system is *marked* in contrast to whiteness.

Race as we now know it began forming centuries ago, built on the relation of colonizers to colonized, slave owners to slaves, and more generally, those controlling resources to those whose worth was limited to their place in the resource system, as chattel or exploitable free labor or, in the case of indigenous inhabitants, simply in the way of people who wanted their land. Economic relations are critical to this historical process but what turned it into what we now recognize as race is the naturalization of origin as an inherent and inherited quality that was seen to fit that type of person for a specific social place. In this way, African slaves, dispossessed native populations, and exploited labor were all subject to racialization, imagined as a natural type signified by physical features shared by people thought to be connected to each other "by blood." These are the historical origins of categories now known as black, Indian, Hispanic, and Asian. (Other once racialized categories like Irish, Jewish, or Italian are now assimilated into whiteness.) Racial classifications and markers change over time. What does not change is the privileged situation of whiteness. Language plays a part in this process every step of the way. Racial thinking and concepts are transmitted through discourse. Racial categories are defined and codified in words and phrases. Racial perceptions are reinforced in everyday uses of language. Language itself may be racialized, standing in for an older notion of "blood."

All languages have distinct varieties which reflect the social conditions in which they formed and exist. This is a reflection of the more general principle that languages do not come in strictly defined packages, that they evolve under specific conditions and never stop changing. This means that language varieties can reflect the conditions that generate racial categories. From a linguistic perspective there is no sharp distinction between a language variety (e.g. dialect) and a language: what people recognize as discrete languages have grown from language varieties. All languages and language varieties have their own coherent grammars and sound patterns. People recognize distinct languages, or high-status ("correct") varieties of a language, because institutional work has been done to present them as such. Thus, what we now know as English exists through the historical accident of Anglo-Saxon settlement of Britain a millennium and a half ago and the eventual emergence of England as a global colonial power. English has always been made up of a wide range of varieties. What people recognize as "proper" English is the result of four centuries of standardization through publication and teaching of dictionaries, grammars, and a great many books and articles about what counts as good English. Much the same has been true throughout Europe and more recently, the rest of the world. The standardization and naming of languages in association with nations (England and English, French and France, Spanish and Spain, and so on) meant that non-standard varieties of the same languages were associated with excluded, often racialized, people and named and explained in terms of their "degraded" association. So the varieties of English that developed among slaves and their descendants became associated in the United States with African Americans. Although William Labov and John Baugh have shown that the varieties of English spoken by African Americans have regular and coherent patterns of grammar and pronunciation, their language has long been perceived and described as sloppy, ungrammatical, and wrong, a marker of racial boundaries. Similarly, code-switching, the rapid alternation of English and Spanish among working-class bilingual Latinos often called "Spanglish" has been heavily criticized as sloppy, lazy, wrong, confused, etc. Yet code-switching is a coherent and patterned form of linguistic behavior, as Ana Celia Zentella has shown in her thorough and complex picture of language use among two generations of New York Puerto Rican bilinguals.

Racialization of language or language variety denies or trivializes the legitimacy of linguistic identity, of how one speaks being an important part of who one is. Latino bilinguals are doubly racialized through language, through non-standard linguistic behavior like code-switching and through their association with Spanish. Here we see vividly the association of U.S. whiteness with English and non-whiteness with Spanish. The association of English, whiteness and American-ness is an old pattern in U.S. history. In the 19th century, Native American languages were forcibly suppressed among native children made to attend off-reservation residential schools, and public figures like Theodore Roosevelt associated immigrant languages with racialized ethnic threat. In this rhetoric, whiteness, American-ness and English all appear vulnerable and in need of protection. The same assumptions appear in more recent rhetoric surrounding bilingual education and the condemnation of the use of Spanish in official channels. In such linguistic racialization, Spanish (or any foreign language "threat") is cast as invasive, a form of pollution much as non-white "blood" had long been seen. There is a parallel social logic between beliefs that mixed "blood" is dangerous and beliefs that mixed language is dangerous; hence the political attractiveness of English-only or official English legislation to "protect" people from Spanish.

Racialization is also reproduced through acts of reference. Each language contains words and expressions that denote race and racial classification: "official" terminology used by institutions, relatively formal terminology used in public venues, and relatively informal terms likely to be used in private. Whether or not a specific term is problematic depends on its discourse history: who has used it with whom to what end. It is through discourse, the process of spoken or written use, that people transmit racialized concepts and terms take on social impact. This happens in official discourses, in publications, and in everyday talk. The very process of writing and publishing laws defining race or of legislating activities on the basis of race or studies explaining race become part of a public discourse shaping notions of race and passing them along. Virginia Dominguez, for example, describes the importance of legal language in Louisiana (not repealed until 1972) specifying black–white boundaries

in terms of blood quanta, the number of white ancestors that one had to document to prove one's whiteness.

References to and beliefs about race inevitably enter into how people use language in the most ordinary ways. This last consideration is the most important and for most people the hardest to grasp, so let me expand a bit. People rarely use language solely to refer, that is, to convey information. As important as reference is, people's use of language is usually motivated by with whom they do what, which is why ordinary talk tends to form around social alliances, and reference is organized by the nature of talk. This is obvious in acts of gossiping, kidding, around, or flirting. It is also true for expressions of thought, opinion, or feeling, especially when responses to such expressions matter. Reference in public discourse is shaped by the same considerations. In addition, how people engage in communication is affected by the social circumstances in which they grow up, what they take for granted as normal and acceptable, and how they assume the world works. All these factors shape the ways in which notions of race turn up in discourse, as generalizations about types of people, as forms of humor, as ways of racially typifying what people do or how people talk, and as beliefs about languages and language varieties spoken by racialized people.

Most Americans recognize the racializing consequences of racist epithets, insults, and slurs insofar as they ascribe the impact of such usage to a speaker's bad intentions. But whatever the speaker's intent, racialization proceeds from the cumulative effects of such discourse in shaping and perpetuating racializing assumptions among those involved. Such effects may be ignored or even unperceived by the participants, particularly when they are not members of the group being racialized. The American cultural tendency to reduce social action to individual acts and intents and to ignore the structures that shape action often leads people to assume that if an act of discourse is "just a joke" or simply a mistake, and if no harm is intended or the speaker apologizes, then there are no racial issues. Jane Hill demonstrates this in her detailed examination of racializing language. Native American team or place names and the rationales defending their use; public figures' comments about someone's looks or preferences or other race-related ascriptions and the media energy expended explaining or excusing them all; metaphors and jokes in ordinary talk that rely on presuppositions about racially marked social groups, and deliberate "joking" misuses of language varieties or languages spoken by racialized people (like the usage Hill terms "mock Spanish"); the rationales linking Spanish, illegal immigration, disorder, and danger often depending on heightened rhetoric and imagery: all these usages cumulatively cast those referred to or joked about as disordered and trivial. Racializing language has few consequences for the unmarked, who can ignore the more subtle manifestations of such discourse and dismiss its serious consequences for people who are racially marked. Racially unmarked whites operate within a value hierarchy in which what they do, think, and say is assumed to be orderly and unproblematic. The value of racialized people is measured against that hierarchy – hence the racializing impact of allegedly positive generalizations like "black but hardworking." This value hierarchy also protects the unmarked from

the consequences of what the marked have to say about them. Racialized people have plenty to say about white people, in the forms of use described above, sketchy jokes and all. But the cumulative impact of such usage on whites is negligible in terms of legal, institutional, or economic consequences.

The relations among language and race are, as we see, complex and multiple, but two principles particularly stand out. Language itself can be racialized: an individual's language variety can be seen as a racial marker, and an entire language can be seen as a race-like threat. And racialized attitudes are routinely passed along, too often as "common sense," through routine, everyday forms of talk. These everyday uses are rarely recognized as racializing by those who engage in them. But all the processes described above operate together, in mutually reinforcing ways, in a social atmosphere where those most in a position to do damage are least likely to perceive or admit the real effects. Whatever individuals may or may not intend, what matters is what happens.

References

Hughes, R.
2010 Tennis Anyone? Race and Class Still Matter in Sports. Diverse Issues in Higher Education, July 12. http://diverseeducation.com/blogpost/278/, accessed July 19, 2011.

Jaschik, S.
2010 Removing an Honor. Insider Higher ED, July 12. http://www.insidehighered.com/news/2010/07/12/klan, accessed July 19, 2011.

Lewis, B.
2010 Sen. Webb decries federal diversity programs. *Associated Press*. July 24.

Pew Research Center
2010 Media, Race and Obama's First Year: A Study of African Americans in U.S. News Coverage. Washington, DC: Pew Research Center.

Troung, S.
2010 Review of Harvard Scholar's Arrest Cites Failure to Communicate. The Chronicle of Higher Education, June 30. http://chronicle.com/article/Review-of-Harvard-Scholars/66099/?sid=at&utm_source=at&utm_medium=en, accessed July 19, 2011.

Worley, Z.
2010 "From Orange Groves to White Hoods: The Origins of the Riverside Ku Klux Klan." Unpublished manuscript. University of California Riverside, Riverside, CA.

Bonnie Urciuoli: Language and Race

Baugh, John
1983 Black Street Speech. Austin: University of Texas Press.

Dominguez, Virginia
1986 White By Definition. Piscataway, NJ: Rutgers University Press.

Hill, Jane
2008 The Everyday Language of White Racism. Malden, MA: Wiley-Blackwell.

Labov, William
1972 Language in the Inner City. Philadelphia: University of Pennsylvania.

Zentella, Ana Celia
1997 Growing Up Bilingual. Oxford: Blackwell.

13

Race and the Census

Figure 13.1   Students and a faculty advisor from Macalester College in St. Paul, Minnesota wearing T-shirts indicating how they would have been "raced" at different points in U.S. history. Front, left to right: Tsione Wolde-Michael, Sarah Ganley, GaoNue Xiong, Kim Wortmann. Back, left to right: Peter Rachleff (faculty advisor), Carmen Phillips, Tinbete Ermyas, Kemi Adeyemi, Jessica Masterson, Dennis Holmes, Romina Takimoto. Courtesy of the Science Museum of Minnesota.

Race: Are We So Different?, First Edition. Alan H. Goodman, Yolanda T. Moses, and Joseph L. Jones.
© 2012 American Anthropological Association. Published 2012 by Blackwell Publishing Ltd.

This chapter will briefly trace the history of the U.S. census and how it has changed over time, especially around issues of race and identity. Since it was first instituted in 1790, each decennial census has been used to take a poll of the number of people in households in the country. We will look at how classifications of race in the census have changed specifically in the 20th century. Material highlighting the lives of recent immigrants will also be showcased. The differences between the 2000 and 2010 census will be highlighted, and readers will be asked to consider future uses of race in the census in the 21st century should be.

History of the U.S. Census and Race

One of the consistencies of the U.S. census over the two hundred plus years during which it has existed has been the fluidity of the concepts of race and ethnicity it embodies and the corresponding changes

Race Categories	Census Year																						
	1790	1800	1810	1820	1830	1840	1850	1860	1870	1880	1890	1900	1910	1920	1930	1940	1950	1960	1970	1980	1990	2000	2010
Indian	■	■	■	■	■	■	■	■	■	■	■	■	■	■	■	■							
Slave	■	■	■	■	■	■																	
White	■	■	■	■	■	■	■	■	■	■	■	■	■	■	■	■	■	■	■	■	■	■	■
Free colored person			■	■	■																		
Black							■	■	■	■	■	■	■	■	■	■	■	■	■	■	■	■	■
Mulatto							■	■	■	■	■		■	■									
Chinese									■	■	■	■	■	■	■	■	■	■	■	■	■	■	■
Japanese											■	■	■	■	■	■	■	■	■	■	■	■	■
Octoroon											■												
Quadroon											■												
Other													■		■	■	■	■	■	■	■	■	■
Mexican															■								
Negro															■	■	■	■	■	■	■	■	■
American Indian																	■	■	■	■	■	■	■
Filipino																	■	■	■	■	■	■	■
Hawaiian																			■	■	■	■	■
Korean																			■	■	■	■	■
Aleut																				■	■		
Asian Indian																				■	■	■	■
Eskimo																				■	■		
Guamanian																				■	■	■	■
Hispanic*																				■	■	■	■
Samoan																				■	■	■	■
Vietnamese																				■	■	■	■
Other Asian or Pacific Islander																					■		
African American																						■	■
Alaska Native																						■	■
Chamorro																						■	■
Latino*																						■	■
Other Asian																						■	■
Other Pacific Islander																						■	■

* The U.S. Census Bureau considers Hispanic and Latino to be ethnicities rather than a race.

Figure 13.2 U.S. census race (and "color") categories, 1790–2010.

in the questions it asks. One of the best ways to see the visual impact of the shifting categories is to look at Figure 13.1, which is taken from the Race exhibit. This picture depicts students from Macalester College enrolled in an academic success program for students of color who want to become teachers. What is striking about this picture is that it shows how each of the students would have been classified in past censuses. Why would they have been assigned to different racial/ethnic categories from one census to the next? The census has been used by the U.S. government over the years to collect data that documents the political power of each state, and the social and economic conditions of its citizens and non-citizens. The notion of race and how it is defined and used in the census gives us a look over time at the processes of racial formation and reformation.

The census was the brainchild of founding fathers of the Constitutional Convention in Philadelphia in 1787. It was originally created to determine the number of representatives each state of the new United States of America would send to Congress. While the census was originally intended for political representation, eventually it came to measure the size of the tax assessment, the size of the military, and even how to design social policy programs among other things. The first U.S. census, carried out in 1790, was conducted by 16 U.S. marshalls and 650 assistants. It took the field marshalls 18 months to visit the colonial households and to compile a final tally of 3.9 million people in the new nation, including nearly 700,000 slaves (Anderson 1988:8). The goal of this scheme was to ensure that states had no more than one representative for every 30,000 free males. The Convention determined that an enslaved individual counted for three-fifths of a free person (Anderson 1988:7–14).

Why Is Race a Question on the Census?

A question asking the race of each resident has been included on every U.S. census since the first national survey was conducted in 1790. Why is race a question on the census? Once used to support discriminatory practices, race data gathered by the census now help enforce civil rights laws.

Figure 13.3   Enslaved African American family. Courtesy of the Library of Congress, Prints and Photographs Division.

1790

In accord with the U.S. Constitution, and in keeping with slaveholding, which was then legal, the first U.S. census counted each enslaved individual as three-fifths of a person when determining state populations. Native Americans were not identified systematically in censuses dating from 1790 through 1840.

1860s

Scientists of the day used census data to assert the inferiority of people seen as being of mixed race. Their claims were used to justify laws preventing interracial marriage.

1920s

Census data were used to establish quotas that blocked immigration from Africa and Asia and favored immigration from northern European countries.

1940s

By identifying areas where large numbers of Japanese Americans lived, data from the 1940s U.S. census were used to help justify the forced internment of Japanese Americans during World War II.

Figure 13.4 Closing the gate on racially undesirable Chinese immigrants. Cartoon from Literary Digest, July 5, 1919.

Figure 13.5 Japanese Americans being relocated to internment camps. Photograph by Clem Albers. Courtesy of the National Archives.

1960s

The 1964 Civil Rights Act made discrimination on the basis of race, color, religion, or national origin illegal in public places. It also called for desegregation of schools and helped protect voting rights.

> If African Americans are 12 percent of the population, but only 5 percent of college entrants or 1 percent of the nation's business leaders, they are under-represented in these areas, indicating the possibility of discrimination. To track the patterns and dynamics of under-representation among minority groups, the nation needs a denominator – that is, the percentage of the total population that African Americans represent. *The Census establishes this denominator.* (Kenneth Prewitt, former director, U.S. Census Bureau, personal communication with Sara Ilse, SMM, August 2006)

Separating Black from White

In the past, determining the race of children of mixed black and white ancestry was a matter of law.

The mathematics of whiteness

In the 1800s, state "blood fraction" laws specified the maximum percentage of African ancestry a person could have and still be considered legally white. The most common fraction was one-eighth. Anyone thought to have more than that was considered black.

The Census and the Science of Racism

To many, it seemed only natural to include race as a census category. Over time, scientists and others realized that census information could be used to support their theories about the nature of race. From the 19th century, they would influence how race was categorized on the U.S. census.

In the mid-1800s, Alabama physician Josiah Nott was among those who sought to prove that different races represented separate species and that people of mixed ancestry were feeble in various ways. Nott and others

Figure 13.6 Alabama physician Josiah Nott. Courtesy of Historical Collections, University of Alabama at Birmingham.

successfully urged that the census include questions about degrees of mixture between blacks and whites as well as about the number of children, living and dead, born to each woman in order to find data that would support this idea.

From 1850 to 1890 the category Mulatto, meaning someone of mixed black and white ancestry, was included on the census. Two additional categories, Quadroon (one-fourth black and three-fourths white) and Octoroon (one-eighth black), were introduced in 1890.

Be particularly careful to distinguish between blacks, mulattoes, quadroons and octoroons. The word 'black' should be used to describe those persons who have three-fourths or more black blood; 'mulatto,' those persons who have from three-eighths to five-eighths black blood; 'quadroon,' those persons who have one-fourth black blood; and 'octoroon,' those persons who have one-eighth or any trace of black blood. (Census workers' instructions, 1890, cited in RACE exhibit, SMM)

Adding Asians

The addition of various Asian nationalities to the census mirrors the history of Asian immigration to the United States.

New immigrants, new categories
Asian categories were added to the census in response to increased immigration from particular countries.

1870: Chinese
Chinese were the first Asians to arrive in large numbers in the United States, in the early 1800s. The California Gold Rush and work on the transcontinental railroad brought thousands more in the 1850s and 1860s. Nearly 37,000 Asian immigrants arrived in 1860 alone, most of them Chinese.

1890: Japanese
Japan and the United States established diplomatic ties in 1854, and in the following years many Japanese immigrants arrived.

1950: Filipino
The Philippines came under U.S. control in 1899 following the Spanish–American War, resulting in increased immigration from the Philippines.

1970: Korean
A wave of Korean immigrants arrived after the Korean War of 1950–53.

Figure 13.7 Asian immigrants arriving at Angel Island, about 1910. Courtesy of California State Parks, 2006.

1980: Vietnamese
Following the Vietnam War, refugees from the Communist governments of Vietnam, Cambodia, and Laos fled to the United States.

Counting all Asians
Since 1977 the various Asian groups have all been combined within one category for purposes of reporting the statistics gathered by the census and other federal agencies.

Figure 13.8 Romina Takimoto. Courtesy of the Science Museum of Minnesota/C. Thiesen.

Both my parents immigrated to the United States as young adults and settled in Hawaii. My mother came from Seoul, Korea, and my father from Yokohama, Japan. Growing up in Hawaii, I never felt any discrimination against me for my race because everyone that I knew was mostly Asian–Japanese, Chinese, Korean, Filipino or Vietnamese. Of course, there are many Caucasian people in Hawaii, too, and we use the word *Haole* (which actually means 'foreigner' in Hawaiian) to refer to the whites.

I realize now that I've moved to Minnesota that Haole, a word I've used without much discretion in the past, is packed with negative connotations. Living in Minnesota has awakened me to a great amount of racial discourse and has made me more mindful of the words I choose to use.

Now I use terms like *Asian American* and *person of color* actively, whereas in Hawaii I would never have had that kind of vocabulary, simply because the racial categories are not so broad. Now that I am living with students who come from multiple corners of the world and am learning more about race, I am trying to relay my knowledge back to my parents in Honolulu. I am trying to show my mom that racial formations like black equals crime and Latino equals poverty are completely false and that there is a whole new world of thinking that she must open up to. (Romina Takimoto: RACE exhibit, SMM)

The Asian Indian Question

The census's classification of Asian Indians reveals confusion about what criteria should be used to establish its racial categories.

White, Hindu, or Asian?
At various times, the census would have classified the girl in Figure 13.9 as either white, Hindu, or Asian.

White?
From the 1600s onward, many scientists classified the people of the Indian subcontinent as either European or Caucasian. In keeping with this, Asian Indians were classified as white on the census until 1920.

Hindu?
Census workers in 1960 were instructed to classify Asian Indians as "Other" and to write in "Hindu." This was in line with the common practice of referring to Asian Indians as Hindus. But that confused race with religion and ignored the fact that many Asian Indian immigrants were Sikhs or Muslims.

Asian?
Since 1980 the subcategory Indian has been included within the larger Asian category on the census. This reflects India's location within the continent of Asia.

Figure 13.9 South Asian girl. © iStockphoto. com/KailashSoni.

"One-drop rule"

In the early 1900s, most states abandoned their blood-fraction laws in favor of ones that designated any person thought to have even "one drop of African blood" as black. People who had been seen as white according to the blood-fraction laws were now said to be "passing" for white.

Self-identification

For most legal purposes today, self-identification is the accepted practice. People of mixed black and white ancestry can decide whether to classify themselves as black, white – or both.

Seeking a separate category

The U.S. census now classifies people from the Middle East and North Africa as white. Before the 2000 census, some Arab Americans asked that a separate Arab category be included. They hoped for data to be collected that would help monitor discrimination against them as a minority group. Their request was unsuccessful.

During the 20th century, there were substantive changes to the census that expanded its categories and incorporated the presence of various racial and ethnic groups that immigrated to the United States in the late 19th and early 20th centuries. Over time the census became longer, but it was shortened again in 2010. It eventually introduced the idea of multiple questionnaires as well, and asked characteristic questions based on birthplace, education, occupation, language spoken in households and race/ethnicity. The 2000 census asked just six questions on the short form that went to about 83 percent of U.S. households. These questions included age, sex, race, Hispanic origin, household relationship and owner/renter status (Population Reference Bureau 2009:2).

Counting Mexican Ancestry

This country's first Mexican inhabitants were not immigrants. They were residents of land that the United States claimed following the 1846–48 Mexican–

Figure 13.10   Deportees waiting at a train station in Los Angeles, March 9, 1932. Courtesy of the Herald Examiner Collection/Los Angeles Public Library.

American War. The changing official classifications for people of Mexican ancestry over the years reflect the powerful role politics plays in the census.

Mexican: a race in 1930 …

The 1930 census categorized Mexicans as a racial group. The Census Bureau explained that the category was added because of increased immigration to the United States in the wake of Mexico's revolution of the 1920s.

… but not in 1940

During the economic depression of the 1930s, nearly 400,000 Mexicans and Mexican Americans living in the United States were deported to Mexico. Many Mexican Americans saw a link between the Mexican racial category on the census and this forced expulsion. They lobbied successfully for its removal, and it did not appear on the 1940 census. That year, census workers were told to count Mexicans as white unless they were clearly Indian or belonged to some race other than white.

Mexican Americans today

Many Mexican Americans feel their status as Americans is still being questioned and that new Mexican immigrants are treated unfairly.

Figure 13.11 Immigration reform activists protest in Washington, DC (May 2010). © iStockphoto.com/rrodrickbeiler

Practically all Mexican laborers are of a racial mixture difficult to classify, though usually well recognized in the localities where they are found. In order to obtain separate figures for this racial group, it has been decided that all persons born in Mexico, or having parents born in Mexico, who are definitely not white, Negro, Indian, Chinese, or Japanese, should be [counted] as Mexican ("Mex."). (Instructions to 1930 Census workers cited in RACE exhibit, SMM)

The long form for the 2000 census had 46 additional questions, which was the shortest long form since the 1940 census. The census was changed over time in very different ways. It has reflected the growth and development of the nation, its westward movement, its absorption of new lands by displacing Native Americans to reservations and inhospitable places, and its growth of new populations, including its absorption of new immigrant groups from Europe in the early 20th century. (For more information on the history or race and immigration and the laws see the website of the Race project, http://www.understandingrace.org/history/text_timeline.html#soc.)

Issues of the 2000 Census

The censuses of 2000 and 2010 represent a new phase of how the United States counts and documents its citizens, especially citizens of color. The 2000 census was mailed out to nearly all households in the country. However, 12 million households did *not* mail back the survey. As a result, the Census Bureau employed more than one million part-time workers to visit those households. The 2000 census cost more than 4.5 billion dollars, and the total tally was 281,421,906 people. There was concern from many groups of color that in that year's census their numbers were significantly undercounted (especially Hispanic Americans, populations who were recent immigrants, and those for whom English was not their first language). Another issue of the 2000 census was how to acknowledge the growing numbers of people in the United States of two or more known ancestries; the federal government finally decided to incorporate a place in the document where people could write in more than one known racial identity. Eventually, little more than 2 percent of the population took advantage of that option. What follows goes some way toward demonstrating how having multiple ancestries has been handled over time by the U.S. census.

The Multiracial Question

The way that people of mixed ancestry fit into Census categories has only recently changed.

Fitting into the boxes

Before the 2000 census, each person had to be classified as belonging to a specific race. Detailed instructions were given directing how a person of mixed ancestry should be classified. In the previous several censuses, respondents could choose which race they wanted to be identified with, but they were still limited to naming just one race.

"Mark one or more"

The 2000 census was the first in which people were allowed to officially acknowledge all the known or recognized sources of their ancestry by selecting more than one racial category. Roughly 6.8 million people chose more than a single race that year.

1930 census instructions defined the following categories:

1 *Negroes* – A person of mixed white and Negro blood should be returned as a Negro, no matter how small the percentage of Negro blood. Both black and

Figure 13.12   Now the children in this family can choose how the census classifies them. © iStockphoto.com/ RonTech2000.

mulatto persons are to be returned as Negroes, without distinction. A person of mixed Indian and Negro blood should be returned a Negro, unless the Indian blood predominates and the status of an Indian is generally accepted in the community.

2   *Indians* – A person of mixed white and Indian blood should be returned as Indian, except where the percentage of Indian blood is very small, or where he is regarded as a white person by those in the community where he lives.

3   *Mexicans* – Practically all Mexican laborers are of a racial mixture difficult to classify, though usually well recognized in the localities where they are found. In order to obtain separate figures for the racial group, it has been decided that all persons born in Mexico, or having parents born in Mexico, who are definitely not white, Negro, Indian, Chinese, or Japanese, should be returned as Mexican ("Mex").

4   *Other mixed races* – Any mixture of white and nonwhite should be reported according to the non-white parent. Mixtures of colored races should be reported according to the race of the father, except Negro-Indian. (RACE exhibit, SMM)

1990 census instruction

Fill ONE circle for the race that the person considers himself/herself to be.

The Multiracial Question: For and Against

Proposed changes to the 2000 census sparked a debate about how to classify individuals of mixed ancestry as well as about the logic underpinning the race question.

The 2000 census and the multiracial movement

In the 1990s a grassroots movement, consisting mainly of the parents of multiracial children, successfully worked to change how the census collects race data – arguing that a new multiracial category should be added. But many civil rights leaders opposed adding a multiracial category, fearing it would make it harder to gather data needed to enforce antidiscrimination laws.

In the end, the Census Bureau adopted a question that allows people to choose more than one category to describe their ancestry. But this push for a change also led to a more basic question: Should the primary purpose of the race question on the census be to gather data needed in order to trace and undo discrimination, or is it more important to allow people to affirm their identity?

What are people saying?

One thing that has come to bother me more and more in recent years is how to classify myself ethnically or racially on applications and surveys. I have trouble deciding whether to check the "white" box or the "Asian" box, because I don't want to deny either side of my heritage. But I have even more of a conflict when I check the box marked "Other." I'm not an "other" and have never been an "other." I would like to be recognized for the racially mixed person I am. So far, I have only had the chance to check a box marked "biracial" once in my life. (Candace Rea, quoted in Gaskins 1999)

People need groups. But now I would be in favor of checking all boxes that apply. I think the worst thing to do would be to put a multiracial category in the census, because, in effect, you would be buying into the system – a system that you've detested all your life, a system that pressures you to fit into some group. So now you have a group, now you fit into it, but what does that do for racial problems in America? I would hate to see the creation of more racial divisions. (Monina Diaz, quoted in Gaskins 1999)

As a kid, filling out applications was an infrequent but distressing occurrence. I felt overwhelmed being forced to pick between white and black and assumed that I was the only one who had to make this choice. I usually chose what was expected (black) and hoped my reality (white) wouldn't get lost. In college, I was exposed to lots of different people with different identities and was given space to express the complexity of my life experiences, space to identify with the positives of "mixed" rather than with the negatives of trying to [fit] neatly into a single box. (Kemi Adeyemi: RACE exhibit, SMM)

Figure 13.13 Kemi Adeyemi. Courtesy of the Science Museum of Minnesota/C. Thiesen.

Another example of how Americans of more than one ancestry see themselves can be found in the work of Kip Fulbeck, an artist and professor at the University of California, Santa Barbara. In the Hapa Project, he explores through photo-essays, the mixed ethnic heritage of people with Asian or Asian Pacific Islander ancestry and some other ancestry.

How Was the 2010 Census Different for Counting Race?

The 2010 census was different from previous censuses in several important ways. First of all, it was composed of a short form only. It also was the first time since 1940 that that the short form was used. Why did the U.S. Census Bureau decide to the use of the short form in 2010? It happened because the long form, historically mailed to a select number of households, had been replaced by a new national survey in 2007 called the American Community Survey. The American Community Survey (ACS) is a nationwide continuous survey designed to provide reliable and timely demographic, housing, social, and economic

The Hapa Project: Conceived and Produced by Kip Fulbeck

"What are you?" It's a common question among multiracial people in a country focused on tidy racial categories.

ha•pa (hä'pä) **adj**. 1. *Slang*. of mixed ethnic heritage with partial roots in Asian and/or Pacific Islander ancestry. **n**. 2. *Slang*. a person of such ancestry. [*der*./Hawaiian: *hapa haole*. (half white)]

I grew up in Los Angeles during the 1970s. My mother and four siblings are from China, as are my cousins. My father is from New York, the son of English and Irish immigrants. He and I are the only non-Chinese members of the extended family.

At home, I was the "American" kid—the one who couldn't speak Chinese, didn't like the food, and didn't understand the culture. When I went to school, however, I was definitely not white. I got called "Chink," "Chinaman" and many other names that weren't kind. In many ways, I felt like I didn't belong in either world. Fitting in is important to everyone, but especially to kids.

No one talked about multiraciality then. I remember filling out forms asking me to identify my ethnicity by checking "one box only." This made no sense – any more than asking me to pick only my mother or only my father. The option of checking an "Other" box wasn't any better. It would have helped to know there were other people out there who felt the way I did. Even now, when multiraciality does get discussed, it's almost always framed in a black–white paradigm, leaving many of us out of the conversation.

I began *The Hapa Project* in 2001, photographing more than 1,100 people of partial Asian-Pacific Islander descent nationwide. All of the volunteers were photographed identically – unclothed from the collarbone up, without jewelry, glasses, heavy makeup, or purposeful expression. I wanted people to look like themselves. Every participant got to okay their image, and then handwrote their individual response to the question "What are you?" I wanted to give the decision to participate in this conversation back to us. The project has culminated in a traveling exhibition and the book *Part Asian, 100% Hapa*. It's the book I wish I'd had as a kid.

Hapa people now permeate pop culture, from Keanu Reeves to Tiger Woods to Ann Curry to Michelle Branch to The Rock. There are millions of us out there, yet awareness about Hapas remains minimal at best. I hope my project helps raise that awareness. (Kip Fulbeck, artist)[1]

Figure 13.14 "I am a person." Used with permission of Chronicle Books LLC, San Francisco. Visit ChronicleBooks.com.

hawaiian, chinese, german

I'm a grown man who just exposed my breasts to a complete stranger :)

Figure 13.15 "I'm a grown man who just exposed my breasts to a complete stranger." Used with permission of Chronicle Books LLC, San Francisco. Visit ChronicleBooks.com.

[1] For more information, visit www.thehapaproject.com.

data every year, rather than every ten years. The ACS was designed to provide a more accurate and ongoing snapshot of life in the United States (Population Reference Bureau 2009:1) The ACS, according to Linda Jacobsen, Vice President for Domestic Programs of the Population Reference Bureau, is already providing very important data to federal and local governments and non-governmental agencies, including tracking the needs of immigrant and migrant children. For example, the survey was instrumental in determining how many bilingual English–Spanish Census forms were needed for the 2010 census. This was the first time that English–Spanish forms were provided for households (Population Reference Bureau 2009: 1–2) The ACS has been criticized, on the other hand, because it uses a smaller sample size than the traditional census. But the fact that the data can be provided separately by age group, race, Hispanic origin, and sex is seen as a plus for policy makers and lawmakers. It is claimed by the Census Bureau that no other census resource will provide such a plethora of social, economic, and housing information about members of American society than will the ACS survey done on a regular basis. (Population Reference Bureau 2009:1)

African or African American?

The category "African American" includes people of very different backgrounds.

African Americans old and new

Until recently, most people who thought of themselves as black or African American were descended from enslaved persons. Although they were a diverse population, they shared a common history. Over the past several decades, many Africans have been immigrating to the United States, bringing with them a wide range of cultures, languages, and histories. In addition, many of their experiences in the United States differ from those of African Americans with a family history in the country of hundreds of years.

For these reasons, African immigrants and African Americans alike have questioned whether it makes sense for all of them to be grouped together on the census. It is likely that in years to come, the Census Bureau will be pressed to consider this question.

The U.S. Census Bureau states that its racial categories "generally reflect a social definition of race recognized in this country. They do not conform to any biological, anthropological or genetic criteria."

(a)　　　　　(b)　　　　　(c)

Figure 13.16　People representing a wide range of cultures, religions, histories, and physical appearances are classified together within the census's "black or African American, or Negro" category. Courtesy of (a) Mary Begemann; (b) © iStockphoto.com/keeweeboy; (c) Chris McGreevy.

How I would classify myself on the census is a complicated question. Along with the fact that my family comes from Ethiopia, they don't see themselves as black or African American, so the majority of my family classified themselves as "other" on the Census and wrote in "Ethiopian." I, however, having grown up in the U.S., have been classified as a number of things. People ask if I am Middle Eastern, Indian, from the Caribbean, biracial or some combination of any of these nations/races – based on the way I look. With that being said, I would classify myself as African American because I feel I am just that: a person of African descent who was born and raised in the United States. But my family and many others here in the U.S. (even African Americans) may not necessarily agree. (Tinbete Ermyas, personal communication with Sara Ilse, Science Museum of Minnesota, July 2006)

Figure 13.17 Tinbete Ermyas. Courtesy of the Science Museum of Minnesota/C. Thiesen.

As was mentioned earlier in this chapter, there was also a series of issues around race and the census held over from the 2000 census that needed to be addressed. First, there was the issue of the underrepresentation or undercounting of minorities in general. Asian Pacific, African American, and Hispanic groups were concerned that comprehensive outreach would not be made to ascertain and to meet those communities' needs. To mitigate that concern, the U.S. Census Bureau spent millions of dollars reaching out to old and newer ethnic communities, both domestic and immigrant. For example, the Bureau created a "turnkey kit" that was designed to be used by special advocate groups called "Complete Count Committees." These kits were designed to be able to tailor the message to the different diverse communities to encourage people to fill out their census forms (the short form) and mail them back (2010 U.S. Census: P.1–4).

In another instance, the Census Bureau teamed up with *Telemundo*, the international Spanish-speaking television conglomerate, which reaches over one million Spanish-speaking persons nightly in the United States, to promote the 2010 census in one of their most popular telenovas, *Mas Sabe El Diablo* (*The Devil*

Knows Best) (Montgomery 2009:1–3). In another example, an attempt to reach out to Native Americans, who are routinely and chronically undercounted, the Bureau partnered with such groups as the National Congress of American Indians. This was a government-to-government approach where the representatives from the Census Bureau made formal presentations to 564 federally recognized tribes and asked permission to conduct operations on tribal lands. In an article written in May 2010, Greg Guedel estimates that through these outreach efforts, the Tulalip Tribes alone boosted their mail-in return rate to 70 percent, even before the census workers got there. This is in contrast to the 2000 census where the final return rate was only 54 percent among the tribes (Guedel 2010:102).

The United States government communicated the importance of gathering the 2010 census data to a broad array of constituent groups. The government cited the following reasons for wanting the census information: (1) the need to know how to allocate over $400 billion dollars to states and communities; (2) the need to know how to allocate resources for new housing, roads, and educational programs; and (3) the need to gather data for use by Native American decision- and policy-makers as they apply for grants and develop business plans for construction of new roads, housing, hospitals, childcare and senior citizen centers, schools, and more (United States Census Bureau 2009). So, the focus on use of the census data collected to help communities that had been underserved in the past hit a positive chord.

LGBT – lesbian, gay, bisexual, and transgendered communities and the census

For the first time in the history of the census, the Census Bureau made a concerted effort to reach out to all of the LGBT communities in the United States, and especially to LGBT communities of color. For example, in the Latino community, the Latino Equality Alliance and The Mexican American Legal Defense and Education Fund (MALDEF) helped to get the word out. The National Queer Asian Pacific Islander (NQAPIA) and the International Federation of Black Prides were organizations that also worked with the Census Bureau to get their constituents counted in the 2010 census. These organizations all wanted the people in their communities counted for the purposes of obtaining resources for them and for their families. As expressed by Matthew Alder of MALDEF, "The Census is extremely important for communities of color and immigrants, especially Latinos. Often it is people at the intersection of minority communities such as the LGBT people of color who are most under-documented and therefore, benefit the least from resources allocated by the Census." (Our Families Count 2010). Benjamin DeGuzman of the National Queer Asian Pacific Islander Alliance echoes the same sentiments when he says "It is a critical time for the Census to be reaching out in our communities. Despite the heightened tension that new laws in Arizona create for immigrants and anyone the state might think 'looks like an illegal immigrant,' we need to respond to enumerations and get counted now more than ever" (Our Families Count 2010)

Concern about homeless and undocumented workers

The census merely counted who was in the country during the weeks surrounding April 1, 2010 – National Census Day. The census counts persons present in households, not necessarily citizens. In other words, there is no requirement to have a permanent residence or to have a legal status as a U.S. citizen to be counted. It was often hard for census workers in previous years to find people to count who were frightened or did not want to be counted. On the other hand, there are those people who think that states like California are violating the Constitution by counting people who will give the state extra seats based on people who are not U.S. citizens. Since 1980, the census has not distinguished citizenship from those people who are present illegally. Baker and Stonecipher (2009) talk in very specific ways about how a state like California benefits, maybe undeservedly so. They note "according to the latest ACS survey, California has 5,622,422 non-citizens in its population of 36,264,467. Based on our round number projection of a decade-end population in that state of 37,000,000 (including 5,750,000 non-citizens) … the Census has drifted far from its constitutional roots, and

the 2010 enumeration will result in a misalignment of Congress" (Baker and Stonecipher 2009:1–2).

Language Issues: Who is Counted and what are they Called?

There are several language and identity issues that have been raised by the 2010 census. Among them is the controversy surrounding the use of the word "Negro." Some people were concerned that the 2010 census used the word "Negro" along with "Black" and "African American." As we indicated earlier in this chapter, racial terms have been used in a very fluid and changing way on the U.S. census, and the census at some level is a reflection of the mores and values of U.S society, particularly as they relate to race, ethnicity, identity, and social status at any given point in time in the nation's history. In 1960 the census did not contain the word black, only Negro was used. At that time in history, many African Americans identified as "Negro." By 1970 you could check "Negro" or "Black" on the census. It was the first appearance of "Black" since 1920. It was not clear why the word black was used in 1920. In 1980 the order was changed to "Black" first and then "Negro." And in 2000, people were allowed to choose more than one racial group on the census form for the first time.

Counting Hispanic and Latino Ancestry

In 1970 a question about Hispanic ethnicity was added to the U.S. Census.

The need

In order to see that the social legislation of the 1960s was working effectively, the federal government had to gather reliable data about the groups of people that the laws aimed to help, including U.S. Hispanics. For example, affirmative action programs used statistics about the number of minority workers in a community to determine if all groups were receiving equal access to employment opportunities.

Adding the question

From the late 1960s through the 1970s, Mexican-American leaders worked to get a Hispanic-ethnicity question added to the census. At first, the Census Bureau resisted the idea because the notion of Hispanic ethnicity seemed too subjective. However, an ethnicity question was added to some 1970 census forms, and ten years later one appeared on all 1980 census questionnaires. For the 2000 census, the question was expanded to include the term Latino.

An ethnicity, not a race

According to the Census Bureau, Hispanic and Latino are ethnic designations, and those who identify themselves as Hispanic can belong to any race. The distinction between ethnicity and race is unclear to many people. A number of those who pick Hispanic in response to the ethnicity question on the census choose "Some other race" and fill in Hispanic, Latino, Chicano, or the name of a Latin American country when answering the race question.

Figure 13.18 Jessica Masterson. Courtesy of the Science Museum of Minnesota/C. Thiesen.

Hispanic leaders … got indigenous bilingual enumerators to work in Hispanic neighborhoods. They got the government to hire aliens as temporary census workers. … They also got public assurances from high federal officials that the Immigration and Naturalization Service would not conduct raids in the barrios while the census was in progress. (Choldin 1986)

I strongly dislike the term *Hispanic* because it implies a tie to Spain that my family does not identify with in the least. Of course, the language we speak was originally theirs, but over time I think it evolved to be much more than the language of the oppressor. It became ours. I definitely prefer *Latina* or *Latino* when talking about people whose ancestry lies in Latin America. (Jessica Masterson, personal communication with Sara Ilse, Science Museum of Minnesota, July 2006)

The second big language issue, and also a problem in the 2000 census, was how to count Hispanics. Despite the long history of Hispanic residence in the United States, there was still no systematic effort to count this group separately in the census until the late 20th century. Hispanics make up 16 percent or 48 million of the people in the United States today and constitute the country's largest minority. There was a one-time inclusion of "Mexican" as a race on the 1930 census. Census takers identified people by race on the census forms prior to 1970. However, in 1970, residents were allowed to identify themselves, or self-identify racially, on the census form, and not have the census enumerator do it. Wording the question relating to Hispanic or Latino identity was problematic. It was apparently very confusing to everyone, not just Hispanics. In 1980 the question of Hispanic identity was moved to the short form and was reworded. The 1980 census counted 14.6 million Hispanic/Latinos and was deemed by the Census Bureau to have worked rather well. In 1990 the Hispanic origin question was virtually identical to the 1980 question and counted more than 22 million Hispanics. However, this census form included a new write-in line to specify "other Spanish/Hispanic" origins. The form also shortened the category name to "Mexican Am" from "Mexican-Amer" which helped to deal with the problem of non-Hispanics answering the "American" portion of the census form.

The 2000 census counted more than 35 million Hispanics and saw some changes in the Hispanic origin item. The term "Latino" was added, and so the question on the census form read, "Is the person Spanish/Hispanic/Latino?" The Hispanic origin question preceded the race question and people were advised to answer *both* questions. People were asked to mark the *No* box if the person was not "Spanish/Hispanic/Latino."

In the 2010 census there were two other changes. The order of the term was different. The word "Spanish" was the third rather than the first word and the word "origin" was added. The wording of response categories was changed to reflect the questions' wording. In the lead-in to the question, respondents were instructed to answer *both* the Hispanic origin *and* race items, and to

United States Census 2010

This is the official form for all the people at this address.
It is quick and easy, and your answers are protected by law.

U.S. DEPARTMENT OF COMMERCE
Economics and Statistics Administration
U.S. CENSUS BUREAU

Use a blue or black pen.

Start here

The Census must count every person living in the United States on April 1, 2010.

Before you answer Question 1, count the people living in this house, apartment, or mobile home using our guidelines.

- Count all people, including babies, who live and sleep here most of the time.

The Census Bureau also conducts counts in institutions and other places, so:

- Do not count anyone living away either at college or in the Armed Forces.
- Do not count anyone in a nursing home, jail, prison, detention facility, etc., on April 1, 2010.
- Leave these people off your form, even if they will return to live here after they leave college, the nursing home, the military, jail, etc. Otherwise, they may be counted twice.

The Census must also include people without a permanent place to stay, so:

- If someone who has no permanent place to stay is staying here on April 1, 2010, count that person. Otherwise, he or she may be missed in the census.

1. How many people were living or staying in this house, apartment, or mobile home on April 1, 2010?

Number of people =

2. Were there any <u>additional</u> people staying here April 1, 2010 that you <u>did not include</u> in Question 1? *Mark ☒ all that apply.*

- [ ] Children, such as newborn babies or foster children
- [ ] Relatives, such as adult children, cousins, or in-laws
- [ ] Nonrelatives, such as roommates or live-in baby sitters
- [ ] People staying here temporarily
- [ ] No additional people

3. Is this house, apartment, or mobile home — *Mark ☒ ONE box.*

- [ ] Owned by you or someone in this household with a mortgage or loan? *Include home equity loans.*
- [ ] Owned by you or someone in this household free and clear (without a mortgage or loan)?
- [ ] Rented?
- [ ] Occupied without payment of rent?

4. What is your telephone number? *We may call if we don't understand an answer.*

Area Code + Number

OMB No. 0607-0919-C: Approval Expires 12/31/2011.

Form **D-61** (1-15-2009)

5. Please provide information for each person living here. Start with a person living here who owns or rents this house, apartment, or mobile home. If the owner or renter lives somewhere else, start with any adult living here. This will be Person 1.

What is Person 1's name? *Print name below.*

Last Name

First Name   MI

6. What is Person 1's sex? *Mark ☒ ONE box.*

- [ ] Male [ ] Female

7. What is Person 1's age and what is Person 1's date of birth?

Please report babies as age 0 when the child is less than 1 year old. Print numbers in boxes.

Age on April 1, 2010   Month   Day   Year of birth

→ NOTE: Please answer BOTH Question 8 about Hispanic origin and Question 9 about race. For this census, Hispanic origins are not races.

8. Is Person 1 of Hispanic, Latino, or Spanish origin?

- [ ] **No,** not of Hispanic, Latino, or Spanish origin
- [ ] Yes, Mexican, Mexican Am., Chicano
- [ ] Yes, Puerto Rican
- [ ] Yes, Cuban
- [ ] Yes, another Hispanic, Latino, or Spanish origin — *Print origin, for example, Argentinean, Colombian, Dominican, Nicaraguan, Salvadoran, Spaniard, and so on.*

9. What is Person 1's race? *Mark ☒ one or more boxes.*

- [ ] White
- [ ] Black, African Am., or Negro
- [ ] American Indian or Alaska Native — *Print name of enrolled or principal tribe.*

- [ ] Asian Indian   [ ] Japanese   [ ] Native Hawaiian
- [ ] Chinese   [ ] Korean   [ ] Guamanian or Chamorro
- [ ] Filipino   [ ] Vietnamese   [ ] Samoan
- [ ] Other Asian — *Print race, for example, Hmong, Laotian, Thai, Pakistani, Cambodian, and so on.*   [ ] Other Pacific Islander — *Print race, for example, Fijian, Tongan, and so on.*

- [ ] Some other race — *Print race.*

10. Does Person 1 sometimes live or stay somewhere else?

- [ ] No [ ] Yes — *Mark ☒ all that apply.*
  - [ ] In college housing   [ ] For child custody
  - [ ] In the military   [ ] In jail or prison
  - [ ] At a seasonal or second residence   [ ] In a nursing home
  - [ ] For another reason

→ If more people were counted in Question 1, continue with Person 2.

Figure 13.19 United States Census Bureau 2010 questionnaire. Courtesy of the United States Census Bureau.

name them, not just number them. The census instruction statement also said "Hispanic origins are not races." Finally, the instructions to "Mark *No*, if not Hispanic" was eliminated. We will have to wait to see what impact, if any, the changes will have. (See Figure 13.19 for a look at the questions on the short form 2010 Census).

Was the 2010 Census Successful on Issues of Documenting Race?

The Race: Are We So Different? initiative posits that the concept of race is not real biologically, but that it is very much real as a social and cultural construct. Our goal as anthropologists is to make sure that our students and the general public understand how the fluid concept has changed over time, and is in the process of changing today as well. There are anthropologists and other scholars who think that the race questions on the U.S. census forms of 2000 and 2010 are cumbersome, inaccurate, and inadequate; especially as they relate to capturing the experiences of mixed heritage people. For example, see Kim William's book, *Mark One or More: Civil Rights in Multicultural* America (2006). This interesting book chronicles the political grassroots movement that resulted in the 2000 census allowing Americans, for the first time ever, to write in more than one identity.

Even more troubling for us as scientists and humanists are the questions of (1) of who gets to decide what is put on the census forms and (2) how useful the census data are for documenting the pulse of the nation as people define who they are for themselves. We have had hours and hours of discussion, dialogue, and debate about this issue among our own Project Advisory Board as we put the exhibit, website, and teaching materials together. In the end, we finally documented the facts that show that people in the United States have moved and live beyond these stationary fixed categories of identity that we find on the current census forms. It is up to the government (with help from the people of the nation) to figure how to capture those changes and new ways of thinking and talking about "race."

Visitors to the exhibit have the opportunity to give their opinions on the future of the U.S. census as well.

They are asked to consider four options: (1) "Stay the course" – continue using current race categories; (2) "Simplify" – use fewer categories and list them in alphabetical order; (3) "Have it your way" – allow each person to define his or her own categories; and (4) "No question at all" – remove the question of race from the U.S. census completely. What option do you think is best?

Ken Prewitt, a member of the RACE Project Advisory Board and former Director of the U.S. Census Bureau, believes that the race questions on the 2010 census were still "broken," especially around the question of race and Hispanic ethnicity. While acknowledging the need to collect census data by race and ethnicity in order to shed light on disparities and discrimination based on color, ancestry, or immigrant status, he indicates that this should be done more carefully. He says, "[if] the census form asked the question, 'What national origin, ethnicity, tribe, language group or ancestry do you consider yourself to be?' (and List all of these that are important to you) then we would be letting the people of the U.S. speak for themselves" (Prewitt 2010). According to Prewitt, this would finally move the census away from the racial hierarchy established in the 1790 survey. Indeed, he argues that it would move us away from the use of the term "race" itself and would allow people to define for themselves who they are and finally, would allow people to claim their multiple identities. He goes on to say,

> This question does not assume that a recently arrived Ethiopian belongs to the same (*social*) race as 10th generation descendants of enslaved people from Africa's Gold Coast. It does not put 5th generation Chinese Americans in the same box as 1st generation Vietnamese. It does not count an Argentinean who speaks only English the same way it treats a Mayan immigrant. (Prewitt 2010)

Unfortunately, he does not believe that either the current Congress nor the Obama White House will mediate a serious discussion or national conversation at this time. While the government may not have the political will to take on the challenge, he puts the challenge to universities, scholars, the media, advocacy organizations, and the informed public to push for these changes.

Prewitt and others, including the contributors to and the editors of this book, would agree that the continual collection of data to understand where to put governmental resources is very necessary. But, how we do it must reflect the racial, ethnic, and identity realities of the 21st-century United States.

We end this chapter with an essay that will help us to reflect on one of these complex realities. Arlene Torres, in "AfroLatina/o Culture in the 21st Century" challenges us to see the linguistic and cultural diversity that exists among this group that we call Latino.

ARLENE TORRES

AfroLatina/o Culture in the 21st Century

Arlene Torres is Director of the Latino Faculty Recruitment Initiative at CUNY, and Associate. Professor in the Department of Africana and Puerto Rican Studies at Hunter College. A cultural anthropologist, Dr. Torres has published on a wide range of topics including race, migration and transnationalism, class, and economic development in the United States and the Caribbean. Dr. Torres also served as a member of the RACE Project Advisory Board. Photograph courtesy of Arlene Torres.

The purpose of this essay is to prompt us to consider the Latino presence in the United States, immigration, the color line, racializing practices, and the development of social relations and institutions.

W. E. B. Du Bois made the following observations in the 1950s: "This newest South, turning back to its slave past, believes its present and future prosperity can best be built on the poverty and ignorance of its disfranchised lowest masses – and these low-paid workers now include not only Negroes, but Mexicans, Puerto Ricans, and the unskilled, unorganized whites. Progress by means of this poverty is the creed of the present South." This excerpt informs some of the issues we are grappling with and will be concerned with in the southern

United States and throughout the nation well into the 21st century. Social analyses have yet to fully grasp how the Latino presence and more specifically migrant, immigrant, and settler communities in the United States are changing the face of the country. How we rise to the challenges this entails will also define how we live in locales that inform the future of all.

Du Bois argued that the central problem of the 20th century was the color line. How do migration, immigration, and settlement inform social relations, one-drop rule, and the black/white color line? In the United States, individuals with any African ancestry were considered black. Individuals of mixed race were classified as mulattoes, as nonwhites. However, the extent to which they were incorporated into their communities was informed by legal, social, and cultural mores that have changed over time. Increases in Latino migration, immigration, and settlement into areas heretofore unseen have prompted us to consider its impact on the nature of the color line. The problem of the 21st century is the shifting nature of the color line. A line that was rather rigidly defined is now more ambiguous and ripe for the promotion and practice of racism and ethnocentrism under the guise of difference based on citizenship, class, color, language, and cultural practices. While some would argue that the color line has begun to disappear, we could argue that a white/nonwhite color line that incorporates the vestiges of the past informs the contemporary racial terrain.

Because race is a social construct, how Americans define who belongs to a racial group is subject to change and it is changing. As immigrants are incorporated into U.S. society they are differentially integrated based on perceptions about their racial heritage and status. Some scholars argue that Latinos, for example, are being differentially incorporated based on perceived notions of racial belonging along the white/ nonwhite color line. Other scholars argue that Latinos are pursuing whiteness. Critical questions emerge. If Latinos are pursuing whiteness, how is that pursuit being defined and realized? Or are Latinos pursuing other strategies toward upward mobility where racial/ ethnic boundaries are crossed and maintained selectively. Moreover, how is this selectivity, informed by history, community, place, and the prevalence of pigmentocracies and the persistence of racism? How are those currently designated as white ethnics responding to this? We know that those who seek to maintain privilege and power do selectively incorporate some ethnic/racial groups and not others to ensure their privileged position in a racial hierarchy. If we pursue this a bit further then it behooves us to continually investigate how members of an ethnic group are incorporated while others are rendered marginal or explicitly discriminated against based on negative ascriptions associated with being black or nonwhite.

The behavior of Latinos is informed by racializing practices historically and contemporaneously from their country of origin whether that is the continental United States, Latin America or the Caribbean. African and indigenous slavery forms part of the legacy of Latin America and the Caribbean. This challenges us to rethink the ways by which slavery in Latin America and the Caribbean informs the experiences of Afro descendant immigrants in the United States. The reification of ideologies of *mestizaje* (of racial intermingling), the social formation of *mestizo* (mixed-race) subjects, and the propensity to render a struggle to affirm a black identity as steeped in the distant past and isolated to specific locales within these nation-states complicates matters.

The sense of dislocation experienced by Latino immigrants to the United States who believe that they are white given racial categories and practices in their home countries is quite profound. Additionally, AfroLatinos whose experience with racism in Latin America and the Caribbean differs also experience disjunctures as they seek to understand how they are socially positioned in a racialized terrain informed by the one-drop rule. This necessitates an exploration of the kinds of

strategies and limitations Latinos contend with in the face of racializing practices and institutions of power in the Americas. In an effort to assert their own identity, some Latinos do distance themselves from African Americans and their AfroLatino counterparts, and in other cases Latinos and those who define themselves as AfroLatinos seek to align themselves with groups who also experience racism and discrimination. As differences are collapsed and subsumed under the category Latino, racialized and ethnic groups have the potential to develop productive alliances with one another.

Who counts as Latino in the 21st century? What is at stake given the U.S. racial framework that has not supported racial intermingling in spite of localized practices throughout the nation's history? Do Puerto Ricans, Dominicans, Panamanians, Mexicans, Columbians, Venezuelans, Nicaraguans, and Brazilians of African ancestry identify as Latinos and as AfroLatinos? How do we determine who is and is not of African ancestry given the legacy of slavery and social and cultural intermingling in Latin America, the Caribbean? Today, stereotypical assumptions, myths, and misconceptions continue to permeate the media in the United States, Latin America, and the Caribbean and they do inform perception. Racializing imagery in Spanish- and English-language television, comic books, and other media reveal the propensity to support a pigmentocracy that devalues blackness. The ideology of whiteness ascribes negativity to features associated with blacks and others who are rendered nonwhite. Even if the ideology of *mestizaje* is at play, there is a racial continuum from black to white that places higher value on those located on the whiter end of the continuum. However, this does not mean that social movements and ideologies of blackness do not exist. Indeed they do. Claims to blackness, Latinidad, and to Afrolatinidad in Latin America, the Caribbean, and the United States are possible. These are complex social and cultural processes that are also informed by changing ideas about race, regional histories, settlement patterns, and social interactions that must be examined via sustained research and scholarship.

References

Anderson, M. J.
1988 The American Census: A Social History. New Haven, CT: Yale University Press.

Baker, S. and Stonecipher, E.
2009 Our Unconstitutional Census California could get nine House seats it doesn't deserve because illegal aliens will be counted in 2010. Wall Street Journal, August 9. http://online.wsj.com/article/SB10001424052970204908604574332950796281832.html, accessed January 24, 2012.

Choldin, Harvey M.
1986 Statistics and Politics: The "Hispanic Issue" in the 1980 Census. Demography, August.

Gaskins, Pearl Fuyo
1999 What Are You?: Voices of Mixed Race Young People. New York: Henry Holt and Company.

Guedel, G.
2010 2010 Census Count Improving For Native Americans. Native American Legal Update, May 28. http://www.nativelegalupdate.com/2010/05/, accessed June 15, 2010.

Montgomery, D.
2009 To engage Latinos about census, telenovela steps up to be counted. The Washington Post, October 7. www.washingtonpost.com/wp-dyn/content/article/2009/10/06/AR2009100601643.html, accessed October 7, 2009.

Our Families Count
2010 LGBT Communities of Color Unite for the 2010 Census Fear doesn't count El miedo no cuenta. Washington, D.C.: Our Families Count. May 6, http://ourfamilies-count.org/, accessed December 13, 2011.

Population Reference Bureau
2009 About the American Community Survey. Washington, DC: Population Reference Bureau.

Prewitt, K.
2010 How to fix Census' broken race question. USAToday.com, July 12. http://www.usatoday.com/news/opinion/forum/2010-07-13-column13_ST_N.htm, accessed January 24, 2012.

U.S. Census Bureau
2009 A Journey of Many Voices, July 2009. July 7. Washington, DC: U.S. Census Bureau.

U.S. Census Bureau
2010 Take 1: Turnkey Kit. Washington, DC: U.S. Census Bureau.

William Kim,
2006 Mark One or More: Civil Rights in Multicultural America. Ann Arbor: University of Michigan Press.

14

Race and Education

This chapter will highlight the story of education and race in the United States, focusing on the impact of school segregation then and now and on the lingering achievement gap between whites and other minorities and looking at the implication of this gap on higher education aspirations, the future of minorities in science, and finally, at the link between education achievement and wealth accumulation. As you have read in part 1, the education of racialized groups and immigrants in the United States has been less than stellar (see chapter 6 for a more detailed look at the provision of schooling, or lack thereof, for Native Americans, freed slaves, and immigrant groups in the 19th and early 20th centuries.)

On the west coast, in San Francisco, California in 1906, an international crisis was set off when the Japanese government protested the fact that the San Francisco Board of Education ordered the segregation of Asian children in all public schools. People are familiar with segregation and Jim Crow laws in the southern states of the United States; however, this educational segregation along racial/ethnic lines in schools was not infrequent in California. As a matter of fact, it was the *Mendez v. Westminster* case, where the Westminster, California school district segregated its Mexican students into certain schools based on skin color, that helped to provide a background case for the *Brown v. Board of Education* Supreme Court case in 1954. The Mendez family challenged the California school segregation law and won. Their case was brought to the attention of Thurgood Marshall, the NAACP lawyer who would later use this successful model to support the NAACP case, *Brown v. the Board of Education of Topeka, Kansas* (See Ian Haney López's essay in chapter 6 for more details).

On May 17, 1954, the United States Supreme Court handed down a 9:0 decision in *Brown v. Board of Education* which stated that separate education facilities are inherently unequal. The decision reversed the precedent set by the Supreme Court's previous decision in *Cummings v. Richmond County Board of Education (1899)*, which had validated the segregation of public schools. *Brown* did not immediately result in the desegregation of America's public schools, nor did it mandate desegregation of public accommodations such as restaurants or bathrooms that were private property. This would not happen until the Civil Rights Act of 1964. In 1955, the Supreme Court completed its ruling and instructed the local states that with "all deliberate speed" they should move to desegregate public schools. Even so, compliance was not immediate, and most states (and northern cities such as Boston, Massachusetts) did not desegregate until the late 1960s or early 1970s. Recent studies have found that public schools, especially in poor urban neighborhoods, are still segregated (understandingrace.org website: Government Timeline, 2007).

The geographic segregation of housing has a negative impact on the quality of the schools many minority children have to attend. Having fewer resources, these

Race: Are We So Different?, First Edition. Alan H. Goodman, Yolanda T. Moses, and Joseph L. Jones.
© 2012 American Anthropological Association. Published 2012 by Blackwell Publishing Ltd.

schools often are underfunded. For example, only 25 percent of poor white families live in neighborhoods of concentrated poverty with levels over 20 percent compared to 75 percent of poor blacks and 66 percent of Latino families.

The 1960s and the 1970s saw the continued push at both the state and federal levels of government to promote school integration across this country. These plans were met with limited success. There were cities in the north, like Boston, whose citizens resisted by showing up and taunting the children who got off the buses in their neighborhoods. Boston was a city where the courts ordered black children to be sent on buses to white neighborhoods while white children would be bused to black neighborhoods. This was repeated and resisted in cities around the nation. One way that white families avoided integration in this instance was to move out of the cities; thus, federally mandated school desegregation was a major boost to white flight in the United States in the late 1960s and early 1970s.

School Segregation

The geographic segregation of housing has a negative impact on the quality of schools that minority students attend.

A race and class issue
Many poor black and Latino families live in areas of concentrated poverty. Only one-quarter of poor white families live in neighborhoods with poverty levels over 20 percent, but three-quarters of poor black and two-thirds of poor Latino families do. Public schools in poorer areas typically have fewer resources than those in middle-class areas. Because white families are less likely to live in such places, poor white children are less likely to attend these schools than poor children of color.

Desegregating schools
During the 1960s and 1970s, federal and state governments passed laws aimed at addressing educational inequalities that had resulted from the segregation of schools. These laws were largely successful in integrating many public school systems nationwide.

Resegregation
In the 1990s the legality of many desegregation efforts was successfully challenged, resulting in the resegregation of some schools. In certain American cities today, school districts are nearly as segregated as they were fifty years ago.

"Segregated schools and neighborhoods isolate children from networks and connections that are important for gaining opportunities for social and economic success" (Myron Orfield, Institute on Race and Poverty, University of Minnesota School Segregation: RACE exhibit, SMM).

Boston: a case study
In 1974 U.S. District Court Judge Arthur Garrity ruled that the Boston School Committee had "knowingly carried out a systematic program of segregation." To remedy the situation, the court ordered black children to be bused to schools in

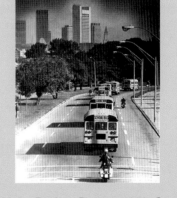

Figure 14.1 Busing. Boston, 1976. Courtesy of the Boston Herald.

mainly white areas of Boston, while white children were bused to schools in largely black neighborhoods.

Response to the busing was heated and at times violent. At some schools in white neighborhoods, rocks were thrown at black children as they got off their buses. Many white parents withdrew their children from the public school system and sent them to private schools.

Judge Garrity's busing order was enforced until 1989, when a policy of "controlled choice" was implemented: parents were allowed some choice in selecting schools, but the racial makeup of each school was matched to the racial makeup of the city as a whole. In 1999 a lawsuit was brought by a group of white parents alleging that the policy was discriminatory, and the racial-proportionality policy was abandoned. Today, as a result of white migration to the suburbs and enroll-

ment in private schools, only 15 percent of Boston public school students are white.

Louisville, Kentucky: a case study

In order to ensure that its schools are integrated, the metropolitan Louisville, Kentucky school district had a policy that dictated that the student body of each school must be 15–50 percent black. In 2002, parents of some white students took the school district to court, claiming that this practice amounts to racial discrimination and violates their children's rights to attend the school of their choice.

In June 2007 the U.S. Supreme Court ruled, in a closely divided 5:4 vote, that public school systems cannot classify students by race for the purpose of school assignments. The implications for this decision are currently being worked out in school districts throughout the United States, and further legal challenges are expected in coming years.

According to educational researchers such as Myron Orfield at the University of Minnesota, segregated schools and neighborhoods isolate children from networks and connections that are important for gaining opportunities for social and economic success.

Data from National Center for Educational Statistics (2010) shows that the racial/ethnic distribution of public elementary and secondary students has changed over time. Between 2000–01 and 2007–08, the number of students enrolled in public schools who were white decreased from 61 to 56 percent. During the same time period, the percentage of black and American Indian/Alaskan Native students remained unchanged at 17 percent and 1 percent respectively, but the percentage of Hispanic students increased from 17 to 21 percent and the percentage of Asian Pacific Islander students increased from 4 to 5 percent.

Closing the "Achievement Gap"

One of the most intractable problems in public education in the United States is the persistent gap in test scores between black and Latino students on one

hand and White and Asian Pacific Islander students as a group on the other hand. For a detailed literature review and academic explanation of the achievement gap see Henze 2007. One of the key messages of this chapter is that the language used to frame the issue is one loaded with negative assumptions. Eschewing the notion that the issue is a natural phenomenon, the authors propose not to talk about the "achievement gap" but instead to use the words "opportunity gap" to describe and locate the persistent racial problem with the institutions and environmental conditions that provide opportunities for certain students and *not* others. The "opportunity gap" is the "logical outcome of hundreds of years of racialized hierarchy in the United States. We are reaping in the 21st century seeds that were sown in the United States centuries ago. It shows us how powerfully cultural constructions of inequality based on race have worked to the point that even now, when most people want to undo the legacy of racism, the legacy persists" (Mukhopadhyay, Henze, and Moses 2007:202).

Many factors are likely to continue to contribute to the racial gap in scores on standardized tests, among them are parents' educational level, lower quality and poor schools, less qualified teachers, and fewer

The Race Gap in Standardized Test Scores

Many factors are likely contribute to the gap in scores on standardized tests.

Testing in schools

Standardized tests are used to gauge student abilities and evaluate the effectiveness of teaching. Increasingly, passing such tests has become a condition for high school graduation. Also, scores on the SAT or ACT are crucial for acceptance at many colleges and universities.

A racial gap in standardized test scores – on average, African American students score lower than white students do – is well documented. Much research has been done to uncover the reasons for this gap. Among the factors that have been found to play a role are socioeconomic differences between students' families, differences in parental educational levels, and racial or cultural bias built into the tests themselves.

Better preparation results in better scores

Minority students are more likely to attend schools in low-income areas that receive less public funding, have less qualified teachers and offer fewer high-level academic courses. Students who attend high-quality schools have an edge when it comes to standardized tests. In addition, test-preparation classes for the SAT and ACT can raise students' scores. But the high cost of these private classes makes them inaccessible to many lower-income students.

"In short, what is being measured by the SAT is not absolutes like native ability and merit but accidents like birth, social position, access to libraries, and the opportunity to take vacations or take SAT prep courses" (Stanley Fish, legal scholar, Florida International University: RACE exhibit, SMM).

The psychology of test taking

A set of five experiments conducted in the 1990s provides a possible explanation for at least part of the disparity in standardized test scores – the fear of confirming negative stereotypes.

In the experiments, African American and white undergraduate students were given a 30-minute test composed of questions from the Graduate Record Examination in literature. Half the students were told that the test was a measure of their academic ability while the other half were told that the test was not a measure of ability but designed to study how difficult verbal problems are solved. The African American students who were told the test was a measure of ability scored lower on average than the white students. But those African American students who were told that it was not a measure of ability scored as well as the white students. The white students scored equally well in both situations. The researchers hypothesize that the performance of African American students who were told the test measured ability was impaired by their fear of confirming negative stereotypes about their intellectual skill.

"Whenever African American students perform an explicitly scholastic or intellectual task, they face the threat of confirming or being judged by a negative societal stereotype – a suspicion – about their group's intellectual ability and competence. ... This additional threat, in turn, may interfere with their performance" (Steele and Aronson 1995).

high-level academic courses. In addition, many students who attend higher quality schools have an advantage when it comes to taking standardized tests because they can afford test preparation classes for the Scholastic Aptitude Test (SAT) or American College Testing (ACT) and have the time and money to take the test multiple times.

Research by social scientist Claude Steele conducted in the 1990s provided another possible explanation for racial disparity in test scores: fear of standardized tests and the resulting stereotype that poor performance may incur. Mica Pollock in the article "From "Shallow to Deep: Towards a Thorough Cultural Analyses of School Achievement Patterns," and in

Going Down the Wrong Track

In schools with ability-based tracking, students of color are often placed in lower-level, non-college-preparatory classes.

Figure 14.2   Students in classroom. © iStockphoto/ bonniej graphic design.

What is tracking?

Tracking is the practice of grouping students and organizing classes according to the level of difficulty. For example, high school students on an advanced math track might take geometry during their freshman year, algebra 2 as sophomores, pre-calculus and trigonometry in their junior year, and calculus as seniors. Meanwhile, those on a lower math track take pre-algebra, algebra 1, geometry, and finally algebra 2 in their senior year. Because each class builds on the previous classes, it is very hard for a student who starts on a lower track to move up to a higher one.

How do students get onto tracks?

Students are placed on tracks through a combination of teacher recommendations, grades, scores on standardized tests, and the preferences of the students and their parents. Most studies of tracking have found that African American, Latino, and low-income students heavily populate the lower tracks, but there is little agreement about why this disparity occurs.

Unfortunate consequences

Typically, lower-track classes tend to have less engaging curricula and lower expectations of student achievement. Combine this with the difficulty of advancing from a low track to a higher one, and the result is that students who start high school in lower-tracked classes are often less prepared for college or higher-paying jobs than their higher-tracked peers.

In many states, concern about the social inequities perpetuated by tracking has led some school districts to de-track schools. However, evidence about whether student achievement is higher at tracked or untracked schools is inconclusive. Ability-based tracking has long-term impacts on students.

> Perceptions of students' suitability for classes at various track levels were also influenced by race, ethnicity, and social class. ...Racial groups had become identified in most educators' minds with particular tracks. Asians, almost uniformly considered by educators to be highly capable and motivated, were strongly identified with the highest tracks. ... In contrast, Latinos ... were almost always judged as the least well-suited for academic work and were most often associated with low-track academic courses and vocational programs. (Oakes and Guiton 1995)

her essay at the end of this chapter, challenges anthropologists and others to counteract what she sees as a shallow analysis of culture. She contends that "these analyses purport in schools to explain achievement gaps by making quick claims about how parents and children from various racial/ethnic, natural origin or class groups react to schools. Such shallow analyses dangerously oversimplify the social processes, interactions and practices that create disparate outcomes for children" (Pollock 2008:369).

One of the structural ways that some students are directed on non-college trajectories in schools is through the process of tracking, which is the practice of grouping students and organizing classes according to level of difficulty in the subject content. Students are placed on tracks because of a combination of teacher recommendations, grades, scores on standardized testing, and the desires of students and their parents. Most studies of tracking have found that African American, Latino, and low-income students in general heavily populate the lower tracks in schools across the country. There is often difficulty moving from one track to another. The unfortunate consequences are that the curricula is often less challenging in the lower-level tracks. Some administrators have decided that tracking is so negative an experience for students that they have decided to detrack their schools entirely.

There are some researchers who suggest that all schools should be detracked. In the book *Detracking for Excellence and Equity* Carol Corbett Burris and Delia T. Garret write about how their school did away with the tracking system. In the place of tracking, they actually put in place a "detracking" process of reform for the Rockville Centre School District. The implementation of their detracking program resulted in the near elimination of the racial socioeconomic gap that existed before. The reform required careful cultural and political work. The authors talked about what the school was like before detracking was introduced: "Minority students and low socioeconomic-status (SES) students were overrepresented in the lowest tracks. In addition, tensions existed between minority and majority students in the low-tract classes, and the classroom focus was on discipline rather than on academics. The learning outcomes reflected this inequity of opportunity as well" (Burris and Garrity 2008:6).

At the end of the book, the authors lay out a list of *beliefs* that must be in place for any school to be successful with detracking. These beliefs and institutional values are laid out here:

- Schools and opportunity matter.
- Acceleration and enrichment improve students' achievements.
- All students have gifts and talents.
- All students deserve access to the best curriculum.
- The achievement gap can close.

- Schools have an obligation to be learning organizations.
- Teaching requires great skill and extraordinary dedication.
- School leadership requires vision and courage.
- Education is the fundamental method of social progress and reform (John Dewey).
- Success can be a beautiful Harvest. (Burris and Garrity 2008:148–155)

Affirmative Action: Undoing Inequality

"One of the most notable accomplishments of liberalism over the past twenty years is something that did *not* happen, the demise of affirmative action," said Randall Kennedy in his recent article, "The Enduring Relevance of Affirmative Action" (2010:1). He is surprised that, given the entire conservative backlash over the last decade in the United States, affirmative action is still around. According to Kennedy, this is not only a triumph for race relations but also for the liberal vision of an inclusive society with full opportunity for all (2010:1). In the box "Affirmative Action: Undoing Inequality" is a time line that will familiarize younger readers with the brief history of affirmative action laws and policies in this country. For example, In 1949 President Harry Truman signed an Executive Order to desegregate the United States armed forces. In 1964, the Civil Rights Act was passed. This landmark law prohibited discrimination in education and employment on the basis of race, color, religion, or national origin. In 1965, Lyndon Johnson, President of the United States, issued an Executive Order directing that "all government contracting agencies take affirmative action to ensure that applicants are employed – without regard to their race, color or national origin." Since 1965, as the authors noted in chapter 12, there has been a segment of the population that has pushed back against these laws as being unfair (read "unfair to white males"). In 1978, a medical student by the name of John Bakke challenged the affirmative action policies of the University of California, Davis Medical School, which had a robust affirmative action plan that Bakke felt discriminated against him as a white male. This case went all the way to the Supreme Court, and a decision was handed down that said that "race" could be taken into account for admissions as one of many criteria. In 1996, the Citizens of California, by referendum, voted on Proposition 209, abolishing all public sector affirmative action programs in the state of California. In 1996, Texas followed suit to ban affirmative action in Texas, in 1998 in Washington and in 2000 in Florida laws were passed following suit. Then, in 2003, the Supreme Court again ruled on two cases involving affirmative action at the University of Michigan, upholding once again, a limited use of race as one factor of many in reviewing student applications at the law school at the University of Michigan (Gurin et al. 2002).

Some social and political conservatives still charge that affirmative action is about "reverse" discrimination that affects innocent whites who had nothing to do with developing and/or benefitting from racial discrimination policies of the past. Most recently, Senator Webb of Virginia has joined the ranks of those calling for an end to diversity programs (Webb 2010). (As the authors pointed out in chapter 12, Senator Webb is also trying to make the case that such programs are unfair to white people.) However, the switch to the use of the broader, inclusive concept of "diversity" is a bit more difficult for people to disagree with. The desire to create more diverse communities and workplaces is in the best interest of the United States on so many fronts. In fact, it was this focus on the value of diversity that, almost 10 years after the passage of Proposition 209, which banned taking race and gender into account in hiring and admissions in public workplaces and in university and college admissions, ultimately led to the passage of the Diversity Policy at the University of California, reaffirming the commitment of the regents of the university to creating a world-class public university with more, not less, diverse faculty, staff, and students, that include among them more women and underrepresented minorities (Regents of University of California Diversity Statement 2009).

It is not clear where the nation as a whole is going on this issue. As long as debates over affirmative action and diversity in higher education are about how scarce resources are divided up and who gets into elite educational institution, there will be conflict around these issues and they will be charged with racial, gender, and class overtones.

Affirmative Action: Undoing Inequality

The legacy of white privilege still runs far ahead of efforts to compensate for it.

Legalized privileges for whites
For most of U.S. history, government policies gave whites extreme preferential treatment. People of color were systematically shut out of schools, jobs, and housing.

The U.S. Social Security Act, 1935
Social Security did not always provide benefits for all. In 1935, when the Social Security Act became law, more than 60 percent of African American workers were farmworkers or maids. Those occupations were excluded from Social Security coverage until the 1950s. They were also excluded from legislation allowing for the creation of labor unions, setting a minimum wage and regulating work hours.

The GI Bill of Rights, 1944
More than any other legislation, the GI bill helped create the American middle class. This law helped millions of veterans go to college, buy their own homes, and start businesses. Although its benefits were supposed to be available to all veterans, regardless of race, in practice most African American, Asian, and Latino veterans were excluded.

Segregated colleges and universities
Colleges and universities were largely racially segregated – by law in the South and by practice in the North. Poorly funded black colleges did not

Figure 14.3 President Franklin D. Roosevelt signs the GI Bill into law. Courtesy of the Franklin D. Roosevelt Presidential Library.

Figure 14.4 Tuskegee Institute (later, Tuskegee University). Courtesy of the Library of Congress.

have the resources to provide the level of education available at many white schools.

Affirmative action

The many laws and programs we now group under the term *affirmative action* began in the 1960s. Their aim was to undo the gross inequalities that had resulted from the legacy of slavery and the discriminatory laws and policies that were in effect from the 1880s until the 1950s.

"You do not take a person who, for years, has been hobbled by chains and liberate him, bring him to the starting line of a race, and then say, 'You

Figure 14.5 Supporters and opponents of affirmative action. Courtesy of Jim West Photo.

are free to compete with all others and still justly believe you have been completely fair'" (President Lyndon B. Johnson, cited in RACE exhibit, SMM).

"In order to get beyond racism, we must first take account of race. There is no other way. And in order to treat some persons equally, we must treat them differently. We cannot – we dare not – let the Equal Protection Clause perpetuate racial supremacy" (U.S. Supreme Court Justice Harry Blackmun, cited in RACE exhibit, SMM).

Debating affirmative action

"Affirmative action benefits all. We are better off as a nation when those who run our schools, our businesses, our police departments, reflect our population as a whole. [An] America that ignores the need for such representatives is a nation asking for social turmoil" (Mills, 1994).

Are we there yet?

Recent national employment and income statistics show that equality remains distant.

The unemployment rate for African Americans remains about twice that of whites. The Hispanic rate is still much higher. Women have narrowed the earnings gap, but still make only 72 cents as much as men for comparable jobs. The average income for a Hispanic woman with a college degree is still less than the average income of a white man with a high school diploma. (President Bill Clinton, 1996 Occupational employment in private industry 2003, cited in RACE exhibit, SMM)

Table 14.1 Occupational Employment in Private Industry, 2003, by percent.

	Total workers	Officials and managers	Professionals
White	69.9	84.5	79.4
Black	13.8	6.5	7.2
Hispanic	11.1	5.0	4.1
Asian/Pacific Islander	4.6	3.6	8.9
American Indian/ Alaskan Native	0.6	0.4	0.4

Source: U.S. Equal Opportunity Commission.

Lingering privileges

Many colleges and universities give extra admission points to applicants whose parents or grandparents attended those schools. This tends to favor white students because many minority students' parents and grandparents were blocked from attending college because of segregation in the past or financial barriers that still exist today.

Also, extra admission points often go to students who took advanced placement classes in high school. But these points are not equally available to all students because many high schools in poorer school districts do not offer such classes.

A brief history
1949
President Harry Truman signs an executive order to desegregate the U.S. Armed Forces.

Figure 14.6 President Lyndon Baines Johnson. LBJ Library. Photograph by Yoichi R. Okamoto.

1964
Civil Rights Act prohibits discrimination in education and employment on the basis of race, color, religion, or national origin.

1965
President Lyndon B. Johnson issues an executive order directing that "all Government contracting agencies … take affirmative action to ensure that applicants are employed … without regard to their race, creed, color, or national origin."

1970
The U.S. Department of Labor issues Order Number 4, authorizing goals and timetables to correct the "underutilization" of minorities by federal contractors.

1978
In its Bakke decision, the U.S. Supreme Court upholds the use of race as a legitimate factor in admitting students to colleges and universities but rules against the use of quotas, or targeted minimums.

1996
Voters pass California Proposition 209, abolishing all public–sector affirmative action programs in the state.

1996
As a result of a Fifth U.S. Circuit Court of Appeals ruling, Texas bans affirmative action in university admissions.

Figure 14.7 2003 U.S. Supreme Court. Courtesy of the Collection of the Supreme Court of the United States.

1998
Voters pass Initiative 200 in Washington State, banning affirmative action in higher education and hiring.

2000
The Florida legislature passes the "One Florida" plan, banning affirmative action.

2003
The U.S. Supreme Court rules on two cases involving affirmative action at the University of Michigan, upholding a limited use of race as a factor in reviewing student applications.

MICHAEL OMI

Asian Americans

The Unbearable
Whiteness of Being?

Michael Omi *is Associate Professor of Ethnic Studies and Interim Director of the University of California at Berkeley's Institute for the Study of Social Change. His research focuses on racial theory and politics and Asian Americans and racial stratification. Among his many publications on these topics is the influential book* Racial Formation in the United States *(Routledge 1994), coauthored with Howard Winant.* Photograph courtesy of Michael Omi.

In his memoir, the author Eric Liu reflects on being the bearer of a strange new status – "white, by acclamation." He writes in *The Accidental Asian: Notes of a Native Speaker* (Random House 1998: 34–35), "Some are born white, others achieve whiteness, still others have whiteness thrust upon them."

Asian-Americans, it seems, are experiencing the last fate. Just as previous "outsiders" – such as the Irish and the Jews – have been incorporated into our collective notions of who is white, some scholars and policy makers believe that Asian-Americans are following such a trajectory of inclusion under an expanded definition of "whiteness."

This essay first appeared in the *Chronicle of Higher Education*, September 26, 2008, B56–B58. Copyright Michael Omi. Reprinted by permission of the author.

The sociologist George Yancey, in *Who Is White? Latinos, Asians, and the New Black/Nonblack Divide* (Lynne Rienner Publishers 2003), argues that Asian-Americans, along with some Latinos, are undergoing significant levels of structural, marital, and identificational assimilation. He draws upon survey data to illustrate that the social attitudes of Asian-Americans on a number of issues are closer to those of whites than blacks. Yancey believes that a black/nonblack divide is emerging in the United States as Asian-Americans and Latinos become "white" and blacks continue to endure a specific form of what he calls racial "alienation."

The question of whether Asian-Americans are becoming white is a complex one. Ostensibly regarded as a "racial minority," Asian-Americans are nonetheless not seen as a "disadvantaged" or "underrepresented" one. The popular belief is that Asian-Americans do not directly experience racial discrimination nor incur social disadvantages by race. Drawing upon select social and economic indicators, it is argued that Asian-Americans have achieved parity with whites with respect to income and levels of education and, correspondingly, have distanced themselves from other groups of color.

Higher education proves an oft-cited example: While Asian-Americans compose less than 5 percent of the U.S. population, a sizable and increasingly visible percentage of students at elite private and public universities throughout the country are Asian-American. In California, such students make up 24 percent of the undergraduate population at Stanford, 39 percent at UCLA, and 42 percent at Berkeley.

While the reported averages for median family income, rates of poverty, and levels of education are relatively high for Asian Americans compared with other groups, the indicators mask the internal diversity within the socially constructed group. Asian Americans exhibit a bimodal pattern; some Asian ethnic groups (notably east Asians like Chinese and Japanese) are doing quite well economically, but others (Southeast Asians like the Hmong and Cambodians) are mired in poverty. Such heterogeneity, however, is often glossed over in the literature in favor of deploying a broad, panethnic category.

Of the key social and cultural indicators evoked, the most popularly cited indicator that Asian-Americans are becoming "white" has been the high rates of Asian-American intermarriage with whites. Currently, more than one-quarter of all married Asians (27.2 percent) have a spouse of a different racial background, and 86.8 percent of intermarried Asians have a white partner, according to a study by Jennifer Lee and Frank D. Bean. By contrast, only 10.2 percent of blacks are intermarried, with 69.1 percent having a white spouse.

In the classic model of assimilation, advanced by the sociologist Milton Gordon in *Assimilation in American Life: The Role of Race, Religion, and National Origins* (Oxford University Press 1968), increasing rates of marriage between minority and majority groups are interpreted as an important indicator of a reduction in group prejudice and discrimination, and a lessening of strict social boundaries. George Yancey says, "With sufficient time and a sufficiently high outmarriage rate, Asian-Americans will lose the social perception that they belong to a different race" [2003:130].

While an optimistic prediction of dissolving racial-group distinctiveness, the meaning of interracial marriages for Asian-Americans in a highly racialized social order can be subject to another interpretation: Asian-American women, for example, are popularly regarded as desirable sexual partners and spouses. Ideas and images about them circulate in a variety of settings from popular films to pornography, and from dating ads to "mail-order bride" services. The point is that "racial difference" can be affirmed, not shed, as the model of assimilation would have us believe. Instead of assimilation, increasing intermarriage might simply reflect inequalities in racial power, and the persistence of stereotypical notions of race, gender, and sexuality that shape marital preferences.

One clear impediment to white status for Asian-Americans is the enduring social perception of Asians as "perpetual foreigners." This image is reflective of the process of racializing people in terms of their presumed affiliation with foreign places. Our nation has not been able to purge itself of a repertoire of cultural and racial representations that are evoked or emphasized in particular historical moments that render Asian-Americans foreign, subversive, and suspect.

Both the Asian campaign-finance controversy of the Clinton–Gore years and the spy-scandal case of Wen Ho Lee underscored the prevalent mistrust of Asian-Americans due to their presumed foreignness and questionable allegiance. A 2001 national survey on American attitudes toward Chinese-Americans found that 32 percent of those surveyed felt that Chinese-Americans were more loyal to China than to America. Those surveyed said they were more "uncomfortable" with an Asian-American as president of the United States, chief executive of a Fortune 500 company, or a supervisor at work than they would be with an African-American, a woman, or a Jewish American.

In a stratified racial order, different groups are positioned and racialized in different ways. In contrast to African-Americans, Asian-Americans are often perceived by whites as a threat not because they are deemed racially or culturally inferior, but because they are seen as unfair competitors who do "too well" and acquire social advantages and secure prized material resources as a result.

Such a belief has ironic consequences. In November 2005, *The Wall Street Journal* ran a news article titled "The New White Flight" that focused on Monta Vista High School, in Cupertino, Calif. – a school with an outstanding academic reputation that was losing white students as Asian student enrollment increased dramatically.

A white woman who was president of the Monta Vista PTA confessed that she had recently dissuaded a family with a young child from moving to Cupertino because there were so few white students left in the public schools: "This may not sound good, but their child may be the only Caucasian kid in the class. … White kids are thought of as the dumb kids." Contrast this with the "old" white flight away from blacks and "deteriorating" school districts and one quickly gets the picture.

Recent scholarship has challenged the view that Asian-Americans can easily be categorized or recognized as "honorary whites" and, in so doing, has emphasized issues of racial hierarchy, racism, and their continued salience.

In *The Racial Middle: Latinos and Asian Americans Living Beyond the Racial Divide* (New York University Press 2008), the sociologist Eileen O'Brien's Asian-American respondents express racial ideologies and assert identities that reveal a distinctive social location within the dominant black/white paradigm of race in the United States.

In *The Myth of the Model Minority: Asian Americans Facing Racism* (Paradigm Publishers 2008), the sociologists Rosalind Chou and Joe Feagin capture how individual Asian-Americans encounter racial hostility and discrimination in different social and institutional sites, and the distinct ways in which they strategically respond to such treatment, including both passive accommodation and active resistance.

But what may be fundamentally missing in the broader debate regarding whether Asian-Americans are becoming "white" is a substantive challenge to the problematic category of "whiteness" itself. The legal scholar John A. Powell (he goes by john a. powell) writes that even if groups are "allowed to pass" into whiteness, "it does nothing to transform the meaning associated with that boundary in the first place." "The very need to pass," he insightfully observes, "indicates the continued salience of racial hierarchy."

The application of his point puts a different spin on the topic of whether Asian-Americans are becoming white. Perhaps the issue to be addressed is not whether the category of "white" is expanding to include Asian-Americans, but why, given the current racial climate, there is a move to expand our notion of whiteness.

MICA POLLOCK

Some Myths about Race that Every Educator Needs to Unlearn

Mica Pollock *is Professor of Education at the University of California, San Diego. As an anthropologist of education, her research and writing have focused on how youth and adults communicate about everyday issues of diversity and opportunity in schools. Her award-winning books include* Colormute: Race Talk Dilemmas in an American School *(2005);* Because of Race: How Americans Debate Harm and Opportunity in Our Schools *(2008); and* Everyday Antiracism: Getting Real about Race in School *(2008). Through* The Oneville Project *(www.oneville.org), Dr. Pollock began studying how commonplace technology can support people in diverse educational communities through to share ideas, information, resources, and efforts.* Photograph courtesy of Mica Pollock.

My research on race talk in education – and my professional development efforts with educators – indicate that educators talking about race today (or refusing to) are often struggling with four myths about race. These myths are common among non-educators, too. They arose over the past few centuries to explain, as natural, the racial inequality being built by human beings. First, are "the races" truly valid biological or genetic subgroups to the human race? (No; see part 2, this volume.) Second, are some "races" smarter than others? (No, as this chapter shows.) Third, are opportunities in America racially equal? (No, as this chapter demonstrates.) Fourth, are achievement gaps caused by groups' "cultural" orientations toward education? (No; I address this issue here as well.) We need to lay out the evidence disproving each myth, so that educators and others have facts at hand.

Some of this material appeared first in "Emphasizing Educators' Everyday Actions," a blog post for Leadscape (http://www. niusileadscape.org/bl/?p=72#more-72), and in "From Shallow to Deep: Toward a Thorough Cultural Analysis of School Achievement Patterns." *Anthropology and Education Quarterly* 39(4): December 2008.

A quick nod to the fundamentally inaccurate Myth 1, covered elsewhere in this volume: *We don't belong to race groups* in any stable biological sense. It is only in our inherited inequality system that we do (Pollock 2004). Starting with colonial expansion and slavery in the 1400s, Europeans began to use physical appearance – visible differences of nose shape, skin color, hair texture, eye shape, and facial bone structure – as short-hand for determining who would gain opportunities and who would lose them (Sanjek 1996; Smedley 1999). Laws, for example, ruled that European-descended "whites" would get paid for their labor and that African-descended "black" slaves would not, and that "whites" and not "Asians" would own property, or be citizens (Smedley 1999; Almaguer 1994; Haney López 1996; Hu-DeHart). Enter Myth 2: such purposeful racial inequality was then supported by racist "science," which rationalized the increasingly unequal status of "the races" by arguing incorrectly that *internal* differences, like "intelligence" or motivation or ethics, justified unequal status (Gould 1981; Smedley 1999). Thomas Jefferson, a champion of freedom for European-Americans, proposed in his *Notes on the State of Virginia* that perhaps black slaves should remain unpaid laborers because they lacked mental capacity for any other kind of work.

So what now? Are opportunities today racially equal? Well, no.

Myth: Opportunities in America are generally now equal regardless of race.
Reality: Opportunities in America are often still unequal along racial lines.

The best tool I have seen for starting a thorough, fact-based conversation about racial inequality in education today is a framework offered by Rebecca Blank, an economist (2005). Blank discusses racial inequality today as the result of three forms of cumulative disadvantage for various people of color and, conversely, cumulative advantage for people whose families have been seen as "white":

cumulative disadvantage and advantage across *generations*;
cumulative disadvantage and advantage across *domains*, like health and housing;
cumulative disadvantage and advantage *across the lives of children* within a single domain, like education.

First, how did race–class inequality accumulate *over generations* in the United States? Well, for centuries, Myth 1 and 2 rationalized a purposefully unfair distribution of life opportunity, often via education itself. Here are a few examples. In the 1830s, free public education was proactively extended to European-descended children in the U.S.: simultaneously, antiliteracy laws denied enslaved African-descended children in the South the right to learn to read at all. Black people were denied publicly funded schools through the 1800s in the North, and often had to pay for their own schools; Chinese people were similarly denied publicly funded schools in 19th-century San Francisco and paid for their own (Wollenberg 1976); and by 1910, black people were still arguing for the extension of public school in the South and only 1 in every 12 black youths of high school age in the South was enrolled in school at all (Anderson 1988). Simultaneously, Native Americans were forcibly removed from economically sustainable ancestral lands by the 1830 Indian Removal Act, and many were later forced to attend white-run schools designed explicitly to "kill the Indian" in children. In 1930, 85 percent of Mexican-American children in the Southwest went to school in purposefully segregated, inferior-resource environments, where, in comparison to "white" peers, they were tracked to vocational education and encouraged to drop out after elementary school in order to work in manual jobs (Donato 1997). In each case, "white" children's experiences of free, higher-quality education had serious consequences for their families' wealth accumulation, as they could then pursue higher-paying jobs than their non-"white" peers.

Throughout, "white" people also experienced a preferential extension of blatantly economic benefits. For example, immigrants not classified as "free white people" were denied citizenship under the 1790 Naturalization Act (not repealed fully until 1952) and thus couldn't own property in many areas or vote for people who could protect their economic interests.

Over time, opportunities provided and denied along the lines of "race" became fundamental inequalities of class. This is precisely why theorist Manning Marable calls the "race or class?" debate a "false debate" (see also Pollock 2004). Here's a personal example of such "cumulative advantage." My own grandfather, who didn't go to school past elementary school, benefited from the GI bill, which, after World War II, extended housing and educational subsidies preferentially to veteran "whites." (As Sacks (1997) shows, Jews were treated as "white" after World War II). He and my grandmother bought a house and helped provide a tax base supporting well-equipped public schools in their neighborhood. This helped my father get to college. When my dad got his first job as a professor, Grandma and Grandpa helped him buy a house, using the wealth they'd accumulated after a series of houses. I attended sufficiently resourced public schools with a similarly adequate tax base. I went to college without even imagining alternatives. When I was ready to buy a house, my down payment included not just my own hard-earned savings, but also small gifts from my family stemming from two generations of accumulated housing wealth. My job then supported reasonable mortgage payments on that house, subsidized health care for my children, and allowed me to send my children to a day care that helped prepare them for school. Zoom out to Blank's aggregated stats: due to the distribution of the GI bill and other post-WW II benefits, "African Americans whose parents came of age in the 1940s and 1950s will receive less than one-tenth the inheritance of their white peers" (Blank 2005:15).

This is "white privilege" in action; it's real money. My grandfather went to work every day, quite literally until the day he died; individuals in each successive generation of his family have worked incredibly hard. Yet after WWII, we all also benefited from a government subsidy assisting us to accumulate wealth.

There's more: in the 1970s and after, courts' and governmental decisions to not fully remedy the inequalities of previously enforced racial segregation ensured that segregation's accumulated race–class inequalities would remain unremedied too. Today, clustered in their still-segregated schools and neighborhoods with higher property tax bases, "white" children still enjoy disproportionately well-financed educations and neighborhood social services (Kozol 1991). White children today are disproportionately not poor, children of color disproportionately are, and many immigrants from Asia and Latin America move into segregated neighborhoods lacking social services or a good tax base. Even people of color who now take

home salaries equivalent to "whites'" do not enjoy similarly accumulated intergenerational wealth (Lareau and Conley 2008). Because of racially driven housing choices, low income white people also share neighborhoods, amenities, and schools more often with wealthier whites than do people of color (Charles 2008). In effect, today's students walk in the door with vast accumulated advantages and disadvantages of wealth. Interventions against cumulative economic disadvantage include universal preschool (Kirp 2007; Rothstein 2004) and neighborhood-wide efforts like Promise Neighborhoods and the Harlem Children's Zone (Tough 2008).

This brings us to Rebecca Blank's second form of "cumulative advantage and disadvantage." How does racial inequality accumulate today *across domains?* Well, in today's schools and neighborhoods, "white" children still most often enjoy not only the cumulative advantages of disproportionately well-financed and resourced public schools (Hochschild and Scovronick 2003; Kozol 2005), but also of privately funded preschool (Kirp 2007), and, extracurricular activities, housing stability, nutrition, and health care (Rothstein 2004; Lareau 2003). Researcher Richard Rothstein (2004) has shown that when you concentrate low income children in a racially segregated school, you concentrate high need and exacerbate unequal educational opportunity – unless you also concentrate responsive supports. If you can't see the board because you have no health care and thus no glasses, you can't do the work, and if you have asthma or haven't eaten you cannot breathe well or concentrate; if you have many such children around you, you have even more trouble concentrating. If you have no stable housing situation you are more likely to be transient; and transience, which disrupts teacher–student relationship and student progress monitoring, negatively affects the schooling outcomes of both the child moving and the children disrupted by his sudden arrival.

Schools often concentrate economic disadvantage and advantage, but what happens to children daily inside schools also shapes children's trajectories. This brings us to Blank's third point. Blank argues that racial inequality of opportunity and outcome in education also accumulate *each day inside schools.* For example, Blank notes, white students (more likely to have attended preschool) are disproportionately likely to be put in a high "ability" reading group in elementary school. Someone put in such a group in elementary school is more likely to get better instruction and to end up in A.P. [advanced placement] classes and then college later on. Even while we talk about early reading groups as naturalized measurements of inherent "ability," they are really groupings of children reading at particular levels for the moment, due to prior educational experiences. (Even something as purportedly "innate" as an IQ test score is the result of life and educational experiences over time. See Mehan 1992 and American Psychological Association: *Intelligence: Knowns and Unknowns* [1995/6].) Those groupings can *then* have major consequences for children's trajectories.

There's more: educators, who are themselves predominantly white and middle-class, tend to react more positively to students with middle-class experiences (Lareau 2003; Heath 1983); they also tend to react more positively to white children, as their styles of talk (Baugh 2008), dress (Carter 2008), and interaction feel more familiar and also more highly valued. Old ideas even about how "smartness" looks and which "groups" are "smart" still play out (even unintentionally) in educators' everyday decisions about gifted placement and ability grouping and tracking, with fundamental consequences for students' academic pathways and for how students think about their own intelligence and potential (Tyson 2008; Ong 2008; Rubin 2008).

Pedro Noguera (2008) shows that educators often discipline students of color disproportionately, and particularly harshly; not only does this everyday act have fundamental consequences for students' motivation, relationships to their teachers, and ultimate sense of their own potential, but repeated suspensions also contribute to truancy (Pollock 2008a) and often, then, to dropout. Dropout is itself not just a sudden decision, but one produced over many years. Think about your own educational experience, and consider the "millions of daily interactions" (Johnson 2004) that contribute to getting a child to the graduation stage. Work by Angela Valenzuela (1999), Nilda Flores-Gonzalez (2002), Prudence Carter (2005), and myself and colleagues (Pollock 2008a; 2008b) all demonstrate how through interactions with school adults, between peers, and between school adults and families, students either build positive relationships to schools or turn off to specific schools over time.

Any close look at actual interactions in schools also explodes Myth 4 – *the myth that children's outcomes are simply the consequence of their "cultural" "backgrounds,"* or relatedly their "cultural" "values," rather than of educational experience. Students' academic fates are built through real time *inter*actions, as children interact with educators and peers and parents and the various other people and situations in their lives. Stated otherwise, *students are reacting to educators on a daily, even moment to moment basis,* even as they react on an ongoing basis to their parents and peers and to their advantaged or disadvantaged experiences outside of schools. In turn, *educators are reacting to children on a daily, even moment to moment basis,* even as they also react to families and to the ways families raise children. It is the *accumulation of these everyday interactions, in a context of preexisting advantage and disadvantage,* that creates student achievement. Everyday actions by educators in hallways and deans' offices (and student responses to educator actions) accumulate to forge students' disciplinary and academic trajectories; the actions of many people aggregate to produce "dropouts" (Ferguson, 2000; Fine 1991). Children get suspended for "defiance" in part because through repeated suspensions for defiance, they become more defiant (Ladson-Billings, personal conversation, 2000; Pollock 2008a; Ferguson 2000; Noguera 2008).

"Shallow" analyses comparing "cultures" in schools ignore such interactional realities and purport to explain "achievement gaps" by making quick claims about how parents and children from various racial, ethnic, national-origin, or class groups react to schools (Pollock 2008c). Such shallow analyses are often stereotypes. They are "shallow" because they dangerously oversimplify the social processes, interactions, and practices that create disparate outcomes for children. Such claims allow speakers to explain achievement outcomes too simply as the production of parents and children without ever actually examining the real-life experiences of parents and children in specific opportunity contexts.

"Cultural" statements also routinely forget not only that people from Group A quite often share foundational school-related beliefs, motivations, and behaviors with people from Group B, but also that group members always are negotiating the task of "achieving" in ongoing formative interaction with people *outside* "the group." The essays in Perry, Steele, and Hilliard's *Young, Gifted, and Black* (2003) show how young black people experiencing U.S. schools interact constantly with *non-black* people and their damaging ideas *about* black people. Analogously, Annette Lareau's book on "middle-class" parental pushing makes clear that to have "middle-class students" be successful, teachers have to react favorably to middle-class parents' styles of pushing. Even student "motivation" or "attitude" is built up or threatened in real-time interactions between group members and others in shared contexts, not just "passed down" inside a "group."

This knowledge can lead to a transformational way of talking about the power of educators' everyday actions. A book I produced with many colleagues, *Everyday Antiracism*, offers 65 short essays, each training educators' attention on one routine action in their work. We show that through attending closely to their everyday interactions with students, educators can also fundamentally counteract racial disparities. Even as generational and cross-domain disadvantages and advantages have accumulated and continue to, the task of the educator is to make sure that in every move, she pushes in the opposite direction.

Educators didn't create racial myths or racial inequality; but they live with these each and every day. Today, many of our inequalities remain unremedied rather than actively ordered (Pollock 2008a), in part because the myths explored here blur clear visions for progress. Like the rest of us, educators need to consider, facts in hand, how student achievement takes shape in a system where racial disparities are hardly "natural," but reinforced over time by many players in interaction inside and outside schools.

References

Burris, C. C., and D. T. Garrity
2008 Detracking for Excellence and Equity. Alexandria, VA: Association for Supervision and Curriculum Development.
Gurin, P., E. L. Dey, S. Hurtado, and G. Gurin
2002 Diversity and Higher Education: Theory and Impact on Educational Outcomes. Harvard Educational Review, 72(3):330–366.
Henze, Rosemary
2007 The Academic Achievement Gap and Equity. *In* How Real is Race?": A Source book on Race, Culture and Biology. Carol Mukhopadhyay, Rosemary Henze, and Yolanda T. Moses, eds. New York: Roman and Littlefield.
Kennedy, R.
2010 The Enduring Relevance of Affirmative Action. The American Prospect. August. http://www.prospect.org/cs/articles?article=the_enduring_relevance_of_affirmative_action, accessed January 29, 2012.
Mills, Nicolaus
1994 Debating Affirmative Action: Race, Gender, Ethnicity, and the Politics of Inclusion. New York: Delta Trade Paperbacks.
Oakes Jeannie, and Gretchen Guiton
1995 Matchmaking: The Dynamics of High School Tracking Decision. American Educational Research Journal (Spring) 32:3–33.

Pollock, M.
2008 From Shallow to Deep: Toward a Thorough Cultural Analysis of School Achievement Patterns. Anthropology & Education Quarterly, 30(4):369–380.
Steele, Claude M., and Joshua Aronson
1995 Stereotype Threat and the Intellectual Test Performance of African Americans. Journal of Personality and Social Psychology, 69(5):797–811.
Webb, J.
2010 Diversity and the Myth of White Privilege. Wall Street Journal, July 22. http://online.wsj.com/article/NA_WSJ_PUB:SB100014240527487037241045753 79630952309408.html, accessed January 29, 2012.

Michael Omi, Asian Americans: The Unbearable Whiteness of Being?

Chou, Rosalind, and Joe Feagin
2008 The Myth of the Model Minority: Asian Americans Facing Racism. Boulder, CO; Paradigm Publishers.
Gordon, Milton
1968 Assimilation in American Life: The Role of Race, Religion, and National Origins. New York: Oxford University Press.
Hwang, Suien
2005 The New White Flight. Wall Street Journal, November 19: A1.

Liu, Eric
1998 The Accidental Asian: Notes of a Native Speaker. New York: Random House.

O'Brien, Eileen
2008 The Racial Middle: Latinos and Asian Americans Living Beyond the Racial Divide. New York: New York University Press.

powell, john a.
2005 Dreaming of a Self Beyond Whiteness and Isolation. Washington University Journal of Law and Policy, 18:13–45.

Yancey, George
2003 Who Is White? Latinos, Asians, and the New Black/Nonblack Divide. Boulder, CO: Lynne Rienner Publishers, Inc.

Mica Pollock, Some Myths about Race that Every Educator Needs to Unlearn

Almaguer, Tomas
1994 Racial Fault Lines: The Historical Origins of White Supremacy in California. Berkeley: University of California Press.

Anderson, J.
1988 The Education of Blacks in the South, 1860–1935. Chapel Hill: University of North Carolina .

Baugh, John
2008 Valuing Non-standard English. *In* Everyday Antiracism: Getting Real about Race in School. Mica Pollock, ed. Pp. 102–106. New York: The New Press.

Blank, Rebecca M.
2005 Tracing the Economic Impact of Cumulative Discrimination. American Economic Review 95(2): 99–103.

Carter, Prudence
2005 Keepin' It Real: School Success Beyond Black and White. Oxford: Oxford University Press.

Carter, Prudence
2008 Teaching Students Fluency in Multiple Cultural Codes. *In* Everyday Antiracism: Getting Real about Race in School, ed. Mica Pollock, ed. 107–111. New York: The New Press.

Charles, Camille Zubrinsky
2008 Who Will Live Near Whom? Poverty and Race Research Action Council Newsletter. September/October.

Donato, Ruben
1997 The Other Struggle for Equal Schools: Mexican Americans during the Civil Rights Era. Albany: State University of New York Press.

Ferguson, Ann Arnett
2000 Bad Boys: Public Schools in the Making of Black Masculinity. Ann Arbor: University of Michigan Press.

Fine, Michelle
1991 Framing Dropouts: Notes on the Politics of an Urban Public High School. Albany: State University of New York Press.

Flores-Gonzalez, Nilda
2002 School Kids, Street Kids: Identity Development in Latino Students. New York: Teachers College Press.

Gould, Stephen Jay
1981 The Mismeasure of Man. New York: W. W. Norton and Company.

Haney López, Ian F.
1996 White by Law: The Legal Construction of Race. New York: New York University Press.

Heath, Shirley Brice
1983 Ways with Words: Language, Life and Work in Communities and Classrooms. Cambridge: Cambridge University Press.

Hochschild, Jennifer, and Nathan Scovronick
2003 The American Dream and the Public Schools. New York: Oxford University Press.

Hu-Dehart, Evelyn
1996 P.C. and the Politics of Multiculturalism in Higher Education. *In* Race, Steven Gregory and Roger Sanjek, eds. New Brunswick, NJ: Rutgers University Press.

Johnson, Deborah J.
2004 The Ecology of Children's Racial Coping: Family, School, and Community Influences. *In* Discovering Successful Pathways in Children's Development. Thomas S. Weisner, ed. pp. 87–110.

Kirp, David L.
2007 The Sandbox Investment: The Preschool Movement and Kids-First Politics. Cambridge, MA: Harvard University Press.

Kozol, Jonathan
1991 Savage Inequalities. New York: Harper.

Kozol, Jonathan
2005 Still Separate, Still Unequal: America's Educational Apartheid. Harper's Magazine 311(1864):1, September.

Lareau, Annette
2003 Unequal Childhoods: Class, Race, and Family Life. Berkeley: University of California Press.

Lareau, Annette, and Dalton Conley, eds.
2008 Social Class: How Does it Work? New York: Russell Sage.

Mehan, Hugh
1992 Why I like to Look: On the Use of Videotape as an Instrument in Educational Research. *In* Issues

in Qualitative Research. M. Schratz, ed. London: Falmer Press.

Mehan, Hugh
1993 Beneath the Skin and between the Ears: A Case Study in the Politics of Representation. *In* Understanding Practice: Perspectives on Activity and Context. Jean Lave and Seth Chaiklin, eds. Cambridge: Cambridge University Press.

Noguera, Pedro A.
2008 What Discipline is For: Connecting Students to the Benefits of Learning. *In* Everyday Antiracism: Getting Real about Race in School. Mica Pollock, ed. pp. 132–137. New York: The New Press.

Ong, Maria
2008 Challenging Cultural Stereotypes of "Scientific Ability." *In* Everyday Antiracism: Getting Real about Race in School. Mica Pollock, ed. pp. 114–119. New York: The New Press.

Pollock, Mica
2004 Colormute: Race Talk Dilemmas in an American School. Princeton, NJ: Princeton University Press.

Pollock, Mica
2008a Because of Race: How Americans Debate Harm and Opportunity in Our Schools. Princeton, NJ: Princeton University Press.

Pollock, Mica, ed.
2008b Everyday Antiracism: Getting Real about Race in School. New York: The New Press.

Pollock, Mica
2008c From Shallow to Deep: Toward a Thorough Cultural Analysis of School Achievement Patterns. Anthropology & Education Quarterly, 30(4):369–380.

Rothstein, Richard
2004 Class and Schools: Using Social, Economic, and Educational Reform to Close the Black–White Achievement Gap. Washington, DC: Economic Policy Institute; New York: Teachers College, Columbia University.

Rubin, Beth C.
2008 Grouping in Detracked Classrooms. *In* Everyday Antiracism: Getting Real about Race in School. Mica Pollock, ed. pp. 90–95. New York: The New Press.

Sacks, Karen Brodkin
1997 How Did Jews Become White Folks? *In* Critical White Studies. Richard Delgado and Jean Stefancic, eds. Philadelphia: Temple University Press.

Sanjek, Roger
1996 The Enduring Inequalities of Race. *In* Race. Steven Gregory and Roger Sanjek, eds. New Brunswick, NJ: Rutgers University Press.

Smedley, Audrey
1999 Race in North America: Origin and Evolution of a Worldview. 2nd edition. Boulder, CO: Westview Press.

Tough, Paul
2008 Whatever It Takes: Geoffrey Canada's Quest to Change Harlem and America. Boston: Houghton Mifflin Harcourt.

Tyson, Karolyn
2008 Providing Equal Access to "Gifted" Education. *In* Everyday Antiracism: Getting Real about Race in School. Mica Pollock, ed. p. 126. New York: The New Press.

Valenzuela, Angela
1999 Subtractive Schooling: U.S.-Mexican Youth and the Politics of Caring. Albany: State University of New York Press.

Wollenberg, C. M.
1976 "Yellow Peril" in the Schools. *In* All Deliberate Speed: Segregation and Exclusion in California Schools, 1855–1975. Berkeley: University of California Press.

Mica Pollock, Some Myths about Race; Further Reading

Abu El-Haj, T. R.
2006 Elusive Justice: Wrestling with Difference and Educational Equity in Everyday Practice. New York: Routledge.

Appadurai, Arjun
1996 Modernity at Large: Cultural Dimensions of Globalization. Minneapolis: University of Minnesota Press.

Bailey, Benjamin
2000 Language and Negotiation of Ethnic/Racial Identity among Dominican Americans. Language and Society 29:555–582.

Barth, Fredrick
1969 Ethnic Groups and Boundaries: The Social Organization of Culture Difference. Boston: Little, Brown.

Cazden, Courtney B.
2005 Agency, Collaboration, and Learning in a Middle-School Program. Paper prepared for the Charles Darwin Symposium Series 2005, Imagining Childhood: Children, Culture and Community, Alice Springs, Australia, September 20–22.

Conchas, Gilberto Q.
2006 The Color of Success: Race and High-achieving Urban Youth. New York: Teachers College Press.

Diamond, John, and K. Williams Gomez
2004   African American Parents' Orientations toward Schools: The Implications of Social Class and Parents' Perceptions of Schools. Education and Urban Society.

Erickson, Frederick
1987   Conceptions of School Culture: An Overview. Educational Administration Quarterly 23(4):11–24.

Erickson, Frederick
1996   Going for the Zone: The Social and Cognitive Ecology of Teacher–Student Interaction in Classroom Conversations. In Discourse, Learning, and Schooling. D. Hicks, ed. Cambridge: Cambridge University Press.

Erickson, Frederick
2006   Culture in Society and in Educational Practices. In Multicultural Education: Issues and Perspectives. 6th edition. James Banks and Cherry McGee Banks, eds. pp. 31–60. Hoboken, NJ: John Wiley/Jossey Bass.

Foley, Doug
2008   Questioning "Cultural" Explanations of Classroom Behaviors. In Everyday Antiracism: Getting Real about Race in School. Mica Pollock, ed. New York: The New Press.

Foley, Douglas A., Bradley A. Levinson, and Janise Hurtig
2000–2001   Anthropology Goes Inside: The New Educational Ethnography of Ethnicity and Gender. Review of Research in Education 25:37–98.

Foster, Michele
1997   Black Teachers on Teaching. New York: The New Press.

Garcia, Eugene
2008   Valuing Students' Home Worlds. In Everyday Antiracism: Getting Real about Race in School. Mica Pollock, ed. New York: The New Press.

Geertz, Clifford
1973   The Interpretation of Cultures. New York: Basic Books.

Gonzáles, Norma, Luis Moll, and Cathy Amanti, eds.
2005   Funds of Knowledge: Theorizing Practice in Households, Communities, and Classrooms. Mahwah, NJ: L. Erlbaum Associates.

Goodenough, W.
1976   Multiculturalism as the Normal Human Experience. Anthropology and Education Quarterly 7(4):4–7.

Gutierrez, K., P. Baquedano-López, and C. Tejeda
1999   Rethinking Diversity: Hybridity and Hybrid Language Practices in the Third Space. Mind, Culture, and Activity, 6(4):286–303.

Gutierrez, K., and Barbara Rogoff
2003   Cultural Ways of Learning: Individual Traits or Repertoires of Practice. Educational Researcher 32(5): 19–25.

Hall, Kathy
2002   Lives in Translation: Sikh Youth as British Citizens. Philadelphia: University of Pennsylvania Press.

Henry, Jules
1963   Culture against Man. New York: Vintage Books.

Ibrahim, Awad El Karim
1999   Becoming Black: Rap and Hip-Hop, Race, Gender, Identity, and the Politics of ESL Learning. ESOL Quarterly 33(3):349–369.

Jacob, Evelyn, and Cathie Jordan, eds.
1993   Minority Education: Anthropological Perspectives. Westport, CT: Ablex Publishing.

Jones, Makeba, and Susan Yonezawa
2008   Inviting Students to Analyze their Learning Experience. In Everyday Antiracism: Getting Real about Race in School. Mica Pollock, ed. New York: The New Press.

Kuipers, Joel, and Ray McDermott, eds.
2007   Fine Description: Ethnographic and Linguistic Essays of Harold C. Conklin. New Haven: Center for Southeast Asian Studies, Yale University.

Ladson-Billings, Gloria
1997   The Dreamkeepers: Successful Teachers of African American Children. San Francisco: Jossey-Bass.

Ladson-Billings, Gloria
2006   It's Not the Culture of Poverty, It's the Poverty of Culture: The Problem with Teacher Education. Anthropology and Education Quarterly 37(2): 104–109.

Lamont, Michèle
2000   The Dignity of Working Men: Morality and the Boundaries of Race, Class, and Immigration. New York: Russell Sage Foundation; Cambridge, MA: Harvard University Press.

Lave, Jean, and Etienne Wenger
1991   Situated Learning: Legitimate Peripheral Participation. Cambridge: Cambridge University Press.

Lave, Jean, and Seth Chaiklin, eds.
1993   Understanding Practice: Perspectives on Activity and Context. Cambridge: Cambridge University Press.

Lee, Stacey J.
1996   Unraveling the "Model Minority" Stereotype: Listening to Asian American Youth. New York: Teachers College Press.

Levinson, Bradley A.
2001   We Are All Equal: Student Culture and Identity at a Mexican Secondary School, 1988–1998. Durham, NC: Duke University Press.

Louie, Vivian S.
2004   Compelled to Excel: Immigration, Education, and Opportunity among Chinese Americans. Stanford: Stanford University Press.

Maira, Sunaina, and Elisabeth Soep
2004   Youthscapes: The Popular, the National, the Global. Philadelphia: University of Pennsylvania Press.

McDermott, R. P.

1997   Achieving School Failure 1972–1997. *In* Education and Cultural Process: Anthropological Approaches. 3rd edition. George D. Spindler, ed. Prospect Heights: Waveland Press, pp. 110–135.

McDermott, R.P., Kenneth Gospodinoff, and Jeffrey Aron

1978   Criteria for an Ethnographically Adequate Description of Concerted Activities and Their Contexts. *Semiotica* 24:3/4.

Moerman, Michael

1968   Being Lue: Uses and Abuses of Ethnic Identification. *In* Essays on the Problem of Tribe. Jane Helm, ed. Seattle: University of Washington Press.

Moll, Luis C., and Stephen Diaz

1993   Change as the Goal of Educational Research. *In* Minority Education: Anthropological Perspectives. Evelyn Jacob and Cathie Jordan, eds. Westport, CT: Ablex Publishing.

Nieto, Sonia

2000   Affirming Diversity: The Sociopolitical Context of Multicultural Education. New York: Addison Wesley Longman, Inc.

O'Connor, Carla

1997   Dispositions toward (Collective) Struggle and Educational Resilience in the Inner City: A Case Analysis of Six African-American High School Students. American Educational Research Journal 34, Winter:593–629.

Olsen, Laurie

1997   Made in America: Immigrant Students in Our Public Schools. New York: The New Press.

Ortner, Sherry

1984   Theory in Anthropology since the Sixties. Comparative Study in Society and History 26(1): 126–66.

Page, Reba Neukom

1991   Lower Track Classrooms: A Curricular and Cultural Perspective. New York: Teachers College Press.

Payne, Charles

1984   Getting What We Ask For. Westport, CT: Greenwood.

Perry, Pamela

2002   Shades of White: White Kids and Racial Identities in High School. Durham, NC: Duke University Press.

Rosaldo, Renato

1993   Culture and Truth: The Remaking of Social Analysis. Boston, MA: Beacon Press.

Schultz, Katherine, ed.

2008   Interrogating Students' Silences. *In* Everyday Antiracism: Getting Real about Race in School. New York: The New Press.

Seyer-Ochi, Ingrid

2006   Lived Landscapes of the Fillmore. *In* Innovations in Educational Ethnography: Theory, Methods, and Results. George Spindler and Lorie Hammond, eds. Mahwah, NJ: Lawrence Erlbaum Associates.

Spindler, George

1997[1974]   Beth Anne: A Case Study of Culturally Defined Adjustment and Teacher Perceptions. *In* Education and Cultural Process: Anthropological Approaches. 3rd edition. George D. Spindler, ed. Prospect Heights, IL: Waveland Press, 246–261.

Spindler, George D., and Louise Spindler, eds.

1994   Pathways to Cultural Awareness: Cultural Therapy with Teachers and Students. Thousand Oaks, CA: Corwin Press.

Teel, Karen Mannheim, and Jennifer E. Obidah

2008   Building Racial and Cultural Competence in the Classroom. New York: Teachers College Press.

Thorne, Barrie

1993   Gender Play: Girls and Boys in School. New Brunswick: Rutgers University Press.

Varenne, Herve, and Ray McDermott

1998   Successful Failure: The School America Builds. Boulder, CO: Westview Press.

Willis, Paul

1977   Learning to Labor: How Working-class Kids Get Working-class Jobs. Farnborough, England: Saxon House.

Yoshikawa, Hiro

2008   Roundtable: How Do We Talk Accurately about the Role of Parents? Harvard Graduate School of Education, February 13.

Further Reading

Chronicle of Higher Education.

2010   College-going rates for all racial groups have jumped since 1980: July 14.

Espinosa, L. L.

2010   Where is the Dialoque? web log comment, July 8. http://diverseeducation.com/blogpost/277/where-is-the-dialogue.html, accessed January 29, 2012.

Hacker, A., and C. Dreifus, C.

2010   Are Colleges Worth the Price of Admission? Chronicle of Higher Education. http://chronicle.com/article/Are-Colleges-Worth-the-Price/66234/, accessed January 29, 2012.

Lewis, B.

2010   Webb Calls for Ending Diversity Programs. Diverse Education, July.diverseeducation.com/cache/print.php?articleId = 13980, accessed January 29, 2012

Malsen, G.

2007   The Academic Achievement Gap and Equity. *In* How Real is Race? A Sourcebook on Race, Culture and Biology. Carol Mukhopadhyay, Rosemary Henze, and Yolanda T. Moses, eds. Roman and Littlefield.

Malsen, G.

2010   US: Degree shortfall will hit economy hard. University World News, 132. http://www.universityworldnews.com/ article.php?story=20100709182339930&query=Degree+shortfall, accessed January 29, 2012.

Palmer, R.T., and K. A. Griffin

2009   Desegregation Policy and Disparities in Faculty Salary and Workload: Maryland's Historically Black and Predominantly White Institutions. The Negro Educational Review 60:7–21.

15

Linking Race and Wealth
An American Dilemma

Immigrants from all over the world have come voluntarily to the United States since its inception because of the promise of a better future. That is, America is the place that if you work hard, you can worship the way you want, espouse differing political beliefs, be successful economically and pass on that wealth and prosperity to your children. But the reality of that claim is and has been very different and difficult to achieve for many Americans, especially when looked at through the lens of race.

In the first instance, in the United States wealth has been, and continues to be, based on many factors including visible assets such as land and money (Gerstle 2001:7; Oliver and Shapiro 1995:2). The calculation of wealth also includes invisible assets such as education, specialized knowledge and skills, opportunity, and privilege. The history of the economic development of the United States is highly racialized as well as class based. This has not only produced a racially stratified social system but an economic as well as that must be understood in order to begin to dismantle it. This chapter will explore and give examples of the role that race and its intersections with class and, to a certain extent, gender and geography have played to maintain wealth disparities. Despite some progress to date, policies and practices of the past around land ownership, home ownership, and wealth accumulation that favored elite Euro-Americans continue to maintain wealth disparities

among racialized groups of color to this very day (Oliver and Shapiro 1995; and Shapiro et al. 2010). But first let's take a look at how this system was started at the time of the birth of our democracy in the 18th century.

Land Ownership in Colonial Times

In colonial times only wealthy white males owned land along the eastern seaboard and eventually in what were to become the southern states. During this period, from 1604 to 1800, land was claimed from Native Americans either through barter, treaty, or confiscation. By 1800, disease, warfare, and colonial U.S. treaties had pushed most tribes west of the Appalachian Mountains. By the mid-1830s the Indian Removal Act of 1830 allowed the government to remove thousands more Native Americans to lands west of the Mississippi River. Many hundreds died on that move, called the "The Trail of Tears." (See chapter 6 for a more thorough look at the U.S. laws pertaining to Native American land confiscation.) By 1900, with the help of the 1862 Homestead Act which granted 160-acre parcels of public land to settlers, thousands of white people were allowed to occupy land that had formerly been occupied by American Indians. In addition, the Dawes Severalty Act of 1887 broke up tribal lands into individual

Race: Are We So Different?, First Edition. Alan H. Goodman, Yolanda T. Moses, and Joseph L. Jones.
© 2012 American Anthropological Association. Published 2012 by Blackwell Publishing Ltd.

allotments. Lands that were designated as surplus were sold to white buyers. As recently as 2007, 60 percent of land that the Native Americans supposedly owned on the Indian Reservation still did not belong to the tribal group. Native Americans have lost 95 percent of their homeland to date, systematically removed by the U.S. Government, which at the same time provided legal opportunities for white settlers to acquire the land as the nation moved west. This process has also been called "Manifest Destiny" by some historians and justified by the need for more land to accommodate the press of white people and immigrants needed to move west and relieve the crowding on the eastern seaboard (Zinn 2003:686).

Whose Land Is It?

Native Americans have lost 95 percent of their homeland.

Early losses
Within decades of the first European colonization of the Americas, disease began decimating native populations. Countless Native Americans died from European diseases such as smallpox, malaria, and measles. In New England alone, native populations plummeted by more than 70 percent. Many settlers from Europe saw the epidemics as evidence that God approved of their claiming and colonizing the land.

The legacy of allotment
During the late 1800s, the U.S. Government began restricting Native Americans to reservations, with the aim of turning them into farmers. But many reservations held vast farming, forestry, and mining resources. The Dawes Severalty Act of 1887 opened much of this land to purchase by whites. Each Indian male was "allotted" 160 acres, with the "surplus" lands sold to homesteaders and businessmen.

Between 1887 and 1934, tribal landholdings plunged from 138 million acres to 48 million acres.

The effects of land allotment continue to be felt today, with many reservations "checkerboarded" among tribes, individual Indians and non-Indians, and state and federal governments. Without effective access to land, Native Americans remain among the nation's poorest citizens.

Land allotment went hand-in-hand with policies aimed at absorbing Indians into white culture. From the 1880s to the 1920s, thousands of Indian children were sent to off-reservation boarding schools. Their contact with families and traditions – including language, religion, and dress – was restricted and often forbidden. Many schools sent students to work as domestic servants in local white households. Many children died from disease and neglect.

"Kill the Indian in him, and save the man" (General Richard Pratt, founder, Carlisle Indian Industrial School, 1892, cited in RACE exhibit, SMM).

"I have a great deal of hope that Indian people will own this land again. It won't be in my lifetime, but perhaps my grandchildren will actually see a day when all of the land in reservation boundaries is owned and managed effectively by Indian people" (Chris Stainbrook, President, Indian Land Tenure Foundation, Minnesota, 2005, Personal communication with Rachel Moritz, Science Museum of Minnesota, September 2006).

Figure 15.1 Native lands today. More than 60 percent of the land on Indian reservations has passed out of tribal ownership. Map courtesy of the Indian Land Tenure Foundation.

The Cherokee provide a very interesting case study in understanding how this process worked on the ground. In 1819, the Cherokee Nation, in an effort to live peacefully with the ever expanding stream of white settlers moving west, decided to try to live with them. They also embraced a federal policy to become "civilized." What that meant was settling on plots of land and becoming farmers. They established a government as a sovereign nation, but their government was never recognized by the state of Georgia. By the second decade of the 19th century, despite their adoption of white civilized ways (including the establishment of racial hierarchies within the Cherokee Nation), there was pressure from the white citizens of Georgia to push the federal government to move the Cherokee to make way for white farmers who wanted the land in Georgia to raise lucrative cotton crops (Yarbrough 2007:30).

Making "Brown Men" White/Cherokee Removal

"The civilization policy was actually designed to assimilate us into America. It was ultimately to make us farmers, to live like the colonists lived. The civilization policy was to make us brown, white men" (Richard Allen, policy analyst, Cherokee Nation, 2003: RACE exhibit, SMM).

The Cherokee story

By 1819 the Cherokee Nation had surrendered more than 90 percent of its land to the U.S. Government and embraced its policy of "civilizing" Indians by converting them into farmers. The Cherokee ran farms and plantations in Alabama, Georgia, and Tennessee and, in the 1820s, began publishing *Cherokee Phoenix*, a bilingual newspaper. Some even owned slaves. They formed a government and constitution patterned after those of the United States. But the State of Georgia did not recognize their sovereign status, seeing them instead as tenants living on state land. As white settlers pushed south, eager to raise cotton, they stole Cherokee livestock, burned their towns, and squatted on their land. They also began pressuring the federal government to acquire Cherokee territory.

"The lands in question belong to Georgia. She must and she will have them" (Report of Georgia state legislature, 1827, cited in RACE exhibit, SMM).

"Our property may be plundered before our eyes; violence may be committed on our persons; even our lives may be taken away, and there is no one to regard our complaints. We are denationalized; we are disfranchised. We are deprived of membership in the human family! We have neither land nor home, nor resting place that can be called our own" (Cherokee chief John Ross, letter to the U.S. Senate and House of Representatives, 1836, cited in RACE exhibit, SMM).

Figure 15.2 The red outline shows Cherokee lands prior to removal in 1838. The blue outer line shows the original Cherokee territory. Courtesy of Roger Boehm/Science Museum of Minnesota.

"Established in the midst of another and superior race, they must necessarily yield to the force of circumstances and ere long disappear" (President Andrew Jackson, Fifth Annual Message to Congress, 1833, cited in RACE exhibit, SMM).

Opportunity for the common (white) man

In 1828 Andrew Jackson was elected president on a platform of creating greater opportunity for the "common man." But his ideas about making America more democratic did not extend to Native Americans. In Jackson's view, Indians should not become like white people but should preserve themselves as Indians – on land far away from white cities and settlements. In 1830 Congress passed the Indian Removal Act, ordering the Cherokee, Cree, Choctaw, Chickasaw, and Seminole to give up their lands east of the Mississippi.

Trail of Tears

For nearly a decade, the Cherokee legally fought their removal, even winning two appeals in the U.S. Supreme Court. But during the winter of 1838, the U.S. Army forced them to leave their homes at gunpoint. They were marched westward to the newly established "Indian Territory," in present-day Oklahoma. By 1840 more than 46,000 eastern Indians had been uprooted, opening 25 million acres of land to white settlement.

Figure 15.3 President Andrew Jackson. Courtesy of the Library of Congress.

Figure 15.4 *The Trail of Tears*, 1942. One-fourth of the Cherokee Nation, about 4,000 people, died of such diseases as measles, pneumonia, and tuberculosis on the forced journey west that became known as the Trail of Tears. Courtesy of the Granger Collection, New York.

In 1823, Andrew Jackson was elected as President of the United States. Jackson was very popular with the working class or "common man," especially small farmers. A hero of the War of 1812, Jackson was seen as someone who would lead the country as it continued to move its people west. His ideas about Indians were shaped by his earlier career as a soldier in the war. This bias led to his decision to remove not only the Cherokee, but also the Cree, Choctaw, Chickasha, and Seminole from their lands. The Cherokee, having learned about the laws and courts of the United States, conducted a legal fight against their removal for over ten years. But in 1840 the removal began in

earnest as all of their legal options had been exhausted. This is the political and economic back story behind the upheaval that came to be called "The Trail of Tears," mentioned earlier in this chapter and in other chapters. This movement of disparate tribal groups to the new territory of Oklahoma conveniently opened up millions of acres of land to those new white farmers and settlers. (Zinn 2003:686)

Another example of land loss and confiscation is that of the land lost by the Minnesota tribes of the Ojibwe or Anishinaabe in the late 19th century. These tribes were forced to give up tribal lands to make way for white immigrant farmers, and were moved to White

The U.S. Conquest Of Mexican California

"[It is] our manifest destiny to overspread the continent allotted by Providence for the free development of our yearly multiplying millions" (John O'Sullivan, columnist and editor, 1845, cited in RACE exhibit, SMM).

The Mexican–American War

In 1846 war erupted between the United States and Mexico after years of tension over the former's expansion toward the Pacific Ocean. By early 1847, the United States controlled California and the rest of what was then northern Mexico. Caught in the middle were thousands of Mexicans living in the border territories.

The Californios

Occupying California were thousands of Spanish-speaking *Californios*; they included descendants of European settlers from Spain and Mexico as well as Native Americans and those of mixed native and European ancestry who had adopted Spanish culture and converted to Catholicism. They had lived there for generations. By 1850 some 200 well-established Californio families owned about 14 million acres of land in the territory. Californios earned their livings by raising

cattle, making wine, and growing citrus fruits – so land ownership was crucial to them.

"Ours is a government of the white man. ... In the whole history of man ... there is no instance whatever of any civilized colored race, of any

Figure 15.6 Del Valle family, Rancho Camulos, Ventura County, 1888. Courtesy of the California Historical Society.

Figure 15.7 *American Progress*, 1872. In this 1872 painting, an angelic personification of the United States carries the light of civilization westward with her settlers, pushing Native Americans and wild animals toward the darkness. Many white Americans saw the Mexican–American War as proof that it was part of the nation's "Manifest Destiny" to claim and populate the West. Chromolithograph © George A. Crofutt 1873, Courtesy of the Library of Congress.

Figure 15.5 The 1848 Treaty of Guadalupe Hidalgo officially ended the war and transferred just under half of Mexico's land to the U.S. Courtesy of the Science Museum of Minnesota/C. Johnson.

shade, being found equal to the establishment and maintenance of free government" (U.S. Senator John C. Calhoun, in debate over annexing Mexican territory, 1850, cited in RACE exhibit, SMM).

The greed for gold

On January 24, 1848, a week before the Treaty of Guadalupe Hidalgo was signed, gold was discovered in northern California. Soon, Californio ranchers found their lands swamped by white Americans and immigrants from around the world. In the wake of the Gold Rush, many newcomers came to see having a parcel of California land as their God-given right. Racial hostilities

ran high and violence grew, in part against Californio landowners.

Law of the land grab

The rapid establishment of a white political majority, hastened by California statehood in 1851, soon left the Californio ranchers powerless. The state legislature hit them with heavy land taxes. The 1851 Land Law burdened them further by requiring them to undergo a slow, costly process of legally confirming their claims – forcing many to borrow heavily. Gradually, the Californio ranchers disappeared. By the end of the century, most of the state's former Mexican citizens worked as poorly paid migrant laborers.

Earth Reservation. But by 1920, White Earth residents saw most of that land illegally sold to lumber companies and to the U.S. Government. For more background information on the modern-day consequences of this specific case see the White Earth Reservation Land Settlement Act 1985 (U.S. Congress 1985).

How did something like this federally sanctioned "land grab" happen? The U.S. Government signed, at least on paper, a treaty to hold land in trust for the tribal members for 25 years. At the end of the 25 years, the government assured that each person would be well enough "assimilated" into American culture that they could manage their own 160-acre land allotment. The exception to this law was that "mixed blood" Indians could bypass the trust period of 25 years and sell the land to whomever they wanted. The assumption being that "mixed blood" perhaps sped up that assimilation and civilizing process so that they were able to think rationally enough to decide what to do with their own land.

One of the very interesting things the authors of this book found out working with the Science of Minnesota curators was the central role of anthropologists in helping to perpetuate this legal fraud against the native people at White Earth. Ales Hrdlicka of the Smithsonian Institution and Albert Jenks of the University of Minnesota, were the two anthropologists in question. Traveling to the White Earth Reservation, the anthropologists used the latest cutting edge race science of their time, craniotomy, skin color charts, and

hair form samples to determine the "blood" status (and thus intellect) of the Native Americans in question (Gould 1996:88). This kind of race science was used in courts in Minnesota and elsewhere to help determine binding legal decisions. So, in this case as in others, there was a very grave consequence in believing that one could tell a person's racial/ethnic identity by those very superficial markers. History tells us that the outcome of these decisions usually benefitted the white power structure and the "racial" status quo. Native Americans were in the way of western expansion, and they were deemed expendable by the federal, state, and territorial governments in the expanding democracy.

Another example of huge tracts of land confiscation took place in the West and Southwest. In the western part of the United States, the Mexican–American War provided the opportunity for the United States to annex just over one-half of Mexico's land through the Treaty of Hidalgo in 1848. The Spanish-speaking former citizens of Mexico became resident in what is today the state of California. In that territory at the time, some well-established Mexican families owned over 14 million acres. The language of the territory was Spanish. Both the Gold Rush of 1848 and the Treaty of Hidalgo paved the way for both massive illegal and governmental land grabs. (Zinn 2003:270) When California became a state in 1850, the heavy land taxes caused many of the formerly wealthy Mexican ranchers who owned those vast tracts of land to have to downscale, lose, or sell their land. By the end of the 19th century, the land ownership, especially farmland, had shifted from former Mexican landowners to white landowners (Velez Ibanez 1996:91).

During the 20th century, one of the most racially motivated confiscations of territory by the U.S. Government was the appropriation of land from Japanese Americans when they were interned in camps in the United States during World War II. (See the chapter "World War II: An American Dilemma" in Ronald Takaki's book, *A Different Mirror: A History of Multi-Cultural America* (2008).) Japanese Americans had been a part of the California population for well over a century, often arguing for recognition as citizens based on their census status as Mongoloid (see Haney López's essay in chapter 6). The Japanese Navy bombed the U.S. Naval Base at Pearl Harbor, Hawaii on December 6, 1942. In the months that followed, the United States joined in the Allied war efforts to fight both against Hitler in Germany and the Japanese. But at home in the United States, there was a government decision to round up nearly 120,000 Japanese Americans, and confiscate their homes, property and businesses. Obviously, this kind of systemic response on the part of the government meant that there were already deep-seated prejudices against Japanese citizens. (Takaki 2008:120) The Immigration Act of 1924 explicitly linked citizenship with immigration status, stating, basically, that people who could not become U.S. citizens by law could not immigrate to the United States. So by the time World War II came around, Japanese immigration had dwindled to about 600 people per year. It then ceased altogether until the war ended. But, it was not until 1988, 45 years later, that the U.S. Government officially apologized to Japanese Americans and paid monetary reparations to the survivors and their families for their property and other losses (Takaki 2008:121).

Japanese American Internment

"I am determined that if they have one drop of Japanese blood in them, they must go to camp" (Colonel Karl Bendetsen, administrator, Wartime Civil Control Administration, 1942, cited in RACE exhibit, SMM).

The roots of internment
Japanese American internment during World War II had its roots in a legacy of racist anti-Japanese sentiment. Japanese people began immigrating to Hawaii and California around 1890, working mainly in agriculture. But Japan's rise on the world scene in the early 1900s led to a rising tide of prejudice among white Americans. In California, laws were passed discouraging Japanese immigration and prohibiting non-citizens from owning or leasing land.

Forced relocation
On December 7, 1941 Japanese air forces attacked the U.S. naval base at Pearl Harbor, Hawaii, triggering America's entry into World War II. In the months that followed, the federal government forced almost 120,000 Japanese Americans, nearly two-thirds of them U.S. citizens, into "War

Figure 15.8 California, c. 1920. Courtesy of the National Japanese American Historical Society, Inc. and the United States National Archives.

Relocation Camps" across the West. The internees lost homes, land, and businesses. They also suffered mental and physical hardships that went far beyond the economic damage.

"Race prejudice, war hysteria"
America's European enemies were typically seen as misguided victims of despotic leaders, while Japanese people were called "yellow vermin," "mad dogs," and "monkey men." It wasn't until 1988 that the United States officially apologized to Japanese Americans, admitting that internment had been based on "race prejudice, war hysteria, and a failure of political leadership." Beginning in 1990, the government paid monetary reparations to surviving internees.

We're charged with wanting to get rid of Japs for selfish reasons. We do. It's a question of whether the white man lives on the Pacific Coast or the brown man. ... If all the Japs were removed tomorrow, we'd never miss them in two weeks, because the white farmers can take over and produce everything the Jap grows. And we don't want them back when the war ends, either. (Austin E. Anson, Salinas Vegetable Grower-Shipper Administration, 1942, cited in RACE exhibit, SMM)

Figure 15.9 Heart Mountain Relocation Center, Heart Mountain, Wyoming, 1942. Photograph by Tom Parker. Courtesy of the Bancroft Library, University of California, Berkeley.

The final example of minority land loss is taken from recent headlines and involves racism, the U.S. Department of Agriculture (USDA), and the lawsuit brought against them by black American farmers. Since the end of slavery in 1868, some blacks, despite deep structural racism, were able to become farmers in the South. Their numbers peaked in 1910, when 218,000 African American farmers had an ownership stake in 15 million acres of land. However, by 1992 those numbers had dwindled to 2.3 million acres held by only 18,000 black farmers. Many black farmers for generations had alleged that they were systematically shut out from the federal benefits and monetary opportunities that helped to shore up and sustain small white farmers (Komm 2010:1). Among those in the U.S. government finally concluding that such racial bias existed were USDA researchers themselves. As a result of the publication of the USDA researchers' findings in 1997 that could not be repudiated, the USDA Office of Civil Rights (which had been virtually defunct due to neglect under the Reagan administration) also found the USDA office for dealing with civil rights complaints was in shambles (Komm 2010:2).

In 1997, a group of black American farmers also filed a class action suit against the USDA. In all, 22,000 farmers were ultimately granted a $2.3 billion settlement, but this was only funds for about one out of every ten farmers who had originally signed on to the lawsuit. Most did not qualify because their cases were looked at very carefully by the government's lawyers and were dismissed on a technicality. Under the new Obama Administration, however, the USDA agreed to re-review the lawsuit and President Obama came up with a second $1.25 billion for farmers who were excluded from the first case. This second settlement and the money to fund it has now become a major battle among conservative Republicans and more liberal Democrats in Congress. (Komm 2010:2) The conservative media also appears to be opposing the payments, as they see the payment of the African American farmers tied to the Shirley Sherrod affair. Shirley Sherrod is the black USDA official whose remarks about her interactions with white farmers in the past were taken out of context and who was called "racist" by the conservative media (see chapter 12 for more details).

The allocation of these resources to the black farmers was still pending in Congress as of fall 2011.

In the next section of this chapter, we will look at how wealth accumulation has worked through home ownership in this country. The focus will be on how institutions such as banks, realty boards, the mortgage industry, and the United States government have all colluded in the past to produce a racially segregated housing market. This collusion has had and continues to have very real consequences for people of color versus Euro-Americans and more recently Asians in terms of accumulating and passing on wealth from one generation to the next.

The Housing Market

As we saw in earlier in this chapter, wealth in the United States is accumulated and passed on through land and home ownership, education, and the benefits from policies designated to enhance economic and educational investments. For example, between 1934 and 1962, the federal housing administration insured $120 billion in new housing loans, but less than 2 percent of these loans went to nonwhites. Melvin L. Oliver and Thomas M. Shapiro's breakthrough book *Black Wealth, White Wealth: A New Perspective on Racial Inequality* (1995) provides a more nuanced way of understanding the intractable nature of racial inequal-ity by looking at the accumulation and heritance of private wealth over time, and not just at income. The reality of this approach shows that discrimination in mortgage lending has limited opportunities for many people of color in the United States, thus limiting their chances to accumulate lasting financial security. So, it is this reality that creates a wealth gap, with whites as a group at the top of the racial and eco-nomic hierarchy.

One of the ways that ordinary working-class Americans were able to get into homes in the 1940s

---

White – The Color Of Money

Discrimination in mortgage lending has limited opportunities for many people of color to gain long-term financial security.

The wealth gap
Owning a home that grows in value over the years is the most common way that Americans build a base of financial security. Yet because access to affordable home mortgage loans is typically made harder for people of color than it is for whites, their opportunities to build that base are far fewer.

Today, the net worth of the average African American family is about one-tenth that of the average white family. Much of that disparity is due to differing rates of home ownership between these two groups and to the generally lower val-ues of homes blacks own compared to homes owned by whites. The gap is perpetuated as wealth – or the lack of it – is passed down from parent to child.

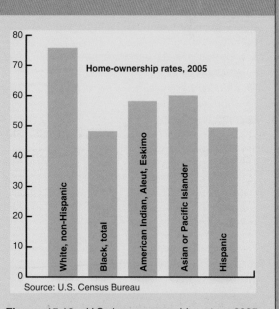

Figure 15.10 U.S. home-ownership rates, 2005. Graph courtesy of the Science Museum of Minnesota.

Mortgage-loan inequality

In 2003 the Federal Financial Institutions Examination Council reported that blacks and Native Americans applying for home mortgage loans were twice as likely to be turned down as whites. Hispanics were 1.5 times as likely as whites to be turned down, yet Asians – stereotyped as the "model minority" – were slightly *more* likely to be approved than whites.

Higher rates for nonwhites

Data gathered by the federal government in 2004 under the Home Mortgage Disclosure Act revealed that even when people of color are approved for mortgages, they are more likely to receive higher-cost "sub-prime" loans. These loans are offered at rates that are 0.1 percent to 0.6 percent higher than standard rates. Although this difference may seem small at first, over time it can mean thousands of dollars in additional interest payments. For example, interest on a 30-year, $180,000 mortgage loan at a 6.5 percent interest rate would total about $21,000 more than the same mortgage loan at a 6 percent rate.

Between 1934 and 1962, the federal government – through the Federal Housing Administration – insured $120 billion in new housing loans. Less than 2 percent of these loans went to nonwhites.

The GI Bill: An Unequal Opportunity

Few minority soldiers benefited from the post–World War II housing and education program known as the G.I. bill.

Home ownership and social change

Commonly known as the G.I. Bill of Rights, the Servicemen's Readjustment Act of 1944 became a powerful stimulus for social and economic change in post–World War II America.

Feeding the dream

Among the many benefits offered to returning military veterans were low-interest mortgages with low down payments. The G.I. bill made the dream of home ownership come true for millions, fostering the growth of the American middle class. Although the legislation specified that every veteran was eligible for benefits, many minority G.I.s were unable to cash in.

The enduring effects of housing discrimination

People whose house increases in market value are often able to use that equity to help finance their children's education or their own retirement. In addition, the increase in their house's value accumulates wealth that is passed on to their children and even to their grandchildren. By contrast, people who are restricted to buying in neighborhoods where home values increase only modestly do not gain much "housing wealth" over the years. In this way, housing discrimination from past decades continues to have financial repercussions today.

Same dream, different endings

Herb Kalisman and Eugene Burnett were of similar age and military experience, but they didn't share equally in the G.I. bill's benefits.

Herb Kalisman

In 1951 Herb Kalisman and his wife, Doris, took advantage of a low-interest G.I. bill mortgage loan to purchase a $9,000 house in Levittown. Among its other attractions, this new suburb on Long Island, New York, provided access to excellent schools for their children. In 2006, the home, where the Kalismans still live, was valued at $420,000.

Eugene Burnett

After the war, Eugene and his wife, Bernice, were kept from buying a house in Levittown. They were told that the "owners of this development have not as yet decided to sell these homes to Negroes."

Eugene worked two jobs in order to qualify for a mortgage. In 1950 the Burnetts bought a $7,000 house in a new development in Amityville, New York, one that promoted itself as welcoming to all races. When they sold the house 10 years later to move to a new town with better schools, it was valued at only $10,100.[1]

Because they were denied access to suburbs where housing values grew quickly, the Burnetts weren't able to accumulate as much financial security through home ownership as the Kalismans.

[1] The houses were both in the median bracket. In 2006, the average price of Amityville house in this range was approximately U.S. $350,000. (See http://www.trulia.com/real_estate/Amityville-New_York/market-trends/, accessed January 17, 2012.)

"There Goes the Neighborhood"

Widespread housing discrimination still goes on today, but it takes subtler forms.

Redlining then

In the mid-1930s, banks nationwide developed a rating system to measure mortgage-lending risks in residential areas. Places where people of color lived were rated lower (meaning they had a higher risk of failing to make mortgage payments) with African American neighborhoods at the bottom of the scale. Banks and insurance companies were hesitant to do business in low-rated areas, limiting people's ability to buy homes there and resulting in lower property values. Because the "undesirable" areas were marked in red on maps that the banks and insurance companies drew up, this practice was called *redlining*. Although redlining was highly discriminatory, it was entirely legal.

Racial steering now

The Federal Fair Housing Act of 1968 outlawed redlining, but housing discrimination continues through the practice of *racial steering*, in which real estate agents guide minority home buyers to neighborhoods where people of similar ethnic and class backgrounds live. This practice limits housing and neighborhood choices and perpetuates patterns of segregation. A study conducted

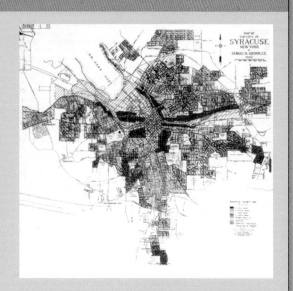

Figure 15.11 1937 map of Syracuse, New York, showing "undesirable" neighborhoods marked in red. Courtesy of the National Archives supplied by Emanuel Carter.

by the National Fair Housing Alliance and the U.S. Department of Housing and Urban Development from 2002 to 2005 found that racial steering occurred among test subjects – both white and black – 87 percent of the time.

White flight

A pattern of whites leaving a neighborhood as people of color move in has marked cities nationwide for several decades. Known as "white flight," this pattern is triggered when a few middle-class families of color move into a largely white neighborhood. Some white residents, fearing their home values will fall, move away. The sudden jump in the supply of houses on the market causes home prices to fall. As this happens, more of the neighborhood's white residents leave and increasing numbers of people of color move in. As the racial and economic makeup of the neighborhood continues to shift, white flight continues to accelerate.

The segregation that results from housing discrimination and white flight limits education and job opportunities. It deeply harms city neighborhoods and older suburbs. And it deepens racial and political divisions in metropolitan America. (Myron Orfield, executive director, Institute on Race & Poverty, University of Minnesota: RACE exhibit, SMM)

and 1950s was through the G.I. Bill of Rights (see Figure 14.3). After World War II, it was a stimulus for serviceman to buy homes. But while this was the goal, very few servicemen of color were able to take advantage of it (Oliver and Shapiro 1995:16). These G.I.s of color, especially black ones, were not able to benefit from "housing wealth." In the 1930s, after the Great Depression was over, an economic depression which caused the crash of the Wall Street stock market, the closure of thousands of businesses, and the unemployment of millions of Americans, the U.S. Government and the nation's banks developed a scheme to assess the risk of mortgage companies when they provided mortgages in residential areas. Places where people of color were living were rated lower, with neighborhoods where blacks lived at the very bottom of the scale (Oliver and Shapiro 1995:17). This policy and the subsequent practice resulted in a process called "red lining," because of the process of coloring in red on residential maps those areas of high risk to banks and mortgage companies, which also happened to be those places with a concentration of people of color. So, both banks and mortgage companies, with the collusion of the U.S. Government, sanctioned the practices for decades. The practice was officially ended by law in 1968, but as researchers tell us, many of those practices still exist today in more subtle ways through racial and ethnic steering (Oliver and Shapiro 1996:185). Most recently, the United States saw once again, the vulnerability of racially segregated and low income communities with the implosion of the

sub-prime housing market. National numbers indicate that once again, the overwhelming number of foreclosures affected owners of color (Estrada 2009:1).

One of the positive ways in which the census is used is to measure segregation on the national level through what is called the "Index of Dissimilarity." Despite the laws on the books, the reality is still that most American cities remain racially divided. The time period of this study is 1980 to 2000. The three cities reviewed for this study are Chicago, San Diego, and New Orleans. These data show that Chicago was the most segregated of the three cities with New Orleans being second (and it may have been even more segregated in 2010, since in 2005 Hurricane Katrina caused the displacement and migration out of state of many poor people, especially African Americans). This is clearly one area where educated citizens, activist community groups, policy makers, and government agencies still have much work to do to level the housing and wealth accumulation playing fields.

How Do Recent Immigrants Manage to Enter the Housing Market?

If recent immigrants are poor, then they have an uphill struggle to raise funds and to establish the credit that they need. The example we will use focuses on the Hmong in Minnesota. Large numbers of Hmong

Measuring Housing Segregation

Despite the end of legalized segregation, most American cities remain racially divided.

Measuring housing segregation
The Index of Dissimilarity is one method of charting segregation in U.S. cities. Scores range from 0 to 100: the higher the number, the higher the level of segregation between any two groups. A value of 60 (or above) is considered very high, while values of 40 or 50 indicate moderate segregation, and values of 30 or below are considered fairly low. Below, we provide dissimilarity data of segregation for three U.S. cities: Chicago, San Diego, and New Orleans.

Chicago
Since the early 1980s, African Americans and Latinos have been moving to Chicago's suburbs in increasing numbers. But they have not been welcomed in all communities. In many areas they experience a level of segregation equivalent to that of the inner city.

> White–Black: 81
> White–Latino: 62
> White–Asian: 44
> (Based on data from the 2000 U.S. census)

San Diego
People of color figured heavily in this area's population growth during the 1990s. However, levels of segregation for blacks and increasing segregation rates for Latinos suggest that much remains to be done to ensure that these populations gain equal access to all housing resources.

> White–Black: 54
> White–Latino: 51
> White–Asian: 47
> (Based on data from the 2000 U.S. census)

New Orleans
Segregation in New Orleans was brought to national attention in 2005, in the aftermath of Hurricane Katrina. The challenge of rebuilding the city presents an opportunity to change its pattern of economic and racial division. Will the 2020 map of New Orleans look dramatically different, or will the city still be largely made up of segregated neighborhoods?

> White–Black: 69
> White–Latino: 36
> White–Asian: 48
> (Based on data from the 2000 U.S. census)

Segregation and Katrina
The destruction wrought by Hurricane Katrina in 2005 dramatically exposed the extent and impact of housing segregation in New Orleans. The neighborhoods most devastated by Katrina were the lower Ninth Ward, where nearly all residents were poor African Americans, and Lakeview, where most residents were middle-class whites. Many Ninth Ward residents lacked the means to evacuate the city and were forced to ride out the storm in the Superdome or the Convention Center. A year later, the lower Ninth Ward still had not been reopened to its residents. By contrast, two-thirds of Lakeview's residents had returned within that time, and city services had been restored there.

Figure 15.12 Displaced New Orleans residents take shelter in the Houston Astrodome. Courtesy of FEMA/Ed Edahl.

One Family's Story

"The Hmong community sees real estate as the key to obtaining wealth in this country" (Kou Vang, St. Paul realtor, 2006: RACE exhibit, SMM).

Figure 15.13 Lynju Yang and John Sou Yang. Courtesy of the Science Museum of Minnesota/ Rachel Moritz.

The Yangs

John Sou Yang and Lynju Yang arrived in Minnesota from Laos in 1979. They found three-bedroomed public housing in St. Paul and there raised their seven children. The Yangs started looking for a house in 1996, when their eldest daughter was nearly 18. In traditional Hmong culture, children live with parents well into adulthood and help support the household. But state public assistance rules assume that children leave home once they reach the legal age of 18. The Yangs faced the possibility of having to move into a smaller public housing apartment as more of their children grew up.

The Yangs bought their home on St. Paul's East Side in 1996 with only a small down payment and the help of a government loan. They were the only Hmong on the block. Almost ten years later, four of their five sons were still living at home,

some with their wives and children. Because of their children's support, the Yangs, neither of whom are employed or fluent in English, are able to afford the house payments.

Race and home ownership in Minnesota

The Twin Cities of Minneapolis and St. Paul have the nation's seventh-highest home ownership rate – 72 percent in 2000. However, large disparities in house value remain between whites and people of color. Although Hmong Americans enjoy the second-highest home ownership rate in the Twin Cities, they mainly live in poorer neighborhoods, so their homes are less valuable. In 2000 more than 60 percent of Hmong Minnesotans were living below the poverty line.

Relative home-ownership percentages and house values in Minnesota

Whites
  Home ownership: 76 percent
  Average house value: $141,200

Hmong
  Home ownership: 55 percent
  Average house value: $93,000

Latinos
  Home ownership: 40 percent
  Average house value: $111,200

African Americans
  Home ownership: 40 percent
  Average house value: $107,500

moved to the United States and to Minnesota from Laos in 1979 (Takaki 2008:284), among them were the Yangs. Initially living in public housing and then in a three-bedroom house with their seven children, the Yangs adjusted to life in the United States. They were eventually able to buy a home, but it took 17 years from the time they arrived in the country for

them to do so. They were finally able to buy a home, with a small down payment and with the help of a government loan, but it was in a poor neighborhood. They were then only able to afford to stay in their home with help from their now grown children who helped to subsidize their monthly payments. In Minneapolis, the 2000 census data showed that 76 percent of whites owned homes, 55 percent of Hmong owned homes; 40 percent of African Americans owned homes; and 40 percent Hispanic/ Latinos. The average house values in Minneapolis at that time were as follows: homes of whites were worth $141,200; homes of Latinos were worth $111,200; homes of African Americans were worth $107,500; and homes of Hmong were worth $93,000.

The Wealth Gap Persists

Melvin Oliver and Dalton Conley explain the difference between wealth and income in one of the videos in the Race exhibit. Their comments on the

wealth gap are presented in the transcript of that conversation in this chapter.

When we talk about the wealth gap in 2011, we are still talking about the fact that the wealth gap between white and African American families increased more than four times between 1984 and 2007. We are also talking about the fact that middle-income white households now own far more wealth than high-income African American households. The four-fold increase in the wealth gap reflects public policies such as tax cuts on investment income and inheritances, which benefit the wealthiest and cause persistent discrimination in housing, credit, and labor markets (Institute on Assets and Social Policy 2010: RACE exhibit, SMM).

Figure 15.14 Race and the wealth gap. These piles of cash represent the average net worth of families based on race. Data was collected by the U.S. Census Bureau from 1997 to 2000. Net worth is defined as a person's assets minus his or her debts. Most middle-class Americans' largest asset is the value of their home. The average net worth of whites is higher largely because their opportunities for owning homes in areas with higher housing values is markedly greater than for members of other racial groups. Source: U.S. Census Bureau, Survey. Courtesy of the Science Museum of Minnesota.

The Race Exhibit portrays the wealth gap through using stacks of money. This has been a very powerful image in this project because it shows in graphic terms that a lay public can understand just how wealth disparities look and work. Tatjana Meschede, one of the coauthors of the report "The Racial Gap Increases Four-Fold" says, "The gap is an opportunity denied and assures racial economic inequality for the next generation" (Shapiro, Meschede, and Sullivan 2010:1). There is still much work to be done!

The way forward to close the wealth gap will take a concerted government, advocacy, and policy effort. Hopefully, with proposals such as Obama's New National Initiative, *Creating Communities of Opportunity*, we have a great place to start (Fox and Treuhaft 2010).

Wealth and Housing

A Conversation

We conclude this chapter with another scholarly "conversation," like those found in part 1. Through a series of edited RACE exhibit video transcripts, leading scholars explain the links between public policy and racial disparities in wealth and housing, past and present. **Dalton Conley** *is Professor of Sociology and Public Policy at New York University, Adjunct Professor of Community Medicine at Mount Sinai School of Medicine and a Research Associate at the National Bureau of Economic Research.* **Melvin Oliver** *is the SAGE Sara Miller McCune Dean of Social Sciences and Professor of Sociology at University of California, Santa Barbara.* **john a. powell** *is Executive Director of the Kirwan Institute for the Study of Race and Ethnicity at The Ohio State University.* **Beverly Daniel Tatum** *is President of Spelman College.*

The wealth gap

MELVIN OLIVER: If there's one thing I'd want people to understand about the asset gap, the wealth gap in America, it's that this was a gap that was created by public decisions for the most part, by public institutions that gave different opportunities for different people to create, nurture, and gain assets.

DALTON CONLEY: There's a long history in America of explicit government policy to exclude African Americans from a piece of the pie, from wealth

Reproduced courtesy of California Newsreel.

accumulation. It goes back to slavery, where, by law, slaves, of course, didn't own their own bodies, let alone other assets. Even after the Civil War, there were policies like the Black Codes in the South, which required enormous licensing fees for blacks to start a business, but nothing for whites.

MELVIN OLIVER: The difference between wealth and income is really highlighted when you look at differences among blacks and whites. While blacks have ten cents for every dollar of wealth that whites have, they have sixty-two cents in terms of every dollar of income. So the gap for wealth is much greater than the gap for income. So if wealth is important for securing life chances, then blacks have a very difficult time doing that compared to whites.

DALTON CONLEY: In the post–Civil Rights era it's very difficult to talk about race and class as two separate entities, because they overlap so much in our society. Many things that we associate with race on the surface of it, like differences in savings rates or differences in education and performance, are really class differences when you get the data and compare individuals coming from similar economic circumstances. But the complicating factor is that those very economic circumstances are determined by race, through historical inequalities, through contemporary dynamics where whites get jobs disproportionately more than blacks do and other minority groups. So race matters, but it often matters indirectly through the class position, the economic situation of a family.

Buying a home

DALTON CONLEY: A family's net worth comes from a lot of sources. But the biggest one, for most American families, is the equity they get in their home. The latter half of the twentieth century has witnessed some incredible rise[s] in housing values, which is [has?] basically been a wealth creation program for most white Americans.

MELVIN OLIVER: In the 1930s the federal government came in to create and sustain the construction industry. And to do that, they created the Federal Housing Administration, whose job it was to provide loans, or the backing for loans, to average Americans so they could purchase a home.

DALTON CONLEY: The American government provided low interest loans to returning veterans and to other white Americans after World War II, to create a boom in home ownership and suburbanization in America, from which blacks were excluded.

MELVIN OLIVER: A perfect example is the communities on the East Coast that are called Levittowns. These were mass market suburban housing tracts, which, when they were built, they were built at very, very reasonable cost.

john a. powell: When Levittown was finished, I think it was over 17,000 units with 82,000 people living there. And it was mass-produced. I mean, some people say Levittown is like the equivalent of the T-Model Ford. It made housing available to working-class America. It made it cheaper to buy than to rent, and it gave people a chance to get out of the city into the suburbs.

MELVIN OLIVER: Most of those communities did not require down payment. So many people just stood in line for days waiting to sign up, and the first one in line got the home. Those were FHA-financed homes. Those homes in Levittowns all had what we call restrictive covenants. Those were legal, binding agreements that no one who was black, Latino, Chinese, and, in some cases Jewish, could get those homes, could purchase those homes.

john a. powell: Until 1960, 82,000 people living in Levittown [… were] supported strongly by public money, which meant not just white people's money, but black people's money. And there wasn't a single black person living in Levittown.

Blacks weren't completely left out of the housing market, but the housing market they were exposed to was largely public housing. And public housing, first of all, was built almost exclusively with some, with a few, exceptions, in the central city. And after World War II, we started building larger and larger public housing projects, which were called "vertical ghettos." All of a sudden you're concentrating large numbers of poor people of color in one place. And then in the

'50s and '60s, there's also this idea of clearing out places where blacks had lived before. Some people called it "urban renewal." Other people called it "urban removal," where we removed whole neighborhoods, and sometimes these neighborhoods were very vibrant.

MELVIN OLIVER: In 1994 when I looked at the survey of income and program participation, you could see a home owner that purchased a Levittown-type home in 1950, which they may have purchased for five thousand dollars, having three hundred thousand dollars in wealth, in equity, home equity in that home. That's an investment that has grown over time. You look at the same similar type of African American family in that survey who did not have an opportunity to buy that home, or who had to purchase a home in the inner city, would have substantially less wealth. So that's how you start to see how this ten-to-one ratio between white and black wealth has created.

Housing market

DALTON CONLEY: The property market is where culture meets economics. Because whites are the majority, they really control the marketplace. They can move from place to place, and because they're the biggest group and because of supply and demand, if whites want to live somewhere, that's going to drive prices up. And if they 'don't want to live somewhere, it's going to drive prices down.

BEVERLY DANIEL TATUM: I might be an individual loan officer who considers herself to be quite progressive, very open-minded, a person with limited, if any, prejudice. And yet I might work for a bank that has the practice of charging higher percentage rates for, yes we make loans, but we charge at a higher rate than a particular … we charge at a higher rate for people who live in particular neighborhoods.

So when, let's say, a person of color from that neighborhood comes to see me, my own inclination might be to give that person a favorable loan. But if the policy of the bank is to give loans at a particular rate in a particular neighborhood, I might enact that policy, apart from my individual attitude, but in my decision-making reinforce the institutional racism embedded in that practice.

MELVIN OLIVER: An interesting case is that of a *Wall Street [Journal]* editor who owned a home in Atlanta and was moved to the headquarters in Washington or

New York. And he had to sell his home. And he put the home up and had an appraiser come out to appraise the value. And when he got the appraisal, he … it didn't fit. It seemed to be ten to fifteen thousand dollars lower than other homes in the community. And when he went to his house, he recognized that even without him there, this house obviously was owned by an African American. It had African American pictures, it had African American art. So he decided to ask the appraiser, another appraiser, to come, and he took out all the photographs that were African American, all of the pictures, anything that would give this home an air of being an African American was gone. The appraisal came in at the appraisal that was consistent with what he knew in the neighborhood. In other words, even today, the notion that a home owned in a community that is all white but owned by an African American has less value than a home owned by a white.

EDUARDO BONILLA-SILVA: Most whites, when you ask them to describe their neighborhood, they tell you, "I live in a nice neighborhood." And then you ask them what proportion of the people in your neighborhood happen to be minorities? And they tell you, "well, it's mostly a white neighborhood." And to be honest, they don't even problematize the fact that they live in white neighborhood, because for them, whiteness is not a race. They are just normal, nice people. The only people who are viewed as being racial in America are people of color.

DALTON CONLEY: Let's take an example of, if I am a nondiscriminating white home owner, and I see that African Americans start to move into my neighborhood, I might not have any sort of social–psychological reason to want to flee, to have white flight and sell off. But if I think that other people in my neighborhood are going to sell off, I have an economic incentive to sell off and escape that neighborhood before others do. Because once a rash of selling starts, then prices are going to drop. And of course, that becomes a vicious circle. Because even if no one in the white community has a psychological interest in selling to avoid integration, they all have an economic interest to be the first one to get out before they perceive a price drop. So it becomes, of course, this huge problem of a vicious circle. And how do you stop the process of white flight and the countervailing trend of gentrification, where whites move in and drive up prices for themselves at the expense of … local black residents?

References

Estrada, Vanessa Correra
2009 The Housing Downturn and Racial Inequality: Executive Summary. Policy Matters, A Quarterly Publication of the University of California, Riverside 3(2):1–11. Fall.

Fox, R., and S. Treuhaft
2010 The President's 2011 Budget. Creating Communities of Opportunity. Oakland, CA: Policylink

Gerstle, Gary
2001 American Crucible: Race and Nation in the Twentieth Century. Princeton: Princeton University Press.

Gould, Stephen Jay
1996 The Mismeasure of Man. New York: W. W. Norton.

Kromm, Chris
2010 The real story of racism at the USDA. *Facing South* (July 22). http://nameorg.org/pipermail/name-mce_nameorg.org/2010-July/006093.html, accessed November 16, 2011.

Oliver, Melvin L., and Thomas M. Shapiro
1995 Black Wealth, White Wealth: A New Perspective on Racial Inequality. New York. Routledge Press.

Shapiro, T. M., T. Meschede, and L. Sullivan, L.
2010 The Racial Wealth Gap Increases Fourfold. Waltham, MA: The Heller School for Social Policy and Management, Brandeis University.

Takaki, Ronald
2008 A Different Mirror: A History of Multicultural America. New York. Back Bay/Little Brown and Company.

U.S. Congress
1985 White Earth Reservation Land Settlement Act of 1985. http://www.welsa.org/pdf/whiteearthlandsettlementact.pdf, accessed November 26, 2011.

Velez Ibanez, Carlos
1996 Border Visions: Mexican Cultures of the Southwest. Phoenix: University of Arizona Press.

Yarbrough, Fay
2007 Race and the Cherokee Nation: Sovereignty in the Nineteenth Century. Philadelphia: University of Pennsylvania Press.

Zinn, Howard
2003 A People's History of the United States: 1492–Present. New York: Harper-Collins.

Further Reading

Cramer, R., M. Huelsman, J. King, A. Lopez-Fernandini, A., and Newville, D.

2010   The Assets Report 2010: An Assessment of President Obama's 2011 Budget and the Changing Policy Landscape for Asset Building Opportunities. Washington, D.C.: New America Foundation.

Cytron, N.

2010   Improving the Outcomes of Place-based Initiatives. San Francisco, CA: Community Investments, Federal Reserve Bank of San Francisco.

Mallach, A.

2010   Facing the Urban Challenge: The Federal Government and America's Older Distressed Cities. Washington, D.C.: What Workscollaborative.

Massey, Douglas S., and Nancy A. Denton

1993   American Apartheid: Segregation and the Making of the Underclass. Cambridge, MA. Harvard University Press.

National Alliance of Community Economic Development Associations

2010   Rising Above: Community Economic Development in a Changing Landscape. Washington, D.C.: NACEDA.

Treuhaft, S., K. Rose, and K. Black

2010   When Investors Buy Up the Neighborhood: Preventing Investor Ownership from Causing Neighborhood Decline. Oakland, CA: PolicyLink.

Wiedrich, K., S. Crawford, S., and L. Tivol

2010   Assets & Opportunity Special Report: The Financial Security of Households with Children. San Francisco, CA: Federal Reserve Bank of San Francisco.

16

Race and Health Disparities

In the previous chapters on the lived experience of race, we considered the various ways that race is linked to wealth accumulation and distribution and how race and class disparities affect education. This chapter focuses on a final arena in which race is of particular salience: disease and death.

As we have argued, race is not the same as or the cause of human biological variation. In that sense, race-as-biology is a myth. However, as we show in this chapter, race and racism are biological in that they have biological consequences. Racing and racism have biological consequences that start prenatally. In fact, recent research suggests that they may even extend backwards to prior generations through a process called epigenetics. These consequences of living in a racist society, or even living daily with subtle everyday consequences of being raced, accumulate and result in wear and tear on the mind and body and higher rates of illness, disease, and premature death. Race and racism not only are out there culturally, they get under the skin. In this chapter we explore some of the mechanisms by which race gets under the skin and leads to racial inequalities in health.

The guest essay in this chapter is by Dr. Susan M. Reverby, a Wellesley College historian and expert on the use of race in medical research. Reverby's essay highlights the racial dimension of one of the more frightening medical experiments done in the name of promoting science: the Tuskegee Experiment. In this long-running "experiment," poor African Americans with syphilis were followed for four decades without treatment to document the consequences of untreated syphilis. What is important about Reverby's essay is the way that she shows that Tuskegee is not an isolated incident. Rather it is imbedded in practices of treating individuals differently depending on their presumed race, and these practices are sadly alive and well today. One way race quickly has biological consequences is in differences in health care.

The field of health care provides one set of clear links between race and health outcomes. Once individuals encounter the health care system, they are treated differently. But neither do they come in on an equal footing. And that is the main reason why health measures are so starkly different by race.

There is no doubt that there is a causal link between race and health. This link, as we will show, goes far beyond disparities of socioeconomic class. In fact, what is interesting about race is that it embodies an economic disparity and a social disparity. Health is patterned by race *and* class. In the first instance, if you are poor and live in a poor community, you are less likely to have access to doctors, hospitals, and clinics. Therefore, poor people get fewer check-ups and so they are more likely to suffer from chronic, often treatable, diseases such as obesity, hypertension, diabetes, and cardiovascular disease. The fact that these health conditions occur more readily in poor communities of color than in white communities is of long standing and appears to be one of the most stable

Race: Are We So Different?, First Edition. Alan H. Goodman, Yolanda T. Moses, and Joseph L. Jones.
© 2012 American Anthropological Association. Published 2012 by Blackwell Publishing Ltd.

and intractable aspects of race. The fact that there are gaps in the diagnosis, care, and treatment of poor people of color speaks just as much to the presence of class disparities as it does to race.

In this chapter, we follow the Race exhibit in presenting a number of places in which race enters into health and health care and the different mechanisms by which living in a racialized society, rather than genetics, leads to racial disparities in health. We start with a study of the health consequences of discrimination, then examine differences in blood pressure that appear to be due to how individuals are raced; we examine the interesting case of BiDil, a heart drug developed specifically for African Americans, and end with an analysis of what is now called environmental racism.

Race, Discrimination, and Stress

While hard to measure, discrimination based on race has been documented by researcher Nancy Krieger Ph.D. and Stephen Sidney, MD at the Harvard School of Public Health. In 1996 they published an article in the *American Journal of Public Health* called "Racial Discrimination and Blood Pressure: The CARDIA Study of Young Black and White Adults." They developed a questionnaire to measure how much discrimination people experience. Their results showed that "overall, 77% of Black women and 84% of Black men reported experiencing racial discrimination in at least one of the 7 specified situations. And more than half of both Black men and women reported experiencing racial discrimination in three or more settings" (Krieger and Sidney 1996:1374).

They show that there is a double negative effect when both race/ethnicity and class come together. When the dynamic of gender is also added, the results show that chronic disease is a constant struggle. Amy J. Schulz and Leith Mullings in their ground-breaking edited volume, *Gender Race, Class and Health* show that "health disparities based on race/racism, class and gender/sexism are matters of life and death." They go on to say that the value of this interdisciplinary work is still rarely done. "In this book we have brought together an interdisciplinary group of scholars from the social sciences and from public health to examine the ways that

gender, class and race are mutually constituted and interconnected." (Schulz and Mullings 2006:3) From the academy to the popular press, the issues of women's health disparities are grabbing center stage. For example, in the article "Women Report Gaps in Healthcare" Molly Hennessey-Fiske reports on the findings of the "Health Indicators for Women in Los Angeles County" a study done by the Los Angeles County of Public Health. This study, reported in the *Los Angeles Times* (Hennessy-Fiske 2010) also showed at least two key examples of the double negative of race and gender in Los Angeles County, California:

- African American women were far more likely to suffer from sexually transmitted diseases including AIDS and to die from chronic illnesses. For example, while white women had higher incidences of breast cancer, African American women were more likely to die from it.
- Latinas reported the poorest health status in women of all ethnic groups. For example, their obesity rate increased from 27 percent in 2005 to 31 percent in 2007.

Part of the problem underlying these alarming data is that a substantive number of these poor women in Schulz and Mullings's volume, and in the health disparities report from Los Angeles County, simply lack health insurance and access to health care. But taking that into account, the coauthor of the public health report, Dr. Rita Singhai, believes that racism is also a factor contributing to high mortality rates of African American women, for example. Singhai said researchers suspect African American and Latinas may suffer racial inequality, discrimination, and stress in trying to maintain healthful diets and to access quality health care (Singhai quoted in Hennessey-Fiske 2010:A37). Therefore, as we think about the issue of race and health disparities, we need to understand that access to health care is a combination of environmental issues as well as the lack of available services (e.g. for free mammograms and free clinics in their neighborhoods).

Latinos, in general, face additional obstacles to receiving quality care. There is more than ample opportunity for reticence on the part of the person who does not speak English; if the person does go to the doctor or nurse, there is a greater chance for

Health Care for Latinos

Barriers exist that can make it hard for many Latinos to get health care.

Language is a barrier for many
According to a 2000 report by the UCLA Center for Health Policy Research and the Henry J. Kaiser Family Foundation, "Almost three in ten (29%) Latinos say they have had a problem communicating with health providers over the past year, including 12% who say this has been a major problem and 17% who say it has been a minor problem."

Figure 16.1 *Salud*, 2003 (acrylic on canvas) by Xavier Cortada (contemporary artist). Private Collection/The Bridgeman Art Library.

In areas with large Latino populations, Spanish-speaking health-care providers may be on hand. However, Latinos who speak only Spanish often have to rely upon translators or bilingual family members. Translators who are not fluent in medical terminology can inadvertently contribute to miscommunication between patients and doctors. In addition, patients may be reluctant to discuss vital personal details when family members or friends are acting as translators.

The working poor face additional barriers to accessing health care
Racial and ethnic minorities, including Latinos, are disproportionately poor and so are more likely to be hindered by

- Difficulty taking time off work for medical appointments
- Difficulty finding child care for appointments
- Difficulty finding transportation to appointments

"Financial barriers to using health services are often compounded by other factors, such as too few providers in a community, long travel times to the nearest provider, and practitioners who do not speak the language or understand the culture of their patients" (Brown et al.:2000).

miscommunication and perhaps misdiagnosis. Adding a language barrier to the already substantial list of obstacles to health care (difficulty getting off work, difficulty finding child care for appointments, difficulty finding transportation to appointments, etc.) creates a robust series of impediments.

Future research into health disparities and gender needs to move away from the current research in which, according to Ruth Zambrana and Bonnie Dill, "tautological arguments that [overlook] the racialized gendered institutional inequities within public health systems contribute to stagnant theoretical approaches that fail to increase our knowledge of the groups"

(2006:217). Zambrana and Dill advocate research that takes into account the "structural and political reality of poorly resourced institutions, particularly schools and health care facilities, in the urban, rural and migrant communities where Latinas live." (2006:217)

Race and Hypertension: The Cultural Meaning of Skin Color

It is a medical fact that diasporic Africans and Native Americans tend to have, on average, higher rates of hypertension than whites or Asian Pacific Islanders.

Is it biological (racial) or environmental or some combination of both? As a matter of fact, in a study published by Robert Cooper, Charles M. Rotimi, and Ryk Ward, it was shown that on a global or transatlantic level African Americans have one of the highest rates of blood pressure in the world. However, in West Africa, where many of the recent ancestors of African Americans come from, some of the lowest rates of blood pressure in the world are found. So, is it biological, race? The clear answer is that the pattern of hypertension in African groups, high in the Americas and low in Africa, suggests that much more than race and genetics is at work.

Anthropologists have weighed in on all sides of the argument. For another example, the "slavery" hypothesis takes the position that African Americans possess a genetic predisposition for high blood pressure based on the consequences of intense selection during the "middle passage" and long period of enslavement here in the United States. The "middle passage" is the harrowing journey that African slaves made on slaver ships crossing the Atlantic from the African continent. The argument goes that these traumatic circumstances caused a biological or genetic "bottleneck" that resulted in the conservation of salt in those persons who survived the middle passage and infectious diseases causing diarrhea and vomiting. Even though the theory has gained prominence in many circles, including the media, there are critics such as George Armelagos, a biological anthropologist, who say that the evidence "is just not there," that "there is no indication of a genetic bottleneck or evidence of 'racial' differences that are genetically determined." According to Armelagos, "it is time to discard the myth of the slavery hypertension hypothesis and begin to examine the issue from a biological and social perspective that reflects a more realistic approach to the disparities that exist in the prevalence of hypertension" (Armelagos 2005:119).

On the other side of the argument are those who say that when one explores the role of history, stress, genes, risk, environment, and other factors may or may not explain the hypothesis. Biological anthropologist Fatimah Jackson says, "the reality is that there are many different types of hypertensions; salt sensitive hypertension is one of those types and certain African Americans appear to develop greater

physiological pathologies than others in response to elevated dietary salt exposures" (2005:125). She goes on to talk about the relationship of human salt tolerance to that of other mammals. She says that most terrestrial mammals will develop cardiovascular, neurological, and renal abnormalities in the presence of extended exposures to elevated dietary salt. The key question for her is then "Why are some humans better able to tolerate exposure to this toxin (salt) without developing these physiological abnormalities?" (Jackson 2005:125) One of her challenges to biological anthropologists who do not believe in the salt hypertension hypothesis is to truly test it; and that means (to her) taking the history of African Americans, especially the middle passage and the vicissitudes of slavery into account.

Did the middle passage leave a legacy of salt sensitivity of African Americans? It is possible, but what is also beginning to be clear from the research is that Africans with no connection to middle passage populations also experience increased stress and illness when they live in the United States. As well, African Americans suffer increased rates of other diseases that are not related to salt sensitivity. In fact, they suffer from increased rates of virtually every disease. Our suggestion is that the causes of these broad disparities are also broad: living in a racial society.

A stunning example of how subtle racial classifications might lead to hypertension comes from recent research by medical anthropologist Clarence Gravlee. Gravlee is interested in understanding how to separate the impact of skin color as a biological trait from how we "race" individuals based on their skin color and other physical features. His research, discussed here, specifically evaluates how the cultural consensus category of "color," or what we might here refer to as social race, effects blood pressure in Guayama, Puerto Rico. Guayama is a logical site because the ascription of *color* is shaped by physical features like hair form, in addition to skin color, and also by markers of social status like wealth. Guayama, is a town of approximately 45,000 people and was the third-highest sugar-producing municipality on the island in the 1800s. One legacy of sugar and slavery is the "racialized landscape" reflected in this map of recent census data.

Especially in the mainland United States and also in Puerto Rico, dark skin color is associated with

High Blood Pressure: Race or Racism?

Studies suggest that the stress of racism contributes to higher rates of hypertension among African Americans than among European Americans.

It's not genetic

Between 1991 and 1995, researchers compared blood pressure levels in Africans from Nigeria and Cameroon with levels of African descendents in the Caribbean and the United States. Despite genetic similarities, the groups had very different rates of high blood pressure. Those differences are likely due to social environment, diet, and lifestyle.

Scientists have known for some time that the rate of hypertension in rural West Africa is lower than in any other place in the world, except for some parts of the Amazon Basin and the South Pacific. People of African descent in the United States and the United Kingdom, on the other hand, have among the highest rates of hypertension in the world. This shift suggests that something about the surroundings or way of life of European and American blacks – rather than a genetic factor – was the fundamental cause of their altered susceptibility to high blood pressure (Cooper et al. 1999).

Racism plays a role

Numerous studies support the claim that the stress of racism on African Americans is linked to high blood pressure among them.

"Race is a very, very powerful social category in the U.S. It influences where we live, what schools we attend, what jobs we have, what kinds of stresses we experience, whether we have access to health care, and many other

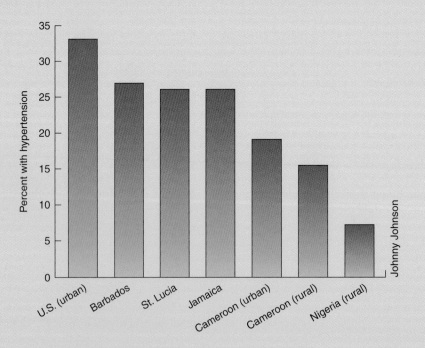

Figure 16.2 Science Museum of Minnesota illustration after "Incidence of Hypertension" graph from Cooper, Rotimi, and Ward (1999). Copyright © 1999 by Scientific American, Inc. All rights reserved.

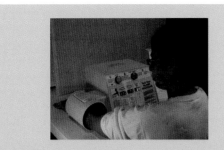

Figure 16.3 Science Museum of Minnesota Director of Community Engagement Joanne Jones-Rizzi measuring blood pressure. Courtesy of the Science Museum of Minnesota/Robert Garfinkle.

aspects of our lives. Because race is such a powerful social category, it can influence our biology and our health"(Pilar Ossorio, medical ethicist, University of Wisconsin Law School, at http://www.pbs.org/race/000_About/002_04-experts-01-12.htm).

"Discrimination that is not directly perceived may also produce changes in health status. For example, individuals may experience economic deprivation that is a result of racism, but they may not consider their economic circumstances as determined by race-related bias"(Brondolo et al. 2003).

increased blood pressure in African diasporic groups. Gravlee notes two very different mechanisms have been advanced to explain the relationship – based on two very different meanings of skin color. The first de facto explanation is that dark skin color is used as a genetic proxy for African admixture. Thus, the association is the result of "African genetics." The second less common explanation is that dark skin color *signifies* decreasing social status and increasing exposure to racism, and these cause increased blood pressure. The key point is that in the first instance, skin color, or pigmentation, may be associated with the second instance, *Color' – the social category*.

Gravlee measured both skin pigmentation – by standard reflectance spectrophotometry – and also classified individuals into color/race categories. Following the work of Marvin Harris in Brazil, Gravlee undertook a series of ethnographic interviews and was able to come up with a consensus classification of race, moving from the lightest category, Blanco(a) to Trigueño(a), Indio(a), to darker categories of Jabao(a) and finally Negro(a) (Gravlee 2005).

Gravlee and colleagues found that a*scribed color* (controlling for skin pigmentation) not skin pigmentation, is associated with high blood pressure. The powerful interaction between ascribed *color* and socioeconomic status (SES) is particularly telling. As SES increases so does blood pressure: those who are classified as negro have higher mean blood pressures, whereas the blood pressure of blancos or trigueños decreases (Gravlee

et al., 2005). These findings are consistent with the ethnographic record in Puerto Rico, which suggests *color* is relatively insignificant in low-SES contexts, and that racism is most pernicious in the middle and upper classes. Respondents who are classified as *negro* in high-SES contexts are *negros* living in a world of *blancos*. As a result, they may experience institutional and interpersonal racism that gets under the skin. One result could be sustained high blood pressure.

In summary, Gravlee's study shows that race is not biological in the sense that it is the same as human genetic variation. However, race is a powerful cultural category that has biological consequences.

Environmental Racism

Another mechanism that clearly leads to decreased health in poor communities is exposure to a wide variety of pollutants and irritants. When the poor communities are also communities of color, this is called "environmental racism."

Research over the last few decades has increasingly pointed to a relationship between the presence of chronic diseases such as childhood and adult asthma in community situations that are highly toxic. Examples of variations in toxins and pollutants by location include air quality (sulfur compounds, particulate matter, cancer-causing organic compounds), waste dumping, and ground water contamination. These toxic sites are often invisible to the eye but are more often found near poor neighborhoods of color. The exhibit panel entitled "Race pollution and health" reaffirms this assertion with statement from the United States Environmental Protection Agency as far back as 1992. The exhibit panel also makes the statement that people of color are more likely to live in areas where air quality does not meet the standards set by the agency. The health problems that this kind of pollution causes include upper respiratory infections, asthma, headaches and nausea, lung cancer, and heart disease.

In 2007 The United Church of Christ Justice and Witness Ministries commissioned a report as a follow up to one they did in 1987 to assess the progress made in identifying and cleaning up toxic waste sites in poor neighborhoods across the United States, "Toxic Race and Waste in the United States." The report was significant then because it found race to be the most important variable in predicting where commercial hazardous waste facilities were located in the United States. Race was a stronger predictor than household income, the value of homes, and the estimated amount of hazardous waste generated by industry (Bullard et al. 2007:x).

The new report was commissioned as part of the 20th anniversary celebration of the first. Among other things the report also examined the environmental justice implications in post-Katrina New Orleans. "Toxic Wastes and Race at 20" was written and designed to "facilitate renewed grass roots organizing and to provide a catalyst for local, regional, and national environmental justice public forums, discussion groups and policy changes in 2007 and beyond." (Bullard et al. 2007:x) The approach taken by the second report was different from that of 1987 in that it employed the use of 2000 census data (still another example of how census data can be used in a positive way) and distance-based methods and applied it to a current database of commercial hazardous waste facilities to assess the extent of racial and socioeconomic disparities in facility locations in the United States. Disparities were then examined by region and state and separate analysis was done for metropolitan areas, where most hazardous waste facilities are located.

The key findings of the report were that with the new application methodology the researchers were better able to see where people live in relation to where hazardous waste sites are located. The report showed that racial disparities in the distribution of hazardous wastes are even greater than previously documented. In fact the data show that people of color make up the majority of people living in "host neighborhoods" within 1.8 miles of the nation's hazardous waste facilities. They found racial and ethnic disparities still to be prevalent throughout the country (Bullard et al. 2007:x). Here are the findings for the national and neighborhood levels:

National disparities More than 9 million people are estimated to live in host neighborhoods within 1.8 miles of the nation's 413 commercial hazardous waste facilities. More than 5.1 million people of color live in neighborhoods with one or more commercial hazardous waste facilities. (Poverty rates in the host neighborhoods are 1.5 times greater than non-host areas (18% vs. 12%).)

Neighborhoods with clustered facilities Neighborhoods with facilities clustered close together have higher percentages of people of color than those with non-clustered facilities (69% vs. 51%). These neighborhoods have high poverty rates. Because people of color and the poor are highly concentrated in neighborhoods with multiple facilities, these groups are exposed to even more risk and negative impact on their health.

The report concludes with the observations that twenty years on from the first report, significant racial and socioeconomic disparities persist in the distribution of the nation's commercial hazardous waste facilities. Even with better technology and sampling techniques, the authors of the report found the conclusions unfortunately to be similar to what they were in 1987 (Bullard 2007:xi). The report also provides a robust set of recommendations that begin at the federal level and descend down to the local community level. A full copy of the report is highlighted in the further reading section at the end of the chapter.

BiDil and Race in Medicine

On June 23, 2005, the U.S. Food and Drug Administration (FDA) reinscribed "race" as a surrogate for genetic variation. The FDA approved BiDil "for the treatment of heart failure as an adjunct to

Race, Pollution, and Health

People of color are more likely to be exposed to pollution and suffer from its effects.

Industrial pollution
Hazardous-waste treatment and storage facilities are more often located in and around where the poor or minorities live than in middle-class or white communities.

The health effects of exposure to toxic dumps and industries vary depending upon the specific contaminants involved and levels of exposure.

Air pollution
People of color are more likely to live in areas where air quality does not meet the standards set by the Environmental Protection Agency. The health problems caused by air pollution include

- upper-respiratory infections
- asthma
- headaches and nausea

- lung cancer
- heart disease

"Racial minority and low-income populations experience higher than average exposures to selected air pollutants, hazardous waste facilities, contaminated fish and agricultural pesticides in the workplace" (U.S. Environmental Protection Agency 1992, cited in RACE exhibit, SMM)

Figure 16.4 Industrial pollutants have a disproportionately high impact on racial minorities and the poorer members of society. © iStockphoto.com/AVTG.

standard therapy in self-identified black patients." BiDil is a fixed-dose combination of two generic drugs, isosorbide dinitrate (a nitric oxide "donor") and hydralazine hydrochloride (a vasodilator and antioxidant). NitroMed, the Lexington, Massachusetts pharmaceutical company that received the patent, believes that BiDil's fixed-dose combination will enhance nitric oxide levels and thereby improve the dilation of large vessels and blood flow.[1]

The FDA Cardiovascular and Renal Drugs Advisory Committee held a day-long meeting the week prior to its approval of BiDil. Two of the coauthors of this book, Jones and Goodman, attended this meeting held in the Gaithersburg, Maryland, Holiday Inn ballroom, and listened to NitroMed's morning presentation of its African American Heart Failure Trial. As reported by Taylor and colleagues (2004) in the *New England Journal of Medicine*, among the 1,050 black patients with advanced heart failure who

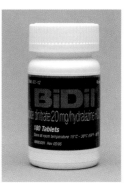

Figure 16.5 BiDil. Courtesy of NitroMed, Inc.

participated in the trial, the group that received BiDil suffered 43 percent fewer deaths than the placebo group. During the following hour of public comment, supporters of BiDil noted the need for better heart medications for African Americans, while academics such as physician and anthropologist Shomarka Keita questioned the logic of approving a drug for such a genetically diverse social grouping. The committee

---

[1] The section on BiDil is modified from Jones and Goodman (2005).

then deliberated, mostly, it seemed, to discuss the proper level of statistical significance of the results of the trial, before unanimously approving the application for BiDil. Two committee members voted for approval for general, non-race-specific use.

The FDA's decision to approve BiDil as an adjunct therapy in "self-identified black patients," in effect made it the first federally approved race-specific patent. It follows a torturously long history of separate and unequal medical treatment by race. It almost certainly will not be the last race-specific FDA patent application.

Healthy distrust?

BiDil's approval seems to owe more to politics than science. NitroMed deftly played politics by wrapping BiDil in the rhetoric of health disparities and enlisting African American groups in its heart failure trial and the FDA approval process: as its co-sponsor, the Association of Black Cardiologists facilitated patient enrollment in the heart failure trial. During the FDA hearing in Gaithersburg, the Association of Black Cardiologists, Congressional Black Caucus Health Brain Trust, NAACP, and the National Minority Health Month Foundation voiced support for the application of BiDil. ABC and NAACP representatives shared their hopes that BiDil would allow children to know their grandparents. And African Americans who participated in the heart failure trial, such as 48-year-old Debra Lee, gave similar supporting testament: "I take 23 pills a day but my joy comes from knowing that my medication is truly working its best to correct something that can't be fixed, my heart … What do I contribute as the cause of this turnaround? It is my strong faith in God and a little pill called BiDil."

Invoking sentiments from current debates on health disparities, Steven Nissen, chair of the committee meeting, applauded the trail's exclusive focus on and high enrollment of African Americans: "There is distrust of the health provider community by African Americans, some of it justified. So, we have to overcompensate in order to make people comfortable in minority groups with participating in clinical trials. … These folks were able to pull it off and I am going to give them some points for that. Let's move on."

Indeed, the hearing did "move on," proceeding without serious discussion of the issues and stakes in approving a drug for one race. Rather, the advisory committee continued a logic of race as an imprecise but necessary marker of genetic difference on the road to an era of personalized medicine. Nissen summarized:

> My view … is that drugs are not racist; people are racist … we are moving forward in medicine toward the era of genomic-based medicine. There is no question that in 10 or 15 years it is going to happen. I know it has been predicted for a long time and hasn't happened yet but it is going to happen, trust me. … So, what we are doing is we are using self-identified race as a surrogate for genomic-based medicine … I wish we had the gene chip. (United States Food and Drug Administration 2005)

In our view, BiDil is a step in the right direction if it meets a fraction of its promise of increasing survival of African Americans (and others) with heart failure. But, as Obasogie (2005) suggested in the *San Francisco Chronicle*, BiDil may represent one step forward and two steps back. It is especially troubling to not have a scientific sense of whether BiDil actually works better in African Americans than in others; interestingly, researchers of the African American Heart Failure Trial acknowledge their trial did not address this question. And if BiDil does work better, as is assumed, we still do not know why. Left without answers to these questions, the Holiday Inn ballroom overflowed with two troubling leaps of scientific faith: that responses to BiDil are genetic, and that genetic differences fall along racial lines.

Race-ing the future

Indeed, not addressing the scientific merits of BiDil's race-specific labeling may have aided NitroMed's application. In a detailed history of the making of a market, Jonathan Kahn (2004) suggests that BiDil "became ethnic" in order to secure FDA approval as a "new" drug with extended patent protection. An earlier effort to secure FDA approval for BiDil's non-race-specific use by Medco, the drug's former patent holder, was unsuccessful. NitroMed's patent on BiDil without reference to race expired in 2007, whereas the "blacks only" label extends patenting to 2020.

In his 1952 *Black Skin, White Masks*, Frantz Fanon classically analyzes what it means to be defined as a racial other, or as always somehow innately deficient. Such an analysis provides a more somber assessment of the FDA's approval of BiDil for "self-identified" blacks. As Fanon (1967) writes, "not only must the black man be black; he must be black in relation to the white man." The "facts" of genetic blackness that are read into health disparities may be managed with medication, and so long as it remains good business to do so, the underlying social insult of racialized difference will be reproduced.

Should Race Be Used in Medical Research?

Using racial categories in medical research is a standard practice that may be problematic.

Many medical research studies are required to collect data on race

The National Institutes of Health (NIH), one of the largest funders of medical research in the United States, requires all the projects it funds to gather information on the race and ethnicity of their subjects using the categories set forth by the White House Office of Management and Budget (OMB) – the same categories used by all federal agencies, including the U.S. census. But since the OMB says the race categories are not scientific, are they useful for medical research?

Some reasons for using race make sense, and some don't

Research into racial disparities in health and health care is important. However, the use of race as a substitute for social environment, ancestry, or genetics is more problematic.

Race as a substitute for social environment

The social experiences of people within one so-called race or ethnic group can vary widely. Think, for example, about how different the diets, lifestyles, and general experiences of a recent immigrant from Ethiopia might be from those of an African American whose family has been in the United States for generations. Although both individuals are classified as "black," they might have widely different health problems.

Race as a substitute for ancestry

Certain diseases are more common among people with a particular ancestry than among the general population. But racial categories are just too big and imprecise to indicate anything medically meaningful about a person's ancestry. In order to be truly pertinent, the data gathered in medical studies must track ancestry at the level of specific country or region.

Race as a substitute for genetics

There is no genetic basis for race. The vast genetic diversity within each so-called race makes race unsuitable as a marker for genetics. A better substitute for genetics is ancestry or family history. "All human groups, however constituted, have particular medical risks. African Americans, Ashkenazi Jews, Afrikaners and Japanese, poor people, rich people, chimney sweeps, prostitutes, choreographers and the Pima Indians all have their particular health risks. And race is not the cause of these risks. Rather, race positively obscures it" (Jonathan Marks, anthropologist, University of North Carolina, personal communication with Sara Ilse, Science Museum of Minnesota, September 2006).

Ancestry, not race, determines risks for genetic diseases

Sickle cell disease

The genetic mutation that causes sickle cell disease, which affects the red blood cells, is found in West Africa, southern Europe, the Middle East, and south Asia. A person from southern Africa is no more likely to have sickle cell disease than someone from northern Europe.

Cystic fibrosis

The genetic mutation that causes cystic fibrosis, a disease of the body's mucus glands, is most common in northern Europeans. Thus southern Europeans, also considered white by the U.S.

census, have very different risks of carrying the cystic fibrosis mutation.

Tay-Sachs
The genetic mutation behind Tay-Sachs, a disease that causes a fatal build-up of fatty substances in the brain's tissues and nerve cells, is most common among people of eastern European and Ashkenazi Jewish ancestry. People of western European ancestry may share the same social race as their eastern European neighbors, but they don't share the same risk of carrying the genetic mutation responsible for Tay-Sachs.

Asians' health statistics demonstrate the need for looking beyond race

When looked at as a statistical whole, Asian Americans are among this country's healthiest citizens. But those statistics hide some serious health problems within particular Asian American sub-populations. For example, although Asians generally have relatively low cancer rates, men of Filipino, Korean, and Southeast Asian descent have the highest rate of lung and bronchial cancer, and Vietnamese men suffer liver cancer at a rate 11 times higher than that of white American males. Such telling statistics might be overlooked in public health education and screening efforts when all Asians are lumped together.

Susan Reverby

Concepts of Race, Practices of Racism

Susan Reverby is Marion Butler McLean Professor in the History of Ideas and Professor of Women's and Gender Studies at Wellesley College and an historian of American women, medicine, and nursing. She has written extensively on the infamous Tuskegee Syphilis Study and its legacy. Her research on government medical study of Guatemalan men and women between 1946 and 1948 led to an apology from President Barack Obama to President Alvaro Colom of Guatemala in 2010. Photograph courtesy of Susan Reverby.

Concepts of race and practices of racism in America have been built on the seeming "logic of difference" embedded in the generic black body (Hammonds, forthcoming). This logic needs the assumption of the biological nature of race whereby multiple and changing natural processes are believed to be different in bodies on which shades of skin tone or curls of hair, can be easily read to have larger enduring meanings (Hammonds and Herzig 2008). This logic did not appear because of religious beliefs, political and economic practices, racial slavery, and folklore alone (Fredrickson 2002). It had to be formed with all the authoritative power that scientific assumptions and research studies could provide. It is through science, and more often the medical care system, that racial differences are often explained, justified, and used as African Americans continue to have their bodies, mental states, and health status measured and judged to be found wanting. The difficulty is to understand the difference between experiences of racism that affect bodies and the assumption that racial differences are created in a pristine biological state.

To find this difference, the seeming availability and vulnerability of black bodies, under slavery and freedom, made African Americans the objects of medical lust and the subjects of countless experiments (Gamble 2000). In 1838, the *Charleston Mercury* ran this advertisement for Doctor T. Stillman:

To Planters and Others—Wanted fifty negroes. Any person having sick negroes, considered incurable by their respective physicians, and wishing to dispose of them, Dr. S will pay cash for negroes affected with scrofula or king's evil, confirmed hypocondriasm, apoplexy, diseases of the liver, kidneys, spleen, stomach and intestines, bladder and its appendages, diarrhea, dysentery, etc. (Weld 1968:171).

In 1972, an Associated Press reporter broke the story that the United States Public Health Service had been deceiving hundreds of African American men for 40 years into thinking they were being treated, rather than just watched and studied, for the sometimes deadly disease of syphilis (Reverby 2000; 2009a). These experiences and many more – some just rumors, others true – added up to what one author called on her book cover "the dark history of medical experimentation on black Americans from colonial times to the present" (Washington 2007).

Not every encounter of African Americans with physicians was an experiment, however, nor every research project built just on racism, especially when poor people of every racial category were assumed to be available for research and teaching purposes in exchange for care (Wall 2006; Emanuel 2007; Reverby 2008b). The complicated use of race by medicine meant that sometimes African Americans were assumed to be different for one purpose, but available, in another, to make generalizations in scientific queries. In the 19th century, educators at the Medical College of Georgia had the graves of both free and slave black bodies robbed to obtain cadavers for their medical students not because they were looking for difference, but because they needed bodies (Blakely and Harrington 1997). Unable to find subjects themselves, University of Pennsylvania researchers in the 1940s relied upon their black janitor to procure his friends as "human guinea pigs" willing "to swallow a flexible twelve-foot tube to which a rubber balloon was attached and inflated once inside the intestine" (Lederer 2000:269). Yet this belief that African Americans have been uniquely vulnerable to questionable medical practices remains part of the link that ties racism and medical care together. By the 1960s, folklorist Gladys-Marie Fry interviewed hundreds of black Americans who told her stories about the dangers of "night doctors," assumed to be physicians, medical students, or their minions who prowled about at night in search of the unwary whose bodies could be snatched up for medical research and dissections (Fry 1975:170–195; Gamble 2000). Memory of the study in Tuskegee is assumed, often without evidence, to affect African American's willingness to participate in clinical trials (Katz and Warren in press; n.d.).

More critical to the relationship between race and medicine has been the ways in which unequal access to treatment and the stresses of racism have been experienced in black bodies (Smedley et al. 2003; Krieger 2010; Kaufman and Cooper 2010). Statistics from the slave period to the present demonstrate what was once called health inequality and is now labeled health disparities to explain the wide differences in the life chances of blacks and whites. To this day, African Americans experience more illness, more maternal and infant mortality, and more early deaths than whites.

An entire health care industry now exists that has documented differences in the kinds of services, interventions, and care offered to patients that break down on racial lines. All of this builds upon overcrowding and poor housing, the existence of "food deserts" in neighborhoods where fast food and small ma/pa stores with few fruits and vegetables are the only eating options, the lack of safety in the streets, and the elimination of public health interventions have all deeply affected the life chances of African Americans who then have to find care in an overcrowded and often unresponsive medical system (DuBois 2007; Roberts 2009; Mapp 2010). When these experiences of racism become embodied in stressors and reflected in the statistics of morbidity and mortality, they are then in turn read as if race were a biological category (Braun et al. 2007; Epstein 2007; Krieger 2010).

It is thus through the medical care system that African Americans become enmeshed in what French theorist Michel Foucault called "biopolitics" and became "biopolitical subjects" in which "concerns about health, medicine and the body are made the simultaneous focus of biomedicine and state policy" (Epstein 2010:66.) The logic of racism and the belief in race as a biological category requires these connections among medical care, medical experimentation, and politics to give it power and force.

All of these categories – experimentation, beliefs about racial difference, lack of care, power of the government, rumors about all of this – come together to explain what happened during what is remembered as the most notorious of American medical experiments: the long running so-called Tuskegee Study of Untreated Syphilis in the Male Negro. Beginning in 1932, United States Public Health Service doctors set up a study to understand what happened in African American men when late latent (third stage and presumed non-contagious) syphilis was left untreated.

Set up in and around the city of Tuskegee in Alabama, the study of this primarily sexually transmitted disease went on for another 40 years and involved 624 men, 439 who already had the disease and 185 who did not. The men thought of themselves as patients obtaining needed medical care for what was known as "bad blood" from the government's doctors. The Public Health Service physicians never told these men they were actually research subjects and controls being followed in a "no treatment" study. Not all of the men in the study died of their disease, but the Public Health Service researchers tried to make sure they did not get treatment (although many did anyway). The only permission asked for was the right to autopsy their bodies after they died (Lederer 2000).

The assumption of racial difference in the disease underlay the need for the study. There had been a retrospective study on whites with syphilis in Oslo, Norway in the early 1900s. This was assumed not to be relevant to African Americans, however, since doctors thought (with very little or misread evidence) that they were more prone to cardiovascular complications than the neurological ones that seemed to be affecting whites (Roy 2000). African Americans were also assumed to be more vulnerable to the disease, although such beliefs failed to consider lack of education and access to safe birth control methods that could stop disease transmission.

Instead, the Public Health Service doctors explained to the Alabama men that the aspirins, tonics, and diagnostic spinal taps given were "free treatment." The enticement at the beginning was decent medical care at a time when it was difficult to obtain and expensive. The study's nurse kept visiting the men's homes, helped them to get medical care for other ills, and promised the families money for decent burials in exchange for the use of the men's bodies for autopsy after their deaths.

The study was not kept secret. More than a dozen medical articles charting its progress appeared over the decades, while several health professionals questioned the study's ethics, especially after penicillin became widely available in the late 1940s and might have helped at least some of the men still alive. In 1972, the research experiment came to an end in a storm of media coverage that brought in federal investigators, a Senate hearing, and a subsequent lawsuit against the Public Health Service, the state of Alabama, and many of the doctors involved.

The study in Tuskegee is often remembered as the moment when American doctors practiced deception and acted like Nazis researchers, doing research that could not benefit their "subjects," requiring painful spinal taps, and even causing dreadful ills and deaths. It is called upon to justify the need for control over the research enterprise, written informed consent of subjects, and special attention for African Americans. All of this matters.

It should also be remembered for the ways in which assumptions about the biological nature of race, the availability of vulnerable people to become bio-citizens for the state, and lack of alternatives for care create the possibilities for a logic of medical racism that seems reasonable and even fair. These men living in rural Alabama came forward for treatment not because they were uneducated and easily duped by their government, but because they needed health care for themselves and their families (Reverby 2009b). Racism affected their life options and their vulnerability; beliefs about race shaped the doctors' understanding of the disease.

More than eight decades since the study in Tuskegee began, how we see racism in medicine and the use of race as a scientific category has, of course, changed. The charting of the human genome in 2000, with its findings of human similarity in 99.5 percent of it, was supposed to bring an end to thinking about racial difference, yet ironically it has given it new life as small differences taken on shifting important meanings (Reardon 2004; Obasogie 2010). The danger of not linking ideas about race to practices of racism came full circle in 2005, for example, when the FDA approved BiDil, a drug supposedly only for "self-identified African Americans" with heart failure. At the FDA meeting where the drug moved on to approval, the study in Tuskegee itself was referenced as an example of medical racism because care was withheld, but not as a way to see how thinking about the biological notion of race might cause medical and political mistakes (Kahn 2004; Reverby 2008a; Obasogie 2010). Without evidence of the true meaning of differences that may come about because of population movement over time and place, vague and differing concepts of race reappears to explain difference. Without much evidence, as anthropologist Duana Fullwilley has argued, "bio-logistical construction of race … statistically derived from genetic markers said to signal continental 'ancestry'" and "safely avoids the politically charged historical baggage of the word 'race' itself" (Fullwilley 2008).

Medicine, because it charts the ills of populations and the experiences of individuals, will always be central to understanding how concepts of race and the effects of racism are felt in bodies as well as in the politics of the body politic. Awareness of the flexibility of racial concepts to link racism to ideas of race will always be necessary.

Race and Health Disparities: Conclusions

In this chapter we have presented some of the diverse paths that lead to racial differences in health care and the creation of health disparities. Most of the examples are drawn from differences between whites and diasporic African groups. The deep problem of black health is one that we have focused on. However, other groups are sometimes even more impacted by race and racism, for example, the epidemic of diabetes and obesity in Native Americans.

What is clear from all of this information is that racial differences in health care are basically economic, and eliminating the health differentials that are the result of these economic injustices is extremely important. Unfortunately, the economic differences tell only part of the story. As Gravlee shows in Puerto Rico, and as Navarro (1990) shows for the United States, racial differences in health persist even after controlling for socioeconomic disparities.

A number of mechanisms seem to contribute to the racial differences in health care and health. These include racial discrimination in and out of health care, unequal access to health care, unequal exposure to environmental toxins, and the constant stress of living in a racialized society. All of these mechanisms are now being actively explored by researchers in a concerted effort to propose solutions to eliminate racial disparities in health. We leave you with a question: when might we live in a society in which life expectancies do not vary by race? Our answer, unfortunately, is not anytime soon.

References

Armelagos, G. J.
2005 The slavery hypertension hypothesis–natural selection and scientific investigation: A commentary. Transforming Anthropology 13(2):119–124.

Brondolo, Elizabeth, Ricardo Rieppi, Kim P. Kelly, and William Gerian
2003 Perceived Racism and Blood Pressure: A Review of the Literature and Conceptual and Methodological Critique. Annals of Behavioral Medicine 25(1): 55–65.

Brown, E. Richard, Victoria D. Ojeda, Roberta Wyn, and Rebecka Levan
2000 Racial and Ethnic Disparities in Access to Health Insurance and Health Care. Report by the UCLA Center for Health Policy Research and the Henry J. Kaiser Family Foundation. Los Angeles, CA: UCLA Center for Health Policy Research. California.

Bullard, Robert D., Paul Mohai, Robin Saha, and Beverly Wright
2007 Toxic Wastes and Race at Twenty 1987–2007: Grassroots Struggles to Dismantle Environmental Racism in the United States. Cleveland, OH: United Church of Christ Justice and Witness Ministry.

Cooper, Richard S., Charles N. Rotimi, and Ryk Ward
1999 The Puzzle of Hypertension in African-Americans. Scientific American, February: 50–58.

Environmental Protection Agency
1992 Environmental Equity: Reducing Risk for all Communities. Washington, D.C.: Division of Policy, Planning and Evaluation.

Fanon, Frantz
1967 [1952] Black Skin, White Masks. Charles Lam Markmann, trans. New York: Grove Press.

Gravlee, Clarence C.
2005 Ethnic Classification in Southeastern Puerto Rico: The Cultural Model of "Color." Social Forces 83(3):949–970.

Gravlee, Clarence C., William W. Dressler, and H. Russel Bernard
2005   Skin Color, Social Classification, and Blood Pressure in Southeastern Puerto Rico. American Journal of Public Health 95(12):2191–2197.

Hennessy-Fiske, M.
2010   Women report gaps in health services. Los Angeles Times, March 7: A37, A46.

Jackson, F. L. C.
2005   A Response to George Armelagos' Commentary. Transforming Anthropology 13(2):125–135.

Jones, Joseph, and Alan Goodman
2005   BiDil and the "Fact" of Genetic Blackness: Where Politics and Science Meet. Anthropology News 46(7):26.

Kahn, Jonathan
2004   How a Drug Becomes Ethnic: Law, Commerce, and the Production of Racial Categories in Medicine. Yale Journal of Health Policy, Law and Ethics 4:1–46.

Krieger, Nancy, and Stephen Sidney
1996   Racial Discrimination and Blood Pressure: The CARDIA Study of Young Black and White Adults. American Journal of Public Health 86(10):1370–1378.

Navarro, Vicente
1990   Race or Class Versus Race and Class. Lancet 336(8725):1238–1240.

Obasogie, Osagie K.
2005   One Step Forward, Two Steps Back. San Francisco Chronicle, July 5. http://www.geneticsandsociety.org/article.php?id=212, accessed December 26, 2012.

Schulz, Amy, and Leith Mullings
2006   Gender, Race, Class and Health: Intersectional Approaches. San Francisco: Jossey-Bass.

Taylor, Anne L, Susan Ziesche, Clyde Yancy, Peter Carson, Ralph D'Agostino, Jr., Keith Ferdinand, Malcolm Taylor, Kirkwood Adams, Michael Sabolinski, Manuel Worcel, and Jay Cohn, for the African-American Heart Failure Trial Investigators
2004   Combination of Isosorbide Dinitrate and Hydralazine in Blacks with Heart Failure. New England Journal of Medicine 351:2049–2057.

United States Food and Drug Administration Cardiovascular and Renal Drugs Advisory Committee
2005   Meeting notes, vol. 2, June 16. http://www.fda.gov/ohrms/dockets/ac/05/transcripts/2005-4145T2.pdf, accessed July 27, 2011.

Zambrana, Ruth E., and Bonnie Thornton Dill
2006   Disparities in Latina Health. In Gender Race, Class and Health: Intersectional Approaches. Amy Schulz and Leith Mullings, eds. pp. 192–227. San Francisco. Jossey-Bass. A John Wiley Imprint.

Susan Reverby, Concepts of Race, Practices of Racism

Blakely, Robert, and Judith M. Harrington, eds.
1997   Bones in the Basement: Postmortem Racism in 19th century Racism. Washington, D.C. Smithsonian Institution Press.

Braun, Lundy, et al.
2007   Racial Categories in Medicine: How Useful are They? PLOS Medicine 4, September:e271.

DuBois, W. E. B.
2007 [1889]   The Philadelphia Negro. New York: Oxford University Press.

Emanuel, Ezekial
2007   Unequal Treatment: Review of Medical Apartheid. New York Times, February 18: Book Review, 1.

Epstein, Steven
2007   Inclusion: The Politics of Difference in Medical Research. Chicago: University of Chicago Press.
2010   Beyond Inclusion, Beyond Difference: The Biopolitics of Health. In What's the Use of Race? Ian Whitmarsh and David S. Jones, eds. pp. 63–90. Cambridge, MA: M.I.T. Press.

Fredrickson, George M.
2002   Racism: A Short History. Princeton: Princeton University Press.

Fry, Gladys-Marie
1975   Night Riders in Black Folk History. Knoxville: University of Tennessee Press.

Fullwiley, Duana
2008   The Biologistical Construction of Race. Social Studies of Science 38(5):695–735.

Gamble, Vanessa Northington
2000   Under the Shadow of Tuskegee In Tuskegee's Truths: Rethinking the Tuskegee Syphilis Study. Susan M. Reverby, ed. pp. 431–442. Chapel Hill: University of North Carolina Press.

Hammonds, Evelynn M.
2009   The Logic of Difference: A History of Race in Science and Medicine in the United States, 1850–1990. Chapel Hill: University of North Carolina Press.

Hammonds, Evelynn M., and Rebecca Herzig, eds.
2008   The Nature of Difference. Cambridge, MA: M.I.T. Press.

Kahn, Jonathan
2004   How a Drug Became Ethnic. Yale Journal of Health Policy and Law 4 (Winter):1–46.

Katz, Ralph, and Rueben Warren, eds.
2011   The Search for the Legacy of the U.S. Public Health Service Syphilis Study at Tuskegee. Lanham, MD: Rowman and Littlefield.

Kaufman, Jay S., and Richard Cooper

2010   Use of Racial and Ethnic Identity in Medical Evaluations and Treatments. *In* What's the Use of Race? Ian Whitmarsh and David S. Jones, eds. pp. 187–206. Cambridge, MA: M.I.T. Press.

Krieger, Nancy

2010   The Science and Epidemiology of Racism and Health: Racial/Ethnic Categories, Biological Expressions of Racism, and the Embodiment of Inequality – an Ecosocial Perspective. *In* What's the Use of Race? Ian Whitmarsh and David S. Jones, eds. pp. 225–258. Cambridge, MA: M.I.T. Press.

Lederer, Susan

2000   The Tuskegee Syphilis Study in the Context of American Medical Research. *In* Tuskegee's Truths. Susan M. Reverby, ed. pp. 266–275. Chapel Hill: University of North Carolina Press.

Mapp, Marqui

2010   Low Income Blacks Stranded in Food Deserts. The Grio, June 22. http://www.thegriot.com, accessed July 5, 2010.

Obasogie, Osagie K.

2010   Reports of My Death Have Been Greatly Exaggerated: Race and Genetics Ten Years after the Human Genome Project. June 18. http://www.geneticsandsociety.org/article.php?id=5262, accessed December 26, 2012.

Reardon, Jenny

2004   Race to the Finish. Princeton: Princeton University Press.

Reverby, Susan M. ed.

2000   Tuskegee's Truths: Rethinking the Tuskegee Syphilis Study. Chapel Hill: University of North Carolina Press.

Reverby, Susan M.

2008a   Special Treatment: BiDil, Tuskegee and the Logic of Race. Journal of Law, Medicine and Ethics 36 (Fall):478–484.

Reverby, Susan M.

2008b   Inclusion and Exclusion: The Politics of History, Difference and Medical Research. Journal of the History of Medicine 63 (January):103–113.

Reverby, Susan M.

2009a   Examining Tuskegee: The Infamous Syphilis Study and its Legacy Chapel Hill: University of North Carolina Press.

Reverby, Susan M.

2009b   A New Lesson from the Old Tuskegee Study. The Huffington Post, December 3. http://www.huffingtonpost.com/susan-reverby/a-new-lesson-from-the-old_b_378649.html, accessed July 6, 2010.

Roberts, Samuel Kelton

2009   Infectious Fear. Chapel Hill: University of North Carolina Press.

Roy, Benjamin

2000   The Tuskegee Syphilis Experiment: Biotechnology and the Administrative State *In* Tuskegee's Truths. Susan M. Reverby, ed. pp. 299–320. Chapel Hill: University of North Carolina Press.

Smedley, Brian, Adrienne Stith, and Alan R. Nelson, eds.

2003   Unequal Treatment: Confronting Racial and Ethnic Disparities in Health Care. Washington, D.C.: Institute of Medicine.

Wall, L. L.

2006   The Medical Ethics of Dr. J. Marion Sims. Journal of Medical Ethics 32 (June):346–350.

Washington, Harriet

2007   Medical Apartheid. New York: Doubleday.

Weld, Theodore Dwight

1968 [1839]   American Slavery As It Is. New York: Arno Press.

Further Reading

Benderly, B. L.

2010   The real science gap. It's not insufficient schooling or a shortage of scientist. It's a lack of career opportunities. Miller-McCune (July/August) 30–39.

Cloud, J.

2010   Why Genes Aren't Destiny. The New Field of Epigenetics is Showing How Your Environment and Your Choices Can Influence Your Genetic Code – and That of Your Kids. Time 175(2):48–58.

Di Leonardo, M.

2004   Human Cultural Diversity. Paper contributed to the Race and Human Variation: Setting an Agenda for Future Research and Education Conference, Alexandria, VA, September.

Hart, D.

2006   Changing Students' Understanding of Race. Anthropology News 47(3):10–11.

Hartigan, J.

2006   Saying "Socially Constructed" is Not Enough. Anthropology News 47(2):8.

McGaghie, W. C.

2007   Medical Education for Cultural Competence: Policies, Initiatives and Student Selection. Paper Contributed to the Race, Human Variation and Disease: Consensus and Frontiers Conference, Warrenton, VA, March.

Margolis, D.

2010   Caring across Cultures: Barnes-Jewish Hospital Reapproached a Diverse Patient Population with

Sensitivity to Any and All Worldviews. Diversity Executive, July 17. http://diversity-executive.com/article.php?article=955, accessed December 4, 2011.

Rose, H., and S. Rose
2010   Darwin and After. New Left Review 63:91–112.

Thompson, E. C.
2006   The Problem of "race as a social construct." Anthropology News 47(2):7.

17

Conclusion

In chapter 1 we made the claim that this book would contribute to a fundamental overhaul of how various publics talk about race in the United States. We wanted to bring a combination of science, history, and the everyday lived experiences of social "race and racism" to our project. We hope we have been successful in untangling that ball and pointing readers in new directions for understanding human variation, how race is socially and culturally constructed, and the contemporary "cultures of race" in the United States of America and beyond. As a companion to the award-winning website and museum exhibit, "RACE: Are we so Different," we wanted to lay bare the roots of the weeds of racism, expose them so we can pull them out of their foundation.

In part 1, we looked at the history of race in the United States of America through the lenses of U.S. laws and policies as well as through the racial science of the 18th, 19th, and 20th centuries. This also included a look at the eugenics movements in the United States and in Europe in the early 20th century to show how socially constructed beliefs in both biological race and in the racial inferiority of some of those races led to the creation of a "scientific racism" that persisted in policy and practice well into the middle of the 20th century. Social and religious beliefs about racial inferiority fueled a science of race that was accountable for the "mismeasure" of humans. A review of the use of science in constructing and maintaining the social stratification of the 17th, 18th, 19th, and 20th centuries on the bases of race and class

provides a powerful commentary on what has been achieved to date by anthropologists, many other scholars, social justice advocates, and others, to overcome not just the racist laws of the United States but also the deeply held assumptions that came out of the beliefs that underlay them, and that still persist in conversations about what race is and isn't even today. What we have not explored explicitly in the book is the link between organized religion, science, and the laws of the United States; this still needs to be done as a part of an ongoing critical historical look at race in America.

In part 2, we looked at what science and the anthropological record had to say about what race is and what race is not. The focus on human origins and the "Out of Africa" themes were designed to destabilize the assumptions that a lot of people have about where we all came from originally as *Homo sapiens*, and just how alike genetically we really are. The second major scientific focus was on how the lay public understand the science of skin color and was designed to destabilize and to put into a scientific context the explanation of why people have different skin tones. Skin color is again related to adaptations of human movement and settlement over thousands of years, and the relationship of those settlements to the ultraviolet sun rays and the ability of people to produce enough folic acid and vitamin D to keep them healthy. Finally, in the science arena, we also wanted to show, through a look at medicine and health, that there are disparities in health among certain ancestral groups based on the realities of the social and cultural construction of race in U.S. society.

While there is a link between biology and the social racial disparities that should not be lost, race is ultimately a powerful social construction, with both social and biological consequences, and not a biological reality.

In part 3, Living with Race and Racism, we focused on the more nuanced understandings of race and wealth accumulation and the reason for the continued disparity between Euro-Americans and Asians on the one hand and African Americans and Latinos on the other. We focused on the intractable nature of health and educational disparities, as well as the contradictions of the classifications captured by the federal government with the use of the United States Census through the years and in the present. Finally, we incorporated some of the voices of people that we interviewed for the project in the text of the book.

This book was not designed to cover all aspects of human variation on the one hand, and institutionalized and structural racism on the other. But, we did want to point out the links, both observed and nuanced, between the biological, historical, and the everyday ways in which everyone experiences "race" in the United States. We also solicited essays from our colleagues from the social sciences, humanities, law, and public policy to help us to round out what we did not cover in the book, to raise new issues, and to enhance, elucidate, and update those issues that we were not able to cover in depth.

What Still Needs to be Done: The Future of Race in America and Beyond

In some ways, this book has only touched the surface of this topic of "Race" as we look at the unfinished business of laying bare, and then eradicating, structural racism. We know it is not enough for us to reveal the breadth and depth of the social and cultural underpinnings of structural racism and the power dynamics that operate to maintain this highly racialized and stratified social system. Sociologist Howard Winant reminds us as we talk about the issue of "postracialism" in America to remember that some of the incorporative concepts of

racial difference tend to actually validate the very identities they purport to question. Rather than serving as catalysts for truly new racial formations they actually "reinforce the racialized social structures such as comprehensive racial stratification, discrimination, xenophobia, etc. that they so loudly repudiate" (Winant 2004:xix).

We would like to suggest that much more critical research and praxis still needs to be done in the following areas: the intersectionality of race, class, and gender; race and immigration; reverse discrimination; the contradictions of colorblindness versus the persistent conversations about race; the impact of national demographic changes and race; the study of whiteness and power from the inside out; race and globalization studies; and the relationship of race and human rights just to name a few areas. Along with this, a deeper and more critical analysis must be made of the continuing educational, housing, and health disparities that exist along both race and class lines.

Intersectionality

The term "intersectionality," coined by Kimberly Crenshaw in the 1970s, is still relevant. Now more than ever before we need to understand the links between race, class, gender, sexual orientation, and religion. We need to understand more deeply the process by which various socially and culturally constructed categories of discrimination interact on multiple levels to maintain systemic, almost caste-like social inequality. This research should be done at both the local, national, and global levels in both contemporary and historical contexts. For example, see the essay in this chapter by Clarke and Thomas for more directions on the research and praxis dynamics on race and globalization.

Race and Immigration

In 2011, an argument is still brewing on the extreme political right that is challenging the meaning of the Fourteenth Amendment once again. In 1868, congress ratified the citizenship clause of the Fourteenth Amendment of the Constitution of the United States. The clause comes as the amendment's first words, stating, "All persons born or naturalized in the United

States and subject to the jurisdiction thereof, are citizens of the United States and the States wherein they reside." The authors of this book believe that there should be more research among anthropologists, legal scholars, and policy makers and NGOs to understand and to educate the general public about how the reinterpretation of laws and of the Constitution today by the conservative right is being used as a foil against the immigration of new populations into this country. For example, in the larger sweep of history, the Fourteenth Amendment was a congressional intervention to overturn the Supreme Court's Dred Scott decision, which held that African Americans were not citizens of the United States and never could be because they were "a subordinate and inferior class of beings" and were never intended to be part of the political community (U.S. Constitution, Fourteenth Amendment). This was reinforced in 1898 in the case of *United States v. Wong Kim Ark* in which the Supreme Court held that a child born in the United States but to alien parents is still entitled to birthright citizenship (Fourteenth Amendment: Annotations: Section 1. Rights Guaranteed: The New Equal Protection Classifications Meriting Close Scrutiny. Alienage and Nationality).[1] There is a need in the 21st century to continue to explore those racial and economic tensions inherent in the ongoing contested American racial narrative about who can truly be American and who cannot. This was an argument of the 19th and 20th centuries, and it looks as though it will be the same in the 21st century as well.

Continued Exploration of White Privilege

In 21st-century America, there is major resistance both from the political Right (in the working and middle classes) to the role of big government in their lives. There is a similar resistance from the moneyed business classes, big business owners, and bankers, but perhaps for different reasons. The current Obama presidential administration is calling for an alignment of economic responsibility with the well-being of all people. But, not since the depression has there been such vitriol and negativity toward the idea of accountability for those captains of industry who took the entire nation to the brink of economic ruin to atone for or to be called to task for what they have done. It is important that future race research studies the links among race, class, and privilege in a way that makes transparent how white privilege (especially for white elites) becomes masked in partisan politics and embedded in an erroneous narrative, not of privilege but of victimization and reverse discrimination against white people (Webb 2010). This misleading narrative has shifted the conversation and attention from whiteness as privilege to whiteness as victim of a run-away government that happens to be led by a black man (who many on the extreme Right think may not even be a citizen of the United States!).

The Cultural, Political, and Economic Implication of Changing Demographics

The 2010 census pointed to a potential problem with changing demographics in the 21st century at several levels. The graying of America and the aging of the Baby Boomers (those Americans born between 1946 and 1966) proposes to pit an aging population of predominately white Americans against a growing younger generation of racially and ethnically diverse Americans of color who may have different political and social views. Minorities now make up more than two-fifths of all children under 18 and William Frey of the Brookings Institute predicts that they will represent a majority of all American children by as soon as 2023 (Frey in Brownstein 2010:1). Frey also says that this contrast of both age and culture may create what he calls a "cultural generation gap." Over time, the major focus of this struggle is likely to be the tension between an older white, more conservative population and a more liberal younger population of color. Issues related to taxes, the role of government in promoting social programs, education, and health care are issues that all call for a deeper look at race and intersectionality through the lenses of age as well as race, class, and geographic region (Frey in Brownstein 2010).

[1] *United States v. Wong Kim Ark*, 169 U.S. 649 (1898), http://caselaw.lp.findlaw.com/scripts/getcase.pl?court=us&vol=169&invol=649, accessed July 14, 2010.

The Paradox of "Colorblindness" and the U.S.'s Continual Focus on Race

In this book we looked at how notions of biological, social, and historical race play out in the institutions and in everyday lives of the United States. In 2010, at the end of the first decade of the 21st century, there are still very real repercussions in the national institutions of American and in the lives of Americans from the power of both the concept and reality of race. While, in the book we have established the fact that "race" is a social construct, the reality is that there are still racial disparities in every aspect of U.S. society. There is no basis in reality for the statements often heard in political and policy circles that we live in a "post-racial world" or that we should be striving for a "colorblind society." As long as structural and institutional racism exist, and there is a racialized social hierarchy in which those in power (economic, social, and political) are still in place, true racial equity is a myth. All of the conversations about race that are held in the United States will not change those racialized status and power dynamics. This continues to be a fruitful area of research well into the 21st century. We still have much to learn about the intractability of this deeply embedded system of privilege in society.

Race and Human Rights

From organizations like Amnesty International to Human Rights Watch to the United Nations globally to the NAACP, MALDEF, and other social justice groups on the national and local levels, racial inequality that results in systemic and systematic disparate treatment of people based on their "race" is more and more considered a violation of the human rights of individuals. What was once a local, state, or federal issue is now being seen as an issue that violates the basic right to be "human" as individuals or as groups. The essay by Faye V. Harrison in this concluding chapter chronicles the work of international groups, grassroots organizations, and scholars as they weave together the strands of race, racism, and anti-racism on both the local and global stage. While each of these areas of research, race, racism, and anti-racism have tremendous bodies of research, there is still research to be done on how racial oppression works across the borders and boundaries of countries. The role of scholars like Harrison has been to show the connections among those oppressions on a global stage.

DEBORAH THOMAS AND
KAMARI CLARKE

Globalizing Race

performance, and transnationalism. She has served as co-editor of Transforming Anthropology. *Photograph courtesy of Deborah Thomas.*

Kamari Clarke *is Professor of Anthropology and International and Area Studies and Chair of the Yale Council on African Studies at Yale University. Her articles and books have focused on issues related to religious nationalism, legal institutions, international law, and the interface between culture, power, and globalization.* Photograph courtesy of Kamari Clarke.

Deborah Thomas *is Associate Professor of Anthropology at the University of Pennsylvania. Her research interests include nationalism, globalization, cultural politics,*

This essay is adapted from Introduction: Globalization and Transformation of Race, Deborah Thomas and Kamari Clarke. In *Globalization and Race: Transformations in the Global Production of Blackness.* Kamari Maxine Clarke and Deborah Thomas, eds. pp. 1–36. Copyright, 2006: Duke University Press. All rights reserved. Reprinted by permission of the publisher.

It has become commonplace to speak of the contemporary intensification of processes of globalization and the ways in which they are continually reconfiguring the structures of everyday life. While scholarly analyses of globalization have proliferated, and while there have been recent attempts within the social sciences to consider the articulations among ethnicity, gender, and sexuality within a global frame of analysis, race and processes of racialization are not usually considered central to academic discussions of global economic and political transformations. Yet, globalization is facilitated by the transmission and reproduction of deeply embedded social prejudices rooted in a past characterized by territorial concepts of belonging that both generated and were generated by racial inequalities. As such, the contemporary redistribution of wealth has exacerbated historically entrenched racial hierarchies. In other words, racial formations dynamically reflect and shape global processes and are not merely effects of them. As a result, the complexity of contemporary global processes can never be fully grasped without a deep understanding of the historically specific and dynamic ways that race has both constituted and been constituted by global transformations. What is clearly critical, then, to a more complete understanding of contemporary global processes is an integrated analysis of the historical precedents of current circulations, of how imperialism and racial ordering have shaped global movements, and of the ways conceptualizations of belonging, membership, and citizenship have been both imagined and institutionalized in racial terms.

Global processes, historical circulations, and racial ordering

The idea of race and the hierarchical institutionalization of racial difference emerged dialectically in relation to sixteenth century economic transformations that ultimately created what we now know as "the modern West" (Holt 2000; Silverblatt 2004; Trouillot 1995). While notions of difference operated prior to this period, the expulsion of Muslims from Europe, the initial European voyages of exploration and discovery, and the development of mercantile trade generated a novel situation whereby, for the first time, racialized labor became "crucial to the mobilization of productive forces on a world scale" (Holt 2000:32). At the same time that the associations between nation building and imperialism and between racial slavery and the development of export-oriented mass agricultural production became more tightly integrated, new ideologies began to circulate in Europe about the Nature of

Man. Within religious, philosophical, scientific, and political discourses, hierarchies of human value were mapped onto gendered, racial, and civilizational difference (Trouillot 1995). In this way, early state formation and mercantile capitalism inaugurated material and ideological processes that indelibly linked the "New World" and the "Old" in a common project of defining modern subjectivity in racial terms. In other words, Western modernity's roots are tangled up with the projects of imperial conquest, plantation slavery, and racial domination. Because these racialized processes also remade Europe itself, this formulation of modernity conceptualizes the Atlantic Ocean as an integrated geohistorical unit in which the structural transformations associated with early European expansion westward created what ultimately became a triangular web of political, economic, and socio-cultural relations joining individuals, communities, and classes on three continents in a single sphere of interaction.

Imperialism, slavery, and colonial exploitation created enduring global linkages that were sustained through the post-emancipation period of the mid-nineteenth century and into the twentieth century. These linkages would also introduce people from south and east Asia to the black–white dichotomy of the world of the plantation through indentured labor schemes. At the same time, science eclipsed religion as the dominant discourse of empire, and advocates for slavery and colonial expansion helped to institutionalize the new science of anthropology, in part to counter abolitionists' claims based on morality and biblical tenets. As the discipline developed during the late nineteenth century, human difference was parsed along a color-coded hierarchy from savage to civilized – from black through brown, yellow and red, to white (Baker 1998). The fact that some researchers documented customs and behaviors while others measured brains and bodies did not change this hierarchy because human diversity and cultural differences were blurred and racially mapped in a way that privileged biology as the basis for human difference.

Though in the U.S. some anthropologists effectively challenged the basis of eugenics research, the institutionalization of anthropological science had the effect of solidifying earlier hierarchical classifications of racial groups. During the early twentieth century, these classifications were further concretized through village studies that conceptualized the distinctiveness of various "peoples" and "cultures" in relation to territorially based conceptualizations of belonging. Yet because racial biology – as the science of empire – was fundamental to the founding of the circum-Atlantic world, these territorially rooted distinctions continued to be racially mapped. Despite Franz Boas' early argument for an analytic (and political) distinction between race and culture, traditional debates within the anthropology of the African Diaspora – and among various activist communities – have often employed 19th century biological notions of race as the predominant basis for connection and continuity.

However, other changes were afoot in the early twentieth century as altered relationships between production and consumption also transformed racial meanings, which now circulated with the movement of both laborers and intellectuals between the United States, Europe, south and east Asia, and Africa. The emergence of race-conscious movements such as Pan-Africanism, Garveyism, and the Niagara Movement, reflected some of these transformations, while further reinforcing a cultural politics of racial belonging and membership. While pre-Fordist socio-economic and political arrangements in the United States required that racialized labor forces remain fixed within the particular (material and ideological) places to which they were transported, by the middle of the twentieth century Fordist models of production and consumption instead relied upon a massive movement of these same labor forces out of their place, "from South to North in the United States, from colony to metropole in the British and French West Indies, from country to city in southern and western Africa" (Holt 2000:70). This movement, facilitated by the liberalization of U.S. immigration laws in 1965, generated a transnational wave of cultural practices from homelands (in particular, the Caribbean, Latin America, and Asia) to new lands (the United States, and to a lesser degree, Europe and Canada).

New culturalist articulations of race

By the mid-twentieth century, these changes spurred the transformation of locally particular notions of difference into discourses of ethnic and national descent and belonging. This re-ordering of human subjectivity in increasingly ethnic heritage terms follows structurally related shifts in the language of contemporary American racial organization particular to the post-

1965 period. During this period, the intensification of civil rights discourses against discrimination generated new ideologies about racial belonging and racial difference. These changes also set the stage for the formation of post-civil rights heritage movements and the development of closely connected corporate interests willing to exploit lucrative markets. The cultural formation of a new commercial politics of linkage between people in the Americas and those in related "homelands" set the stage for the establishment of a heritage category through which linkages to origins were used to supplement national identity and citizenship. In the social sphere, this emphasis on diasporic interconnection redefined prevalent notions of biological race to that of cultural race, here shaped by conceptions of ethnicity, or ancestral heritage. Though it manifested in deterritorialized contexts, this notion of heritage was actually deeply territorial but reflected a historical rather than ontological or biological notion of race.

In the current period, rights discourse is on the wane because states are less powerful in some locations, and in others, less willing to hold "equality" as a value. At the same time, the postcolonial context is one in which migration, movement, and media – though unevenly experienced – have created a situation in which "the nation-based dimensions of racial solidarity have atrophied" (Winant 2000:180). We are confronting a world in which larger and larger percentages of national populations are illiterate, where the avenues for self-advancement have become increasingly limited, where remittances constitute ever greater percentages of developing countries' GDPs, where sexual tourism and sex trafficking is on the rise, where the availability of critical social services is on the decline, where a commitment to social equality becomes framed as anti-capitalist, and where an assertive call for peace is seen as suspiciously unpatriotic. Global economic restructuring has thus resulted in the immiseration and displacement of huge numbers of people from Asia, Africa, Latin America, and the Caribbean who, in search of some degree of economic stability, have concentrated within the formerly imperial European centers and the currently dominant United States, especially in urban areas.

Many researchers have ethnographically considered the (sometimes unexpected) links between migration, racial formation, processes of ethnic identification, the development of political consciousness, and cultural production. More recent research on migration has also examined the ways changing conceptualizations of the relationships between ethnicity, race, culture, and citizenship in the United States and Europe have been critical in terms of shaping migrants' public presence and political life in the countries to which they migrate. Central to these processes has been the circulation and innovation of popular cultural forms among and within groups, forms that themselves carry histories of racialized representations. Yet, migration and technological shifts have also meant that notions of race and Diaspora are more instantaneously debated across space and time, particularly in the realm of popular culture which is now, to a degree (because of U.S. mass media domination) shared. As a result, a new common language has emerged, and this is a language that is differently political – not the civil and political rights discourses of the mid-twentieth century, but something else rooted in changed notions of racial community.

What we are seeing is that in the contemporary period belonging is being recognized as contingent and incomplete, and commonalities are being rethought in relation not only to historical specificities that position people who are differently racialized, nationalized, classed, and sexualized in complex relationships to each other, but also to contemporary processes that seem to solidify particular kinds of hierarchy within diasporas. Given these changes over time, contemporary transformations command us to think about racial formation as a process – and as a process that articulates with other processes – rather than as a stable (and knowable) category. Recent ethnographic approaches to these various processes have made significant contributions to understanding how new developments at local, regional, national, and trans-

territorial levels have generated shifts in ideas about and experiences of citizenship, belonging, and racial difference. Scholars who use ethnographic methods – such as anthropologists, sociologists, oral historians, and cultural studies theorists – are in a unique position to bring to light such processes because long-term field research can enable complex insights into global – local interrelationships. Increasingly, therefore, ethnographic accounts of global processes have offered a simultaneous focus on the specificities of particular locations (and hierarchies of locations) – whether these locations are villages, invented communities, nation-states, networks, or imaginative processes – and on the particular institutional and ideological matrices that exist at national, regional, and global levels, influencing and being influenced by local developments. We have thus been able to write about processes that are having similar effects across a wide range of locations, without intimating that these processes are enacted everywhere in the same way. As a result, we have been able to demonstrate that "race" is neither fiction nor fixed. Instead, we have focused on how people understand, perform, or subvert racial identities by mobilizing knowledges gleaned both from the particularities of their local circumstances and from the range of ideas and practices that circulate within their public spheres. Through this focus it is becoming clearer than ever that race and its related imaginaries have been central to the shaping of global processes and, in that regard, the history of cultural interactions over time. Through these dynamic formations, race has been constituted as social reality and it therefore continues to transform global processes while also being transformed by them.

FAYE V. HARRISON

Race, Racism, and Antiracism

Implications for Human Rights

Faye V. Harrison *is Professor of Anthropology at the University of Florida, Gainesville. Her research addresses*

social inequalities and the politics that emerge in response to them. Her many publications explore social disparities of race, gender, class, and (trans)national identity and "the way they interact and operate simultaneously in everyday life" in the United States, Great Britain, and the Caribbean among other places. Dr. Harrison is past president of the Association of Black Anthropologists and a former (two-term) member of the Executive Committee of the American Anthropological Association. She has chaired the International Union of

Race, culture, and power in the 9/11 era

Race is a historically specific distinction of social stratification assigned to categories of people presumed to share physical or other biological traits or, in the absence of visible differences, a socially salient ancestry from which descent is traced according to culturally constituted and selected criteria. Some scholars have claimed that, historically, race making and its closely related hierarchy have their origins in contexts of colonial expansion and empire building, which have been characterized by land alienation, coerced labor, and repressive, even dehumanizing, forms of state power. Variations on these invidious colonial and later postcolonial themes developed in the Americas, Africa, and Asia (Greenberg 1980). With the voluntary and involuntary criss-crossings of population flows over the past several centuries, racial orders (also called racial formations or systems of race relations) can be mapped globally, with Europe, the historic locus and height of imperial power, becoming more culturally and racially diverse than Western nations have been imagined to be in the past (Anderson 1991). While small numbers of racial (or racialized ethnic) minorities, including stigmatized Europeans such as Jews and Roma, have long had a presence in those so-called homogeneous societies, more recent (trans)migrations have especially contributed to the contemporary multi-racialization of Europe, in many cases igniting intense public debate and political backlash over the authentic boundaries of national and regional belonging. Xenophobia, not uncommonly with racializing meanings and effects, has increasingly targeted Muslim immigrants since the homeland security crisis prompted by Al Qaeda's terrorist attacks of "9/11" (September 11, 2001) in the United States and the later "7/7" bombings in London's "tube" or subway (July 2005). Whether in Europe, the Americas, southern Africa, or elsewhere the culture, politics, and political economy of race figure prominently, though recent discourses claim the achievement of a postracial or nonracial moment. Contrary to such wishful thinking, political naïveté or discursive sleight of hand, the contemporary juncture is marked by "racialized conflicts [that] appear to be escalating rather than declining in many places around the world" (Harrison 2005b).

In many contemporary contexts, the language of race is one in which some notion of culture rather than biology has come to play a central ideological role. In other words, presumptions about intergroup relations and the rationale for social boundaries and distances have been recast in terms of fundamentally unbridgeable cultural differences. In worst case scenarios such differences are pathologized or demonized. These notions provide the discursive basis for punitive practices and policies that target particular populations, both native born and immigrant, for varying sorts of discrimination, profiling, scapegoating, persecution, mass incarceration, or, in the case of immigrants and refugees, deportation. Across many contexts, race is integral to popular perceptions of social reality and the classifications and logics through which those perceptions operate to make common sense. Despite its commonsensical character, intrinsic to an uncritically embraced worldview, "race is an ideologically charged [and shifting] cluster of contradictory and contested meanings" (Harrison 1997:392) shaped by dynamic cultural processes mediated by disparities of power. It is a socially constructed nexus of relations with cognitive, emotional, and material dimensions. Its structures of feeling and materiality permeate sociocultural, economic, and political domains and, ultimately, implicate the structural violence and pathologies of power (Farmer 2003) that are constitutive of *racism* in its various registers and modalities. Some of these have been described in terms of cultural racism, institutional racism, structural racism, and global apartheid (Booker and Minter 2001; Harrison 2002). Given the dialectics of structure, agency, and change, the feelings and material relations that are integral to race's lived reality are not all negative. They have also inspired modalities of cultural and political resistance from which more enabling antiracist identities are constructed and mobilized for goals including freedom from slavery and post-emancipation repression, racial uplift, civil rights, and human rights, as the experiences and struggles of African Americans demonstrates.

Racial oppression is more than prejudice

Racism is a volatile issue whose meanings, forms (which can be subtle), and effects are highly disputed. Often reduced to bigoted intentionality, racism is more than mere prejudice. It is also more than ideology and worldview (Smedley 2007). Ruth Frankenberg (1993:70), who specialized in the critical study of how whiteness is socially constructed, defined racism, whose dominant guise is white supremacy, as "not only an ideology or political orientation … but also … a system of material relationships with a set of ideas linked to and embedded in those material relations." Based on their research in New Zealand/ Aotearoa, Margaret Wetherell and Jonathan Potter (1992) offer a view of racism as "whatever actions, whether intended or not, that perpetuate and reinforce an oppressive structure of uneven power relations." As Harrison puts it, in other words, "racism can be the unintended outcome of everyday discourses and behaviors, despite the absence of race-centered prejudice, and even actions intended to be antiracist may unwittingly have racializing rather than deracializing effects" (1997:395).

Given that racism results in, reinforces, sustains, or *is in itself oppression*, and that this oppression, operating in conjunction with intersecting injustices (e.g. those based on class, gender, and sexuality), often dehumanizes the peoples it targets, racism is a problem that is central to the concerns of the international community and movement for human rights. *Racism is a violation of human rights and dignity*. Human rights are "the morally and legally justifiable claims to dignity, liberty, personal security, and basic wellbeing that all persons can make by virtue of being human" (Harrison 2005a:11). International human rights standards and ideals are delineated in declarations, covenants, and conventions to which states are signatories – when they sign. Holding states – and supra-state parties such as transnational corporations – accountable for enforcing human rights principles is a difficult matter, especially in a globalizing "conflict-laden world where disparities of wealth, health, and power are widening" (Harrison 2005a:11). Nonetheless, since the end of the Cold War, "human rights have come to be the most globally intelligible and accepted political values in the world. In some important respects, the language

of human rights fills the vacuum that the 'demise of [the former] grand political narratives' (Wilson 1997:1)" has created (Harrison 2005a:11).

Racial discrimination codified as a human rights violation

The International Convention on the Elimination of All Forms of Racial Discrimination (ICERD) was ratified in 1965 and took effect four years later, a decade before the adoption of the Convention on the Elimination of All Forms of Discrimination against Women (CEDAW), which went into force in 1981. Although ICERD "was the first of the core international human rights treaties to be adopted by the international community" (Amnesty International 2001:2), it has had less visibility and influence than CEDAW and other conventions. It received the unanimous vote of the United Nations General Assembly; however, its "widespread support … [stemmed from its being] viewed primarily as … aimed at apartheid, racist practices of colonialism and the treatment of African Americans in the USA. Most states did not view it as being applicable or even needing application, within their own territories. Such denial of racial discrimination continues to be a serious problem to this day" (Amnesty International 2001:2–3). Social anthropologist Michael Banton (1996), who served on the United Nations's Committee on the Elimination of Racial Discrimination (CERD), has also written about ICERD's foreign policy significance during the 1960s and the concerted struggle since those beginnings to compel states – including the United States – to comply with its terms as a legally binding treaty.

ICERD's relatively low profile is clearly but unfortunately reflected in the literature on human rights. One example is Micheline R. Ishay's *The History of Human Rights: From Ancient Times to the Globalization Era* (2004) and its sequel of sorts, *The Human Rights Reader: Major Political Essays, Speeches, and Documents from Ancient Times to the Present* (2007). Although basically useful sources of information, these books are conspicuous in their neglect of the forces leading to the 1963 declaration and then the 1965 convention, which defined and codified racial discrimination as a violation of human rights and a denial of fundamental freedoms. Ishay's reader, even in its second edition, contains such important documents as the 1215 Magna Carta, the 1776 United States Declaration of Independence, the French Declaration of the Rights of Man and Citizen (1789) as the philosophical and political background to the other documents anthologized: the 1945 United Nations Charter and a long series of covenants, conventions, and protocols to conventions, including the Declaration on the Rights of Disabled Persons (1975) and CEDAW (1979/1981). Of course, the editor had to be selective. However, in her choices she repeats a common pattern of erasure, silencing, or in some cases perhaps a form of de facto censorship. In her first book, however, there are passing mentions of racism and antiracism in the context of slavery, abolition of slavery, and later the anti-Semitism of the World War II era. ICERD is included in the book's appendix, "A Chronology of Events and Writing Related to Human Rights" (2004:365), but nowhere in the book is it discussed, though Martin Luther King, Jr.'s "I Have a Dream" speech is excerpted in the part of the book on new social movements. Ishay simply missed an opportunity to make linkages with the antiracist work within and beyond the United Nations related to ratifying and enforcing ICERD and other related treaties and United Nations conference programs of action.

Related to this pattern of erasure is the manner in which news coverage and political discourse on the World Conference against Racism (WCAR), which was held in Durban, South Africa in 2001, and the 2009 Durban Review Conference in Geneva have tended to underestimate the import of these events for international human rights. To a great extent, these conferences along with all the research, lobbying, and other organizing activities associated with them have been discredited in mainstream media. This has occurred, in good part, because of the conferences' controversial position on reparations for transatlantic slavery, which WCAR deemed "a crime against humanity," and their critique of Israeli policy toward Palestine and, by extension, U.S. foreign policy in the Middle East. According to the U.S. government, international relations are beyond the legitimate scope and purpose of the United Nations' antiracism conferences and non-governmental (NGO) forums, which have inappropriately addressed these issues in terms of racism. In many respects, this response reso-

nates with conventional approaches to international relations, which tend to deny the relevance and workings of race in modern international affairs. International relations scholar Robert Vitalis (2000) argues that an implicit "norm against noticing race" prevails in foreign policy and, as anthropologist Kristin Loftsdóttir (2009) shows, also in the related field of economic development. W. E. B. Du Bois and Ralph Bunch set important scholarly and activist precedents in contesting this norm (see Harrison 2002).

Much closer to the interests of anthropologists is the limited dialogue and cross-fertilization between the anthropology of human rights and critical anthropological studies of race and racism. For instance, the extensive literature on indigenous peoples and their rights rarely explicitly interrogates race and racism as components of the oppression and, at worst, genocide that indigenous peoples confront. Peter Wade's treatment of "structures of alterity" (i.e. difference, Otherness) that subject both Latin America's indigenous people and Afro-descendants to different forms of racialization – but racialization nonetheless – is one of the few instances in which the conventional application of "ethnicity" to indigenous peoples and "race" to blacks is viewed as problematic and erroneous (Wade 1997:36–37). Jonathan Warren (2001) and Charles Hale (2006) are two other Latin Americanists who have analyzed the culture and politics of race in indigenous peoples' mobilizations for justice and rights.

The Declaration on the Rights of Indigenous Peoples adopted in 2007 was in good part made possible because of anthropological advocacy and the ground cleared by the struggles of a much broader coalition of antiracists to draft and implement ICERD and the *Declaration and Programme of Action* adopted at the WCAR in Durban, South Africa in 2001 (World Conference Against Racism, NGO Forum Secretariat, South African Non-Government Coalition 2002). The latter document includes sections on "Indigenous Peoples" (2002:23–24, 59–62), and it strongly recommended the adoption of the Declaration on the Rights of Indigenous Peoples. Anthropologists' advocacy on behalf of – and in partnership with – indigenous activists has played an important part in advancing indigenous rights as human rights. NGOs such as Cultural Survival and Survival International have been exemplars in this praxis.

Antiracism and rights in the African diaspora

There are other anthropologists who bring a concern with race into the analysis of human rights discourses and practices – or human rights into the study of racism and antiracism. Besides Michael Banton (1996), some of whose work is mentioned earlier, João Costa Vargas (2008) has boldly elucidated the genocidal continuum (Scheper-Hughes 2000) that operates in African diaspora contexts, notably in the United States and Brazil where he has conducted research, synthesizing the multi-sited results in ways that shed light on the common denominators or parallels of oppression and human rights abuse. Keisha-Khan Perry (2010), based on research on Afro-Brazilian women's grassroots struggles in Salvador, Bahia, demonstrates how black women-led neighborhood organizations mobilize "to fight racial and gender oppression and to claim access to resources particularly land" and water (2010:143). She shows how these women play major roles in "reinvent[ing] notions of citizenship" and "employ[ing] the discourse of rights and claims to resources in organized responses to spatially determined racial hegemony" (Perry 2010:148).

My own research (Harrison 2000; 2002; 2005a and b; 2008) also examines antiracism as a site for human rights consciousness, discourse, and practice. I have followed a southern regional social justice network whose leaders, most of whom are African American and other African descended women (e.g. Caribbean and Latina women in Atlanta and south Florida), participated in WCAR – and in the 1995 Beijing Fourth International Conference on Women. They brought lessons learned in Durham back home with them to the local and regional settings in which they do their everyday social, economic, and environmental justice work. As activists, they work to build bridges linking a number of intersecting struggles against racism and related oppressions – as manifested in substandard schools, exploitative work conditions, health disparities, violence against women, repressive policing, and mass incarceration. As I have written elsewhere, "these multiple yet overlapping struggles are being rethought and reframed in terms of an interrelated web of connection based on international human rights" (Harrison 2008:11). My goal is to find out how the

ideas and strategies circulated in transnational contexts (such as those of the United Nations and international NGOs like Amnesty International and Minority Rights Group International) are translated and vernacularized (Merry 2006) in everyday lives and struggles in specific local and regional settings. My multifocal ethnographic lens is directed at human rights activists in the U.S. South, especially the black women who consciously map themselves and their increasingly multiracial constituencies of citizens and immigrants at the intersection of race, gender, and class situated on a sociocultural landscape where the U.S. South meets the global south (Harrison 2005b).

The network's leading activists are deeply aware of the history of human rights consciousness and advocacy in the African American freedom struggle. An annual report of the Atlanta-based National Center for Human Rights Education (2000) highlights that Frederick Douglass addressed the "human rights of Negroes" in the 1850s. During the 1940s and early 1950s, a human rights agenda was at the center of the antiracist campaigns of the NAACP and other more leftist civil rights organizations, notably the National Negro Congress and the Civil Rights Congress (Anderson 2003). These organizations prepared United Nations' petitions documenting human rights violations, with William Patterson's petition going so far as to claim genocide (Civil Rights Congress 1951). Eventually, the NAACP moved to the right, aligning itself to the Truman administration and distancing itself from the radical positions of W. E. B. Du Bois, William and Louise Patterson, and Paul and Eslanda Robeson, who, by the 1950s' McCarthy era, were demonized as "un-American." This Cold War climate forced Du Bois to emigrate to Ghana where he died right before the 1963 March on Washington. That very next year Malcolm X continued to call for human rights. In a 1964 interview with *Monthly Review* magazine, he had the following to say:

> Now my address to [the civil rights leadership] was designed to show them that if they would expand their civil rights movement to a human rights movement it would internationalize it. Now, as a civil rights movement, it remains within the confines of American domestic policy and no African independent nations can open up their mouths on American domestic affairs, whereas if they expanded the civil rights movement to a human

rights movement then they would be eligible to take the case of the Negro to the United Nations the same as the case of the Angolans is in the United Nations and the case of the South Africans is in the United Nations. Once the civil rights movement is expanded to a human rights movement our African brothers and our Asian brothers and Latin American brothers can place it on the agenda at the General Assembly that is coming up this year and Uncle Sam has no more say-so in it then (Spellman 1964).

The significance and legacy of this historical trajectory, documented most cogently in Carol Anderson's historiography (2003; 2008), continues to reverberate in African American and Afro-Atlantic consciousness, political activism, and social analysis today. It is not at all accidental that of the four first-person accounts included in *From Civil Rights to Human Rights*, the second of the three-volume *Bringing Human Rights Home* (Soohoo, Albisa, and Davis 2008), three of the human rights activists are African Americans – Ajamu Baraka, founding director of the U.S. Human Rights Network; the antiracist feminist and reproductive rights activist Loretta Ross, who founded the National Center for Human Rights Education; and activist legal scholar and Howard University professor, Lisa Crooms (Albisa 2008:49–70). This speaks to the centrality of the black experience and antiracism to the struggle for universal human rights. It also signals the degree to which the advances of U.S. liberal democracy and the expansion of constitutional rights have not achieved the full extent of human rights, which extend beyond civil and political dimensions and, increasingly in international debates, underscore expanded understandings of abuse that implicate the structural violence that poverty, unjust work conditions, and environmental degradation exert on human survival and wellbeing.

The black experience in the United States and throughout the African diaspora – notably in the exemplary case of the Haitian Revolution – has long stretched and nuanced the meanings of rights in ways beyond the visions and intentions of the proponents of the French Revolution, the American Revolution, the defeat of Nazism, and other world-changing events. This kind of effect remains necessary today when the lives of some people are still reduced to infrahuman status. The progressive impact of the Enlightenment and its legacy on how rights have been conceptualized and deployed politically is something that the postcolonial Jamaican theorist Sylvia Wynter (2002; 2003) has seriously contemplated. She advocates for a theory of knowledge and social being premised on "conceptual grounds other than those established in the image and within the parameters of the legacy of the Western Enlightenment" (Harrison 2008:14). She argues that the "model of Man derived from that universalism-claiming trajectory presumes the radical Othering and inferiorization of the African and African-derived. As a consequence, full humanity cannot be achieved without the fundamental reconstruction of the terms and conditions of what is human" (Harrison 2008:14). She claims that this radical "after-Man" reconstruction of human has implications for assumptions made about African and Afro-disasporic people's standing even in the contemporary period within global development, international affairs, and, I infer, human rights.

A serious examination and theorization of the black experience – as well as the experience of indigenous peoples and others who have been racially dehumanized – presents a constructive challenge to rethinking and further understanding the contours and boundaries of human rights along with the actors and practices that substantiate their importance and necessity in today's world.

References

Brownstein, R.
2010 The Grey and the Brown: The Generational Mismatch. *The National Journal*, July 24. http://www.nationaljournal.com/magazine/the-gray-and-the-brown-the-generational-mismatch-20100724, accessed July 7, 2010.

Webb, J.
2010 Diversity and the Myth of White Privilege. The Wall Street Journal, July 22. http://online.wsj.com/article/SB10001424052748703724104575379630952309408.html, accessed August 14, 2010.

Winant, H.
2004 The New Politics of Race: Globalism, Difference, Justice. Minneapolis, MI: University of Minnesota Press.

Deborah Thomas and Kamari Clarke, Globalizing Race

Baker, Lee D.
1998   From Savage to Negro: Anthropology and the Construction of Race, 1896–1954. Berkeley: University of California Press.

Holt, Thomas C.
2000   The Problem of Race in the 21st Century. Cambridge, MA: Harvard University Press.

Silverblatt, Irene
2004   Modern Inquisitions: Peru and the Origins of the Civilized World. Durham: Duke University Press.

Trouillot, Michel Rolph
1995   Silencing the Past: Power and Production of History. Boston: Beacon.

Winant, Howard
2000   Race and Race Theory. Annual Review of Sociology 26:169–185.

Faye V. Harrison, Race, Racism, and Antiracism: Implications for Human Rights

Albisa, Catherine
2008   First-Person Perspectives on the Growth of the Movement: Ajamu Baraka, Larry Cox, Loretta Ross, and Lisa Crooms. In Bringing Human Rights Home, vol. 2: From Civil Rights to Human Rights. Cynthia Soohoo, Catherine Albisa, and Martha F. Davis, eds. pp. 49–70. Westport, CT: Praeger Pubishers.

Amnesty International
2001   Using the International Human Rights System to Combat Racial Discrimination: A Handbook. London: Amnesty International Publications.

Anderson, Carol
2003   Eyes off the Prize: The United Nations and the African American Struggle for Human Rights, 1944–1955. Cambridge: Cambridge University Press.

Anderson, Carol
2008   A "Hollow Mockery": African Americans, White Supremacy, and the Development of Human Rights in the United States. In Bringing Human Rights Home, vol. 1: A History of Human Rights in the United States. Cynthia Soohoo, Catherine Albisa, and Martha F. Davis, eds. Pp.75–101. Westport, CT: Praeger Publications.

Anderson, Benedict
1991   Imagined Communities: Reflections on the Origin and Spread of Nationalism. London: Verso.

Banton, Michael
1996   International Action against Racial Discrimination. Oxford: Clarendon Press.

Booker, Salih, and William Minter
2001   Global Apartheid. The Nation 9(July):11–17.

Civil Rights Congress
1951   We Charge Genocide: The Historic Petition to the United Nations for Relief from a Crime of the United States Government against the Negro People. New York: Civil Rights Congress. Papers of William Patterson, Moorland-Spingarn Research Center, Howard University. Washington, D.C.

Farmer, Paul
2003   Pathologies of Power: Health, Human Rights, and the New War on the Poor. Berkeley: University of California Press.

Frankenberg, Ruth
1993   White Women, Race Matters: The Social Construction of Whiteness. Minneapolis: University of University Press.

Greenberg, Stanley B.
1980   Race and State in Capitalist Development: Comparative Perspectives. New Haven: Yale University Press.

Hale, Charles
2006   Mas que un Indio: Racial Ambivalence and the Paradox of Neoliberal Multiculturalism in Guatemala. Santa Fe: School of Advanced Studies (SAR) Press.

Harrison, Faye V.
1997   Entries on "race" and "racism." In The Dictionary of Anthropology. Thomas Barfield, ed. pp. 392–396. Oxford: Blackwell.

Harrison, Faye V.
2000   Facing Racism and the Moral Responsibility of Human Rights Knowledge. Annals of the New York Academy of Sciences 925:45–69, December.

Harrison, Faye V.
2002   Global Apartheid, Foreign Policy, and Human Rights. Theme issue, "Race & Globalization," Souls: A Critical Journal of Black Politics, Culture, and Society 4(3):48–68.

Harrison, Faye V.
2005a   Introduction: Global Perspectives on Human Rights and Interlocking Inequalities of Race, Gender, and Related Dimensions of Power. In Resisting Racism and Xenophobia: Global Perspectives on Race, Gender, and Human Rights. Faye V. Harrison, ed. pp. 1–31. Walnut Creek, CA: AltaMira Press.

Harrison, Faye V.
2005b   What Democracy Looks Like: The Politics of a Woman-Centered, Antiracist Human Rights Coalition. In Resisting Racism and Xenophobia: Global Perspectives on Race, Gender, and Human Rights. Faye V. Harrison, ed. pp. 229–250. Walnut Creek, CA: AltaMira Press.

Harrison, Faye V.

2008 The Politics of Antiracism and Social Justice: The Perspective of a Human Rights Network in the U.S. South. North American Dialogue 12(1):8–17, October.

Ishay, Micheline R.

2004 The History of Human Rights: From Ancient Times to the Globalization Era. Berkeley: University of California Press.

Ishay, Micheline R., ed.

2007 The Human Rights Reader: Major Political Essays, Speeches, and Documents from Ancient Times to the Present. 2nd edition. New York: Routledge.

Loftsdóttir, Kristin

2009 Invisible Colour: Landscapes of Whiteness and Racial Identity in International Development. Anthropology Today 25(5):4–7, October.

Merry, Sally Engle

2006 Human Rights and Gender Violence: Translating International Law into Local Justice. Chicago: University of Chicago Press.

National Center for Human Rights Education

2000 Bringing Human Rights Home: Linking the Individual Dignity with Mutual Destiny; 1996–2000. Atlanta: National Center for Human Rights Education.

Perry, Keisha-Khan Y.

2010 Racialized History and Urban Politics: Black Women's Wisdom in Grassroots Struggles. In Brazil's New Racial Politics. Bernd Reiter and Gladys L. Mitchell, eds. pp. 141–163. Boulder: Lynne Rienner Publishers.

Scheper-Hughes, Nancy

2000 The Genocidal Continuum. In Power and Self. Jeannette Mageo, ed. pp. 29–47 Cambridge: Cambridge University Press.

Smedley, Audrey

2007 Race in North America: Origin and Evolution of a Worldview. 3rd edition. Boulder, CO: Westview Press.

Soohoo, Cynthia, Catherine Albisa, and Martha F. Davis, eds.

2008 Bringing Human Rights Home, vols 1–3. Westport, CT: Praeger Publications.

Spellman, A. B.

1964 Interview with Malcolm X. Monthly Review 16(1) May. http://www.monthlyreview.org/564mx.htm, accessed April 5, 2008.

Vargas, João Costa H.

2008 Never Meant to Survive: Genocide and Utopias in Black Diaspora Communities. Lanhan, MD: Rowman & Littlefield Publishers.

Vitalis, Robert

2000 The Graceful and Generous Liberal Gesture: Making Racism Invisible in American International Relations. Millennium: Journal of International Studies 29(2): 331–356.

Wade, Peter

1997 Race and Ethnicity in Latin America. London: Pluto Press.

Warren Jonathan W.

2001 Racial Revolutions: Antiracism and Indian Resurgence in Brazil. Durham: Duke University Press.

Wetherell, Margaret, and Jonathan Potter

1992 Mapping the Language of Racism: Discourse and the Legitimation of Exploitation. New York: Columbia University Press.

Wilson, Richaerd A., ed.

1997 Human Rights, Culture and Context: Anthropological Perspectives. London: Pluto Press.

World Conference against Racism NGO Forum Secretariat

2002 Declaration and Programme of Action. Johannesburg: Progress Press on behalf of WCAR NGO Forum Secretariat, South African Non-Government Coalition.

Wynter, Sylvia

2002 After Man, towards the Human: The Thought of Sylvia Wynter. Keynote Response at conference in honor of Sylvia Wynter. Centre for Caribbean Thought. University of the West Indies, Mona campus, June 14–15.

Wynter, Sylvia

2003 Unsettling the Coloniality of Being/Power/Truth/Freedom: Towards the Human, After Man, Its Overrepresentation – An Argument. CR: The New Centennial Review 3(3):257–337, Fall.

Further Reading

Ambramsky, S.

2010 Look Ahead in Anger. Hyperbolic Rhetoric Threatens to Swamp our Politics. The Chronicle of Higher Education, July 11. http://chronicle.com/article/Look-Ahead-in-Anger/66152/, accessed August 15, 2010.

Barash, D. P.

2010 Hey, Wait a Minute! Biological Roots of Today's Anger. The Chronicle of Higher Education, July 11. http://chronicle.com/article/Hey-Wait-a-Minute-/66156/, accessed August 15, 2010.

Darity, W. A., J. Dietrich, and D. Hamilton, D.

2005 Bleach in the Rainbow: Latin Ethnicity and Preference for Whiteness. Transforming Anthropology, 13(2): 103–109.

Durrenberger, P. E., and D. Doukas

2008 Gospel of Wealth, Gospel of Work: Counter Hegemony in the U.S. Working Class. American Anthropology, 110(2):214–224.

Friedman, A.

2010 All Politics is Identity Politics. The American Prospect, 22(7), August 10, http://www.prospect.org/cs/articles?article=all_politics_is_identity_politics, accessed August 14, 2010.

Keaton, T. D.

2010 The Politics of Race-Blindness. (Anti)Blackness and Category-Blindness in Contemporary France. DuBois Review, 7(1):103–131.

Mullings, L.

2005 Resistance and Resilience: The Sojourner Syndrome and the Social Context of Reproduction in Central Harlem, 13(2): 79–91.

Sen, R., and Mamdouh, F.

2008 The accidental American. San Francisco, CA: Berrett-Koehler Publishers, Inc.

Truong, K.

2010 Review of Harvard Scholar's Arrest Cites Failure to Communicate. The Chronicle of Higher Education, June 30. http://chronicle.com/article/Review-of-Harvard-Scholars/66099/, accessed December 9, 2011.

Wellman, D.

2009 Reconfiguring the Color Line: Racializing Inner-city Youth and Rearticulating Class Hierarchy in Black America. Transforming Anthropology, 17(2):131–146.

Glossary

ABO blood system. A human blood typing system that consists of four distinct types: A, B, AB, and O. ABO blood type is determined by the **alleles** present at a single **locus**, which are inherited from parents.

abolition. The abolition movement consisted of organized efforts to do away with legalized slavery in the United States. Emancipation was gained gradually in northern states, and slavery was abolished throughout the country by the Thirteenth Amendment to the U.S. Constitution.

acculturation. The cultural exchange and change that results from sustained contact between different groups.

affirmative action. First established by the federal government in 1965, this legal mandate consists of special actions in recruitment, hiring, and other areas designed to eliminate the effects of past discrimination.

African replacement model. The hypothesis that modern humans evolved as a new species in Africa between 150,000 and 200,000 years ago and then spread throughout the Old World, replacing archaic populations; sometimes called the recent African origin model.

allele. The alternative form of a gene or DNA sequence that occurs at a given locus. Some loci have only one allele, some have two, and some have many alternative forms. Alleles occur in pairs, one on each chromosome.

Allen's rule. The biological rule that states that mammals in cold climates tend to have shorter and bulkier limbs, allowing less loss of body heat, whereas mammals in hot climates tend to have long, slender limbs, allowing greater loss of body heat.

anatomically modern *Homo sapiens*. The modern form of the human species, which evolved in Africa between 150,000 and 200,000 years ago.

anthropology. The study of humans and their cultures, both past and present. The field of anthropology includes archaeology, biological anthropology, cultural anthropology, linguistic anthropology, and applied anthropology.

anthropometrics. The study, especially comparative, of the measurements of the human body.

anti-miscegenation laws. U.S. laws that forbade sexual relations or marriage between people of different races. Declared unconstitutional in 1967 (*Loving v. Virginia*).

anti-Semitism. Prejudice or discrimination against Jews.

applied anthropology. The subfield of anthropology that applies the knowledge and methods of anthropology to present-day problems.

archaeology. The subfield of anthropology that focuses on cultural variation and power relations in past populations by analyzing material remains (material culture or artifacts).

assimilation. The process of change that occurs when an individual or group adopts the characteristics of the dominant

Race: Are We So Different?, First Edition. Alan H. Goodman, Yolanda T. Moses, and Joseph L. Jones.
© 2012 American Anthropological Association. Published 2012 by Blackwell Publishing Ltd.

culture and is fully incorporated into that culture's social, economic, and political institutions.

base pairs. A strand of DNA contains four bases – adesine (A), thymine (T), guanine (G) and cytosine (C) – which connect via hydrogen bonds to form pairs with bases on an opposite DNA strand, like the rungs of a ladder. "A" always pairs with "T," and "G" always pairs with "C".

behaviorism. A school of thought in psychology emphasizing the importance of overt behavior responses over conscious experience for understanding human social interactions

Bergmann's rule. The principle that states that (1) among mammals of similar shape, the larger mammal loses heat less rapidly than the smaller mammal, and that (2) among mammals of similar size, the mammal with a linear shape will lose heat more rapidly than the mammal with a nonlinear shape.

biocultural approach. The use of biological and cultural research methods and interdisciplinary theory to study human biological variation and other factors such as health in relationship to social and cultural practices, environment, and change.

biological anthropology. The subfield of anthropology that focuses on the biological evolution of humans and human ancestors, the relationship of humans to other organisms and to their environment, and patterns of biological variation within and among human populations. Also referred to as physical anthropology.

biological determinism. The philosophy or belief that human behavior and social organization are fundamentally determined by innate biological characteristics, so that differences in behavior within and between groups are attributed to genetic variation rather than influences of environment and learning.

Blumenbach, Johann Friedrich (1752–1840). German naturalist who developed one of the earliest, non-scientific human **racial classification** systems, which included geographically defined "Caucasian," "Mongolian," "Ethiopian," "American," and "Malay" races. See also **Linnaeus, Carolus**.

caste system. Closed, hereditary system of hierarchy, often dictated by religion and occupation; status is ascribed at birth, so that people are locked into their parents' social and economic position.

Caucasian. A non-scientific term invented by German physician Johann Blumenbach in 1795 to describe light-skinned people from Europe (and, originally, from western Asia and North Africa as well), whom Blumenbach mistakenly thought came from the Caucasus Mountains. The term became synonymous with "white."

cell. The smallest unit of life. Our human bodies are composed of more than 100 trillion cells. Inside the cell membrane is the nucleus. The cell nucleus is surrounded by cytoplasm.

census. An official count of a population and collection of demographic data. The United States Census is conducted every ten years.

chromosome. Long strands of DNA found inside the **cell** nucleus. Human cells each contain 23 pairs of chromosomes, inherited from our parents.

civil rights movement. Legal and other efforts led by African Americans against racism and segregation and for the enactment of legislation ensuring their full civil and human rights. The modern civil rights movement dates to the mid-1950s and proceeded in earnest throughout the 1960s.

classification. The ordering of items into groups on the basis of shared attributes. Classifications are cultural inventions and different cultures develop different ways of classifying the same phenomena (e.g. colors, plants, relatives, and other people).

cline. A gradual, continuous change in a particular trait or trait frequency over space.

codominant. Both **allele**s affect the phenotype of a heterozygous genotype, and neither is dominant over the other. For example, in the ABO blood type system, alleles A and B are codominant and, together, produce blood type AB.

complex trait. A physical trait affected by multiple loci which interact with environmental conditions. Most studied human traits are complex (e.g. height, body size, and skin color).

continuous trait. A characteristic that is measured on a scale that is ordered and does not have gaps or divisions (e.g. skin color).

creationism. The belief that the universe was created by God.

cross-cultural comparison. The method of comparing characteristics of one culture to another. This is one of the hallmarks of anthropological knowledge.

cultural anthropology. The subfield of anthropology that focuses on describing and understanding human cultures, including human cultural variability (over time, throughout the world).

cultural construct. An idea or system of thought that is rooted in culture. It can include an invented system for classifying things or for classifying people, such as a racial system of classification.

cultural determinism. The belief that human behavior and social organization are fundamentally determined by cultural factors.

culture. The full range of shared, learned, patterned behaviors, values, meanings, beliefs, ways of perceiving, systems of classification, and other knowledge acquired by people as members of a society; the processes or power dynamics that influence whether meanings and practices can be shared within a group or society.

culture shock. The disorienting experience of realizing that the perspectives, behaviors, and experiences of an individual, group, or society are not shared by another individual, group, or society.

cultural relativism or cultural relativity. The belief that the values and standards of cultures differ and cannot be easily compared with the values and standards of other cultures.

discordance. Disagreement, see **nonconcordance**.

discrete trait. A biological characteristic that takes on distinct values and properties (such as ABO blood type).

discrimination. Policies and practices that harm and disadvantage a group and its members.

DNA (Deoxyribonucleic acid). The molecule that encodes heredity information.

dominant allele. An allele that masks the effect of the other allele (which is recessive) in a heterozygous genotype.

double helix. DNA looks like a long twisted ladder. The sides of the ladders are composed of phosphates and sugars.

emancipation. Freedom from legalized slavery gained by most enslaved persons of African descent immediately following the American Civil War. The Emancipation Proclamation made slavery illegal in Confederate states.

essentialism. The idea that all things have an underlying or true essence. Racial essentialists argue that all members of a specific racial group share certain basic characteristics or qualities that mark them as inherently different from members of other racial groups.

ethnicity. An idea similar to race that groups people according to common origin or background. The term usually refers to social, cultural, religious, linguistic, and other affiliations although, like race, it is sometimes linked to perceived biological markers. Ethnicity is often characterized by cultural features, such as dress, language, religion, and social organization.

ethnocentrism. The deeply felt belief that your own cultural ways are universal, natural, normal, and even superior to other cultural ways.

ethnography. Anthropological research in which one learns about the culture of a society through fieldwork, the data-gathering methods that are combined with and/or built upon first-hand participation and observation in that society.

eugenics. From Greek *eugenes* meaning wellborn; the eugenics movement of the late nineteenth and early twentieth centuries sought to "improve" the human species and preserve racial "purity" through planned human breeding. Eugenicists supported anti-miscegenation laws and other, sometimes more extreme, measures such as sterilization.

evolution. The transformation of a species of organic life over long periods of time (macroevolution) or from one generation to the next (microevolution) due to four evolutionary forces. Anthropologists study both the cultural and biological evolution of the human species.

evolutionary forces. The four mechanisms that can each cause changes in allele frequencies across generations: mutation, natural selection, genetic drift, and gene flow.

exogamy. Choosing mates and marriage partners from outside the local population.

fieldwork. A form of data collection. Anthropological fieldwork involves a number of techniques and strategies that rely upon the firsthand observation of social interaction (in cultural anthropology) or the conducting of excavations (in archaeology).

founder effect. A type of genetic drift that occurs when all individuals in a population trace back to a small number of founding individuals. The small size of the founding population may result in very different allele frequencies from those found in the original population from which the founders came. Examples of populations exhibiting founder effect include the French Acadians, the Amish, and the Hutterites

gene. A unique combination of bases (see base pairs) that creates a specific part of an organism.

gene flow. A mechanism for evolutionary change involving genetic exchange across local populations. Gene flow introduces new alleles into a population and makes populations more similar genetically to one another.

genetic distance. An average measure of relatedness between populations based on various traits. Genetic distances are used for understanding effects of genetic drift and gene flow, which should affect all loci to the same extent.

genetic drift. A mechanism for evolutionary change resulting from the random fluctuations of gene frequencies (e.g. from one generation to the next). In the absence of other evolutionary forces, genetic drift results in the eventual loss of all variation. See **founder effect**.

genetics. The study of heredity, its mechanisms, and related biological variation. Heredity may be studied at the molecular, individual (organism), or population level.

genome. One complete copy of all the genes and DNA for a species.

genotype. The genetic endowment of an individual from the two alleles present at a given locus. See **phenotype**.

HapMap. An international research effort to find genes associated with human diseases and response to pharmaceuticals.

heritability. In biology, the proportion of variation of a trait due to genetic variation in a population.

heterozygous. Having two different alleles at a given locus, i.e. two different alleles for a particular trait. See homozygous.

holistic. The perspective that understanding human variation requires understanding how its different aspects (e.g. biological and cultural) are interrelated. This is one of the hallmarks of anthropological knowledge.

homozygous. Situation in which the two alleles at a given locus are identical.

Human Genome Project. An international research effort to sequence and map the human genome: all of the genes on every chromosome. The project was completed in 2003.

human variation. The differences that exist among individuals or among groups of individuals regarded as populations. Anthropologists study both cultural and biological variation.

human biological variation. The observable differences among individuals and groups that have resulted from the processes of human migration, marriage, and environmental adaptations. Human biological variation is often referred to as "human biological diversity."

hypothesis. A proposed explanation of observed facts. A scientific hypothesis must be testable.

immigration. The act of entering a country of which one is not a native to become a permanent resident. In the United States and elsewhere, immigration and immigration policies are often racially charged issues.

institutional racism. The embeddedness of racially discriminatory practices in the institutions, laws, and agreed upon values and practices of a society.

intelligence. The innate potential to learn and solve novel problems.

intelligent design creationism. The idea that the biological world was created by an intelligent entity and did not arise from natural processes. This idea is somewhat different from that proposed by "creation scientists."

interfertility. The ability to interbreed or mate and produce fertile offspring. All humans are members of the same species and are interfertile.

linguistic anthropology. The subfield of anthropology that focuses on the nature of human language and the relationship of language to culture.

linguistics. The comparative study of the function, structure, and history of languages and the communication process in general. Linguistics is also referred to as linguistic anthropology.

Linnaeus, Carolus (1707–1778). Swedish botanist and physician who developed the system for sorting living organisms into major (genus) and then more specific (species) categories (e.g. *Homo sapiens*). In the 1758 tenth edition of *Systema naturae* (*Natural System*), Linnaeus created the first formal, non-scientific human racial classification scheme. It included five varieties of *Homo sapiens* – "Americanus," "Europaeus," "Asiaticus," "Afer," and "Ferus" – based on physical and cultural descriptions that favored Europeans. Linnaeus's human classification system influenced the way race is conceptualized in the United States. See also **Blumenbach, Johann Friedrich**.

locus. The location of a particular gene or DNA sequence on a chromosome.

macroevolution. The study of macroevolution focuses on biological evolution over many generations and on the origin of higher taxonomic categories, such as species.

malaria. A group of diseases caused by any of four different microorganisms called plasmodia (*Plasmodium falciparum*, *vivax*, *ovale*, and *malariae*), which are transmitted by certain species of mosquito. Malaria is potentially life-threatening and is found mostly in tropical and subtropical regions of the world.

Mendelian genetics. The branch of genetics concerned with inheritance. This field was named after Gregor Mendel who discovered the basic laws of inheritance in the nineteenth century.

meritocracy. The idea that merit and individual effort, rather than one's family or social background (including race, gender, class, and legacy), determine one's success, one's social and economic position. Similarly, the idea that social inequalities are the result of individual differences in merit and effort.

microevolution. The study of microevolution focuses on changes in allele frequencies from one generation to the next.

mitochondrial DNA. A small amount of DNA that is located in the mitochondria of cells. Mitochondrial DNA is inherited only through the mother.

Monogeny. A pre-evolutionary scientific argument that human biological "races" all descended from a single source (or biblical "Adam"). See **polygeny**.

Mulatto. Originally from Spanish *mulato* meaning hybrid; a person of European and African parentage or a descendant of European and African ancestors; also used to refer to a person whose phenotype suggests mixed African and European ancestry.

multiregional evolution model. The hypothesis that modern humans evolved throughout the Old World as a single species after the first dispersal of *Homo erectus* out of Africa. According to this model, the transition from *Homo erectus* to archaic humans to modern *Homo sapiens* occurred within a single evolutionary line throughout the Old World.

mutation. A mechanism for evolutionary change resulting from a random change in the **base** sequence of a DNA molecule. Mutations are the ultimate source of all genetic variation but must occur in sex cells to cause evolutionary change.

natural selection. A mechanism for evolutionary change favoring the survival and reproduction of some organisms over others because of their particular biological characteristics under specific environmental conditions. Natural selection does not create variation, but acts on existing variation.

nonconcordance. The tendency of some human traits to vary independently, often in response to environmental or selective conditions. For example, skin color and ABO blood type are nonconcordant.

non-random mating. Deliberate patterns of mate choice that influence the distributions of genotype and phenotype frequencies. Non-random mating does not lead to changes in allele frequencies. Arranged marriage is a form of non-random mating.

phenotype. The observable or detectable characteristics of an individual organism. A person's phenotype includes easily visible traits such as hair or eye color as well as abilities such as tongue-rolling/curling.

philology. The comparative study of human speech and literature, especially those aspects useful for understanding population movements and cross-cultural interactions in the past. See also **linguistics** and **linguistic anthropology**.

physical anthropology. The study of the non-cultural, or biological, aspects of humans and our fossil ancestors. Physical anthropologists are usually involved in one of three different kinds of research: (1) non-human primate studies (usually in the wild); (2) recovering the fossil record of human evolution; and (3) studying human biological diversity, inheritance patterns, and biological adaptation to environmental stresses, and cultural means of adapting to environmental stressors that impact biology. Physical anthropology is also referred to as biological anthropology.

physiology. The organic or bodily processes of an organism.

polygenic. Affected by two or more loci. See **complex trait**.

polygeny. A pre-evolutionary scientific argument that human biological "races" are separate species, each descended from different biblical "Adams." See **monogeny**.

polymorphism. A discrete genetic trait in which there are at least two alleles at a locus having frequencies greater than 0.01.

polytypic. A species with physically distinguishable regional populations. The human species (*Homo sapiens*) is polytypic.

populational model. In reference to humans, an outdated classification system based on the assumption that the only biologically distinct groups are long-isolated breeding populations with distinct evolutionary lineages. In practice, populations are difficult to define scientifically.

primary African origin model. A variant of the multiregional evolution model of the origin of modern humans that suggests most of the transition from archaic to modern humans took place first in Africa and then spread throughout the rest of the species across the Old World by gene flow.

race. A recent idea created by Western Europeans following exploration across the world to account for differences among people and justify colonization, conquest, enslavement, and social hierarchy among humans. The term is used to refer to groupings of people according to common origin or background and associated with perceived biological markers. Among humans there are no races except the human race. In biology, the term has limited use, usually associated with organisms or populations that are able to interbreed. Ideas about race are culturally and socially transmitted and form the basis of racism, racial classification and often complex racial identities.

racial classification. The practice of classifying people into distinct racial groups based on certain characteristics such as skin color or geographic region, often for the purpose of ranking them based on what are believed to be innate differences between the groups.

racial endogamy. Marriage within one's own racial group (see also **anti-miscegenation laws**).

racial identity. This concept operates at two levels: (1) self identity or conceptualization based upon perceptions of one's race and (2) society's perception and definition of a person's race.

racialization. The process by which individuals and groups of people are viewed through a racial lens, through a culturally invented racial framework. Racialization is often referred to as racialism.

racial profiling. The use of race (and often nationality or religion) to identify a person as a suspect or potential suspect. Racial profiling is one of the ways that racism is manifested and perpetuated.

racial stratification. A system of stratification and inequality in which access to resources (political, economic, social) depends largely upon one's racial classification.

racism. The use of race to establish and justify a social hierarchy and system of power that privileges, preferences, or advances certain individuals or groups of people usually at the expense of others. Racism is perpetuated through both interpersonal and institutional practices.

recessive allele. An allele whose effect is masked by the other allele (which is dominant) in a heterozygous genotype.

RNA (Ribonucleic acid). The molecule that functions to carry out the instructions for protein synthesis specified by the DNA molecule.

selective pressure. Environmental pressure on individuals within a population that results in evolutionary change; the driving force of natural selection. Extreme temperature and ultraviolet radiation are examples of selective pressure.

sickle cell allele. An allele of the hemoglobin locus. Individuals homozygous for this allele have sickle cell anemia, while heterozygotes have sickle cell trait. In areas of the world where malaria is endemic, people with the sickle cell trait have a selective advantage (see **natural selection**).

sickle cell anemia. A genetic disease that occurs in a person homozygous for the sickle cell allele which alters the structure of red blood cells, giving it a "sickled" shape. These abnormally shaped red blood cells are less efficient in transporting oxygen throughout the body, which can cause pain and even organ damage.

single-nucleotide polymorphisms (SNP; pronounced "snip"). A single base pair within a DNA sequence that can vary among individuals. An example of a SNP is the change from A to T in the sequences AATGCT and ATTGCT.

slavery. An extreme form of human oppression whereby an individual may "own" another person and the rights to his or her labor. In the colonial Americas, a form of racial slavery evolved that would eventually distinguish only persons of African descent as "slaves."

social class. A social grouping of people based on common economic and other characteristics determined by society and reflecting a social hierarchy.

stereotyping. The process of attributing particular traits, characteristics, behaviors, or values to an entire group or category of people, who are, as a consequence, monolithically represented; includes the process of negative stereotyping.

stratification. In reference to society, a system by which social, economic, and political inequalities are structured in society.

subspecies. Physically distinguishable populations that are genetically distinct within a species. *Humans do not conform to the subspecies criteria.*

symbol. A sign or attribute that stands for something else, to which it may or may not have any relationship. For example, the bald eagle and "Uncle Sam" are symbols of the United States.

taxonomy. The science of describing and classifying organisms.

trait. A characteristic or aspect of one's phenotype or genotype.

typological model. In reference to humans, an attempt to classify people based on the *false* assumption that humans can be unambiguously placed into discrete groupings on the basis of selected traits such as skin color, hair form, and body shape.

universalism. The belief that values and standards are commonly shared among cultures.

white privilege. A consequence of racism in the United States that has systematically, persistently, and extensively given advantages to so-called white populations, principally of European origin, at the expense of other populations.

Whiteness studies. The investigation of white racial identity, defined differently throughout U.S. history, but usually based on the maintenance or pursuit of white privilege.

Index

Race: Are We So Different?, First Edition. Alan H. Goodman, Yolanda T. Moses and Joseph L. Jones.
© 2012 American Anthropological Association. Published 2012 by Blackwell Publishing Ltd.